C000184155

Eric Hobsbawm was born in Alexandria in 1917 and educated in Austria, Germany and England. He was a Fellow of the British Academy and of the American Academy of Arts and Sciences, and a Foreign Member of the Japan Academy, with honorary degrees from universities in several countries. He taught until retirement at Birkbeck College, University of London, and then at the New School for Social Research in New York. In addition to *The Age of Revolution*, *The Age of Capital*, *The Age of Empire* and *The Age of Extremes*, his books include *Bandits*, *Revolutionaries*, *Uncommon People*, his autobiography *Interesting Times*, *Globalisation*, *Democracy and Terrorism* and *How to Change the World*. Eric Hobsbawm died in 2012.

Leslie Bethell is Emeritus Professor of Latin American History at the University of London and Emeritus Fellow of St Antony's College, Oxford.

Viva la Revolución

On Latin America

ERIC HOBSBAWM

Edited by Leslie Bethell

ABACUS

First published in Great Britain in 2016 by Little, Brown
This paperback edition published in 2017 by Abacus

1 3 5 7 9 10 8 6 4 2

Copyright © 2016 The Trustees of the Eric Hobsbawm Literary Estate

Introduction Copyright © 2016 Leslie Bethell

The moral right of the author has been asserted.

All rights reserved.
No part of this publication may be reproduced, stored in a
retrieval system, or transmitted, in any form or by any means, without
the prior permission in writing of the publisher, nor be otherwise circulated
in any form of binding or cover other than that in which it is published
and without a similar condition including this condition being
imposed on the subsequent purchaser.

A CIP catalogue record for this book
is available from the British Library.

ISBN 978-0-349-14129-9

Typeset in Baskerville by M Rules
Printed and bound in Great Britain by
Clays Ltd, Elcograf S.p.A.

Papers used by Abacus are from well-managed forests
and other responsible sources.

MIX
Paper from
responsible sources
FSC® C104740

Abacus
An imprint of
Little, Brown Book Group
Carmelite House
50 Victoria Embankment
London EC4Y 0DZ

An Hachette UK Company
www.hachette.co.uk

www.littlebrown.co.uk

Contents

III: PEASANTS

IV: REVOLUTIONS AND REVOLUTIONARIES

V: MILITARY REVOLUTIONARIES IN PERU

Contents

VI: THE CHILEAN ROAD TO SOCIALISM

VII: LATE REFLECTIONS

Preface

Before his death in 2012, at the age of ninety-five, Eric Hobsbawm brought together in *How to Change the World* (Little, Brown, 2011) a collection of his writings from 1956 to 2009 on Marx and Marxism. At the same time, he organized a collection of his writings and lectures (from 1964 to 2012) on culture and society in the twentieth century, which was published posthumously as *Fractured Times* (Little, Brown, 2013). And he left instructions that he would like a collection of his articles, essays and reviews on Latin America to be published. Eric's literary executors, Bruce Hunter and Chris Wrigley, invited Leslie Bethell, a historian of Latin America and a friend of Eric's for more than fifty years, to locate, select and edit Eric's writings on the region, from an article in the *New Statesman* on the Cuban Revolution (October 1960) to his chapter on the Third World, mainly Latin America, in his autobiography *Interesting Times* (2002), and to contribute an introduction on Eric's forty-year relationship with Latin America. Eric's widow Marlene gave her enthusiastic support to the project.

Keith McClellan generously made available to the editor his Bibliography of the writings of Eric Hobsbawm (to February 2010). Andrew Gordon, Eric's literary agent at David Higham Associates, together with his assistants Marigold Atkey and David Evans, undertook the digitisation of many of the texts. At Little, Brown Zoe Gullen prepared the book for publication, and Sarah Ereira compiled the index.

Introduction: Eric and Latin America

Leslie Bethell

In his autobiography *Interesting Times: A Twentieth-Century Life*, published in 2002 when he was eighty-five years old, the historian Eric Hobsbawm (1917–2012) wrote that the only region of the world outside Europe which he felt he knew well and where he felt entirely at home was Latin America.

Eric had first been attracted to Latin America more than forty years earlier because of its potential for social revolution. After the triumph of Fidel Castro in Cuba in January 1959, and even more after the defeat of the US attempt to overthrow Castro in April 1961, 'there was not an intellectual [of the left] in Europe or the United States who was not under the spell of Latin America, a continent apparently bubbling with the lava of social revolutions'.[1] In an unpublished introduction to a volume on twentieth-century revolutions, Eric wrote (in January 1967):

> The Second World War produced a sort of chain-reaction of movements of revolutionary liberation ... The liberation movement finally began to advance in the informal

empire of the largest and most powerful of the surviving capitalist powers, among the nominally independent but in practice semi-colonial countries of Latin America. Here, revolutionary movements had failed to develop into more than anarchic civil wars (as in Colombia after 1948) or succeeded in the rather exceptional circumstances of Bolivia (1952). However, the victory of Fidel Castro in Cuba (1959) was soon to bring the first socialist regime into the American continent, and to open an era of unrest there *which has not yet concluded* [my italics].

It was above all the expectation, or hope, that there would be social revolution, or at least significant social change, particularly in Peru and Colombia, briefly in Chile, later in Central America and Venezuela, finally in Brazil, that sustained Eric's interest in Latin America throughout the following decades.

A member of the Communist Party of Great Britain since his student days in Cambridge in the late 1930s, Eric visited Cuba in the summer of 1960 at the invitation of Carlos Rafael Rodríguez, a leading figure in the Cuban Communist Party who had joined the 26 July Movement in the Sierra Maestra and become one of Castro's closest allies. Eric had just spent three months at Stanford University, and he joined forces in Havana with two friends from the United States, the Marxist economists Paul Sweezy and Paul Baran, editors of the *Monthly Review*. It was, he later recalled, 'the irresistible honeymoon period of the young revolution'.[2] On his return to London in October, besides briefing the International Affairs Committee of the CPGB, he wrote an article for the *New Statesman* in which he described the Cuban Revolution as 'a laboratory specimen of its type (a nucleus of intellectuals, a mass movement of peasants)', 'remarkably endearing and encouraging', which 'unless the Americans intervene with arms' will make

Cuba, 'fairly soon', 'the first Socialist country in the western hemisphere'.[3]*

In April 1961, along with Kenneth Tynan, the drama critic, Eric mobilized the great and the good to sign a letter to *The Times* denouncing US aggression against Cuba. The two of them also organized a demonstration in solidarity with the Cuban people in Hyde Park, memorable, Eric later recalled, for 'the largest concentration of stunning-looking girls – from theatre and model agencies presumably – that I've ever seen on a political demo'.[4] Eric was also a founder-member of the British Cuba Committee and he revisited Cuba in December 1961–January 1962 with 'a British left-wing delegation of the usual composition: a left-wing Labour MP; unilateral nuclear disarmers; a hardnosed, usually Party-line union leader, not without an interest in foreign nooky; the odd radical conspirator; CP functionaries and the like'.[5]

Curiously, apart from a few remarks in an entertaining account of the Cultural Congress of Havana in January 1968, a heterogeneous assembly of five hundred intellectuals of the international New Left from seventy countries, in the *Times Literary Supplement*, and a few pages in *The Age of Extremes, 1914–91* (1994), his history of the short twentieth century, Eric wrote very little on the progress of the Cuban Revolution in the 1960s – or, for that matter, later. In the *TLS* he described Cuba as 'an embattled and heroic country, [and] a remarkably attractive one, if only because it is visibly one of the rare states in the world whose population actually likes and trusts its government. Moreover, the free and flourishing state of cultural activities at

---

* It was in London in October 1960, soon after his return from Cuba, that I first met Eric. We were both living in Gordon Mansions, Huntley Street, Bloomsbury, close to the university. I was a graduate student in history at University College and a tutor for the London branch of the Workers' Educational Association (WEA). I had just returned from my first visit to Brazil, researching for my Ph.D. thesis on the abolition of the Brazilian slave trade. Twenty years older than me, Eric was a Reader in History at Birkbeck College and, which impressed me even more, jazz critic of the *New Statesman* (under the pseudonym Francis Newton).

present, the admirable social and educational achievements and the endearing excursions into anti-materialist utopia, can hardly fail to appeal to intellectuals.'[6] However, for all its achievements, by the late 1960s Cuba was not exactly a show-case for successful socialist revolution in Latin America. And it would soon no longer be true that 'those who do not like the place are free to emigrate'. Moreover, as we shall see, Eric was a fierce critic of the guerrilla movements the Cuban Revolution inspired throughout the region – and beyond.

On 31 October 1962 Eric embarked on his first journey to continental Latin America, a three-month visit to Brazil, Argentina, Chile, Peru, Bolivia and Colombia.* He had been awarded a Rockefeller Foundation travel grant to research into 'archaic' forms of social revolt, the subject matter of his recent book *Primitive Rebels* (1959), which had focused mainly on southern Europe. In his grant application, he had argued that in Latin America 'modern' political ideologies and political parties had long been accepted by the local elites but without making much apparent impact on the masses, whose emer-gence into political consciousness had only taken place in recent decades. He therefore expected to find in Latin America not only 'numerous genuinely archaic movements' but also 'com-binations of the superficially modern and the archaic'. These were, in his view, invariably misinterpreted

> as when the Gaitán movement was described as 'Liberal' because its leader happened to operate within one of the traditional Colombian parties, or 'Fascist' as in Perón's case [in Argentina], or very likely 'Communist' in the case of Castroist movements ... As the ideological indeterminacy of intellectual elites in recent decades shows (e.g. the shifting

---

* Eric had married Marlene a few days before leaving for South America, and he told her that if the Cuban Missile Crisis turned really serious she was to buy a ticket to Buenos Aires and meet him there.

of labels and co-operation of nominally Trotskyist, Peronist, Communist, etc. elements in Bolivia), description in terms of formed European movements of the twentieth century may be more misleading than illuminating.*

On his return to London, between April and July 1963 Eric published a series of articles in *Labour Monthly*, *New Society*, the *Listener* (the texts of two broadcasts for the Third Programme of the BBC) and the *World Today* (based on a paper given to the Latin American seminar at Chatham House) in which he explored demographic, economic and social change in Latin America since the world depression of the 1930s, in particular the disintegration of traditional agrarian societies (the collapse of the 'old Latin America', 'the end of the Middle Ages'), and the political awakening of the masses – the urban working class, the urban poor and, above all, the peasants – in the 1940s and 1950s. Eric had returned from his first visit to Latin America convinced that in the next decade or so it was destined to become 'the most explosive region of the world'.[7] Several Latin American countries, he believed, were 'ripe for upheaval', indeed, except perhaps for Argentina and Uruguay, ripe for social revolution, if properly organized and led.

He was especially impressed by the potential for revolution of

---

* Eric's visit to Latin America, as we now know, aroused the suspicions of the British Security Service, better known as MI5, which had been monitoring his every move – as well as his correspondence and telephone calls – for years. See the article by Frances Stonor Saunders in the *London Review of Books* (9 April 2015) on Eric's MI5 file which was released at the end of 2014 (to December 1963, and still with numerous blank pages). Saunders is, however, mistaken in claiming that MI5, by alerting the CIA and the FBI, tried and failed to block Eric's Rockefeller travel grant. Such was its incompetence that it only learned (from 'an extremely delicate source') that Eric, 'a hard-line Communist', was 'due to leave' for 'twelve months' 'to write a book about South American revolutions', supported by 'an unidentified foundation', when he had already been in Latin America for over a month. And they only took up the matter with the US authorities, first when he was about to leave Latin America, and then again some months after he had returned home.

peasant movements in Peru and, above all, in Colombia, which were 'virtually unknown to the outside world'. Beginning in the late 1950s and reaching a peak in the early 1960s, the central and southern highlands of Peru had witnessed the largest mass insurrection and political mobilization of Indian peasants since the Tupac Amaru rebellion in the late colonial period. 'If any country is ripe for and needs a social revolution,' Eric wrote, 'it is Peru'. In Colombia, exceptionally in Latin America, a social revolution had been 'in preparation' since the 1920s. '[It] ought logically to have produced something analogous to *Fidelismo*, a populist left-wing regime working closely with the communists.' The insurrection in Bogotá in April 1948, the *Bogotazo*, was a 'phenomenon of revolutionary proportions'. But with no one to direct and organize it a 'classic social revolution' was aborted by the assassination of the Liberal leader Jorge Eliécer Gaitán. However, in the civil war and anarchy that followed, the beginnings of what became known as *La Violencia*, Colombia witnessed 'the greatest armed mobilization of peasants (as guerrillas, brigands or self-defence groups [organized by the Communist Party]) in the recent history of the western hemisphere', with the possible exception of periods during the Mexican Revolution of 1910–20. A revolutionary situation persisted in Colombia in the early 1960s, Eric argued, and, because of its size, population, 'balanced all-round economy' and strategic location between the Caribbean, Central America and Venezuela and the Andean republics and Brazil, Colombia 'can make a decisive difference to the future of Latin America, whereas Cuba is not likely to do so'.

In Brazil Eric had been shocked by the economic backwardness and poverty he found in Recife, the first city he visited on his South American journey. But he also recognized the 'immense' potential for peasant organization in the north-east of Brazil, 'that vast area of some 20 million inhabitants which has given the country its most famous bandits [and] peasant revolts'. Peasant Leagues, which represented the first stirrings of political mobilization in Brazil's countryside, had been active there since 1955. The movement, however, 'had little national presence' and was, he later recalled, 'clearly already past its peak'.[8] The Brazilian Communist Party (PCB) was at the end of the Second World War the biggest Communist party in Latin America. It had, however, been declared illegal at the beginning of the Cold War in 1947. (Eric seemed unaware that the PCB was nevertheless active, alongside progressive Catholic priests, in the organization of agricultural wage-labourers into rural unions in the north-east.) In any event, in March 1964, a year after Eric's visit, all hope of social revolution in Brazil would be crushed by a military coup leading to the establishment of a military dictatorship which lasted for twenty-one years (1964–85).

Eric wrote relatively little on the potential for revolution in Brazil. Typically, however, he did find time to contribute a perceptive article on *bossa nova*, the latest development in Brazilian popular music, for the *New Statesman*. It was, he wrote, 'a cross between Brazilian urban music and jazz, bred in the playboy set of rich young Brazilians ... [and] among those professional musicians most likely to meet visiting American players ... The visiting student of jazz observes it with awe and a sense of the historical occasion. For *bossa nova* is the first major conquest of new territory by jazz ... [significantly] in the one Latin American country which looks as though it has definitely entered the age of modern industrial civilization.' Moreover, he concluded, 'it will not only last, but develop'.[9]

From the mid-1960s to the mid-1970s, the possibilities for social revolution (in Spanish America, if not Brazil) were the main focus of Eric's writing on Latin America. In an essay on the role of peasants and rural migrants in politics, he argued that the urban working class and the urban poor of Latin America, the 'gigantic and constantly expanding proletariat and sub-proletariat' of 'internal immigrants' and 'displaced peasants', were 'a potentially explosive force' because of their poverty, insecurity and appalling living conditions. For the most part, however, they were politically 'immature', relatively passive, more easily mobilized from above by populist parties and politicians (Haya de la Torre and APRA in Peru, Acción Democrática in Venezuela, Perón in Argentina, Vargas in Brazil) than by the left, communist or non-communist.[10] Eric therefore wrote surprisingly little about the urban workers of Latin America. He was more interested in the potential revolutionary role of organized peasant movements, especially in the Andes.

In scholarly articles based on both first-hand observation and research in an edited volume published in Paris, *Les Problèmes agraires des Ameriques Latines* (1967), the *Journal of Latin American Studies* (1969) and *Past and Present* (1974), he focused on La Convención province in the Cuzco region in the central highlands of Peru, where the neo-feudal, *hacienda* system was collapsing ('we may hope for ever') in the face of peasant mobilizations, land invasions and occupations. 'The potential for revolution of a traditional peasantry is enormous,' he concluded, 'but its actual power and influence are much more limited.' Peasant revolutions only become effective, he warned, 'either when unified and mobilized in a sufficiently large number of politically crucial areas by modern organization and leadership, probably revolutionary, or when the national structure and crisis is such that strategically placed regional peasant movements can play a decisive part in its affairs. This happened in Mexico in 1910–20 with Pancho Villa's northerners ... and with the followers of Zapata ... in Morelos ... Neither of these things happened in Peru.'[11]

In an essay on peasant movements in Colombia, written in 1969 but first published in 1976, Eric argued that Colombia had 'a record of armed action and violence by peasants (e.g. guerrilla war) second perhaps only to Mexico', but until the middle of the twentieth century relatively few social movements of the peasantry *as a class*. In this essay he traces the history of Colombian peasant movements, 'unusually decentralized and unstructured, [but] nevertheless extremely powerful', from the 1920s to the *Bogotazo* of 1948, with some emphasis on the influence of the Communist Party. (In 1935, he recalls, the Colombian party complained to the Comintern that most of its members were Indians and peasants rather than urban workers!) But although peasant resistance persisted after 1948, Eric was less optimistic in 1969 than he had been in 1963 about the prospects for revolution in Colombia. 'Instead of social revolution, or a populist regime, there was anarchy and civil war. The hopes of the left were buried in the *Violencia*.'[12]

Eric believed that the choice for Latin America in the 1960s and early 1970s was not between gradual change and revolution, but between revolution and stagnation or chaos. While an inspiration to all social revolutionaries, the Cuban Revolution, however, was unlikely to be replicated elsewhere in Latin America: 'its conditions were peculiar and not readily repeatable', he wrote.[13] And in a series of articles in the *Socialist Register* (1970), the *New York Review of Books* (1971) and the *Latin American Review of Books* (1974), Eric was strongly critical of the Cuban-inspired guerrilla movements of the 1960s and early 1970s – in, for example, Guatemala, Venezuela, Colombia, Peru and Bolivia, as well as Uruguay and Brazil.[14]

The strategy of the young middle-class ultra-left intellectuals who, inspired by the example of Fidel Castro and Che Guevara (and the writings of the French intellectual Régis Debray), believed that revolutions throughout Latin America could be precipitated by the action of small groups of armed militants was, in Eric's view, 'spectacularly misconceived'. The various guerrilla *focos* were doomed to fail – as they uniformly did (except, as we will see, in Colombia). There was no single recipe for a Latin American revolution, but certainly, he believed, it could not be made at will. To be successful it would need a combination of various factors: rural guerrillas, with a solid peasant base (the guerrilla movements of the late 1960s and early 1970s, he later wrote, 'neither understood nor wanted to understand what actually might move Latin American peasants to take up arms'[15]); urban insurrection ('No revolutionaries who fail to develop a programme ... for capturing the capital cities' he wrote in the *Socialist Register* essay, 'are to be taken very seriously'); probably, dissident armed forces; and, absolutely indispensable, political analysis, organization and leadership. In a review of John Dunn's *Modern Revolutions*, Eric commented that though Dunn did not believe that Marx threw much light on twentieth-century revolutions or their consequences, 'he freely admits that Lenin remains by far the best guide to how they came about, and Communist revolutions have been by far the most formidable and successful'.[16]

Cuba may have been a false dawn, but there was no need to be unduly negative about the prospects for radical political and social change in Latin America. Revolutions were not 'around the corner', as Debray and Guevara thought, but neither were they 'beyond the range of realistic politics', Eric wrote. Latin America remained a revolutionary continent. The prospects for the Left were encouraging if it would only recognize that there was more than one way forward. The Marxist left, including the communist left (except perhaps in Colombia), had always misunderstood Latin America and therefore had always been insignificant in the politics of the region. Instead of remaining ideologically pure – and ineffective – it was obliged to make the best of unfavourable and unproductive situations and join forces with other progressive political movements. As Eric wrote in the article in the *New York Review of Books*,

> The history of the Latin American left is (with rare exceptions such as Cuba and Chile [where Allende had been elected president in September 1970]) one of having to choose between an ineffective sectarian purity and making

the best of various bad jobs: civilian or military populists, national bourgeoisies, or whatever else. It is also, quite often, a history of the left regretting its failures to come to terms with such governments and movements before they were replaced by something worse.

Eric had greater expectations of the Revolutionary Government of the Armed Forces under General Juan Velasco Alvarado which had assumed power in Peru in October 1968 than any of Latin America's guerrilla movements at the time. Peru was a country 'whose social injustice and plain misery made the blood run cold', he wrote in the *New York Review of Books*, a review article on several books on Peru written before the military takeover. 'If ever a country needed, and needs, a revolution, it was this. But none seemed likely.'[17] The peasant movements and land invasions of the late 1950s and early 1960s had brought about the collapse of the highland *hacienda* system but, as he wrote in his article on peasant land occupations in Peru in *Past and Present*, 'unlike Marx's proletariat, the spontaneous force of the peasantry, though capable of killing landlordism, was unable to dig its grave'. It took an army coup (in 1968), 'after several years of shilly-shallying, to bury the corpse of the highland *hacienda*'.

Eric was sympathetic to the anti-oligarchical and anti-imperialist military regime in Peru from the outset, though always with a measure of scepticism. It was the first to recognize the mass of Peruvians, the Quechua-speaking Indians in and from the high Andes, as potential citizens and the first to institute a radical agrarian reform, albeit imposed from above, without peasant mobilization. But, without revolutionary cadres linked to the mass of the population, 'is this a revolution?', he asked himself. After the military revolutionary regime had been in power for three years, he was somewhat more critical, more pessimistic. Unlike the Peruvian left, however, he did not write it off. If it remained united there was no foreseeable prospect of replacing it. Certainly there was no alternative of Marxist mass revolution.[18] In an article comparing the experience of military revolution of, among others, Peru and Portugal, and recognizing their political and institutional limitations, Eric insisted that Peru was 'fundamentally different' from what it had been in 1967 and that 'the changes were irreversible'.[19]

In the meantime, the election of Salvador Allende in September 1970 had opened up for Eric the 'thrilling prospect' of an unprecedented, peaceful transition to socialism via democracy in Chile. In an article written as a special supplement of the *New York Review of Books* he expressed his hopes for the success of the Unidad Popular, a coalition of socialists and communists firmly based on one of the strongest working-class movements in Latin America.[20] Privately he believed that the odds were against it: six to four against, perhaps two to one against if his sympathy for Allende was factored in. Allende faced three difficult years; he might not even survive; there was a real danger that he would be overthrown by a military coup supported by the Chilean bourgeoisie. When the coup came in September 1973, Eric wrote: 'However tragic the news ... it had been expected and predicted. It surprised nobody.'[21] The Allende government had not committed suicide, it had been murdered. Like the Latin American left in general, it had underestimated the fear and hatred of the right, its willingness to abandon legality when legality and constitutionalism no longer worked to its advantage and to risk civil war. Eric was always impressed by the ease with which 'well-dressed men and women' acquired a taste for blood and the ferocity of the violence they were prepared to unleash.

The military dictatorship in Chile was not unique in South America. Brazil had been under military rule since 1964, Argentina since 1966. (The return of Perón in 1973 provided a short respite, but the military took power again in 1976 – and proved even more murderous than the Chilean military.) There had been military coups in Bolivia in 1971 and Uruguay in

1972, both supported by the Brazilian military (as was the coup in Chile). And in August 1975 the radical phase of the military regime in Peru came to an end with the ousting of Velasco and his replacement by a more conventional military junta. These right-wing military regimes of the 1970s, characterized by 'executions or massacres, official and para-official, systematic torture of prisoners, and the mass exile of political opponents', were the consequence, Eric believed, of the local oligarchies' fear of the urban masses mobilized by populist politicians and the rural armed guerrilla movements inspired by Castro, together with the US fear of the spread of communism in Latin America in the aftermath of the Cuban Revolution and in the context of the Cold War. The South American coups were all 'strongly backed, perhaps even organized, by the United States'.[22]

The 'old-fashioned' dictatorship of General Alfredo Stroessner, who had been in power in Paraguay since 1954, was an exception. Eric went there in 1975 and wrote a piece for the *New York Review of Books* which was given the unfortunate title 'Dictatorship with Charm'.[23] The *stronato* was the 'longest lived and most right-wing of Latin American dictatorships', but not excessively repressive of the political opposition (at least those members not already in jail or in exile) and for the most part prepared to let the peasants, two-thirds of the population, get on with their lives. 'By the miserably modest standards of the South American poor,' Eric concluded, 'they have not done too badly.' However, in *Interesting Times*, he confessed that he had been excessively kind to Paraguay, largely because it was the only Latin American state officially recognizing an Indian language, Guaraní, and also because he discovered he was known to the editor of the 'somewhat unexpected *Revista Paraguaya de Sociologia*' as the author of *Rebeldes Primitivos*. 'What scholar,' he asked, 'can resist fame in Paraguay?'[24]

Eric had been 'permanently converted to Latin America'.[25] He had made regular visits during the 1960s and 1970s, including in 1971 a six-month visit to Mexico, Colombia, Ecuador, Peru and Chile with Marlene and the children – the longest unbroken period he had spent outside the UK since he arrived from Berlin in April 1933.* And he continued to travel to Latin America, especially to Peru, Mexico, Colombia, Chile and Brazil, in the following decades – to lecture, to participate in seminars and conferences, to promote his books, all of which were translated into both Spanish and Portuguese, to receive homages from public authorities (for example, from the legislature of Buenos Aires in November 1998 at a ceremony in the Teatro San Martin which seated fifteen hundred, with seven hundred watching on a *tela* in the street outside) and to be given honorary degrees (for example, by the University of Buenos Aires in November 1998 and by the Universidad de la República in Montevideo in July 1999). In *Interesting Times* he claimed to have visited every country in the region except Venezuela and Guyana.

He remained primarily interested in the economy, society, politics and, above all, the revolutionary potential of Latin America. At the same time, he wrote, 'I did not even try to resist the sheer drama and colour of the more glamorous parts of that continent, even though it also contains some of the most anti-human environments on the globe – the high Andean *altiplano* on the limits of cultivability, the cactus-spiked semi-desert of northern Mexico – and some of the most uninhabitable giant cities – Mexico City and São Paulo.'[26] He became close friends with many prominent academic and cultural figures: for example, the Colombian sociologist Orlando Fals Borda, whose early writings were so influential

---

* Eric had distant family connections with Chile. His father's brother, Uncle Berkwood (Berk, Ike or Don Isidro), a mining expert, had emigrated to Chile with his Welsh wife and five children during the First World War. At the outbreak of the Second World War in 1939, his Uncle Sydney had also emigrated to Chile, taking with him Eric's sister Nancy and cousin Peter. Sydney remained in Chile, but Nancy and Peter left at the end of the war.

on Eric's thinking about peasants in the Andes and *La Violencia* in Colombia; the Peruvian historian Pablo Macera; the Argentine political scientist José Nun, with whom he made a long trip through the Argentine Chaco; the Mexican novelist Carlos Fuentes; his Brazilian publisher Fernando Gasparian (indeed the entire Gasparian family). He attracted to Birkbeck several Latin American graduate students. Latin America, he wrote in *Interesting Times*, 'is a continent on which I have many friends and pupils, with which I have been associated for many years, and which, I do not know quite why, has been remarkably good to me'. Latin America was also the only part of the world 'where I have found myself not surprised to meet presidents, past, present and future [in Chile, for example, Salvador Allende, in Brazil, both Fernando Henrique Cardozo and Luiz Inácio Lula da Silva] ... the first one I met in office, the canny Víctor Paz Estenssoro of Bolivia, showed me the lamp-post on the square outside his balcony in La Paz from which his predecessor Gualberto Villaroel had been hanged by a rioting crowd of Indians in 1946.'[27]

After the mid-1970s, however, Eric wrote relatively little about the contemporary problems and revolutionary prospects of Latin America. Brazil, Argentina, Uruguay, Paraguay, Chile, Bolivia and Peru, not to mention most Central American republics, were all living under military dictatorship. The one country with which Eric remained engaged was Colombia. There an old-style guerrilla movement led by the Communist Party and based on the support of the peasants and rural labour, the 'formidable and destructive' FARC (Fuerzas Armadas Revolucionarias de Colombia), had survived the 1960s and, alone in South America, gained in strength during the 1970s and early 1980s. Moreover, it had been joined by other guerrilla movements: the Maoist EPL (Ejército Popular de Liberación), the Cuban-inspired ELN (Ejército de Liberación Nacional) and the Movimiento 19 de Abril (M-19). But the armed struggle had brought Colombia no closer to social revolution. There seemed to be no end to the 'endemic and pointless state of sub-civil war' until in 1984, President Belisario Betancur initiated the policy of negotiated peace, with the FARC and EPL at least (it was rejected by the ultras in the ELN), that has continued at intervals ever since. Eric discussed the situation in Colombia (and also in Central America) with Betancur in his presidential apartments in Bogotá for an article published in the *Guardian*.[28] And Colombia's thirty-five-year guerrilla war and the troubles of a nation with 'an altogether exceptional proclivity to homicide' were the subject of a long essay in the *New York Review of Books*.[29]

It was Brazil, however, that increasingly attracted Eric's interest – and affection. Like most people, it seems, Eric liked Brazilians. In *Interesting Times*, he wrote: 'Nobody who discovers South America can resist the region, least of all if one's first contact is with the Brazilians.'[30] And Brazilians certainly admired and appreciated him. In May 1975, during the military dictatorship, he had visited Brazil for the first time since 1962 to attend an international conference on history and social sciences held at the State University of Campinas (Unicamp). It was, reported *Veja* (4 June 1975), a leading Brazilian news magazine, 'after eleven years of silence [since the 1964 *golpe*] the first sign of the resurrection of the social sciences in Brazil'. The conference brought together several international 'stars', 'the greatest of them – at least judging from the admiration shown by the audience – the historian Eric Hobsbawm'.[31]* Eric, who spoke on 'Pre-political movements in peripheral areas', made a huge impression on an entire generation of Brazilian social historians and social scientists, and the extensive coverage the

---

* *Veja* went on to comment on Eric's love of jazz, but then, bizarrely, criticized him for 'intellectual megalomania' on the grounds that the name under which he wrote as a jazz critic, Francis Newton, was an amalgam of Francis Bacon and Isaac Newton! In fact, the name was a homage to Frankie Newton, the black jazz trumpeter who had accompanied Bessie Smith in her final recordings and Billie Holiday in her original recording of 'Strange Fruit', and who was a communist.

conference received in the press brought him to the attention of the general public. He discovered that Marxism was not just the label for a small academic minority, but the prevailing ideology among the younger Brazilian intellectuals.

After the end of the dictatorship, in December 1985 Eric visited Brazil on holiday with Marlene. And in June 1988 he returned to Unicamp for a conference to mark the centenary of the abolition of slavery in Brazil at which he presented two papers: 'On the concept of citizenship' and 'On the concept of race'. In December 1992 he spoke to audiences of hundreds in the open air in Porto Alegre and at the Federal University of Santa Catarina in Florianópolis, and discussed politics with Luiz Inácio Lula da Silva, the leader of the Workers' Party, in a São Paulo restaurant. In August 1995, again with Marlene, he was in Angra dos Reis and Paraty (for a holiday), São Paulo (for a public lecture at the Museum of Art), Rio de Janeiro (for a public lecture to an audience of a thousand, with hundreds queuing outside, organized by Globo, the media conglomerate), and Brasília (to meet President Fernando Henrique Cardoso). And in 2003 at the first International Literary Festival in Paraty, on the coast south of Rio – where he and I shared a platform – Eric (aged eighty-six), astonishingly, was received like a visiting rock star by people on the streets, who shouted 'Eric, Eric' (pronounced Eriky), some women even asking for a kiss (*'Eriky, Dê-me um beijo'*). The bookshops of São Paulo and Rio de Janeiro were, and are, full of his books, which are virtually all best-sellers. He claimed that at one stage he was selling more books in Brazil than in any country outside the UK. 'I'm big in Brazil,' he would say.

Eric was interested in Brazilian history, of course, but also in Brazilian art, architecture, literature, football ('Who having seen the Brazilian team in its days of glory [1970]', he wrote in *Age of Extremes*, 'will deny [football] the claim of art') and, above all, music. He once told me he thought there were two true geniuses of twentieth-century popular music: Duke Ellington

17

and Antônio Carlos (Tom) Jobim. When I visited him in hospital in 2012, Eric (at the age of ninety-five) greeted me with news of a radical young black Brazilian rapper, Criolo, of whom I had to confess I had never heard (and I was living in Brazil at the time). But, as always, his main interest was political. Brazil, it seemed, was Latin America's last chance, if not for social revolution at least for significant social transformation.

In 'The Forward March of Labour Halted?', his influential Marx Memorial Lecture in 1978, later published in *Marxism Today*, Eric had argued that European labour movements were no longer capable of playing a transformative role and as a result the socialist and social democratic left was losing ground all over the world. But two years later in 1980 the Partido dos Trabalhadores (PT), Workers' Party, was formed in Brazil. Eric recognized the PT as a classic socialist party with its roots in organized labour such as had emerged in Europe before the First World War. And uniquely in Latin America, and almost everywhere else in the world, it was a socialist party based on organized labour established since the end of the Second World War. Even more noteworthy, its leader, Lula, was himself an industrial worker. In the light of Brazil's political history, political culture and political system (and the defeat of the socialist left almost everywhere in the world in this period), the growth of the PT in the 1990s was a remarkable story. Although he lost all three presidential elections Lula increased his personal vote from 17 per cent in 1989 to 27 per cent in 1994 and 32 per cent in 1998. Moreover, in every election the PT increased its seats in both the Senate and the Chamber of Deputies as well as the number of states and major cities it controlled. The steady rise of the PT led by Lula was enough, Eric wrote in *Interesting Times*, to 'warm the cockles of all old red hearts'.[32]

Looking back on more than forty years' engagement with Latin America, Eric admitted in *Interesting Times* that 'the expected, and in so many countries necessary, revolution had not happened, strangled by the indigenous military and the USA, but not least by domestic weakness, division and incapacity'. Moreover, he added, 'it will not happen now'.[33]

Eric had some sympathy for Hugo Chávez in Venezuela, but more for his anti-Americanism and the fact that he was supported by the remnants of the Venezuelan Communist Party than for any confidence that he would build a socialist society in that country. He never visited Venezuela in the Chávez era, but just as he always questioned me closely about Brazil when we met he questioned our mutual friend Richard Gott, the author of a study of guerrilla movements in Latin America, a history of Cuba and a biography of Chávez, about Venezuela. When Chávez returned to power in 2002 after the coup against him, Eric sent Richard a postcard saying simply 'Chavez's Bay of Pigs?'[34]

There was, however, still some hope for Brazil, although in the years since its defeat in the presidential election of 1998 the Partido dos Trabalhadores had moved steadily to the centre ground (indeed it dropped the word 'socialism' from its programme) and the Marxist, Trotskyist and Socialist left had been expelled or outmanoeuvred. Nevertheless, in October 2002 I drove from Oxford to celebrate with Eric, in the garden at his house in Nassington Road, north London, Lula's election to the presidency at the fourth attempt. The bottle of champagne empty, Eric, a lifelong optimist in his hope for social revolution in Latin America, but in later years, as we have seen, increasingly pessimistic about the possibilities of achieving it, looked at me and said: 'Now I suppose we wait once again to be disappointed.' We did, and we were.

As a professional historian, Eric was mainly interested in modern Europe. But, from his extensive reading and his conversations with academic and intellectual friends and colleagues, he accumulated an astonishing knowledge of the history of the rest of the world, especially the Third World – Africa, India,

China and, not least, Latin America. He regarded Latin America as a 'laboratory of historical change', 'a continent made to undermine conventional truths', the study of which enriched and changed his perspective on global history. Almost everything Eric wrote on Latin America had a historical dimension, but it was as a contemporary observer and analyst of social and political change in the middle decades of the twentieth century, and especially the critical period following the Cuban Revolution, rather than as a professional historian, that he made his distinctive contribution to our knowledge and understanding of Latin America. He never tried to become or regarded himself as a historian of Latin America.

His first book *Primitive Rebels*, a study of archaic forms of organized social protest, reform and revolution in the nineteenth and twentieth centuries, published in 1959, focused on southern Italy. No examples were drawn from Latin America, although in the preface there is a reference to Euclídes da Cunha's literary masterpiece *Os Sertões* (1902; translated into English as *Rebellion in the Backlands*), a 'classic study of primitive social rebellion' dealing with the War of Canudos (1896–7) in the interior of the state of Bahia in the north-east of Brazil. And the epilogue to the first Spanish edition, *Rebeldes Primitivos*, in 1968, and the preface to the third English edition, in 1971, both mention new research since 1959 on millennial and messianic movements, mainly in areas outside Europe, and in particular the work of Maria Isaura Pereira de Queiroz on Brazil.

Eric expanded the first chapter of *Primitive Rebels* ('The Social Bandit') into a book, *Bandits*, published in 1969, which incorporated studies of several *cangaçeiros* in the *sertão* (backlands) of the north-east of Brazil between the 1870s and the 1930s, especially Virgulino Ferreira da Silva, the famous Lampião. Bandits, or at least 'social bandits', were, Eric argued, not simply criminals; they were peasant outlaws. And banditry, or at least 'social banditry', was an expression of peasant discontent, a form of peasant action. He was interested in the emergence of social bandits in traditional agrarian societies, their relationship to rural messianic movements and organized peasant movements. They could be precursors of major social movements, and absorbed by them, but because of their ambivalent relationship with local power structures and their ideological and military limitations, they were more often a substitute, even an obstacle to their formation. 'The bandits' contribution to modern revolutions was thus', he concluded, 'ambiguous, doubtful and short. That was their tragedy.'[35]

In *The Age of Revolution* (1962), the first of Eric's four-volume history of the modern world from the French Revolution to the end of the Cold War, the subtitle of which was, after all, *Europe 1789–1848*, there are only passing references to Latin America. The Latin American revolutions for independence are treated with brevity, primarily as reactions to events in Europe, and 'the work of small groups of patricians, soldiers and gallicized *évolués*, leaving the mass of the Catholic poor white population passive and Indians indifferent or hostile. Only in Mexico was independence won by the initiative of a popular agrarian, i.e. Indian, movement.'[36] In *The Age of Capital, 1848–1875* (1975) there are half a dozen pages on Latin America in the chapter entitled 'Losers', in which Eric concludes that, despite some foreign, mainly British, capitalist exploitation of the region's natural resources, 'very little had changed in the backlands of Latin America by the 1870s, except that the power of the landlords had been strengthened, that of peasants weakened'.[37] In *The Age of Empire, 1875–1914* (1987) Latin America appears mainly in comments on the negative consequences of the region's insertion into the international economy and on the local elites as subordinate (and collaborative) agents of foreign exploitation. Four pages are, however, devoted to the Mexican Revolution, a 'major armed popular revolution ... the first of the great revolutions in the colonial and dependent world in which the labouring masses played a major part'. Here Eric was clearly influenced by the work of Friedrich Katz on the role of Pancho Villa in the north and of John Womack on the role of Emiliano Zapata in the centre-south.

Only in *The Age of Extremes, 1914–1991* (1994) does Latin America feature prominently as part of the emergence of the Third World in the revolutionary politics of the 'short twentieth century'.* There is some consideration of the Mexican Revolution; the revolutionary student movement in Córdoba, Argentina, in 1918 which, Eric claimed, 'soon ... spread across Latin America and ... generat[ed] local revolutionary Marxist leaders and parties'; the 'Long March' of Luís Carlos Prestes, the future leader of the Brazilian Communist Party, and the rebel *tenentes* in the late 1920s; the resistance to the US Marines in Nicaragua led by César Augusto Sandino (1927–33); the short-lived 'Socialist Republic' in Chile in 1932 under the leadership of the 'splendidly named Colonel Marmaduke Grove'; the Alianza Popular Revolucionaria Americana (APRA) in Peru; in Colombia, the Liberals and the 'people's tribune' Jorge Eliécer Gaitán, whose assassination in 1948 provoked popular insurrection, the *Bogotazo*; the political mobilization of urban workers by nationalist-populist leaders – Getúlio Vargas in Brazil, Perón in Argentina; the Movimiento Revolucionário Nacional (MNR) in Bolivia and the revolution of 1952 which nationalized the tin mines and introduced radical agrarian reform; and finally the Cuban Revolution and the tragedy of Allende's Chile.

---

* Paulo Drinot, a historian of Latin America at University College London, made a study of Eric's treatment of Latin America in his great tetralogy for the 'History after Hobsbawm' conference held at Birkbeck in April 2014. In *The Age of Revolution*, Drinot concluded, Latin America 'hardly features'. In *The Age of Capital* references to Latin America are 'rare and incidental'. In *The Age of Empire* Latin America 'appears fleetingly'. But in *The Age of Extremes* Latin America does finally receive 'more extensive treatment'.

In the meantime, Eric had written a long essay in which he argued that the development of the modern capitalist world economy 'generated or regenerated in various places and at various times dependent social relations which were not capitalist, [but] recognizably feudal'. In the case of Latin America the phenomenon of 'neo-feudalism', though both marginal and transitional, deserved serious consideration in the period from the late nineteenth century to the world crisis of the 1930s in which Latin America became fully integrated into the expanding capitalist/imperialist world economy, but not after the 1930s, 'except in rather unusual circumstances, such as those prevailing in the Amazonian valleys of Peru between the 1930s and early 1960s (e.g. La Convención)'.[38]

He had also become very interested in nationalism, about which he had very negative views. His book *Nations and Nationalism Since 1780* (Cambridge, 1990), based on the Wiles Lectures delivered at the Queen's University of Belfast in May 1985, had nothing at all to say about Latin America. However, he contributed an essay on 'Nationalism and nationality in Latin America' to a *Festschrift* for Paul Bairoch,[39] published in Geneva in 1995. The essay concluded: 'For the time being, lucky Latin America' – for having so far escaped, as he put it in *Interesting Times*, 'the world epidemic of linguistic, ethnic and confessional nationalism'.

Finally, he continued to revise and expand his book *Bandits*. In the postscript to the third edition (1981) and in the preface and postscript to the fourth edition (2000) he took account of some of the extensive research on the subject since the book was first published in 1969 and answered some of his most cogent critics, who were mainly concerned to make the point that, despite the myths surrounding them – and Hobsbawm's analysis, they argued, was too dependent on literary sources – most bandits were not necessarily or typically social rebels, let alone revolutionaries. In a review of Richard Slatta's *Bandidos: The Varieties of Latin American Banditry* in the *Hispanic American Historical Review* (1988), Eric described the book, 'the first comprehensive treatment of the subject for Latin America', as 'essentially a critique of my writings on banditry'. He was, he wrote, proud to be 'the founding father of an entire branch of history'.[40]

Leslie Bethell is Emeritus Professor of Latin American History, University of London and Emeritus Fellow, St Antony's College, Oxford. He was Director of the Institute of Latin American Studies, University of London (1987–92), Director of the Centre for Brazilian Studies, University of Oxford (1997–2007), Editor of the *Cambridge History of Latin America* (12 volumes, 1984–2008) – and a friend of Eric for more than fifty years.

Notes

1 *Interesting Times*, p. 363.
2 Ibid., p. 255.
3 Chapter 1 'Cuban Prospects', below.
4 Letter to Andrew Weale, 21 April 1984. Weale had enquired about Tynan and Cuba on behalf of Tynan's biographer, his widow Kathleen. (Hobsbawm archive, Warwick University, Box 1.) An online catalogue of the papers of Eric Hobsbawm is now available (https://mrc.epexio.com/records/EJH).
5 *Interesting Times*, p. 255.
6 *Times Literary Supplement*, 25 January 1968.
7 Chapters 2 'South American Journey', 4 'Latin America: The Most Critical Area in the World', 5 'Social Developments in Latin America', 6 'The Revolutionary Situation in Colombia' and 7 'The Anatomy of Violence in Colombia', below.
8 *Interesting Times*, p. 371.
9 Chapter 3 'Bossa Nova', below.
10 Chapter 17 'Peasants and Rural Migrants in Politics', below.
11 Chapter 13 'Peasant Land Occupations: The Case of Peru', below. Also chapters 9 'A Case of Neo-Feudalism: La Convención, Peru' and 14 'A Peasant Movement in Peru'.
12 Chapter 15 'Peasant Movements in Colombia', below.
13 Review of Claudio Véliz's *Obstacles to Change in Latin America* in *New Society*, 29 October 1965.

14 Chapters 21 'Guerrillas in Latin America', 22 'Latin American Guerrillas: A Survey' and 23 'US Imperialism and Revolution in Latin America', below.

15 *The Age of Extremes, 1914–1991* (1994), p. 440.

16 *Guardian*, 16 March 1972.

17 Chapter 25 'What's New in Peru', below.

18 Chapters 24 'Generals as Revolutionaries' and 26 'Peru: The Peculiar "Revolution"', below.

19 *New Society*, 22 May 1975.

20 Chapter 27 'Chile: Year One', below.

21 Chapter 28 'The Murder of Chile', below.

22 *Age of Extremes*, p. 442.

23 *New York Review of Books*, 2 October 1975.

24 *Interesting Times*, p. 369.

25 Ibid., p. 376.

26 Ibid.

27 Ibid., p. 362.

28 *Guardian*, 27 July 1984.

29 Chapter 29 'Murderous Colombia', below.

30 *Interesting Times*, p. 369.

31 *Veja*, 4 June 1975.

32 *Interesting Times*, p. 382.

33 Ibid.

34 Personal communication from Richard Gott.

35 *Bandits*, fourth revised edition (2000), pp. 118–19.

36 *Age of Revolution*, p. 185.

37 *Age of Capital*, p. 121.

38 Chapter 8 'Feudal Elements in the Development of Latin America', below.

39 Chapter 30 'Nationalism and Nationality in Latin America', below.

40 Preface to *Bandits*, fourth revised edition, p. x.

I

FIRST IMPRESSIONS

1

Cuban Prospects

Unless the Americans intervene with arms Cuba will fairly soon be the first socialist country in the western hemisphere. Already about 70 per cent of its small industry, nearly all the sugar-mills, and 60 per cent of Cuban agriculture (including sugar) are controlled by government or co-operatives, not to mention foreign trade. Already there are upwards of two thousand people's shops (*tiendas del pueblo*), almost all in the countryside, selling the peasantry consumer goods at little more than cost. Recently the speed of the transformation has increased, most notably with the expropriation of the American oil companies and banks, the nationalization of the tobacco industry and the seizure of sugar mills, big stores and textile factories.

Two things are remarkable about this process. The first is the overwhelming popular support which the government has maintained – and among the workers even increased – throughout. A non-official public opinion poll in June showed the astonishing figure of 88 per cent who gave the government total or virtually unqualified support: 94 per cent in the countryside, 91 per cent in the 20 to 30 age group, 92 per cent in the working class. On the other hand the province of Havana gave 'only' 72 per cent of totally uncritical support, the white collar and office workers 73 per cent (a sharp fall since 1959), and the small class of owners, executives and the professions, 61 per cent.

Asked what they thought the best achievements of the government, 49 per cent listed the agrarian reform, 42 per cent the provisions of more schools and teachers, 37 per cent the building of new houses, roads, etc., 30 per cent the lowering of the urban cost of living (by means of the 50 per cent rent cut, electricity cuts, etc.), and 57 per cent an indefinable combination of things best called 'liberation', 'benefiting and helping the poor', 'paying attention to the peasants', 'democracy and liberty', 'peace, security and happiness for all', 'looking after the people', 'governing well', 'making a real revolution, breaking with the past', 'revolutionary justice' and so on.

Asked what they thought the worst thing the government had done, the only grievances expressed by more than 1 per cent of the answers concerned arbitrariness and incapacity in the agrarian reform (2.5 per cent) and the government's alleged pro-communism (1.5 per cent). Asked 'what the government had so far omitted to do', the citizens made a number of suggestions, but by far the largest single bloc – 34 per cent – answered simply 'everything is perfectly all right'. For those who have not been to Cuba, these figures may seem well-nigh incredible. For those who have visited that remarkable endearing and encouraging revolution they merely confirm everyday impressions.

The second fact is that socialism was clearly not the conscious aim of the 26 July movement. Like most Latin American intellectuals, the original *Fidelistas* were Marx-tinged, but the 'economic thesis' of the movement (1957) was in no sense a socialist document. Nor does the actual propaganda of the revolution stress socialism. It could be summed up by the sentence: 'A free and prosperous Cuba must be free of imperialism, poverty and ignorance.' The keynote slogans – all revolutions produce public aphorisms in incredible profusion – are either simply patriotic like 'Fatherland or Death', 'We shall win through', or 'Cuba si, Yanqui no'; vaguely pro-poor like 'Who betrays the Poor betrays Christ', or anti-imperialist. No doubt the socialists in the *Fidelista* movement and the influential Communist Party had a socialist objective in mind. But what actually imposed it was the force of practical need.

All the government's plans for improvement required planned action: revolutions cannot wait. In effect, a large section of the officer corps of the Rebel Army immediately turned itself into INRA (the National Institute of Agrarian Reform), organizing co-operative and state farms, building houses and schools, running factories, planning industrialization and opening shops. Once Castro had made the crucial discovery that the landless labourers did not actually want small peasant holdings, but could be formed immediately into larger units, the overwhelming technical advantages of planned agricultural improvement simply cried out to be utilized. Not doctrine, but empiricism is turning Cuba socialist.

The speed and smoothness of the transformation so far is due to a combination of Cuba's historical luck and the classically pure nature of its revolution. Cuba is lucky in possessing a fabulously fertile, under-populated and poorly cultivated soil which makes large immediate increases in production possible; in its abundance of communications (notably TV) which can produce something close to direct democracy. Its Catholicism is more than usually nominal: only 10 per cent even of women attend mass. Its Spanishness enables it to draw on experts from other Latin countries with ease: most of its top economic men seem to be Chileans. Above all, a century of plantation monoculture has saved Cuba from the most intractable peasant problems. In brief, the peculiarities of economic slavery have turned into their revolutionary opposites.

At the same time the Cuban Revolution was not only a laboratory specimen of its type (a nucleus of intellectuals, a mass movement of peasants), but one unclouded by preconceived notions. While most socialists accepted the impossibility of moving straight from latifundium to co-operative, Castro saw the Cuban facts. While thirty years of international complexity had blurred the problem of state and revolution, the men from the hills spontaneously rediscovered the classical solution. The very waiters will explain to you that Fidel saw how the old army must be totally destroyed, the people armed, if the paralysis of Betancourt in Venezuela, or the defeat of Arbenz in Guatemala were to be avoided. And the old army is utterly dispersed. A vast urban militia (maybe, to judge by its looks, not yet a very formidable fighting force) and four hundred thousand armed peasants safeguard the revolution against exiles and Caribbean *condottieri*. What would most governments not give for so free a political hand, so zealous a mass support?

So remarkable is the record to date, that the difficulties which will increasingly arise are likely to be overlooked in an excess of Cubatopianism. These are both technical and political, though the technical ones will be lessened by the obvious readiness of the USSR and China to keep the small Cuban economy afloat at present. After all, it will not cost much and the political gains are enormous. But much of Cuban administration is still an inefficient tangle that will take some straightening out. Politically the government faces, with increasingly rapid socialization and growth, not merely the dissidence of the small middle- and white-collar classes, but some peasant opposition. And the economic programme holds out no prospect for rising urban wages in the next few years, while the American boycott (which affects spare parts and most durable consumer goods especially) will be most sharply felt in the towns. How fast the revolution should advance in these circumstances – insofar as the international situation does not determine its movements – is the chief problem facing the revolutionaries. Though the cautious and the dashing are to be found in all groups, my guess is that (paradoxically) the *Fidelistas* incline more towards speed, the communists to caution.

However, none of these problems is insuperable, or need be very serious. None of them is likely to produce, within the foreseeable future, any important body of Cuban opinion in favour of counter-revolution, which American policy has successfully identified with fifth columnism. There is no conclusive reason why my friend Pepe, an anglophile, Bevanite, Protestant Spanish refugee, should not continue to explain to all who care to listen: 'This is a good revolution. There was no bloodbath, as in Spain. Nobody is being tortured any more. We have the rule of law. This is the first government which acts for us and does not lie to the people.'

Unless, of course, the world permits the Americans to turn Cuba into another Suez.

October 1960

2

South American Journey

Brazil: Recife

Anyone who wants to know what an underdeveloped area is, might as well start with Recife, the capital of Brazil's impoverished north-east – that vast area of some twenty million inhabitants which has given the country its most famous bandits, peasant revolts, and still gives it a stream of undernourished migrants. Recife has eight hundred thousand inhabitants, which is well over double the population in 1940; half of them live in the unspeakable shacks and hutments which surround every big South American city, amid the characteristic smell of the tropical slums: filth and decaying vegetable matter. How they live nobody can tell. As in most other South American cities, there is not enough industry to absorb these floods of immigrants.

There is desperate poverty everywhere. The population looks as though nobody has had a square meal for ten generations: stunted, undersized and sick. At the same time there are signs of rebellion. The news-stands are full of left-wing literature: *Problems of Peace and Socialism, China Reconstructs,* and the newspaper of the Peasant Leagues, which are strong in these parts. (But there are also plenty of bibles.) The state of which Recife is the capital has just elected a fairly left-wing governor, mostly by the votes of the city's workers. The country people – former slaves on the sugar and cotton estates, small peasants in the back country – are largely illiterate and so voteless. The strength of the peasant leagues is patchy and one does not get the impression that they have made much progress lately, but the potential of peasant organization is immense.

The peasant leagues here have learned to talk to peasants in their own language. They use the travelling guitarists who make up their own songs as propagandists, and their newspaper prints a weekly 'peasants' almanac' with the saints' days, religious and lay 'holidays' (such as the anniversaries of the Russian and Cuban revolutions), a weekly ballad, horoscope, medical advice and proverbs or 'famous sayings'. This week they come from the Bible – the one about the camel and the eye of the needle – from St Ambrose, and Fidel Castro. St Ambrose, we are reminded, said that God created all things to be common to all men, Fidel Castro that the workers must fight not just for improvements, but for power. If any part of the world needs such useful advice it is this terrible area.

Brazil: São Paulo

It is astonishing to think that I am in the same country as Recife. The skyscrapers sprout, the neon lights glow, the cars (mostly made in the country) tear through the streets in their thousands in a typically Brazilian anarchy. Above all there is industry to absorb the 150,000 people who stream into this giant city *every year* – north-easterners, Japanese, Italians, Arabs, Greeks. São Paulo is a sort of nineteenth-century Chicago: brash, fast, dynamic, modern – anything over twenty years old is ancient history – and corrupt. A leading local politician

[Ademar de Barros], now cherished by the Americans for his anti-communism, used to campaign under the disarming slogan: 'Of course I steal, but I deliver the goods too.' At the same time São Paulo is the capital of the militant labour movement, in which the Communist Party is powerful, especially among the best organized and most skilled. But the party is technically illegal; it cannot put up its own list of candidates, though in fact – such are the complexities of Brazilian politics – some candidates advertise themselves as having the backing of Luís Carlos Prestes, the party's famous leader.

São Paulo's industrialization – a unique case in South America – is leaping ahead. But one cannot help being struck by the slenderness of its basis. The home market for Brazilian industry is desperately poor: here even shirts and shoes are sold on the never-never. The export market does not exist. Inflation keeps the expansion going, but while it makes the rich richer, it impoverishes the poor. Here in São Paulo, where the workers are by Brazilian standards quite well off, this is not so obvious, because the big firms seek to strengthen their monopoly by giving regular wage increases which the lesser firms outside cannot afford. But the whole business still has the air of a pyramid balanced on its point. The one thing industrialization has definitely produced is a national bourgeoisie confident in Brazil's future, and of its power to overcome the feudal estate owners and make itself independent of the USA. They are even prepared to make common cause with labour and the peasants for this purpose, for, of all the rich in South America, the Brazilian industrial interests are the only ones who do not appear to be afraid of social revolution, or of Castro. They may be too optimistic, but at present imperialism is what they are worried about and not expropriation from below. In a way, they remind me of the old Radical industrialists of nineteenth-century Britain, who had the same driving sense of having history with them. Until independence from US imperialism is achieved, it looks as though this alliance between the national bourgeoisies and the left will continue; but Brazil is too strange a country for predictions by casual visitors.

Peru: Cuzco

It has been said before, but it needs to be said again: if any country is ripe for and needs a social revolution it is Peru. Down in Lima the luxury hotels among the shanty towns, the Peruvian landed aristocracy, which flies over to the South of France for brief holidays; up here, twelve thousand feet in the thin air, the tourists arrive by the daily flights to gaze at the cathedrals built by those heroic ruffians, the Spanish conquerors, and at the relics of the Inca empire. Half the population of Peru consists of Indians, like those who pad through the Cuzco mud barefoot in ragged coloured home-spun, the women wearing men's hats over the regulation two black plaits, with babies on their backs. The agencies adver-tise them as picturesque, but they are as poor as any people I have ever seen.

Indians have been serfs for as long as man remembers. Any landlord can beat them or take their wives and daughters, anyone wearing European dress treats them like dogs, every policeman or official is their enemy. Yet now they are stirring. Nothing is more impressive than the long queues of Indian men and women waiting silently inside and outside the Cuzco Peasant Federation at night, waiting for the offices to reopen the next morning. They are delegations, come from distant *haciendas* and communities, to ask advice, to report injustice. A few days ago three hundred of them – as usual men and women in compact columns – invaded the estate of Dr Frisancho to divert the irrigation canals which ought rightly to serve their common lands. The landlord had mobilized the police, who used tear-gas, but the Indians advanced, protected by impro-vised gasmasks made from rags soaked in water. The police then fired and shot Clara Huaranca Puclla and her baby, and the peasant Guillermo Huamán Huamantica. Three police-men were wounded – with stones. Every day there are such incidents. The Peasant Federation (aided by the strong and militant Cuzco Labour Federation) has organized the Indians, and for the first time in history they have discovered that union is strength. Indians are not helpless.

A hundred miles along the narrow-gauge railway which the Japanese are now completing, past the gorges, into the long winding subtropical valley which leads towards the remote Amazon river, lies the valley of La Convención, where 110 out of the 160 estates now have union branches and the owners have fled to Lima, leaving estates of up to four hundred thou-sand acres in the hands of their stewards. Quillabamba, the capital of the province, is a wide, dusty, rotting market town linked to the world by the trucks which leave at 4.30 a.m. and return at night. Here the real lords of La Convención have their offices: El Banco Gibson, Anderson, Clayton & Co, coffee buyers, etc. Our truck is stopped by policemen, for there are armed peasant self-defence units in the region and the authori-ties are tense.

Most of the peasants cannot speak Spanish, or talk it hesitantly with a slurred whistling Indian accent which is hard to follow. Luckily there is a local carpenter who can help with the translation. I ask: why have the peasants started to organize? Because they are unjustly treated, like beasts. Why now? Because the trade union movement is now active. Are there not any problems in organizing for the first time? A quiet, flat-faced, tough man intervenes, explain-ing patiently. 'No, it is quite simple. You see, there are two classes. One has nothing, the other has everything; money, power. The only thing the working people can do is to unite, so that is what they do.' I ask: 'But are you not afraid of the police and the soldiers?' 'No, not now,' says the carpenter. 'Not any more.'

On the railway from Peru to Bolivia

My neighbour is a sharp young man with a briefcase. 'I am an insurance agent, cattle is the main business here, so I get around the country a good bit. If you ask me, these estate owners have brought it on themselves. They do not invest anything. They think because they are *duenos de vida y hacienda*, lords of life and livelihood, they have nothing to worry about. Now the hour is striking they run to Lima weeping. There are the Indians walking barefoot, even in the houses of the estate owners, and sleeping on the floor while the lord blows two or three thousand *soles* a night on a party. And they are not even aware of the contrast. Now the chickens are coming home to roost. Now there is nothing except the troops and the jails between them and the Indians. But it will not last for ever.'

No, it certainly will not. All over South America the poor and oppressed are stirring. What form their awakening will take one cannot yet tell. But the hour of the lords on their estates is indeed striking. When it does strike there will be great changes in Peru, and all over South America.

July 1963

3

Bossa Nova

The quarter of São Paulo, Brazil where the pop music industry
has its home is hard to distinguish from its London counterpart,
except for the skyscrapers. The same sharp, maudlin, slightly
wolfish characters hang round the same sort of offices, over-
flowing with records and back copies of *Billboard* and *Cashbox*.
The same mixture of lyric-writers, disc-jockeys, journalists and
guitar-players fill the bars, grabbing sandwiches, telephoning
and talking shop. Mr Enrique Lebendiger, the boss of *bossa
nova*, who has now left Brazil for the wider horizons of world
pop success, could be transplanted from the Avenida Ipiranga
to London without introducing a specially Latin note into the
Charing Cross Road.

And this in fact is the secret of *bossa nova*'s international
appeal. It is a cross between Brazilian urban music and jazz,
bred in the playboy set of rich young Brazilians and in the most
Westernized milieu of Brazilian big city entertainment, among
those professional musicians most likely to meet visiting American players. The interesting thing is that, in its short life of four
or five years, it has had three altogether different functions.

The origins of *bossa nova* go back to the war, when the

40

discovery of the big US swing bands of the thirties (reinforced later by that of 'progressive' and 'cool' jazz) first made local musicians aware of the instrumental and harmonic limitations of their own popular groups. *Bossa nova* therefore began in Brazil as an attempt to get more complex colour and harmony into the local music: one of those spurts of musical ambition which are so characteristic of the evolution of communities of self-educated craftsmen-musicians. In São Paulo the point about *bossa nova* is not merely that it has a new accent (an element of syncopation and, in commercial forms, an increasing suggestion of the square northern beat over the samba rhythm, which makes it acceptable to the gringos), but that in addition the chord progressions of the accompaniment are more skilled and 'educated' than before. They require *study*.

The new amalgam gained some popularity among local upper-class hipsters (a leading singer, Maysa Matarazzo, comes from millionaire stock and a leading composer, Vinicuis de Moraes, is a diplomat-poet), and also in those circles where Brazilian musicians met American ones. The name itself (it means 'the new style') is said to have been invented by one Joe Carioca, who worked with the late Carmen Miranda and later in Los Angeles.

Bossa nova was discovered for the world by visiting American avant-garde jazzmen, led by Dizzy Gillespie. It is revealing that the jazz avant-garde should have made the running in this new pop style, a very rare thing indeed. The top-selling *Desafinado* record (a number of which Mr Lebendiger claims with sober satisfaction that there are twenty-five recorded versions) is by such unlikely figures as Stan Getz and Charlie Byrd. For the jazz vanguard the attractions of the new style were twofold. First, it provided remarkable rhythmic interest and stimulation, and second, this very rhythmic interest enabled a man to get back, after years of increasingly unrewarding harmonic experiment, to blowing a straightforward nice tune without feeling philistine. And it is just sufficiently modified by jazz to be readily used by jazzmen. Hence the unaffected pleasure with which such leaders of the forward march as Sonny Rollins have turned to *bossa nova*. That this very combination of an unfamiliar yet not wholly unusual rhythm and good tunes should appeal to the public is a welcome bonus.

And so we come to the tin pan alleys of New York and points east. For them *bossa nova* is neither a way of making technically more exacting music nor a way out of a musical impasse. It is the possible successor to the twist. It is a new dance in an era of pop music in which, for the first time in a generation, dances as such are once again the basis of pop fashion. Now in Brazil *bossa nova* is in no sense a dance. It is a way of playing and singing. When I showed the ballroom diagrams which US radio stations have been distributing in order to help their listeners learn the new steps, local musicians burst out laughing. For them it is no more a special dance than jazz is.

This is why *bossa nova* in Brazil will certainly survive the ruins of the craze in the USA and Europe; for the pop industry is already engaged in its usual task of killing every new fashion it discovers by over-exposure. It will not only last, but develop. And the visiting student of jazz observes it with awe and a sense of the historic occasion. For *bossa nova* is the first major conquest of new territory by jazz. Hitherto the regions with a strongly rooted, rhythmically powerful, urbanized and expansionist popular music – and most of all Latin America – have proved impervious to jazz. If anything, jazz has been influenced by them. *Bossa nova* marks their first retreat. It is perhaps significant that this retreat should occur in the one Latin American country which looks as though it has definitely entered the age of modern industrial civilization.

December 1962

4

Latin America:
The Most Critical Area in the World

In the years after the Second World War, Asia was the region of the world's great political and social changes. In the 1950s we were all preoccupied by what was happening in Africa and the Arab world. No sane man cares to make firm predictions in politics, but one forecast seems reasonably safe. In the next decade or so [1960s and 1970s] the most explosive region of the world is likely to be Latin America. The twenty republics south of the United States – one French, one Portuguese, and the rest Spanish-speaking – are probably the parts of the world about which least is known in Britain. [. . .] However, when one begins to investigate Latin American affairs, one immediately discovers an obstacle even greater than simple ignorance. By our standards – not merely British, but, if you like, North American or even Russian standards – and in the terms in which we usually analyse political phenomena, the place simply makes no sense.

Consider the sort of thing which confronts the unhappy student of Latin America. We think we know what fascists, men directly inspired by Hitler and Mussolini, stand for. But in Bolivia a coalition of local followers of the Nazis, less classifiable nationalists and Trotskyists, made a social revolution which nationalized the mines, distributed the land to the peasants, gave equality to the Indians, and partly replaced the army by an armed workers' and peasants' militia. We think we know what a parliamentary system of Liberals and Conservatives looks like. But in Colombia, where such a system is traditionally strong – there have been, by Latin American standards, comparatively few military coups and dictatorships – it has produced massacre as a permanent political institution, at least in the past fifteen years. As recently as last 22 December, a Conservative gunman by the name of Efraín González entered a small town on market day, sorted out fourteen local Liberals, and shot them, though failing to cut off their heads, which is otherwise a not uncommon sequel to such political disagreements.

Again, we think we know what political ideology a solid, class-conscious, not particularly revolutionary trade-union movement is likely to have. But in Argentina such a movement is almost entirely Peronist, and conversely, Peronism is about as firmly based on the trade unions as is the Labour Party in Britain. We think we can recognize what separates socialists from communists. But where socialists exist at all in Latin America – which is only in a few countries – they are today often distinguished from the communists by being more revolutionary in, at any rate, their phraseology. Fidel Castro is a communist and Cuba the first 'people's democracy' of the American continents. But even his most ardent admirers would not claim that either his political career or his behaviour since coming to power is particularly orthodox by traditional communist standards.

Obviously we cannot expect the well-known political movements and institutions of our part of the world to be particularly successful in Latin America; and they have not been. Perhaps it is not surprising that Western liberal democracy has an unimpressive record there, for this form of government has never been easily transplanted. Indeed, over there it has in general been extremely feeble in strength and unimpressive in performance. Even where it has been strong, it has also by our standards been rather odd, as in Uruguay, where until the recent victory of the Blanco party, the Colorados had monopolized government for just under one hundred years. What is more surprising is that such movements as socialism and communism have on the whole been equally feeble. If mass communist movements could come into existence in countries like China and Indonesia, which have little in common in their social structure with Europe, why is it that outside of Chile, Cuba, and perhaps Brazil, no mass communist party has ever established itself permanently in countries which are fertile territory for movements of social revolution? (Chile is almost the only country in Latin America whose political structure and parties look reasonably familiar to the visiting European, though this familiarity is probably misleading.) What is more, even the Asian or African student will be puzzled by Latin American politics. He will, for instance, generally look in vain for such things as the 'national movement' with which he is familiar – the strongly organized front for national independence, generally under a charismatic leader, which virtually embraces and replaces all political life in a country.

On the other hand the unprejudiced observer will soon discover that there is a characteristic, Latin American form of political movement other than periodic military dictatorship. It is what might be called 'populism'; a mass movement of the poor against the rich, but supported also by military men and intellectuals, at once – if the terms are not too misleading – nationalist and socially revolutionary, sometimes poorly or hardly at all organized, generally built round or taking shape round some demagogue or leader-figure. In a broad sense, populist movements of this kind exist or have existed in several countries. Peronism in the Argentine, the movement of Getúlio Vargas in Brazil, the National Revolutionary Movement in Bolivia, the APRA (Alianza Popular Revolucionaria Americana) in Peru, the Acción Democrática in Venezuela,

45

the movement of the late Jorge Eliécer Gaitán in Colombia, are or were phenomena of this sort. Perhaps the Mexican revolutionary movement and *Fidelismo* have something in common with them also. The heyday of such movements was between the late 1930s and the middle 50s, though some – like APRA in Peru – go back rather longer. Around 1945–50 unbiased observers would probably have concluded that, for good or ill, such movements represented the coming trend in Latin American politics. Today we can no longer be sure even of this, for all of them are in an obvious state of stagnation, decline or disintegration, or else they have changed their character fundamentally.

Why European terms are inapplicable

It will therefore be clear that any attempt to analyse Latin American politics in European terms merely creates confusion. This confusion becomes even worse when we judge them not merely in our terms but by our preferences; for instance, by whether they have free elections or are anti- or pro-USA. To make sense of the countries between the Rio Grande and Cape Horn, we have to look at them not in our light but in theirs.

Still, one cannot help asking why European terms really are quite so inapplicable, why the classic movements and institutions of the Western world have hitherto been such failures in Latin America. And the answer can perhaps give us a valuable clue to the solution of the bigger problem. If I had to sum it up in a sentence I would say that Latin American politics are determined by the fact that national independence came to the continent more than a century before the great majority of its people entered national life. By 1830 all former Spanish and Portuguese colonies except Cuba and Puerto Rico were already independent states, though they immediately became informal economic dependencies of Britain. However, the social structures and colonial status of the continent remained virtually unchanged. The masses of its slaves or ex-slaves (that is, the Negroes), its peons and serfs (that is, the Indians), its inland communities of self-sufficient medieval *mestizo* peasants, its urban craftsmen and labourers, normally took no interest in national liberation and were not asked to. Some of them – for instance among the Indians on the Andean *altiplano* – almost certainly remained unaware that they were even living in one state rather than in another until the 1950s, for the nationality of the lords and officials who battened on them was irrelevant to their lives. I know of at least one old gentleman in the interior of Brazil who had not discovered in 1953 that his country had ceased to be ruled by an emperor more than sixty years earlier.

Independence, then, was the work of a small stratum of the westernized and educated, that is to say of the rich Creoles or, as we would today say, white settlers ('white' is a relative term in a continent which has always defined its colour bar in social rather than biological terms). The French and British liberal ideas and institutions which Latin America adopted in the early nineteenth century made no sense in the feudal and colonial society; or rather, they merely became yet another method of enriching those who were already rich, strengthening those who were already strong – for instance, by depriving Indians of common lands, by the corruption of deputies, and ministers, by the interminable delays of a theoretically lucid and codified law. What was liberal about them was turned into rhetoric, or into an excuse for local feuding. It is therefore not surprising that when the masses of Latin Americans entered politics they were generally inoculated against liberalism.

An unrepresentative minority

Socialist and communist ideas have proved rather more influential, but socialist and communist movements have suffered from a similar time-lag. For even during their formative period – say between 1890 and 1920 – Latin American politics still remained, apart from Mexico and a few other special cases, the affair of an unrepresentative minority. Socialist ideas belonged to European immigrants (as in the Argentine), to the odd model of organizable craftsmen and industrial workers, and to a few intellectuals from rich families. Roughly, where there was scope for trade unions of the European type, there was also scope for socialism, but not elsewhere. And 'elsewhere' included the great bulk of the Latin American peasantry, whom the traditional socialists and even communists mostly neglected, and with whom they could not come to terms even when they tried to. It was not easy for the simple, rationalist, secularist Spanish or Italian artisan anarchists, who did so much of the socialist agitation on the continent, to come to terms with, say, Brazilian inland peasants whose intellectual universe was, as near as makes no matter, that of Europe in the age of St Francis of Assisi. When, in turn, the peasants began migrating to the cities, they would also sometimes associate socialism and communism with the comparatively affluent labour aristocracies there, as like as not composed of European immigrants.

All this changed with the great slump of the 1930s, which marks the real end of the Latin American middle ages. If ever there was a crucial decade in the history of any continent, this was it. Broadly speaking – and always excepting the special cases like Mexico – it was only twenty-five years or so ago that the bulk of Latin Americans began to be the subjects rather than the mere objects of their countries' history. Their own movements of social revolt were slow to take shape, but the collapse of the colonial economies led almost immediately to the formation of nationalist and anti-imperialist movements led by middle-class politicians, intellectuals or officers. These were the people who sometimes borrowed ideas freely, and superficially, from fascism, which was at that time the most influential nationalist-demagogic ideology in Europe, though in fact the general trend of their movements was towards the left, for their power lay in mobilizing the poor against the rich (who were in turn associated with the colonial economy).

Populist movements

These populist movements were the equivalents of the national liberation movements of Asia and Africa. But they were inevitably rather more complex, or if you like rather more muddled, phenomena. For they lacked the obvious purpose of national political independence, which holds such movements together and gives them an easily realizable programme. Latin American states were already independent, at least on paper. Only the smallest, or those nearest the USA, knew foreign troops as actual occupiers, foreign bodies of men as actual – though perhaps unofficial – rulers, as in the banana republics of Central America. It is no accident that the nearest thing to a straightforward national movement against the foreigners is Fidel Castro's in Cuba. What strikes the observer most about such movements is a sort of groping, a sort of playing it by ear – a search, and often an extremely muddled and inefficient search, after a programme which would give reality to the formal independence of their nations. Such a programme would imply social reforms, if only to satisfy the masses without whose support the nationalists were bound to fail. It would also imply economic development. And, whatever the personal views of its leaders, it would be against the *gringos* from the USA, because nobody likes Big Brother, and even the habit of talking about 'America' when they mean the United States irritates Latin Americans as deeply as the habit of saying England instead of Britain irritates the Scots and the Welsh. But beyond that it was far from clear where the populists were going, and even less clear whether they would get there.

It is not clear yet. Only three things are clear. The first is that the awakening of the people in Latin America has begun. Nobody can go back to the years before 1930, or even before the Cuban Revolution of 1958. The second is that hardly any Latin American countries have yet found a reasonably permanent form of social and political organization. And the third is that Latin America is undergoing remarkably rapid social and economic changes under our very eyes.

May 1963

5

Social Developments in Latin America

I have suggested that it is useless, and indeed dangerously misleading, to think of the future of Latin America in the political
terms of Europe and North America. I want to consider here
what is actually happening in this continent today [1963]. This,
as I suggested, is not something unprecedented in itself. It is, in
fact, in many respects familiar to the European student, especially if he is a medieval historian and also knows something
about the modern colonial economies. What is original in Latin
America is a peculiar combination of, as it were, different historical epochs; the particular institutional setting – which is a
good deal more European than in most other underdeveloped
areas – and the time in world history in which matters are
starting to move, and to move at great speed.

First impressions are never complete, but not always, as one
is apt to think, insignificant. Most people, for instance, must
travel through Latin America by air, because often there is no
other choice. In Brazil there is a plane from Rio to São Paulo
every half-hour, but there are few railways and even fewer
roads. Most such plane journeys will almost certainly start or
finish at the airport of some large city, its skyscrapers, neon

signs and traffic jams rising like a mirage from among the plains and deserts, the jungles, and the wild, naked eighteen-thousand-foot peaks of the Andes. Mexico City, São Paulo, Buenos Aires, Rio are bigger than any European city except London, Moscow and Paris. But in between one flies over huge and apparently uninhabited areas. Latin America, except for a few areas such as part of the Caribbean zone, is in fact an empty continent, with incredibly poor communications, dotted with giant towns.

But not altogether: if it is empty, it is also filling up at an unbelievably rapid rate, faster than any other part of the world. By the year 2000, at the present rate, the number of Latin Americans should be approaching six hundred million, which is almost three times the present figure. Today there is about one North American for every Latin American. Tomorrow there will be two people south of the Rio Grande for every one north of it, and neither the Anglo- nor the Latin-Americans are unaware of the fact.

That is what the statisticians tell us. But one does not need to be a statistician to be horrified by the most striking aspect of this demographic revolution, the fantastic surge from the villages and backwoods into the cities. Forty per cent of the population of Lima or Rio, half the population of Recife live – if that is the right word – like refugees fleeing an earth-quake, in shanty towns and encampments. In ten years the size of vast cities may double. Already, in an overwhelmingly non-industrial continent, there are more townsmen than coun-trymen in five states: Argentina, Chile, Cuba, Uruguay and Venezuela. By 1970 they will have been joined by Colombia, Mexico and Peru. It took all of seventy years of the British industrial revolution and forty years of Soviet industrializa-tion to produce an urban majority in these two countries. This explosion of the cities has not yet produced social as distinct from demographic upheaval in the towns, though there have been rumblings and eruptions here and there – in Buenos Aires under Perón; in Bogotá the great insurrection of 1948; in Caracas, the capital of Venezuela, today. If anything the peasants flooding the cities have drowned the small local nuclei of socialists and communists there. In spite of appearances, peasants in shanty towns are often better off than in medieval backwoods, for the average consumption per head in a Latin American city can be several times that of the countryside. It will take time for these people to measure the gap between what they have – which is little enough – and what they could and ought to have. They are politically ignorant and innocent, and it costs little to buy their votes, where they have any. But the passion which is at present unloaded chiefly in the support of football teams will not remain non-political for ever.

In a traditional society millions of peasants do not start to stream away from the hinterland unless some profound changes are taking place in their lives. And so they are. Broadly speaking, there are two types of rural Latin America: the production of colonial cash crops of the world market, such as coffee and bananas, and a backward economy of large estates and dependent peasants rather like that of the European dark ages. The colonial cash crops are better known outside than in the medieval estates, but both are in a state of crisis.

To call much of rural Latin America medieval is not a metaphor but the strict truth; for in many cases there is still substantially the mental world of the European middle ages, which is after all the world the sixteenth-century conquerors brought with them. A religious revival or peasant rebellion in the Brazilian back country (which starts a few dozen miles from the big city) is often still a medieval heresy, led by a local prophet who patterns himself on Franciscan friars. The guitar-players still recite verse epics about Roland and Charlemagne to illiterate listeners. But even without this heritage, it is hardly misleading to call a society medieval in which feudal lords run ramshackle estates, often cultivated by serfs doing labour service, in which peasant communities live in a subsistence economy often hardly using money, linked together by feudal dependence and by the mutual aid between neighbours which is their basic social institution.

All this has been deeply disturbed by the rise of commercial agriculture which partly supplies food for the new cities, and partly supplies us with the coffee, the bananas and the other tropical foods we want, and on which the foreign trade of several Latin republics depends almost entirely. This rise of market agriculture is a comparatively recent phenomenon, and its direct and indirect effects are cataclysmic. Some peasants take hold of the new opportunities and become small commercial farmers. Some escape towards the vast unsettled frontier, where free men can still squat on virgin land. (Both these groups take readily to rebellion and communism.) Many give up and move to the cities. The remainder live increasingly restlessly in a social framework which is collapsing about them: an unpredictably explosive mass.

But even the colonial economy of the export crops (and of mining and petrol) is not what it was. The great slump of 1929 broke it, for it demonstrated the instability of the world market on which they depend. In almost every Latin country the year 1930, when the prices of the unique commodities on which their trade depended collapsed, is a landmark as visible as the date of liberation from Spain or Portugal. Never since then has there been even the illusion of economic stability, though the period between 1940 and the end of the Korean War produced a temporary boom, from which a crop of contemporary dictators benefited heavily. Never since 1930 has the oligarchy of large estate owners and middlemen merchants, which is the typical ruling class of most of Latin America, ruled unchallenged. Today, when changes which seem trivial to us, such as the rise of a taste of instant coffee, can take away more income from a half-dozen Latin republics than astronomic foreign loans can put back, people are more aware than ever of the crisis in economies which are in

54

fact colonial or semi-colonial, whatever the official status of their governments.

The old Latin America is collapsing. Something radically new must take its place. But so far in most places it has not yet done so. To take an obvious case: there are vast cities but as yet little industrialization, and what there is, is still largely concentrated in the typical old-fashioned food, drink and textile trades. A fistful of skyscrapers and luxury hotels, or even (as the Middle East shows) a flourishing oilfield, do not mean that a country has moved economically or socially into the twentieth century. There is thus a sense of oppressive tension, a feeling that things cannot go on this way, everywhere, especially among the educated and the intellectual. Like so much else in this continent it recalls the mood of Russia before 1917. For instance, though only one in five of the students at the National University of Colombia are Fidelists, nine out of ten believe that there must be 'a radical economic, social, and political change' in their country. These, as it happens, are young men and women who are personally rather optimistic about their future prospects; perhaps unduly so, for, as in many underdeveloped countries, there is a distinct shortage of opportunities for those with professional training. No, the discontent of these students is simply an extreme and unusually explosive form of the discontent which all except a handful of the very rich feel with the present situation of their countries. The most vocal and active of such potential rebels are students and sometimes young officers (who are a middle-class and very under-employed species, because few Latin armies have fought anybody for a long time, or are likely to). There are Nasserites as well as Fidelists between the Rio Grande and Cape Horn.

It is not only a sense of social justice which creates rebellion. It is also a general sense of backwardness and foreign domination, no less real for being informal. This is something felt even by the growing new middle classes of Latin America, who are torn between this feeling and the ubiquitous fear, which Castro has intensified, of expropriation. These are the classes which feel themselves constricted by the oligarchies of landowners and export merchants which stand in the way of industrial development, because their own interests lie in the semi-colonial export economy of coffee or bananas, meat, copper or oil. These are the people who would resent the old rulers anyway, for – though there are no monarchies – few aristocracies today are prouder or more powerful than the 'traditional families' of South American republics. They resent the sloth and ignorance of their countries and are very angry indeed about the comic opera image of sombreros, carnivals and epaulettes which attracts the North American tourist trade. They do not require communist prodding to be anti-North American any more than middle easterners needed it to be anti-British in the days when we were the economic Big Brothers of that region.

What are these discontents hoping for? Insofar as they think clearly about the subject, all of them, irrespective of their politics, are convinced that four important changes must take place. There must be agrarian reform – that is, the expropriation and division of the vast estates which dominate so much of the continent. There must be an end of the dependence of countries on one or two primary products – that is, an end of the semi-colonial economy. There must be systematic economic development – that is, in practice, industrialization. Lastly, whether they sympathize with it or not, there must be wholesale social reforms. There are no two opinions about this programme. President Kennedy's advisers are urging it in a moderate form upon the sometimes recalcitrant oligarchies in order to forestall communist revolution, just as Fidelists are urging it as part of such revolutions. The United Nations urges it in their own way. The only question is, who can bring it about and in what ways it can be brought about.

In fact the experience of the Latin republics is as discouraging as it is long, and the prospects for them are obscure. But a few of them have already made some sort of a break towards

56

the future, and they are watched with great attention by the rest. There is Cuba, which has chosen the frankly social-revolutionary way, on the assumption that the Latin middle classes are too weak, or too closely geared to economic dependence, to solve the continent's problem. (There is also Bolivia, which had a rather home-grown social revolution in 1952, but since this backward country has worked itself into a blind alley, nobody seriously considers it a model for progress). On the other hand two large states have shown some dynamism in economics in the tradition of private enterprise: Mexico and Brazil. Neither is a capitalist economy in the classical liberal sense. Both rely on large-scale government financing, on nationalized industries, and on state control to a substantial extent. The middle classes of both are far from conservative. Mexico rests on the greatest social revolution achieved in Latin America before the Cuban one, a revolution which lasted from about 1910 to 1938; and in Brazil the champions of industry are also the deliberate mobilizers of labour and peasant unrest against the old oligarchy.

Moreover, while both Mexico and Brazil are obviously out of sympathy with communism, the United States has been far from happy about their attitude – especially the Brazilian attitude – on the Cuban question. Neither country is by any means out of trouble, and anyone who has seen the horrifying shanty slums of Brazil will hardly advertise the place as a monument of social justice. It is possible that they may be unable to keep up their present rhythm of economic development, or even that they may stagnate or relapse, as the Argentine has done, from a level of social development which was in some ways more advanced than anything achieved elsewhere in Latin America. All one can say is that at present Cuba on the one hand, Brazil and Mexico on the other, provide home-grown models of change. No other country does.

At this point we must resist the asking of prophetic and loaded questions such as: will liberal-democratic institutions prevail in Latin America? What are the chances of communism there? Is a new crop of populist dictators likely to arise? It is not that such questions are unanswerable, though any forecast is likely to be wrong. It is rather that in asking them we almost inevitably project on to Latin America our own wishes and dislikes about world affairs. The important thing is not that Latin American changes should satisfy our political or social preferences. Those whose desires they must satisfy are the Latin Americans.

May 1963

6

The Revolutionary Situation in Colombia

The thesis of this article is that the history of Colombia in the past fifteen years can be understood only in terms of the failure, or rather the abortion, of a classic social revolution. From at least 1930 onwards, by a coherent historic evolution, a social revolution was in preparation in Colombia which ought logically to have produced something analogous to *Fidelism*, a populist left-wing regime working closely with the communists. In fact, this movement reached its climax, a plainly insurrectionary situation, at a moment when the taking of power was feasible. More than this: insurrection actually broke out spontaneously in April 1948 and was freely supported by the police of Bogotá. But there was no one to direct and organize it. The populist movement of Jorge Eliécer Gaitán, being entirely unorganized, was decapitated by the assassination of its leader; the communists did not recognize what was happening until it was too late. In consequence the country subsided into the state of disorganization, civil war and local anarchy which has obtained during the last fifteen years.

The situation in Colombia today is therefore far more significant than most students of Latin America have supposed, not merely because a straightforward advance towards a classic social revolution is very exceptional on that continent and because the degree of spontaneous mass mobilization achieved in Colombia, especially in the years from 1948 to 1953, is greater than anywhere else in the history of Latin America, with the exception of Mexico. (The *Bogotazo* of 1948 was, by all accounts, the most impressive spontaneous insurrection of the urban poor, and the mobilization of peasant guerrillas – and virtually *all* guerrillas in Colombia were and are peasants – has been incomparably greater than in Cuba, for instance.* The main reason why the Colombian situation was and remains so crucial is the fact that Colombia is a country which can make a decisive difference to the future of Latin America, where Cuba is not likely to do so. Colombia is a large country; in terms of population it is the fourth largest in the continent, and, at the present rate of increase, will soon have passed Argentina to become the third largest. It is a rich country with a potentially balanced all-round economy. Its situation makes it the strategic link between the Caribbean and Central America and at least the Andean mass of the South American continent. It borders on Venezuela, on Ecuador, on Peru and on Brazil, that is to say, on countries several of which are ripe for upheaval. And it would be far harder to bring pressure to bear upon a Colombian revolution than upon a Cuban one.

That Colombia, in common with most Latin American countries, with the possible exception of Argentina and Uruguay, contains the raw material for a social revolution both of the peasantry and of the urban poor is patently obvious. As in other Latin American countries, the problem is not to discover

* There is no solid statistical base for the estimates of Monseñor Guizmán in his book *La Violencia en Colombia* (Bogotá, 1962) that there were at one time up to thirty thousand armed guerrillas in action in the country. But it is a fact that, during a mere five days of 1953 at the end of the civil war, 6500 rebels laid down their arms; this is a considerable figure for irregular forces.

inflammatory material but to explain why it has not yet burst into flames, or – as in the Colombian case – why, having spontaneously flared up, it has settled back into a smoky mass showing only an occasional glimmer.

Background to the present situation

Modern Colombian history can be said to begin with the slump of 1929 and the return of the Liberals to power in 1930 which marked the opening of a new political era.

Colombia has had a rather special political structure with a stable two-party Liberal–Conservative oligarchy; this structure has to a large extent excluded the usual forms of *caudillismo*, and has also – and this is exceptional – sunk deep roots among the rural peasantry. In Colombian terms, therefore, political evolution has tended to proceed not by leaving the traditional parties high and dry as islands of the rich, but by infiltrating and transforming them. Thus, between 1930 and 1948 the Liberal Party was transformed into a people's party, partly through its adoption by the rising urban, industrial, non-*comprador* middle class, which, as usual, was boosted by the collapse of the cash-crop economy, and partly through the deliberate effort made by a New Deal wing of the traditional Liberals to capture the political awakening among the urban and, to a lesser extent, the rural poor.

Alfonso López, perhaps under Rooseveltian influence, pursued this course with great success in his presidencies from 1934 to 1938 and, to a lesser degree, from 1942 to 1945. More important, the independent populist mass movement organized by Gaitán moved back within the orbit of Liberalism, out of which Gaitán had himself emerged; in fact, Gaitán eventually captured the Liberal Party in 1946. It ought perhaps to be added that the Communist Party, also founded in 1930, tended to operate under the general wing of the Liberal New Dealers. It was not, however, particularly influenced by Gaitán and his

61

supporters. For various reasons, it treated *Gaitanismo* with deep suspicion until too late, and this, as it turned out, was a decisive error.

This trend in Colombian politics undermined the entire basis of the two-party oligarchy, for it threatened to turn the parties into social movements and, what is more, to transform the Liberal Party, with its appeal to the poor, into the permanent and overwhelming majority party.* This development can be regarded as the root cause of the civil wars of 1949–53. Faced with virtual long-term eclipse, the Conservatives had to fight back, and, after the insurrection of 1948 had shown them the full danger of their position, they did so by means of a systematic attack on the Liberal regions of the country, combined with a deliberate conversion of the state apparatus, notably the police and the army, into a Conservative vested interest.

The civil wars and the Pinilla dictatorship

In April 1948 Gaitán was murdered, and an insurrection broke out almost immediately. It was met by a national coalition of the two parties, that is, by a switch of the moderate Liberals to the Conservatives; this move was opposed by the left-wing Liberals and by the *Gaitanistas* and produced wild dissension within the party.

The coalition broke down shortly before the 1949 elections. The Conservatives attempted to seize the opportunity provided by a deeply divided Liberal Party to establish their own power. This could be done, however, only by extra-electoral methods, especially since the Liberals were still strong enough, though only just, to win the 1949 elections. The army was purged of Liberals, and all administrative and military means were used

---

* The Church and certain traditionally conservative areas, like Boyacá, would probably have kept a certain following among the peasantry for the Conservatives, though probably not much in the cities.

by the Conservatives, under the right-wing presidential candidate Laureano Gómez, to render Liberal politics impossible and to smash the Liberal strongholds in the countryside. The countryside had already been considerably disturbed since the death of Gaitán, and the Conservative attack produced, in effect, a movement of Liberal self-defence, ranging from the spontaneous formation of peasant guerrillas against government forces and strong-arm squads to the collective dissidence of entire Liberal regions, such as the Llanos Orientales. The civil war soon developed beyond a mere armed party struggle. Broadly speaking, at its peak it involved all the inhabited areas of the country, with the exception of the Atlantic and Pacific coastal zones. The Conservative regime moved steadily towards a semi-fascist dictatorship.

In 1953, however, the military, under Rojas Pinilla, took over the government in order to end an intolerable situation, for by then it was clear that the experiment of right-wing government under Laureano Gómez had been a total failure. The civil war was ended by an amnesty, and political life was at least formally re-established at the centre, though only as a sort of adjunct to military rule.

But Rojas's dictatorship also failed. Rural violence was resumed after 1954, though only in a limited sector of the country, and it became clear that Rojas's attempt to introduce a regime modelled on a kind of *Peronismo* was entirely hopeless. It lacked the essential basis of populist military rule, namely mass support, the Colombian masses being, not virgin soil politically, but traditionally Conservative, Liberal or, in a minority of cases, communist. Rojas also lacked the other asset common to Latin American dictators of the early 1950s such as Perón in Argentina and Odría in Peru, namely, ample reserves of foreign exchange or the support of a boom in the price of the basic export commodity. Coffee prices (on which 95 per cent of Colombia's foreign exchange depended) fell from 80 cents a pound in 1954 to 45 cents in 1958. Moreover,

Rojas's mismanagement of the economy did not help. By 1957 there was a severe exchange crisis, and it was necessary to cut imports heavily. The Church abandoned its support of Rojas, the two parties formed a solid bipartisan front in exile, and in 1957 the dictatorship fell and the present regime took over, ostensibly as a temporary measure.

The conclusion of the civil war can therefore be explained in very similar terms to its beginning. The civil war was in danger of turning into social war. In the Llanos Orientales, for instance, it began as the armed self-defence of a solidly Liberal region against the Conservative government and was organized by the ranchers, led by the ranch foremen, and fought by the cowhands and peons. But within a short time the social cleavage within the Plains people began to trouble their leaders: the war against Bogotá showed signs of turning into a war against the cattleless men, who favoured social change. The magnates preferred, therefore, to make their peace with the capital, once they had secured a guarantee of non-interference. Since 1953 the Llanos have been quiet, though they are now said to contain a strong communist underground.

It is worth adding that, in the course of the war, a few communist areas – notably the important and strategically situated so-called 'Republic of the Tequendama', within a few dozen miles of Bogotá – made themselves virtually autonomous, though the more orthodox among them made no attempt to do more than prevent the incursions of all outsiders, governmental or otherwise.

The dictatorship of Rojas Pinilla in 1953 put an end to the civil war, but unrest revived again. In 1957, however, the two traditional parties agreed on the twelve-year truce under which Colombia is still governed. Only Liberals and Conservatives can now stand for election (although, in an arrangement rather reminiscent of Uruguay, organized political groups within each party can put up candidates, and the Communist Party, though disenfranchised, is legally tolerated). Liberal and Conservative presidents alternate.

This truce arrangement has greatly reduced the *violencia*, though it has recently tended once again to revive, this time entirely free from party loyalties though encouraged by the mere fact of elections. It is, however, fairly certain that the Liberals are and will remain the majority party – in 1960 they gained about 1.5 million votes against 1 million for the Conservatives – the balance now being made up by the conservatism of the armed forces. The revolutionary element has passed to the support of the so-called Revolutionary Liberals under López Michelsen, the son of the New Deal president, and such members of the extreme left as were or are elected, such as the peasant leader Juan de la Cruz Varela of Sumapaz, have sat or are sitting as Movimiento Revolucionario Liberal (MRL) deputies.

The situation today

What has been the consequence of the civil war and the rural unrest which has persisted ever since? In effect, it has been to destroy the attempt, made during the Conservative era, to set up effective centralized administration. At present the only genuinely all-Colombian organization with the power to enforce its central orders locally and to collect income from the whole country is the Church (which is, of course, a Conservative vested interest). A semblance of central administration exists, but it depends largely on a *de facto* withdrawal of the government from certain purely local functions, which are left to the local administration – in some instances communist, in most Liberal or Conservative. This situation, reminiscent of medieval feudal states, is perhaps no worse in Colombia than in several other Latin American countries, though the geographical complexity of Colombia makes it appear rather more obvious.

What, in terms of the forces which might have been expected

to support a social revolution, is the situation today, fifteen years after the *Bogotazo*? In the cities, which have grown at an unbelievably rapid rate – the five largest have together doubled in population in the past ten years – all is quiet. Gaítan is dead, and no leader capable of mobilizing the urban poor has emerged. The urban and industrial labour movement has been split, through demoralization and ideological or cold-war divisions, into three main groups: the Colombian Labour Federation linked with the International Confederation of Free Trade Unions, a Catholic body, and an alliance of the surviving communist and independent unions.

In the countryside the situation is different, for *violencia* has not been eliminated, but is endemic in five or six departments – Valle, Tolima, Calda, and the adjoining parts of Huila, Cauca and Cundinamarca, as well as in sections of Antioquia and Santander-Boyacá. It is dormant in a great many other places. Fifteen years of anarchy have turned it into an institution or a racket – sometimes, as in the coffee areas of Caldas, strikingly similar to the Sicilian Mafia, insofar as it is an organization of the rural middle class working for economic ascent. It is not an institution aiming at social revolution. Recently, however, abandoned by both the two great political parties, the surviving groups of brigands and the new groups constantly forming from among the second generation of violent men have been discovering a mission to fight for the poor against the rich, and it is said that communist influence has increased among them. This is true only in a very qualified way, however. The Communist Party has no enthusiasm for the brigands, even when they are not frankly anti-red, and shows the utmost reluctance in its contacts with them.

The communist areas

On the other hand, the quasi-autonomous communist areas and nuclei persist. They are of three kinds. First, the 'Republic of the Tequendama', which is similar in social structure to the neighbouring area of *violencia* lying between it and Bogotá. Its population consists of former small tenant farmers who forced the landlords to sell them their plots before the war. It has become a sort of communist William Tell Switzerland, consisting of independent 'cantons', such as Viotá, run by an admirable party functionary and former brewery-worker, Victor Merchan, and Sumapaz, run by a grassroots peasant leader, Juan de la Cruz Varela, who has passed successively through the stages of Liberalism, the Communist Party, *Gaitanismo*, his own agrarian movement, and the Revolutionary Liberals, which appear to be in his case a camouflage for more advanced views.

This area adjoins the second type of communist stronghold, consisting of the empty spaces stretching from the mountains towards the plains and the Amazon basin. These have gradually been settled by independent groups of peasant pioneers, who, as masterless men, have much sympathy for communism. In these inaccessible territories of the Metá and the Caquetá there are guerrilla training bases and other centres, such as the training base for the Sumapaz people on the Rio Duda, in the El Pato area of Metá, and in Belen (south-west of Florencia). There are also some communist centres in Tolima (Villarica, Icononzo, Chapparal), and some – less active than before – in the Indian zone of Cauca. The third communist stronghold is the semi-underground nucleus in the Llanos Orientales.

Communist areas are armed, organized, disciplined, with a regular system of administration, education and law, and are invariably recognizable because, even in the middle of areas of bloodshed, they are free from *violencia*. Their chief advantage lies in their attraction for the neighbouring peasantry because of the evident efficiency and justice of their arrangements; the best expert in the field, Monseñor Germán Guzmán, considers that they may become increasingly attractive. Their chief weakness is the very spontaneous peasant character which gives them their appeal; for, in fact, their political horizon is completely local. If left alone they concentrate on their own region, and hardly even challenge the higher levels of administration and economic activity. Viotá, for instance, lives in a state of informal coexistence with the central government.

Seizures of land

However, a more direct form of agrarian agitation has recently revived, namely, the occupation of land. This development is strikingly similar to what is happening all over Latin America, and it has no direct correlation with *violencia*. The move to occupy land, whether spontaneous or organized by the communists, has not occurred to a great extent in the coffee zone of small tenant farmers which is the centre of *violencia*, but mainly in the latifundist zones of the south: Nariño, Cauca, Huila, part of Tolima, and – a new phenomenon, or rather a revived one – on the Atlantic coast in Bolívar, Atlántico and Magdalena. The seizures are undertaken less by landless labourers, who are, on the whole, a rather passive class all over the continent, than by sharecroppers and tenants.

The chief characteristic of this activity is that it cuts entirely across politics. Thus, at the end of 1961, and in the Cunday area – part of the old zone of influence of the Tequendama and Juan de la Cruz – Conservatives, Liberals, communists and priests united to invade the estates, and the owners preferred (as in very similar situations in Peru) to retire to the city.

Broadly speaking, the areas with active land occupations are the ones in which the government has decided to implement agrarian reform. With the exception of a zone in Santander, all the nine projects of agrarian reform under way in 1962 – partly colonization (as in Nariño and Antioquia), partly division of estates (as in Cunday) – affect such areas. This fact, incidentally, underlines the weakness of all Latin American plans for land reform from above; in general the only means of actively bringing about the implementation of such plans is through active agrarian unrest.

The situation among the students

As regards the last of the insurrectionary classes, the students, the present situation in Colombia is quiet. Unlike several other countries of Latin America, Colombia has not seen a striking left-wing movement among students in the past two or three years. The left (including the MRL) is distinctly in a minority in Bogotá, and even in the Universidad Libre, a secular and quite strongly Marxist-orientated institution, *Fidelistas* form less than half the student body, as they do in the most politically minded faculty of the Universidad Nacional, Law and Economics. The general mood of left-wing intellectuals appears to be pessimistic and disoriented, though student strikes, spreading from one university to another as in 1962, are popular and influential.

One important fact must be noted, however: between 1948 and 1958 the number of university and secondary-school students rose by about 140 per cent. In 1958 there were more than nineteen thousand university students. Moreover, several new universities have been founded in various cities, thus constituting several new centres of potential revolutionary activity.

The political parties

What is the present situation of the parties and such other political groups as exist? There is, in the first place, evidence that all parties have been somewhat weakened. Thus in the elections of 1960 only 4.4 million voters registered out of 7 million, and only half of these voted. In 1962 the percentage of the total electorate actually voting was also only about half.

The Liberal Party is, broadly speaking, divided between

the official Liberals of Lleras Restrepo and the MRL of López Michelsen, which is to some extent, though against much internal resistance, also the legal front for the disenfranchised left. (Juan de la Cruz was one of its first leaders and sat for it in the Chamber.) The MRL scored an unexpected success in 1960, gaining 20 per cent of the Liberal vote, and an even greater success with 36 per cent of the vote in 1962. Its strength lies in the countryside and in the medium-sized towns with Liberal traditions, and perhaps also in its links with guerrillas and ex-guerrillas who have considerable political power locally. In the big cities it failed lamentably in 1962. Its appeal is broadly *Gaitanista*, though Gaitán's daughter, who has tried to revive his movement, is usually in opposition to it. It manoeuvres carefully between identification with the *Fidelistas* and communists and opposition to them which might cause the loss of their support. At present the tendency is to the right. It is thus a coalition of revolutionaries and reformers; its leader, López Michelsen, is perhaps to the right of his father and certainly no revolutionary. Insofar as the left has a mass expression, however, it is through the MRL.

The Conservatives have one major asset, the support of the Church, though its actual allegiance to this or that politican or (Conservative) movement is unofficial and conditional. Beyond that the party is fragmented, in the main between the bipartisan followers of Ospina Pérez and the right-wing *Laurenistas*. The former dictator Rojas is also a power to be considered. It is perhaps misleading to read too much social significance into the eighteenth-century type squabble between political clans and connections, since personal relations, family loyalties and tactical alliances between local blocs probably have a major influence in such combinations. Of late they have once again tended to combine.

It is, however, probable that outside the electoral framework a socially conscious wing is forming somewhere within Conservatism, composed perhaps largely of young Falangist intellectuals and officers. In the circumstances of Latin America, such a quasi-fascist right may quite easily turn into a potentially social-revolutionary force, as it did in Bolivia, or throw up a strong Nasserist current, as in Peru. It is true that the Colombian army has not the tradition, common to several other Latin American countries, of military coups and *caudillos*, but the breakdown of the party system has once already put a General – though perhaps rather a reluctant one – into temporary power: Rojas Pinilla in 1953–7. It may do so again. The persistence of the *violencia* rather militates against this possibility, however, for attempts to control it keep the army occupied.

The Communist Party, very much smaller and more localized than the other two parties, is weakened by internal dissension and also by lack of central control over outlying districts. Its leadership, under Gilberto Vieira, is of the orthodox stamp, but the party has never reached the stage of monolithism, and remains not far removed from the early phase when groups split and remerge as the political situation changes. At present the chief dissidents are intellectuals who consider the party policy too moderate, though until recently Maoism seemed to have very little influence. Beyond them are the *Fidelistas*, the name being largely a synonym for left-wing opposition to the communists. They have formed a Frente Unido de Acción Revolucionaria (FUAR), a coalition of various local groups with the revived *Gaitanism* of Gaitán's daughter and son-in-law, which appears to be its directing force. It is probable that a few *Fidelista* groups remain outside it. All these attempt to instigate direct action and to link up with existing guerrillas. The FUAR is composed entirely of intellectuals, and so far its activities are not of great moment.

Outlook for the future

It cannot be said that any existing political party or movement is likely at present to succeed in rousing the masses, or that any individual leader has gained a national reputation such as

71

that of Gaitán. (The existing non-communist leaders belong to the traditional political families, such as Lleras or López or Ospina, with all the accompanying advantages and limitations this implies.) The MRL is the nearest thing to a mass left-wing movement, but its sphere of influence is limited.

It is possible, indeed probable, however, that the rigid framework of bi-partisan rule will be broken by a joint defection of Conservative and Liberal malcontents, and that full party agitation will resume before the unofficial end of the truce. Another possibility, in this or a different situation, is some sort of military dictatorship. There are left-wingers who pin their hopes on the reaction against such a dictatorship, but this is merely another way of expressing their pessimism about the actual situation.

It seems clear that the net result of the aborted social revolution of 1948 has been to produce a disorganized anarchy. Superficially the situation looks stable, but this is plainly an illusory phenomenon, for beneath the surface social change is taking place at a staggering rate. The population, as mentioned above, is increasing fast; over the past decade it has risen by 27 per cent. The urban population is rising even faster. By 1970 the population of Colombia will be predominantly urban, and, what is more unusual, divided between several giant cities: even now Bogotá, Medellín, Cali and Baranquilla each have upwards of half a million inhabitants. The living conditions of the working class are poor, as is shown by the fact that Colombian urban workers spend a higher proportion of their income on food than Brazilian workers, and a rather lower proportion on clothing than even their neighbours in Ecuador. There is evidence that in the big cities, and notably in Bogotá, the standard of living of the working class has deteriorated. The capital has, for instance, a lower per capita consumption of proteins and calories in general than all but one of the major cities of the country, and, after Cali and Pasto (Nariño), shows the widest gap between middle- and working-class consumption.

72

It is inconceivable that this situation will not sooner or later lead to a revival of mass unrest in the capital, and, for that matter, in the other cities. Industrialization is modest and relatively slow: the percentage of industrial workers in Colombia, in comparison with the rest of the South American continent, is higher only than that in Bolivia, Paraguay and Ecuador.

The disintegration of traditional rural society is proceeding at an accelerated rate, as the rush into the cities demonstrates; and the structure of land tenure and the standard of agriculture remain archaic. It is too early to judge the possible effect of agrarian reform, which is for the moment planned mainly to affect one or two particularly critical zones.

Above all, the conviction that something must change, and radically, is universal. Though the students are relatively passive, 82 per cent (91 per cent after their first year) are convinced of the need of such a change; and 72 per cent would be *Gaitanista* if Gaitán were alive.

It is difficult to predict the form of the political and social change that is likely to come or its consequences. But any observer who believes that Colombia is living through anything but a pause of exhaustion is likely to have a very sharp awakening.

June 1963

7

The Anatomy of Violence in Colombia

For the past fifteen years the South American country of Colombia has been ravaged by a combination of civil war, guerrilla action, banditry and plain massacre which is no less catastrophic for being virtually unknown in the outside world. This phenomenon is known as *La Violencia* for want of any better term. At its peak, between 1949 and 1953, it amounted to a civil war which involved about half the country's area and most of its population. At its lowest point (1953–4) it was probably reduced to parts of two departments (which are the main administrative subdivisions of Colombia). At present it affects parts of six or seven departments, which between them comprise 40 per cent of the population and is probably dormant, but not extinct, in several more.

The total human costs of *La Violencia* are startling. The latest monograph, published by the Faculty of Sociology of the National University of Bogotá[1] rejects the wilder estimates of 300,000 or so killed (in 1958 the government's guess was 280,000) but suggests no less than 200,000. However, this lacks reliable statistical foundations. On the basis of the latest (January 1963) official government and provincial figures the total can hardly be much less than 100,000 and may well be much higher. There are no figures for lesser casualties. On the other hand the effect of the *Violencia* in specific areas can be gauged by local studies such as R. Pineda Giraldo's for El Libano (Department of Tolima).[2] Of 452 families interviewed in the poorer quarters of this city in 1960, 170 had between them lost 333 relatives in the various massacres. The effect of the *Violencia* on internal migration has also been measured in one or two enquiries. It is very considerable, for, to quote Father Camilo Torres, who has studied it for Bogotá, 'as in feudal times the peasants come to the city to seek security'.

But what is most interesting about *La Violencia* is the light it throws on the problem of rural unrest and rebellion. If we omit the period of formal civil war (1949–53) the *Violencia* is an entirely rural phenomenon, though in one or two cases (as in the Departments of Valle and Caldas) its origins were urban, and certain types of government or Conservative gunmen – the *pajaros* – remained city-based, as is indicated by their use of motor transport. It represents what is probably the greatest armed mobilization of peasants (as guerrillas, brigands or self-defence groups) in the recent history of the western hemisphere, with the possible exception of some periods during the Mexican Revolution. Their total number for the entire period has been estimated as high as thirty thousand, though all such statistics are highly unreliable. Of the actual armed men almost all are peasants, between the ages of fourteen and thirty-five, and probably above the average in illiteracy. (One sample of one hundred guerrillas in the Tolima department contained only five illiterates.) No workers and only the odd intellectual or middle-class person are found there. Except for a few Indians (in specific localities) and a very few – disproportionately few – Negroes, they are the usual type of scrawny, undersized, under-fed, but astonishingly resistant *mestizo* peasants or pastoralists who may be seen anywhere outside the coastal regions of the country. Politically they divide very much as the country does: into Liberal and Conservative groups – the latter probably rather smaller – and a much smaller communist sector, un-involved in the *Violencia* proper, and concentrating on armed self-defence against irruption by the government or hostile groups. The areas of dormant *Violencia* probably have the same pattern. The most important of these are the Eastern Plains (Llanos Orientales), a solidly Liberal region of cattlemen, though now containing also a communist contingent, which laid down but did not abandon its arms in 1953 after the (Conservative) government ended its attempt to impose central control. I shall not consider this wild western scene here.

In any Latin American country there are, fundamentally, two types of agricultural zones: those of extremely backward subsistence farming, which is virtually outside or only marginally within the range of the economy, and those of production for the market, which means partly food for the rapidly growing cities, but still mainly the growth of cash crops for the world market, such as coffee. The systematic production of coffee (as of bananas and some lesser crops) began in Colombia [at the beginning of the twentieth century], and the country is today second only to Brazil as a producer. There are also two basic types of agrarian organization, the large estate cultivated by wage-labour or some similar device, and the peasant family unit, whether operated by an owner, tenant or sharecropper. The actual pattern of land ownership has no direct relation to the structure of agricultural enterprise, which may explain why there is no significant correlation between the *Violencia* and the distribution of landed property. This, by the way, is latifundist as in many other parts of Latin America, but with large patches of dwarf holdings. The combination of large estates and tiny peasant holdings affects the Colombian social situation chiefly in two ways. It accentuates the inequalities of income: 4.6 per cent of the population receives 40 per cent of the national income. It also perpetuates a quasi-feudal social structure in the countryside.

The general picture of the Colombian countryside is therefore one of extraordinarily backward, isolated, ignorant and custom-dominated peasant communities, dominated by feudal landowners and their henchmen. This traditional society, based on a semi-subsistence agriculture, is now in headlong disintegration. As elsewhere in Latin America, the main agent of disintegration is a cash-crop economy geared to the world market. Its advance, prepared in the first thirty years of this century, has accentuated sharply since 1940.

Until the Conservative and Liberal parties formally withdrew from the *Violencia* in 1957, its general social shape was to some extent obscured by national and local political feuds. However, in the past five years it has been little affected by such factors, and some tentative generalizations about it can therefore be made. In the first place, it has hardly touched the region of large estate cultivation. As elsewhere in Latin America, the landless rural labourers are among the less rebellious elements in the countryside. In the second place, it has taken a particular hold in the area of rapidly advancing cash crop farming by small operators, notably in the coffee country. At present it is largely confined to an area covering all or part of the Tolima, Valle and Caldas departments, which are the three leading coffee producers in the country. Caldas and Valle are among the three departments with the most rapid population increase, Tolima is well above the median. It may be added that some of the leading communist areas, armed though non-violent, are contiguous with this zone and belong economically to it.

A third armed, but quiescent zone ought also to be mentioned. It consists of the remote empty country stretching from the mountains to the Amazon basin, in which groups of independent pioneer settlers have established strongly communist nuclei, and provide locations for guerrilla training bases. This phenomenon also has its parallels in other Latin American countries. The independent pioneer, breaking away from a traditional setting – often of feudal domination – is one of the most potentially militant peasant elements, and – as in Peru and some parts of Brazil – one of the most accessible to left-wing organizations.

On the other hand, in its main centres the *Violencia* is not a simple movement of the poor against the rich, of the landless for more land. To some extent of course it is an expression of land hunger, though it takes the form of Conservative peasants massacring and expelling Liberals from their holdings, or the other way round. More obviously, in the course of fifteen years of anarchy, it has been utilized by a rising rural middle class (which might otherwise find social ascent hard in a quasi-feudal society) to gain wealth and power. This aspect of the *Violencia* has developed in forms strikingly reminiscent of the very similar Sicilian Mafia, especially in the coffee department par excellence, Caldas. There the opposite numbers of the Sicilian *gabelotti*, the estate administrators and middlemen, have even established a formal organization for blackmailing landlords – and terrorizing peasants – the Cofradia de Mayordomos (Brotherhood of Estate Managers). In such areas the *Violencia* has become economically institutionalized. It revives twice yearly with the coffee harvests, and determines the redistribution of farms, estates, of the coffee crop and the trade in it. It is significant that the perpetual massacre in these areas has made no difference at all to the increase in coffee cultivation. As soon as a peasant is expelled from his holding, someone else immediately takes over this lucrative asset.

Of course the *Violencia* is often revolutionary and class-conscious in a more obvious sense, especially in recent years, when the armed men, deprived of the justification of fighting for the two big parties, have increasingly tended to see themselves as champions of the poor. Moreover, in the nature of things the armed men and outlaws tend to be either young men without property or ties, or victims of massacre and expropriation, whether by the state or political opponents. In most recorded cases, self-defence or (what amounts to the same thing in such societies) vengeance pushed them from the legal into the outlaw life. On the other hand the mere fact that the arming of peasant bands arose not out of a straight social rebellion, but out of a combination of traditional party civil war and police or army terrorism, has obscured the class issues. For the Liberal guerrilla the *chulavitas* (originally soldiers and policemen from the department of Boyacá, who have gained a sad reputation for ferocity in the service of the Conservatives) are more obvious enemies than local Liberal lords, though on the Eastern Plains the Liberal ranchers came to conclude, in the course of the rebellion of 1949–53, that the cattle-less men and the rank and file cowhands were a more serious danger than the Conservative government. The 'clean' Liberal guerrilla might often spend more time fighting the 'dirty' *communes* or communist groups, than the Conservatives, on the grounds (which come oddly from poor peasants) that 'those who affirm that all belongs to all, and that things are not the lord's, but ought to go to those who have need of them, are bandits'. For the traditional communal loyalty of some settlement to the Liberals (or Conservatives), the traditional feuds with neighbouring areas of different complexion were strengthened rather than weakened in the years of civil war. What most of the guerrillas and bandits express is rural social disorganization, rather than social aspiration.

It so happens that we have a few examples of what such spontaneous social aspirations of the peasantry are, notably the complex of semi-autonomous communist peasant areas lying between the capital and the great centres of *Violencia*, and known (half jokingly) as the 'Republic of the Tequendama'. Here the peasant movement goes back many years; in the case of Viotá to the late 20s and early 30s. Well before the war the local tenantry, under communist leadership, forced the landowners to sell them their plots. Since then the region – or rather the homesteads and hamlets, for the market town is not communist – has been one of small, relatively equal peasant proprietors. The communism of Viotá is entirely a matter of peasant autonomy, independence and self-government at the local level. When the government sent an armed expedition into the valleys during the period of repression, the men of Viotá – all armed and mobilizable – ambushed it and killed all the invaders. Thereafter the government left them in peace, thus confirming their proud boast that 'Over there they kill each other; here nobody is persecuted.'

Such islands of peasant autonomy are rare. Outside them terror rules between men and in the souls of men. For the most striking and awful aspect of the *Violencia* is the wild, purposeless, destructive savagery of the armed men. The victims of *Violencia* are not merely killed but tortured, chopped into small pieces (*picados a tamal*), decapitated in a variety of horrible ways and otherwise disfigured. Above all the killers 'leave not even a seed' (*no dejar ni semilla*). Entire families, including the babies, are massacred, the foetus ripped out of pregnant women, surviving males castrated. In Colombia, local genocide – the word is used to describe such incidents – occurs constantly. In the last five months of 1962 there were seven such massacres, with an average of just over nineteen victims each. Of late there appears (according to government statistics of January 1963) to be a distinct tendency for such genocides to increase.

There is of course some functional reason for such barbarism. Guerrillas or brigands depend on the absolute complicity of the local population, and where half of these happen to be bitterly hostile, their silence is most easily extorted by terror. Yet one cannot escape the impression that the killers know that their actions – for instance the tearing out of a foetus by rough caesarean and the substitution of a cock (as occurred in two widely separated departments) – are not merely savage, but wrong and immoral by the standards of their traditional society. There are isolated examples of deliberately anti-social initiation rituals or other practices. There are chieftains whom close observers frankly describe as mentally unhinged, or whose killings plainly exceed even the norm of the outlawry, such as Teófilo Rojas ('Chispas'), who was recently killed. Rojas is held responsible for an average of two murders a day for the past five years. But even without such direct evidence, it is difficult to see the pointless sadism of so many bands as anything except a symptom of deep social disorganization.

To what extent does it represent a general collapse of traditional values in areas undergoing exceptionally rapid social change, or subject to exceptional tension, to what extent only the exceptional troubles of men who have been, as it were, thrown into a void by the whirling disc of their formerly stable universe? In the first instance it is obviously the latter. The freelance guerrillas or bandits are lost people, especially lost youths: for the older men, past thirty or thirty-five, tend, if they can, to retire from the hills. The infamous 'Chispas' was thrown into illegality at the age of thirteen, his father killed, his mother and brothers in hiding, his neighbourhood destroyed.

Such men, lacking an ideological hold – for even Liberals and Conservatives (i.e. the Church) have now withdrawn from them – easily turn into professional criminals, or into blind, savage avengers of their private fate on anybody. They are joined by the groups of lost youths who form the most recent (1958–63) generation of recruits to *Violencia*, joining in gangs about the age of fifteen: boys whose families were very likely massacred before their eyes, whose childhood job was to finger local enemies for the gunmen, whose migrant sisters form the armies of prostitution in the cities. Fifteen years of *Violencia* set up their mechanism of self-perpetuation like the Thirty Years War.

However, there is no sharp distinction between these extreme cases and the shaken local communities from which they spring. There are plenty of examples, in and outside Latin America, of violence beyond the traditional measure (which is large enough) arising in traditional communities whose world goes out of joint. The profound crisis induced in the mentality of subsistence peasants by the growth of a market economy has perhaps not been as adequately studied in Colombia as in Brazil, but there is little reason to doubt that the emergence of violence may be the same; perhaps even greater, for Colombia, with its all-powerful crusading sixteenth-century Spanish church, lacks the safety valve which apocalyptic sectarianism often provides in the Brazilian backwoods. In his section of Colombia the unspeakable Efraín González has become a folk hero, as the bandit Lampião did in the Brazilian north-east: cruelty belongs to the public image of both, in sharp contrast to the almost universal image of the 'noble brigand' of peasant tradition, which invariably stresses his moderation in killing.

For reasons peculiar to the history of Colombia, it may be suggested, the latent violence of such situations was encouraged to emerge fully in the course of a bitter civil war, which in turn reflected the economic, social and political crisis of the country. The result was the *Violencia*. The special circumstances which led to this development in Colombia, but not elsewhere, do not concern us here. It would in any case take us too far afield to analyse the peculiar nature of the Colombian two-party system, the crisis of the economy since about 1930, the growing conversion of the Liberal Party into a mass party of the poor under the impulse of New Dealish politicians and of the charismatic mass leader Jorge Eliécer Gaitán, who captured it; the murder of Gaitán in 1948 and the spontaneous mass insurrection in the capital which followed it and initiated the era of civil war and massacre. It will be sufficient to conclude with Professor Orlando Fals Borda that the *Violencia* arises out of a frustrated social revolution. It is what may happen when social revolutionary tensions are neither dissipated by peaceful economic development nor harnessed to create new and revolutionary social structures. The armies of the dead, the expelled, the physically and mentally maimed are the price which Colombia pays for this failure.

April 1963

Notes

1   G. Guzmán, O. Fals Borda and E. Umaña Luna, *La Violencia en Colombia*, Vol. I (Bogotá, 1962).
2   R. Pineda Giraldo, *El impacto da la violencia en el Tolima: el caso de Libano* (Monografias Sociologicas 6, Universidad Nacional, Bogotá, 1960). See also Departamento de Tolima, Secretaria de Agricultura, *La Violencia en el Tolima* (Ibagué, 1958).

II

AGRARIAN STRUCTURES

8

Feudal Elements in the Development of Latin America

Feudalism lies outside the range of interest of historians who specialize in the nineteenth and twentieth centuries, or at best at its margin. Nevertheless, we cannot escape it. In the first place, we cannot avoid some concern with the problem of the transition from feudalism to capitalism, which has been the subject of considerable discussion, especially among Marxists. Even those who deny that the economic system which preceded the industrial revolution in the west can be called feudal can hardly deny that the specific development of certain capital-ist economies and societies – e.g. the Japanese – was affected by a historical background which can be plausibly described as feudal. In the second place, feudalism is perhaps the only system of socio-economic relations within class society which can be found in all parts of the world, and (one might add) during a variety of historic periods. The development of the modern capitalist world economy therefore inevitably pene-trated, and in conquering transformed, numerous local societies with predominantly feudal relations – e.g. among the Rajputs in India, or the emirates of northern Nigeria. But in the third place, the development of capitalism on a world scale itself generated or regenerated in various places and at various times dependent social relations which are not capitalist. Some of these are recognisably feudal, i.e. indistinguishable from those prevailing in unquestionably feudal societies. This essay will briefly discuss this last phenomenon in Latin America.

It may be convenient to begin with some clarifications. In the first place the process by which any part of the globe, outside the original centres of capitalist development, was drawn into the capitalist world market must be distinguished from the creation of economic structures and relations characteristic of modern capitalism. This process was lengthy and, allowing for variations in speed, gradual. In other words for a long period the 'world market' was far from global. Consequently at any moment of its history between the sixteenth century (or whenever we choose to date the start of such a world market) and at least the twentieth century, sectors transformed in different degrees by capitalism coexisted. In extreme cases enclaves totally transformed by this market (e.g. oilfields and refineries) could coexist with sectors virtually unaffected by any outside economic factor (e.g. hunting and gathering tribes in inaccessible jungles), though it is doubtful whether any part of the population of even the most remote area can be today considered unaffected by the modern economy. To this extent all the economies with which even the nineteenth-century historian deals outside certain 'developed' countries were multiple economies or, if we choose to put all the parts of population affected in some degree by the capitalist world market into one group, dual economies. Though the distinction has been made and hotly denied, the debate on this issue is not of great interest. What is important is (1) that the process by which world capitalism penetrated other economies was uninterrupted and irresistible and (2) that at any moment it involved various types and degrees of penetration and consequent transformation.

These transformations, conscious or unplanned, can be divided into two broad types, so far as they affected the social relations of production. They could utilize or adapt already pre-existing institutions and relations, or they could establish new ones. Thus the Spanish conquerors of Peru utilized the already existing system of labour services in the Inca Empire, but modified it in significant ways. In the first place they eliminated the element of reciprocity and redistribution which was essential (at least ideally) to the Inca system. Henceforth the movement of goods and services was in one direction only, from Indians to Spaniards, without any returns in the other direction. In the second place they asked not merely for labour, but also for deliveries of products. (Insofar as the Incas had asked for such deliveries, e.g. of textiles, they had also been merely demands for labour, since the state supplied the raw material.) In the fourth place [*sic.*], insofar as the extraction of the labour surplus operated directly for a world market (e.g. by the production of precious metals) or indirectly for a wider market it ceased to be conducted essentially as a system of localized labour services, as it had been previously. In the fifth place, this appropriation now operated largely for the private benefit of a set of individual Spanish *encomenderos* who formed an exploiting class for which there was little precedent. Finally, the requirements of the Spaniards necessitated changes in the actual balance of production – e.g. the substitution of forced production and manufacture of cotton for that of wool, as well as changes in the rhythm of tribute payments (several times a year instead of annually) and an increase in obligations. Yet, so far as the Indians were concerned, these were modifications of already existing social relations of production, though undoubtedly changes for the worse, and above all changes which deprived the system of its old legitimacy. On the other hand the introduction of a separate class of individual lords, very likely with their own private lands, and lacking any organic relation with the peasant community, was an innovation in Peruvian terms, though in Spanish terms it may be merely considered an adaptation of familiar European pre-capitalist institutions.

The distinction made here is, of course, historical rather than functional. Had the Spaniards been unable to use a pre-existing system of *mita** they would undoubtedly have devised some other arrangement to provide forced labour for the royal mines or the needs of *encomenderos*, as indeed they did elsewhere, and as was done in the nineteenth and twentieth centuries in Africa. Nevertheless, the historic availability of certain established techniques of exploitation is not without significance. It may bias the choice of exploiters towards one form of exploitation rather than another, both performing the same function. Thus (as Witold Kula has demonstrated for Poland) the choice of a *corvée* system has the tendency to restrict the contacts of a permanently large part of agricultural production – that produced on the peasants' own plots – with the market. Conversely, where the system of forced labour is established and a large labour supply is available, increased demands of the market are likely to be met by an intensification or extension of forced services and prestations rather than by other means, insofar as this is possible. All this may in turn affect the structure of the economy, at least for a time.

Another more recent example may illustrate this. Coffee is not a traditional crop in Latin America. Indeed, outside Brazil it was not cultivated on any scale before the 1880s at the earliest. Moreover, in its production, as it developed in the nineteenth and twentieth centuries, there were no obviously decisive economies of scale. Indeed in some circumstances the opposite was the case. In both Guatemala and Brazil, as indeed in most other countries of the continent, coffee cultivation takes place essentially on large estates. In the former country this is presumably an adaptation of an older quasi-feudal type of

* In the Inca Empire *mit'a* was a form of reciprocal labour exchange. Under Spanish rule *mita* became mandatory forced Indian labour for a proscribed number of days in public works.

'traditional *hacienda*', marked by an absentee landlord, management by an administrator and foremen who control the permanent hired hands in charge of the continuous work, and the seasonal harvest labour consisting chiefly of temporary peasant migrants from the subsistence peasantry of the interior. In the latter coffee was originally a slave crop, and after abolition grown by a combination of *colonos* (at times little different from servile labour) sharecroppers and, increasingly, free labour.

However, in Colombia, the second-largest coffee producer on the continent, 80 per cent of coffee land in 1960 was in units of under 50 hectares. The department of Caldas, with 40 per cent of the total national output, in 1952 had only twenty-eight coffee fincas of more than 60 hectares.[1] In this country part of the coffee zone had initially also been cultivated on large estates until broken up by the combined pressures of the world depression of 1929 and of peasant rebellion.

It would clearly be illegitimate to suppose that the present structure of coffee production is due only to historical differences, however modified by subsequent operation of the economics of capitalism. However, it would be equally illegitimate to deny that these historical differences have not played a major role. The fact that, e.g., the settlement of São Paulo was organized in a manner which led to the predominance of large landowners, while that of Antioquia in Colombia largely took the form of peasant colonization, evidently influenced the structure of coffee cultivation in those areas. Indeed, there are areas where geographically similar regions are simultaneously settled in different ways and under different institutional conditions – but for similar economic purposes – e.g. various parts of the subtropical and tropical valleys on the east side of the Peruvian Andes. There the variations of economic structure due to 'historical' factors – e.g. the existence of a landlord economy in one case, its absence in another – can be observed with particular clarity.

The second type of transformation did not utilize pre-existing methods of exploitation, or rather, their existence was irrelevant to it. Yet it does not follow that the development of a world capitalist economy had to proceed directly, or until the twentieth century at all, by means of the characteristic social relations of production of capitalism everywhere. The only exception to this are the relations between buyers and sellers in a supra-local market. This applies with particular force to agrarian production, though it is probably also true up to a point of the production of manufactured commodities, which can also be substantially expanded while continuing to be conducted by independent petty commodity producers, i.e. even without more than a very partial transformation into some type of *Verlagsystem*. There is, of course, no doubt that these non-capitalist relations, local or sectoral, were part of a generally capitalist market or a capitalist world economy, and subordinate to it. Nor is there any doubt that such producers can be regarded as economically rational, though their rationality may not have been capitalist, perhaps because such a rationality was not within their reach for technical reasons.

The most dramatic example of a non-capitalist form of exploitation, subordinate to the development of a world capitalist system, is productive slavery, which, in the western hemisphere, is plainly an entirely novel institution. Indeed, while the development of feudal relations in the context of world capitalist development are modifications or recreations of a type of relations of production which can and does occur almost universally in certain circumstances – at least until the triumph of modern industrial capitalism – slavery (except in the economically trivial form of domestic slavery) occurs only occasionally or marginally in history. Probably the only real example of a socio-economic system essentially based upon slavery occurs in the Caribbean zone and its hinterland and in certain coastal zones of South America between the sixteenth and nineteenth centuries. Since the slave plantation, which was its characteristic unit of production, was essentially designed to produce commodities for export overseas, the slave system clearly arose as a subordinate part of capitalist development. However, though a plantation owner evidently had to make economic calculations similar to those of any other producer for a world market, he cannot be identified with a capitalist entrepreneur, either economically or socially. This error vitiates the technically very sophisticated enquiries into the economics of slavery by Robert Fogel and others, at least from the point of view of the historian.

The slave plantation was a highly specific response to the demands of the capitalist world market under certain conditions, which may perhaps be summarized as the mass production of fairly standardized export crops (most notably sugar) in the absence of a locally available labour force and of available or willing immigration. The absence of alternative labour forces may be due to the sheer lack of population (as in the West Indian islands after the extermination of the original natives), to the refusal of free labour to migrate on any terms or on the terms offered, or (where its physical coercion is for one reason or another impossible) the refusal of local labour to work on the plantations. Hence the continued importance of quasi-slavery arrangements, such as the import of indentured labourers from Asia and Oceania to former slave plantation areas such as the sugar island of the Indian Ocean, Trinidad and Guyana, Cuba and the isolated plantation oases of Peru. The absence of alternative labour forces is illustrated by the discussions on immigration in mid-nineteenth-century Peru, which considered all possible sources of labour for coastal plantations except the one which in the twentieth century has come to supply the great bulk of it, namely seasonal and eventually permanent emigration of Indians from the highlands to the coast.

*

93

Feudal and quasi-feudal arrangements are more complex, given that they are virtually always imposed on a pre-existing population with its own social structure and, though to a much lesser extent, that they were themselves likely to be influenced by traditions, institutions and laws brought over by the conquerors and derived from feudal Europe. On the other hand the actual seignorial estate (*hacienda*) in the Americas was an innovation, not provided for by the institutions of the Conquest, developed independently of government policy and largely against it, though eventually recognized by and after independence largely replacing government.[2] Its very name was novel, having originally indicated merely any kind of liquid assets, real or movable property, without special reference to rights over land and men.

Two propositions about the *haciendas* of colonial America (and the independent republics) can safely be made. First, in their external relations they were not feudal in either an institutional or economic sense. Estate ownership did not carry with it or imply noble status. Estates (though rarely diminishing in nominal size from an early period)* were freely bought and sold, often on a speculative basis by merchants and others. According to data by H. Favre, out of eleven *haciendas* in Huancavelica (Peru) documented for 1690 and 1760 only one remained in the possession of a single family for at least three generations, whereas seven were sold at least three times. Above all, the purpose of a *hacienda* was production for sale on a supra-local market, and consequently profit.

Paradoxically enough, under American conditions, this very purpose might lead to an apparent and sometimes a real diversion of entrepreneurial behaviour in a non-capitalist direction; except perhaps for the most rationally conducted properties of large institutions, such as the Jesuits. This was due both to the

---

* For reasons discussed below, a clear distinction must be made between the nominal area owned by a *hacienda* – insofar as this was known – and the actual area utilized at any time.

94

limitations of the market and – outside the major world export crops normally produced by slave-plantations – the uncontrollable uncertainties to which producers were subject. In extreme cases the market was so negligible that profit maximization was not an option at all. Thus the Hacienda del Monde in Michoacan (Mexico) simply had no adequate body of purchasers within reach for its meat and hides, and clearly never became economically viable at all.[3] More commonly, the *haciendas'* policy was twofold. They sought to monopolize what markets existed – mainly round substantial cities and mining areas – by excluding peasant producers from them, i.e. by expanding the area of the *hacienda* to cover all the better lands, possibly reducing former self-sufficient peasants to the status of consumers and certainly to exclude them from the area of competition. (The development of *haciendas* in the neighbourhood of markets naturally also drove remoter ones out of effective competition.) They also sought to establish an area sufficiently large and containing a sufficient variety of resources and products to offset any possible fluctuations. As a *hacendado* of the Porfirian period in Mexico put it:

A good hacienda must have everything, water, tillage land, pastures, woodland, cactus, quarries, lime-kilns etc. Thus the products will complement one another. The income from the pulque (alcoholic drink) produced by the cactus will help to pay wages and supplies for the labourers. The income from the pastures will help with the harvest. What the Indian charcoal burners produce on the mountains will help pay taxes. Some of what the other crops provide, will help with extraordinary expenses. Thus the income produced by selling the main harvest can pay for next year's expenses and at least leave something over for profit. The hacienda which does not have everything is likely to go short. To avoid shortages, one must have everything, and the way to do this is to expand the hacienda.[4]

But, as Florescano points out, it also followed under these circumstances that the logical policy for landowners was 'to obtain a regular and fixed income from their *haciendas* rather than great profits in one year and losses in another', the potential profits not being so large as to offset the risks of climate, fluctuations in output, and limited markets. Hence the attitude of the *hacendado* could easily converge with, or be transformed into, that of a sort of rentier, seeking to derive an income suitable to his social status, and not bothering too much with estate administration so long as he enjoyed this,[5] or even the quasi-feudal attitude of the man who cared not so much about the wealth his land procured, as about the prestige of owning large territories and the control over large numbers of people living on them or under their domination. In the vast areas remote from really profitable markets (or during periods of general recession) these attitudes were likely to predominate. In short, *haciendas* might be within or on the margins of a capitalist market economy, but were not necessarily capitalist enterprises.

Second, the internal organization and relations of *haciendas* can only be described as feudal. The similarity between the services and prestations required by lords in the Andes from their peasants is so close as to leave no room for doubt. It should be observed, however, that these relations of villeinage or serfdom are not merely (or not at all) relics of a traditional past, but are under certain circumstances reinforced and elaborated due to the increasing production for the market. In La Convención 'feudalism' was clearly much more highly developed in the 1950s than it had been in 1917. A similar phenomenon is observable in Chile during the second half of the nineteenth century, with the growth of the export market for wheat.

However, this type of 'dependent feudalization' has some peculiar characteristics and obvious limits. As already suggested, in some senses it was actually reinforced by the triumph of world capitalism. Thus the tendency of *hacendados* to behave like feudal magnates, i.e. to exercise independent politico-military power, was strictly controlled by the crown in the colonial period, but is much more frequent in the period of independence, at least until the very tardy re-establishment of effective central state power – in Peru not before the era of Leguía (1919–30). Macera cannot recall any case in colonial Peru where '*peones* are mobilized as soldiers to satisfy some political purpose of their masters'.[6] Conversely, lords might find it convenient to expand market production by a more systematic exploitation of labour services by their peasants.

The limitations on feudalization were both economic and social. We have already observed the effects of remote markets, e.g. excessive transport costs. Production of food for cities and mining areas – the bulk of the rural population was self-sufficient – did not invite major agricultural development, except of a very localized kind. For practical purposes the only products marketable on any scale over most of the area of the Americas were those of livestock (e.g. hides and perhaps wool), and the bulk of the seigniorial economy consisted of extensive cattle-ranching of the kind which, even in 1962, occupied more than half the total Colombian area '*de utilización agropecuaria*', maintaining in that country an estimated 10 million cattle as against an estimated 15 million human beings.[7] In terms of manpower, its demands were slight. The major export products (other than those of the mines) were, until the mid-nineteenth century, produced by slaves rather than serfs: notably sugar.

In considering the limits of this method of exploitation within the context of capitalist development we must, of course, bear in mind two somewhat different things: the limited scope for any large-scale production for a capitalist market and the limitations of agrarian enterprise based upon labour services. The first is often overlooked. Even in 1950 the area under coffee in Colombia, the second-largest producer of this crop in the world, and from which it derived 80 per cent of the value of all its exports, amounted to only 650,000 hectares or 0.5 per cent of the national territory or, more realistically, in the early

1960s 5 per cent of the area exploited for agrarian purposes in the major regions of the country (the Andean and Caribbean).[8] In the small Central American republic of Honduras only 15 per cent of the territory was agriculturally exploited in 1952. Of this 70 per cent was under subsistence crops and 30 per cent under commercial crops.[9] A fortiori the market sector of the agrarian economy in the pre-imperialist period was at least equally restricted. It should also be borne in mind that a large part of the normal food requirements of local towns were met from the immediate neighbourhood, and largely by purchases from relatives, friends and compadres.

At the same time a 'manorial system', being based on the assignment of subsistence plots to peasants against services and prestations, automatically removes a large proportion of land from more than marginal market production. [. . .] As late as 1959 in the main Indian-inhabited departments of the southern highlands of Peru, the land used directly by *hacendados* amounted to 12 per cent in the department of Cuzco, 7 per cent in Puno and 4 per cent each in Apurimac and Ayacucho.[10]

A large part of the land and population were therefore irrelevant to exploitation by means of agricultural enterprise, though not to other forms of exploitation – e.g. direct coercion for non-economic services, forced deliveries of products, and economic exploitation by (white, *mestizo* or mulatto) traders, usurers, alcohol dealers, etc. In extreme cases a purely dual economy could develop, as in the Mexican Huasteca region, where self-sufficient Indian communities in the more densely populated mountains coexisted with hardly any interaction with extensive cattle *haciendas* operated by non-Indian labour on the coastal plains, until non-Indian settlers penetrated and exploited the communities from within during and after the eighteenth century.[11] But the resistance of the peasantry itself must not be underestimated, all the more so since its communal organization was, within limits, legally recognized and maintained by colonial legislation. There is overwhelming evidence that *comuneros*, however involved in the *hacienda* economy, cherished their relative independence and considered themselves superior to *colonos* or *hacienda*-peasants. In Indian areas the community, whatever its legal status or economic function, is a device to ensure rejection of the non-Indians and counter-acculturation. As Macera observes, during the colonial period the multiplication of religious and civil offices within it served, and was intended to serve, as a means of removing Indians from the obligations of serving the Spaniards. For the same reason the Indians of Paez (Colombia) consider it disgraceful to sell on the local markets: it 'is a sign of subservience to the white intruders'.[12] One should perhaps add that resistance to the lords was not confined to independent peasants. All Indians, within or outside the *hacienda*, considered it an intrusion on land they believed to be theirs. Like the old Russian *muzhiks*, of whom the observer is constantly reminded, the Andean *hacienda* serfs were not as powerless in practice as in theory. They possessed the invaluable collective capacity to drag their feet. Above all: they were always there and much of what they did, especially on large and traditionally managed estates, was beyond the control or even the knowledge of the lord. From outside and inside, they were always testing and infiltrating the lord's economy. Hence the curious feeling among both traditional *hacendados* and their peasants that each 'exploits' the other.

In fact, so far as we can tell, the number of peasants exclusively within the *hacienda* system was only a minority.

[. . .]

The independent peasants were not, of course, entirely outside the *hacienda* economy, which relied on neighbouring communities for much of its labour. Moreover, a survey taken on any specific date conceals the considerable fluctuations of the relationship over any lengthy period of time. Furthermore, any peasant, independent or not, was, especially if an Indian, subaltern to any member of the (non-Indian) landlord class, and subject to non-economic domination. Nevertheless, it seems clear that the scope of the memorial economy was limited.

The essential limit on the development of large-scale agriculture of any kind was therefore a peasantry most of whom neither needed nor wanted to work in a seignoral or capitalist sector of agriculture. Expropriation, in one form or another, was an obvious method of turning them into a labour force. However, though the process of *hacienda* expansion (largely through encroachment on peasants' lands) continued at a varying pace for some centuries, there are only comparatively few examples of wholesale expropriation, and these generally not before the late nineteenth century. In some of them the demands of the market are clearly visible, as in Yucatan, where by 1910 90 per cent of the heads of Maya families appear to have been landless, and in the sugar areas of Morelos (Mexico) under Díaz. In others, such as the systematic holocaust of communities in Bolivia during the rule of Melgarejo (1866–71) and after, the market element is less clear. Nevertheless, it is unwise to assume that such examples are representative, or that even the enormous extension of latifundism, or more precisely, the monopolization of good land by large estates, by itself produced a landless or submarginal rural population which was economically obliged to labour on them.

The existence of a system in which landlords (a) possess considerable powers of extra-economic coercion and (b) can establish property rights over large stretches of territory, naturally produces a bias in favour of forms of economic exploitation which utilize these advantages; at least in areas of relatively dense population not within easy reach of unsettled land.* However, it does not follow that even so the development of demesne production with servile labour is necessarily the most advantageous form of

---

* The very low man/land ratio in much of Latin America and the availability of unoccupied land outside – and sometimes within – the *hacienda* system for long periods, should not be forgotten.

exploitation. Indeed, one might suggest that, with certain exceptions, some sort of combination of share-cropping tenancies and
cultivation by low-paid wage-labour would be more suitable.
Share-cropping (or rent in kind) has the advantage that marketable surpluses can be extracted from peasants who do not wish
to work on the demesne or at times when work on cash crops is
slack. [. . .] Wage-labour has the advantage over labour services
that it is far more flexible, an important consideration given the
enormous seasonal variations in labour requirements of many
cash crops. Moreover, there seems very little doubt that wage-
labour is cheaper than serf-labour. Such calculations as have
been made for relative incomes suggest this, as well as the fairly
general evidence that serfs were or are better off than landless
labourers, and that the position as *colono* was regarded as desirable, and the threat to expel a peasant from his labour holding
was held over rebellious serfs. This does not, of course, imply that
the conditions of serfs were in any sense satisfactory.

[. . .]

The major problem of wage-labour was that of any labour:
how to obtain it at all. A specific difficulty during part of the
colonial period must, however, not be forgotten. For much of
it there was an absolute shortage of small denominations of
money (the wages of labourers being far below anything payable in silver or gold). This encouraged credit-advances, the use
of private monetary tokens outside the range of public currency
and the use of truck-payment and truck-shops (*tiendas de raya*),
all of which helped to bind labour to the *hacienda* through debt
relationships. It would also, naturally, encourage non-monetary
remuneration e.g. through the granting of subsistence plots.

However, even without this special factor it seems likely
that various forms of debt bondage (peonage) would have
been developed to recruit and hold labour. Whether it was the
main method of binding a labour force to the *hacienda*, as such
eminent authorities as Chevalier and Macera have held, has
recently been doubted on various grounds, though at least one

of the arguments does not deny that debt establishes permanence of labour relationships. The truth is that we know little about peasant debt to lords in the colonial period and practically nothing about it in the nineteenth century. It is probably a mistake to seek for any single favour responsible for bonding peasants. Each can be legitimately shown to be too weak for the purpose. Thus the thesis that expropriation of community lands was 'the main method' of obtaining labour is as vulnerable to criticism as the thesis that debt-peonage was. In an economy as underpopulated, as relatively undeveloped on the landlord side and as relatively self-sufficient on the peasant side as most of Latin America before the imperialist period, both the scope of landlord exploitation and the impact of income incentives or compulsions on peasants was rather limited. On the other hand in a society in which landlords were unquestionably the (rural) ruling class, with substantial extra-economic powers of command and domination, their scope for establishing some degree of peasant dependence by one method or another or a combination of several, was bound to be considerable, so long as peasants could not escape from the universe of lords and rulers by mass migration. And it can probably be shown that collective migration, as distinct from individual evasion, resulting perhaps in small free settlements on the uncultivated frontier, was not very practicable. In any case, peasants who (rightly) regarded the land they lived on as theirs, even if encroached upon or expropriated by foreign conquerors, would not lightly wish to abandon it. The history of their age-old and tenacious struggles for it demonstrates this.

In short, so long as the economic incentive for landlords to modernize their economy remained (or became intermittently) weak, the typical 'traditional' *hacienda* had no overwhelming labour problems. It could normally establish enough labour tenants on its land – which was normally far larger than the area actually exploited by the lord – for its modest regular requirements. It could call upon or make arrangements with neighbouring communities for extra labour, possibly by extra-economic compulsion, probably by offering the use of resources monopolized by the *hacienda*. (This is the implication of Martínez Alier's arguments.)[13] It could draw upon income extracted in one form or another from mostpeasants within the range of its power. And it required little beyond this. *Haciendas* engaged in economically more advanced production, e.g. for the export market, undoubtedly had labour problems, especially after the abolition of slavery. But these were special cases.

The situation changed dramatically with the real entry of the Latin American hinterland into the world economy – from the middle of the nineteenth century onwards; a change whose significance is concealed both by the apparent similarities of the *hacienda* system before and afterwards, and by the attempts to prove that it was 'essentially capitalist' since the conquest. The old *haciendas* had – at least for long periods – functioned, to quote John Womack, 'more as symbols than as businesses'. Now the incentive to turn themselves into businesses became pressing, even when the estate did not actually fall into the hands of capitalist foreigners.

Yet in considering the labour problems of the increasingly commercialized *haciendas* we ought to bear in mind not only the demand for it, but also its supply. For demographic growth (producing increasing pressure on land) and the impact of capitalism on the peasant economy and within the communities were highly significant. Thus the typical method of hiring migrant labour for mines and plantations, the *enganche*, in which labourers work off advances made by labour contractors, operated mainly among small peasants – at least in Peru – and assumed both the existence of a village 'bourgeoisie' from among whom the *enganchadores* were recruited, and that cash advances were a sufficient incentive to make people migrate. And cash requirements arose in the villages not only out of poverty, and the need for large outlays on marriages, deaths or status competition for fiestas and communal offices, but also out

of a more active peasant land market. This in turn was stimulated – at least in Central Peru, where the subject has been well
studied – both by the growth of the market for small producers
and by the concentration of large-scale agrarian enterprise on
extensive livestock ranching in the highlands, leading to the
sale of small and medium (white) estates and ecclesiastical land
in the agricultural valleys. The significance of purchasers of
land and other commodities as migrants is indicated by the
surprising degree to which these were – in this area – drawn
from among the better-off peasantry.

Still, the element of coercion or (what amounts to the same
thing) personal dependence, retained its importance, both
because it was ready to hand, and because of the reluctance
of the peasantry to abandon its independence. This was
particularly marked in areas lacking a dense local population, i.e. a rural proletariat. The most marked use of labour
services – whether by the granting of labour tenancies or by
other means – occur in such areas. Thus the sugar estates of
Jujuy (Argentina) bought up by the uneconomic latifundia of
the neighbouring Andean highlands from the 1920s in order
to convert the rents of their Indian tenants from money into
labour, i.e. to compel them to work as cane-cutters. The sugar
plantations of Porfirian Morelos (Mexico), especially in the
remoter areas, preferred to concentrate large permanent populations of expropriated peasants on the estate compound as a
completely landless and dependent force of resident servants,
relieving managers of 'the dangerous and humiliating reliance
on local villagers, who hated them and who might desert them
for a higher wage elsewhere'. For extra labour they might rely
on contracted immigrants from Puebla and Guerrero, whose
indebtedness also guaranteed dependence.[14] (The policy was
not unsuccessful: the resident labourers of Tenango, cowed
and secure, took no part in Zapata's rising.[15]) Where labour-
tenancies were already established, the incentive to increase
services and, where possible, to diminish peasant holdings, was

obvious, as is evident in Chile. Conversely, as Martínez Alier has pointed out, where the local peasantry had the *de facto* use of *hacienda* resources, they might make it difficult for landlords who would have preferred to transfer to ordinary hired labour to do so.

The major gap in the system of labour coercion and dependence was, of course, the need for large temporary supplies of labour, most readily supplied by rural landless workers or minifundist peasants, to whom it would have been uneconomic to offer permanent labour tenancies. The *enganche* provided a means of acquiring a labour force of outsiders, where no sufficient local reserve army was available. Its 'foreignness' and the constraints of debt-contracts prevented it from effectively exploiting its bargaining position at peak seasons. One might suggest that the most lasting use of bonding and coercion was to keep the wages of hired labour below market levels.

'Neo-feudalism' was thus one response to the changed economic situation. It may be suggested that it was most likely to occur (a) where the *hacienda* system was well established, (b) where alternative land for peasants was not readily available or desired, (c) where landlords suffered from a degree of labour shortage and (d) where the expansion of commercial production was unusually rapid. Where a choice existed, and the economic advantages of alternative methods of exploiting the estate were clear to the landlord (as might not always be the case), these might be offset by the exploitation of the lord's monopoly of resources or power, or even by the more traditional and unquantifiable advantages of the social status and influence which has come from the possession of estates. However, it is clear that neo-feudalism was (or is) both a marginal and a transitional response to the development of a capitalist world economy, at least in Latin America.

It was marginal because, unlike the slave plantation in its characteristic areas and for the commodities associated with it, the estate cultivated by labour-tenants never became the universal unit of agricultural production for the wider market. There are no convincing a priori reasons why it could not have done so, and evidently the tendencies to develop labour tenancies from the eighteenth century and their systematic utilization in nineteenth-century Chilean wheat production suggest that, under certain circumstances, it might have done so. It was transitional partly because the economic advantages of a large permanent labour force attached to the estate diminished with the rise of capital-intensive cultivation, the availability of a large rural proletariat or body of seasonal migrants, and the estate's increasing utilization of land, and partly because the *hacienda* system, always unpopular among all except *hacendados*, became increasingly vulnerable to the pressures of its competitors, its victims (not least the peasantry) and those who considered it an obstacle to the general economic development of their country.

In fact the development of large-scale market agriculture in the mid-twentieth century can no longer be considered neo-feudal in any sense, if ever it could. Thus in Colombia labour tenancies appeared to be of very small importance at the time of the CIDA enquiry, in Guatemala the large estates (*fincas*) investigated 'depend totally on wage-labour', in Brazil, where labour services appear to be more widely distributed – partly as adjuncts to share-cropping tenancies, partly in connection with other tenancies – they are clearly to a large extent historical relics.[16] The three countries are mentioned because no agrarian reform had taken place at the time of these enquiries. Except in rather unusual circumstances, such as those prevailing in the Amazonian valleys of Peru between the 1930s and early 1960s (e.g. La Convención), we need not seriously consider neo-feudalism in any discussion of mid-twentieth century agricultural development in Latin America.

It may be suggested that, insofar as it has to be seriously considered, it is in the period in which Latin America became part of an expanding imperialist world economy, i.e. from the late nineteenth century to the world crisis of the 1930s. During this period the incentive to pursue the expansion of agrarian production by utilizing the resources available to a traditional *hacienda* economy – expansion of the estates, expropriation of peasant and community land, non-economic coercion, labour services, debt-peonage, etc. – were at their maximum, the support of governments for planters and *hacendados*, local or foreign, almost unlimited, the resistance of the rural population at a low ebb, and the tensions which were to make themselves felt subsequently in revolutionary and other movements still accumulating. Neo-feudal methods could also be utilized to some extent (as in Brazil) to fill the gaps left by the abolition of slavery. However, this period of Latin America is still very insufficiently known, especially insofar as it falls into that darkest of all historical eras in the post-Colombian history of the continent, the nineteenth century. Only further research will be able to show how important neo-feudal adaptations were during this period, and in what areas or types of production.

1976

Notes

Some notes in the original essay have been omitted from the version that appears in this volume.

1 CIDA, *Tenencia de la tierra ... Colombia* (Washington, 1966), p. 46; E. Guhl, 'El Aspecto economico-social del cultivo del café en Antioquia', *Revista Colombiana de Antropologia*, I (1953), pp. 197ff.
2 The fullest analysis of its genesis is F. Chevalier, *La formation des grands domains au Mexique* (Paris, 1952), translated in a shortened version as *Land and Society in Colonial Mexico: The Great Hacienda* (Berkeley and Los Angeles, 1963).
3 Luis González, *Pueblo en vila* (1968), pp. 52, 56ff., 91ff.
4 Cited in E. Florescano, *Estructuras y problemas agrarios de México (1500– 1621)* (1971), p. 142.
5 Ibid., p. 141.
6 P. Macera, *Feudalismo colonial americano: el caso de las hacienda Peruanas* ('Acta Historica', XXXV, Szeged, 1971) p. 4.

7   CIDA, *Tenencia de la tierra ... Colombia*, p. 18.

8   Ibid., p. 45.

9   L. Becerra, *El problema agrario en Honduras* (Havana, 1964), pp. 14–15.

10 Plan Regional del Desarrollo del Sur del Peru II, quoted in R. Montoya, *A proposito del caracter predominantemente capitalista de la economia peruana* (Lima, 1970), p. 105.

11 G. Stresser-Péan, 'Problèmes agraires de la Huasteca ou region de Tampico (Mexique)', CNRS, *Les problems agraires des Amériques Latines* (Paris, 1967), p. 202.

12 Macera, *Feudalismo*, p. 17.

13 Joan Martínez Alier, *Relations of production in Andean haciendas* (1972).

14 J. Womack, *Zapata and the Mexican Revolution* (1969), p. 47.

15 A. Warman (ed.), *Los campesinos de la tierra de Zapata I Adaptación, cambio y rebelión* (1974), pp. 108–9.

16 CIDA, *Tenencia de la tierra ... Colombia*, p. 130; ... *Guatemala*, p. 74, ... *Brazil*, pp. 198–9, 221, 227. Thus in the north-east, according to the former leader of the peasant leagues, 'the days (of compulsory labour service) required, represented very little in the year, what the peasant resented was not the actual work, but the humiliation of compulsory and unpaid work for a landlord to whom he paid rent for his holding'. Francisco Julião, *Cambão* (Paris, 1968), p. 75.

9

A Case of Neo-Feudalism: La Convención, Peru

I

The province of La Convención, department of Cuzco, in Peru became familiar to citizens of the outside world in the early 1960s, when it was the scene of the most important peasant movement of that period in Peru, and probably in the whole of South America. This might legitimately attract the attention of the social historian. At the same time La Convención is a special version of a more general phenomenon, which ought also to interest the economic historian. It is 'frontier territory' in the American sense of the word, i.e. it belongs to the large zone of undeveloped land on the eastern edge of the Andes (the western edge of the Amazon basin) which has come under settlement and cultivation in recent decades, mainly for the cultivation of cash crops for the world market, but also for other economic purposes. Along the Andean slopes there are a number of such regions, into which, in their different ways, landlords and entrepreneurs penetrate with estates and trade, peasants in search of land and freedom. Mostly they are Indian peasants from the highlands, and the socio-economic background of the *sierra* and *altiplano* determines to some extent the forms of the new

109

economy which take shape on the semi-tropical and tropical eastern slopes.

Broadly speaking, these zones provide us with examples of colonization covering a wide range of possibilities: penetration into totally unoccupied (i.e. legally ownerless) territory, into territory partly under private ownership or providing legal scope for small settlement, and into territory wholly occupied by *haciendas*; *haciendas* of the traditional feudal or the modern capitalist type, or intermediate; settlement by Indian *comunidades* or by individual colonists; settlement for the purpose of extending or re-creating the subsistence economy of the traditional peasantry or a market economy; the operation of such a market economy by means of serfdom, small peasant agriculture, share-cropping, and/or short pioneer tenancies, by seasonal labour migrations or indentured labour, and even by modern capital-intensive and labour-saving mechanized development. The La Convención area combines two extremes: the penetration of individual, market-oriented peasant settlers – future *kulaks*, it has been said – into an area wholly dominated by large *haciendas*, whose policy it was to develop production through labour-service tenancies, i.e. serfdom. Probably it is the conflict of extremes which accounts for the unusual sharpness of social collisions there. I shall deal mainly with this very interesting region, observing variations in other areas only incidentally.[1]

The study of such a region is illuminating for several reasons. One of them may be mentioned immediately. It is the total unreliability of all statistics which concern it, a fact which even the historian needs to be reminded of and which the economist must never forget. The most elementary data such as censuses, or even estimates of the size of the area, are quite uncertain. [...] The censuses fluctuated wildly, and used to be taken, when at all, at irregular intervals, and intercensal estimates differ even more widely. The 1940 census simply added one third to allow for the *población selvatica* beyond the reach of the enumerators; for all we know they might as well have added 10 per cent or 40 per cent. Figures for the total production of the province are given with confidence, but if we compare them with the statistics of the quantities of various goods transported by the Cuzco–Santa Ana railway, which provides the only link of the province with the wider world, we shall find considerable divergences. And so on. Hence *all* figures can be used only as approximate orders of magnitude, and they may not even be reliable for this purpose.

II

The province of La Convención, which has existed as an independent administrative unit since 1857, is a vast region to the north of Cuzco, and along the river system which eventually joins the Amazon. (It begins just beyond the celebrated Inca ruins of Machu Picchu.) It is a region of subtropical hills and forests dipping rapidly towards the tropics, from perhaps 2000 metres at the top to perhaps 700 metres at the limit of cultivation. It thus shades off into the tropical *selva*, and indeed during the rubber-boom of the early twentieth century it was one of the gateways into the Peruvian part of the rubber areas. It is isolated from the rest of Peru by high mountains, through which a mule-path (constructed by the Peruvian government under pressure from the *haciendas*) has passed since 1890[2] and the railway from Cuzco to Huadquiña since the 1930s. However, even in the early 1960s the railhead was still 3–4 hours' truck-drive from the provincial capital Quillabamba (also founded in the 1890s), the only real township of the region. The entire road system in 1959 amounted to only 298 kilometres. It is not surprising that only a tiny fraction of the land – some 11,000 hectares – was then actually known to be under cultivation.

The population has fluctuated considerably, though all estimates are little better than guesswork. Censuses (taken irregularly) suggest a rise from about 12,000 in 1862 to between 27,000 and 40,000 in 1940, and there were said to be some 60,000 landless inhabitants in the early 1960s. The one unquestioned fact is that the population was decimated by an epidemic of what it described as 'malaria' which entered the valleys in 1932–3.[3] This catastrophe, which reduced large areas of the province to a human desert, is of crucial importance in its recent history. The fundamental situation of the province has thus always been the combination of abundant land, poor communications and an acute shortage of labour.

For practical purposes we can regard La Convención as having remained outside the world economy until the twentieth century, outside any economy until well into the nineteenth, except insofar as parts of it were involved in the regional market of the Cuzco highlands. The area was sufficiently near Cuzco for its potentialities to be known and exploited in the way which would occur naturally to Spaniards in hot climates: sugar plantations, of which we have record as far back as the early seventeenth century, but which, for obvious economic reasons, concentrated entirely on the production of aguardiente for sale in the highlands. The second standard crop was coca, also for the highland Indians. Indeed these two drugs constituted practically the only consumer goods purchased by them.

How far this sugar-and-coca economy developed in colonial times is immaterial. It was under constant threat from the forest Indians, and it seems that, perhaps in connection with the rising of Túpac Amaru, perhaps linked with the disruptions of the independence period, there was a retreat of settlements in the *montaña* in the late eighteenth and early nineteenth centuries. When they began slowly to expand again, it was on the old basis of sugar and coca, together with a little cocoa, which was produced for the manufacture of Cuzco chocolate, a well-known luxury article, and perhaps a certain amount of cattle. The travellers of the early twentieth century do not bother to mention any other agrarian products, and indeed transport costs precluded any others. It took five days to travel the 190 kilometres from what is now Quillabamba to Cuzco even after the construction of the mule-trail, and transport costs for coca ranged from one-sixth to one-third of the cost of production per arroba, depending on the distance of travel, or 25 per cent of the selling price of aguardiente, 10 per cent of that of coca, according to another source of the same period. On the other hand the market was stable or expanding. It is quite evident [...] that this archaic type of economy still prevailed at the time of the First World War.

Though production for the world market had evidently begun before the First World War, it remained on a small scale and there was little monoculture, except on one or two *haciendas* which began to specialize in tea from 1913. It seems to have been left largely to peasant tenants, while the estate owners relied on the older staples. Evidently (though statistics are scarce) it made no startling progress in the 1920s, and almost certainly suffered a setback under the double impact of crisis and demographic catastrophe in the 1930s. It is possible that the cultivation of sugar-cane was already on the decline between the wars, but this cannot be established with any certainty.

In the 1940s and 1950s on the other hand output rose very rapidly indeed, except for forest products, which need not concern us. The main growth occurred in coffee, cocoa and tea. Of these coffee was produced mainly on mixed *fincas*, though a tendency towards monoculture (and production by the estates themselves) was evident, tea was always produced by a few monoculture *haciendas* of relatively modern outlook (which, incidentally, paid somewhat better wages than the rest), cocoa was grown mainly on several hundred monoculture peasant holdings, but also on some mixed estates. Even coca, the old staple, continued to grow satisfactorily, though its acreage does not appear to have increased and may have begun to decline. [...] Sugar, however, declined very rapidly in the later 1950s.

[...]

The unusually rapid development of La Convención since 1940 is due to a combination of circumstances. The first is the construction of a railway (contracted in 1921, opened not before 1933), the absence of which precluded any very large commercial development. (It would seem that Quillabamba hardly grew between 1917 and 1940.) The second is the demographic catastrophe of the 1930s, which delayed development but eventually gave rise to a disproportionately large and rapid growth. Third and most important, this recovery coincided with the long primary commodities boom of the Second World War and the Korean War period, which launched similar – and equally striking – development in other parts of Peru and indeed of Latin America. It is worth observing that this sudden expansion caught many of the La Convención landowners by surprise, as it were. They had for decades, indeed for generations, adapted themselves to the traditional coca–alcohol economy. They were now given the opportunity of exploiting the lucrative, but also potentially much riskier, economy of coffee–cocoa–tea and other tropical exports to the world market.

III

By about 1960 there were upwards of 100 such *haciendas* in La Convención (and the valley of Lares, which, though administratively in another province, belongs economically to its neighbour); forty-six of them had been in existence a century earlier, eighty-seven were recorded in the middle 1950s. They ranged in size from the giant Huadquiña of probably about 150,000 hectares and certainly no less than 80,000 hectares, the relic of a gigantic estate of some 500,000 hectares acquired by a certain Mariano Vargas in 1865 and subsequently divided into various family portions under the Romainville family, through almost equally impressive estates of 45,000, 35,000 or 30,000 hectares, to relatively modest properties of

2000 hectares.[4] (Even so only 15 per cent of the total area of the province was legally private property, the rest being still state property.) Only a small proportion of these estates was cultivated at all – perhaps 8–10 per cent according to *CIDA: Peru* (1966).* An even smaller proportion was cultivated by the landlords themselves. This was evidently due primarily to the perennial problem of the La Convención estates – the shortage of labour, needed both for production and transport.

It seems that the landowners at first tried to solve the labour problem by impressing the forest Indians of the Machiguenga (Machiganga) tribes. They had to pay for their conversion to Christianity by being forced to work whenever they came to the only available churches, which were in the *haciendas*. There were not many of them – around 1914 only 1000–1500. There are signs that the landlords also tried wage-labour in the form of the *enganche* – temporary imports of labour via labour contractors, such as appears to form the main estate labour force in the comparable areas of central Peru. Evidently they had little success; perhaps because La Convención was less accessible from areas of labour surplus than central Peru, or because the highland *haciendas* resisted the competition from the valleys for their own labour force; perhaps also because of the inefficiency and high wastage rate of highland labour in the semi-tropical environment, not to mention the reluctance of the La Convención landowners to pay a free market rate of wages. Indeed, as we shall see, the essence of their characteristic serf-tenancies is not to get labour *gratis*, but to get it at a fixed rate below that obtaining in the open market.

Under the circumstances, i.e. in the absence of both enough free wage-labour or forced- and slave-labour, the estates had to rely on such peasant settlers as filtered into the valleys or could

* This would seem to be a considerable overstatement, even if the cultivated area has increased substantially since 1954; or else the figures for the 1950s grossly understate the area under cultivation. As so often, there seems to be an element of fantasy about statistics relating to La Convención.

be attracted into them. There were in fact only two choices: share-cropping or some combination of peasant colonization and serf-labour on the estates' own land. For reasons which are not wholly clear, share-cropping was hardly developed. One may perhaps guess that the original bias of the landlords towards a plantation economy of sugar-cane determined this choice, for such plantations have heavy periodic labour requirements such as cannot be met by a basically share-cropping system. (It is probable that sugar production was always a seignorial privilege, since tenancy contracts in the twentieth century, when it had lost importance, still often specifically forbade it to peasants.) Neither coca nor cocoa or coffee automatically impose a system of demesne agriculture. At all events, the system which the lords of La Convención adopted was a form of villein tenure surprisingly similar to medieval European villeinage. Tenancies which are paid for in labour services are common enough in Peru under the general name of *pongaje*, but this term is not used in La Convención, where the labour tenants are known as *arrendires*, their tenancy as the *arriendo*, a colourless word which may suggest that serfdom in the province is not so much the child of a feudal tradition as the response by powerful landlords to an economic situation.

The classic *arriendo* has been described by various observers, and most completely by Cuadros (1949) and *CIDA: Peru* (1966). The following description is based mainly on Cuadros, who described the system before the intervention of the peasant syndicates. The length of the tenancy varied, but seems to have been mainly 9–10 years, as was necessary if the tenant was to cultivate plants like coffee or cocoa which do not begin to yield the first crop for four or five years. Normally payments (the *canon*) were excused for the first year, and indeed pioneer settlers, at least during the period of the *rozo* (the clearing of virgin soil and its preparation for cultivation), may well have enjoyed somewhat more favourable conditions than those holding already cultivated land. However, after cultivation was established, the *canon* could be increased as the tenant's holding became more productive. Alternatively landlords would get rid of tenants in order to cultivate the land themselves. There seems to have been no conventional or official limit to such increases in payment.

The *arrendire*'s *canon* consisted of money rent, ranging from 8–10 soles to 80–100 soles a year, but perhaps averaging 20–30, plus a more important set of labour services, plus various other obligations. The universal or almost universal services (*condiciones*) were:

1. A certain number of days' work a year (not necessarily consecutive) at a fixed wage which seems to have been 0.40 soles per day from at least 1914 to the middle 1950s. (Since the agrarian revolt of 1961–2 it has been 1–1.5 soles, which demonstrates the divergence between the servile and the free market wage.) The amount of this *turno* was 8–10 days a month on average in 1942, and might be higher – up to 12 days.

2. The *palla*, an obligation to furnish at least one woman coca-leaf picker for each coca harvest, payable (from at least 1900 to the middle 1950s) at 0.2 soles a day. One *hacienda* in 1918 obliged tenants to send from one to five *palladoras* four times a year. [. . .]

3. The *huata faena* (annual work), an obligation to work 10–15 days without pay, except for food, drink and possibly a conventional *gratificación* of 1 sol. This obligation might include the labour of all the *arrendire*'s dependants and peons, whom he was obliged to pay 0.5–1.2 soles a day plus food and *chicha* – the local fermented drink – as on the Hacienda San Lorenzo in the 1940s. It could also mean a separate obligation to work on the demesne with all his hands when needed for 3–6 days at a fixed wage of 0.7 soles.

4. The duty to undertake *comisiones* of various kinds for the lord when required at a wage of 0.5 soles.

The following obligations were not so universal and are given in order of frequency as recorded by Cuadros (1949).

5. *Fletas cosechas* (transport duty), an obligation to transport a load of 6 arrobas (66 kg) for each pack animal in the tenant's possession up to three times a year, at a fixed rate inferior to transport costs on the open market.
6. The duty to provide house servants to work unpaid for a fixed period.
7. Road and maintenance work, including on the lord's house, for not more than two weeks a year.
8. *Herbaje*, i.e. a money payment (normally 2 soles) for each head of livestock in the tenant's possession above a certain minimum.
9. Payment for timber and other raw materials taken from the *hacienda* by the tenant at a price fixed by the landlord.
10. The prohibition of certain crops on the tenant's land; alternatively the obligation to plant certain crops.
11. The obligation to consume goods produced on the *hacienda* and/or to sell the tenant's crop exclusively to or through the *hacienda*.

These were clearly very heavy obligations, and the lords' labour shortage tended to make them even heavier, particularly in the period after the 1930s, when the province was unusually depopulated and the boom in the primary commodities market unusually big. Indeed, the immediate roots of the peasant revolt of 1958–63 lie in the systematic attempt of the provincial lords to reimpose the system of serf-labour after the malaria epidemics (i.e. in a situation theoretically extremely favourable to the labourer), and later, to take over the land brought into effective cultivation by the pioneer peasant settlers. Historians of the European middle ages may be left to think of parallels. Apart from revolt, the tenant had the choice only of leaving part of his land uncultivated because of his duty to work on the demesne or to employ labour to fulfil his own obligations as well as the labour requirements of his plot. The peculiar feature of La Convención is the development of such subcontracting. The *arrendire* let part of his plot to one or more *allegados* who might (as on Hacienda Echarate) undertake a third or more of his labour services in return, and he also attracted a growing number of free landless labourers (*habilitados, peones, maquipuras,* etc.). This development is recent. In 1917 Rosell listed only *arrendires, gente de rancho* (i.e. direct estate servants) and small independent peasant squatters or settlers as the three types of labour in La Convención, and subtenancies are still technically prohibited in most contracts, though the system of *allegados* is accepted in practice, if only because they increased the number of 'his' workers which the tenant was obliged to put at the disposal of the landlord on the required occasions. Conversely, the official labour services of the *arrendires* and their dependants became increasingly inadequate for the growing estate economy, and consequently arrangements intermediate between labour services and wage-labour seem to have developed. Such is the *maquipura* or *extra*, the obligation to work a certain number of days (up to twenty) with all the tenant's dependants, not for a customary or fixed wage, but for a wage agreed before each duty-period. (Today it might be 2 soles per day.) Similarly, the prosperous *arrendire* might today hire labourers to do his labour services, paying them a cash wage.

The labour structure of La Convención therefore consists of three levels: *arrendires, allegados* and *habilitados*. We have no idea how many of each there are, since the figures are either absent or unreliable, but it would seem that the number of labour-tenants (*arrendires, allegados* and others holding similar tenancies) is probably considerably smaller than the number of landless hired labourers.

IV

It will be clear that this situation was unusually favourable to the estate owners, and indeed became increasingly favourable with the extension of market production and the growing labour shortage – so long as the landlords were able to maintain their traditional power. Thus the $0.40 day-wage was supposed to be about 20 per cent below the market rate in 1918, but in the early 1940s it was no more than a third or a fourth, a few years later a fourth or a fifth, of the open market wage. This is confirmed by the sudden leap of day-rates to $1–1.50, in the case of *maquipura* to $2 after the agrarian revolt of 1961–2. As for the $0.20 of the women workers, which remained unchanged for fifty years, we may imagine the gain to the employer from this secular wage-freeze. We may add that the landlords had long been in the habit of extracting cash payments as well as labour services from tenants, partly in the form of a modest cash rent, partly in the form of payments such as *herbaje*, i.e. the head-tax on the tenants' animals.

[...]

Kuczynski Godard (1946) estimated the rate of return on capital in the Hacienda San Lorenzo at 12–16 per cent, not counting the profit on its products. [...] If the Hacienda Chancamayo were to be sold at 150,000 soles, he estimated that the new owner would from the first day have a 7 per cent return on his investment in the difference between his actual outlays for labour (i.e. in this instance nothing) and what he would have had to pay for labour on the open market. In actual fact, any experienced *hacendado* expected a two- or threefold return on his investment. This situation may explain the remarkable sluggishness of the landlords to undertake improvements. For anyone with enough money to buy an estate, let alone the good fortune to inherit one, a high rate of profit without risk, or indeed without major current outlays, was almost certain. Even if the bottom temporarily fell out of some market, he risked no actual loss, but merely forwent his usual gain. Few gamblers have had the luck to toss two-headed coins so consistently.

The only limits to the *hacendado*'s prosperity were those of the traditional feudal lord: managerial and financial incompetence and a tendency to throw money out of the window for purposes of luxury or status-competition. These were real limits. Under the conditions of La Convención they would inevitably lead estate owners to exploit their feudal rights more intensively whenever they were under economic pressure.

V

Why did the tenants accept such unfavourable terms until the agrarian movement of 1958–63? Their bargaining position was very strong. After all, manpower was the scarce factor of production and land abundant. Even if (as is likely) the landlords might refuse to compete with one another for scarce labour, in theory the tenants might simply have gone beyond their reach and settled on unoccupied land; or they might (as in central Peru) have squatted on the uncultivated areas of the great estates, defying the lords to expel them.

The chief reason why they could not or would not do any of these things was that labour-tenancy brought considerable potential advantages to the peasant. If it is true that, from the landlord's point of view, the traditional latifundium of La Convención is a mere adaptation of the highland *hacienda* to the conditions of the *selva*, the peasant-settlers are no longer traditional highland peasants. They were and are overwhelmingly individual pioneers, modernizers, with a keen appreciation of the possibilities of market agriculture, Indians who rapidly learned to understand or even to speak Spanish, who adopted white man's costume, abandoned their native *comunidades* and were prepared to exploit the profit opportunities of the new situation. At the very least they were men who appreciated that in La Convención serfdom or wage-labour could immediately or eventually achieve *land*. La Convención differs from some more northerly regions of the high *selva* in that its hinterland is not the economically developed coast, but the backward *sierra* of Cuzco; but it appears to differ from other such regions abutting on the *sierra* in that its peasant colonization is individualist rather than communal, and aimed at market agriculture rather than the simple transfer of subsistence farming to a new area.

In the early stages there seems to have been some filtering in of traditional settlers who brought the highland communal Indian organization into one marginal area (Vilcabamba), but this soon ceased to be typical. Unlike central Peru, we find no examples of highland *comunidades* sending a body of colonists en bloc to the frontier territory. (This affected the agrarian situation in two ways: *comuneros* from the highlands, unused to working on *haciendas* and looking down on *colonos* who were forced to do so, tend to refuse labour-service tenancies, thus forcing landlords to make other arrangements for labour, and a large bloc of Indians 'invading' a *hacienda* – i.e. discovered cultivating an unoccupied corner of it – are much harder to browbeat by the forces at the disposal of an estate than individual squatters.) The La Convención settlers are not necessarily only men in search of better economic opportunities, though it is evident that among the *arrendires* there are better potential *kulaks* and agrarian capitalists than among the *hacendados*, and the evidence suggests that (with the exception of tea) the original pioneering of the world market crops – coffee and cocoa – was done at least as much by peasants as on demesnes, and probably more so. The area has also attracted, by its combination of nearness and inaccessibility, a number of recalcitrant or rebel elements, unwilling to accept the constraints of peasant life on the highland *hacienda* or in the highland *comunidad* and moving into the interior rather than to the remote and inaccessible coast.

The search for economic improvement inevitably put the

peasant at the mercy of the *hacienda*, because the only means of communication with the outside world passed through the *haciendas* or close to them. To go into the interior meant to exchange the prospects of a prosperous holding of a few hectares of export crops, for freedom and poverty as a subsistence farmer. This was not necessarily very attractive, all the more so since the immigrant from the highlands might find even subsistence agriculture difficult, since he might not readily adopt the kind of food which could be grown without trouble in the climate of the subtropics and tropics. His preference for his customary highland diet, which observers have noted, would perhaps also help to fix him in the neighbourhood of the large *hacienda*, which could provide it more easily. In any case, even potential Indian *kulaks* from the *altiplano* of Peru were only too accustomed to exploitation, submission and the inability to assert their rights. They might resent the excessive use of the lords' power over life, death and women, and the power of their *gamonales*,* but in this respect La Convención was no different from the highlands and certainly no worse. It might actually be better. If a peasant stayed within the radius of the *hacienda*, he knew that he was going to be exploited and that he had to do the lord's bidding. Only in La Convención he also knew that he might stand a good chance of getting land and – by his standards – wealth.

Evasion was thus no solution, and so long as the peasant stayed where his chances of profit were greatest, he could not use his theoretical scarcity-value to more than a small extent. The only real alternative was collective organization, which could come only from outside. It did come, from the 1930s on, in the form of communist propaganda and organizers from Cuzco, possibly later also in the form of Protestant agitation.[5] By the late 1950s the exploitation of the lords, temporarily veiled by the booms of the 1940s and early 1950s, when plainly

* *Gamonales*: *caciques*, rural bosses.

the *arrendires* also did pretty well for themselves, would appear increasingly intolerable. The leases of the new post-war holdings would begin to run out. The widening gap between the forced and the free wage-rates would become increasingly irksome. With the end of the boom-supported dictatorship, the political possibility of organizing peasant unions improved. The conditions for the mass peasant agitations of the early 1960s came into being. The era of neo-feudalism in La Convención was about to end. It is not the purpose of this paper to deal with the peasants' rebellion itself.

VI

Can we analyse the economic advantages and disadvantages of the form of agricultural development exemplified by La Convención? Not with any degree of realism. For, quite apart from our lack of adequate statistics, the major fact about the latifundia of this region is that they are *not* designed for the maximization of agricultural production, or even of the marketable surplus of such production. As we have already observed, they are overwhelmingly 'traditional', rarely even 'transitional', virtually not at all 'modern' in character, and the medium-sized commercial farms of about 50 hectares which, according to *CIDA: Peru* (1966), seem to be the most efficient units of production in the *selva* region are not of any numerical importance. According to *CIDA: Peru* (1966) the family holding is not less productive than the latifundium in the output of coca per hectare, and very much more efficient than the latifundium (or than the national average) in the cultivation of coffee. The *arrendire*'s holding analysed in the same document sells 90 per cent of its output on the market; the latifundium retains as much as 25 per cent for its own consumption. And this in spite of the fact that the large estates virtually monopolize the high-quality land for themselves. Clearly we cannot assume that the large estates of La Convención even set out to make their profits by the most efficient development of their resources. They are essentially parasitic on their serfs. Consequently there is little point in comparing the possible efficiencies of large-scale estate production and peasant production in this region. So long as the *haciendas* retained their powers of non-economic coercion, they were not obliged to make themselves more efficient. For instance, so long as a *hacendado* could force his peasants to sell their coffee to him at 7 soles per kilo, and prevent them by armed guards from crossing the river to sell it at 11 soles to the merchants, he made 4 soles a kilo profit without so much as lifting a finger. In effect, all one can say in general is that in such regions the major form of production is the small peasant holding, producing its own subsistence and a marketable surplus of the export crops, large parts of the latifundia being in effect left to such peasant cultivation.

These considerations do not easily permit us to compare the development of La Convención, with its specific form of neo-feudalism, with other regions of the high *selva* which have preferred different methods. Such a comparison is difficult, and its results are uncertain. It would seem that the rate of increase of coffee production in La Convención (1950–62) was a little slower than the national average for Peru, though possibly in the 1940s it was rather faster. The increase in cocoa production, which can only be estimated for a much shorter period (1956–60 to 1962) was much slower, that of tea rather faster than the national average, but all these figures are unreliable. The productivity of coffee cultivation was apparently higher than in central Peru (817 kilograms per hectare as against 460 kilograms), that of cocoa much lower (205 kilograms as against 660 kilograms). Central Peru seems to have expanded the area under cultivation more successfully, for the equivalent climatic areas there were about six times as large as in La Convención, but the areas under coffee, cocoa and tea about ten times as large. The only thing that seems reasonably clear is that the La Convención method was wasteful of manpower.

In six comparable areas of central Peru there is about one rural inhabitant per hectare of cultivated land; in La Convención, on the most conservative estimates, at least 2.5 inhabitants. We may perhaps conclude from this that under different conditions of land ownership, such an input of labour could have been expected to bring considerably more land under cultivation, and to produce either a much greater increase in output or a much more striking improvement in the social infrastructure, such as transport and housing; or both.

We may therefore conclude – and this is not surprising – that neo-feudalism seems to be a rather inefficient way of expanding agricultural output in frontier areas, quite apart from its social disadvantages. But we must also note that none of the frontier areas of the *ceja de la montaña* or high *selva* has a very impressive record of economic development. Not because the pioneer settlers showed any reluctance to engage in economic enterprise. Quite the contrary is true. What is striking about these areas is the readiness of colonists from a most traditional type of peasantry to turn themselves into something like commercial cultivators. (This ought to make us suspicious of those who see 'entrepreneurial dispositions' as something that has to be injected into a traditional economy from outside.) The real bottleneck in such areas is in the economic and social infrastructure, most obviously transport, but also sanitary organization, education, etc. Without social investment and planning these are not provided. And even if they were to some extent provided out of the profits of the large *haciendas*, these would still have to be supplemented by public enterprise and planning.

We may conclude that the experience of La Convención does not tell us much about the problem of agrarian development under capitalism that we did not already know. Nevertheless, untypical though it is, this remote province of Peru suggests some lessons which students of economic development ought not to be allowed to forget. In the first place, it demonstrates the danger of isolating economic analysis from its social and historical context. If La Convención had not been partitioned into large private estates, if Spanish lords in the tropics had not automatically thought in terms of a plantation economy, if the immigrants into the valleys had brought their communal institutions with them, the agrarian structure of La Convención would have been quite different, even though it would probably have ultimately also developed into a producer of the characteristic twentieth-century tropical export crops. In the second place, however, it is equally unwise to rely too much on historical or sociological explanations. Though it may be tempting to explain the peculiar neo-feudalism of La Convención by the historic facts of the Spanish conquest (the transfer of European medieval institutions, practices and values), by survivals of pre-Columbian forced labour, by the character of social relations between lords and dependent peasants, or in similar terms, there is no need for such explanations. It is perfectly possible to assume that (within a given framework of society) the development of this specific form of neo-feudal agriculture is a necessary consequence of the decision to undertake demesne cultivation under conditions of labour shortage and inadequate communications. Insofar as La Convención allows us to observe the emergence of an agrarian system surprisingly similar to some of those of European feudalism, it will probably interest the historian of the European middle ages more than the typical economic historian of our century. On the other hand, insofar as it is the offspring of a peculiar marriage between the twentieth and (in West European terms) the thirteenth centuries, it holds a final lesson for the student of capitalist development, though perhaps a familiar one. For it demonstrates once again that the very growth of the capitalist world market at certain stages produces, or reproduces, archaic forms of class-domination on the frontier of development. The slave-societies of eighteenth- and nineteenth-century America were the products of capitalist development, and so, on a more

modest and localized scale, is the neo-feudalism which prevailed in La Convención, until it collapsed, we may hope for
ever, under the revolt of the peasants.

1969

Notes

*Some notes and an Appendix on Production in La Convención 1862–1962 in the origi-
nal essay have been omitted from the version that appears in this volume.*

1 The major sources on the economic development of La Convención,
which will be used extensively below are: Unión Panamericana,
Tenencia de tierra y desarallo sócio-económico del sector agrícola: Peru (Wash-
ington, 1966) (cited as *CIDA: Peru* [1966]), especially Chapter VII, ii
'Caracteristicas generales de los sistemas de tenencia en la selva con
referencia especial al valle de La Convención'. D. D. Enrique Rosell,
'Fragmentos de las Monografias de la provincia de La Convención',
Revista Universitaria, VI (Cuzco, 1917) (cited as Rosell [1917]). F. Ponce
de Leon, 'Formas del arriendamiento de terrenos de cultivo en el
Depto de Cuzco, y el problema de la distribución', *Revista Universitaria*,
VII (Cuzco, 1918) (cited as Ponce de Leon [1918]). Isaac Tupayachi,
'Un ensayo de econometria en La Convención', *Revista Universitaria*
(Cuzco, 1959) (cited as Tupayachi [1959]). C. F. Cuadros y Villena, 'El
"Arriendo" y la Reforma Agraria en la provincia de La Convención',
Revista Universitaria, XXVIII (Cuzco, 1949) (cited as Cuadros [1949]). J.
Kuon Cabello, 'Industrias alimenticias en el Cuzco', *Revista Universita-
ria*, LI–LII (Cuzco, 1965) (cited as Kuon [1965]). Kuczynski Godard,
A propósito del saneamento de los Valles Yungas del Cuzco (cited as Kuczynski
Godard [1946]).

2 H. Bingham, *Inca Land* (1922), p. 324. See also I. Bowman, *The Andes of
Southern Peru* (1920). The expedition of 1911, which discovered Machu
Picchu, provided us with some useful data on La Convención at this
time. It is fortunate, incidentally, that the upper part of these valleys
was visited by several early European travellers, thanks to its proxim-
ity to Cuzco, so that we have descriptions of two of the great *haciendas*,
Huadquiña and Echarate, dating back to at least the 1830s.

3 Between 1933 and 1945 it killed or forced into emigration in one
hacienda for which we have figures, 65.5 per cent, 87 per cent and 83.4
per cent of various classes of tenants. Kuczynski Godard (1946), p. 32;
CIDA: Peru (1966), p. 209.

4 For figures see *CIDA: Peru* (1966), p. 208; *Guerra a Muerte al Latifundio*: Proyecto de ley de Reforma Agraria del M.I.R. Estudio del Ing. Carlos Malpica S.S. (Lima, s.d.), pp. 221–3.

5 Wesley W. Craig, *The peasant movement of La Convención*, Cornell University, 1966, mimeo, notes that the first Secretary-General of the Federación Provincial de Campesinos in 1958 was a Protestant, subsequently jailed as a 'communist', and I have certainly encountered Protestant peasant militants from La Convención. How early this phenomenon appeared, I do not know. The first peasant union seems to have been that of Maranura in 1934, which long remained a fortress of the Communist Party.

III

PEASANTS

10

Peasants as Social Bandits

Social bandits are peasant outlaws whom the lord and state regard as criminals, but who remain within peasant society, and are considered by their people as heroes, as champions, avengers, fighters for justice, perhaps even leaders of liberation, and in any case as men to be admired, helped and supported. In the cases where a traditional society resists the encroachments and historical advance of central governments and states, native or foreign, they may be helped and supported even by the local lords. This relation between the ordinary peasant and the rebel, outlaw and robber is what makes social banditry interesting and significant. [...]

Socially [banditry] seems to occur in all types of human society which lie between the evolutionary phase of tribal and kinship organization, and modern capitalist and industrialist society, but including the phases of disintegrating kinship society and transition to agrarian capitalism. [...] Modern agrarian systems, both capitalist and post-capitalist, are no longer those of traditional peasant society and cease to produce social bandits except in countries of what has been called 'settler capitalism' – the USA, Australia, Argentina. [...] Social

133

banditry is universally found wherever societies are based on agriculture (including pastoral economies), and consist largely of peasants and landless labourers ruled, oppressed and exploited by someone else – lords, towns, governments, lawyers, or even banks. It is found in one or other of three main forms: the *noble robber* or Robin Hood, the primitive resistance fighter or guerrilla unit, and possibly the terror-bringing *avenger*.

[...]

Banditry may be the precursor or companion of major social movements such as peasant revolutions. Alternatively, it may itself change by adapting to the new social and political situation, though in doing so it will almost certainly cease to be social banditry. In the typical case of the past two centuries, the transition from a pre-capitalist to a capitalist economy, the social transformation may entirely destroy the kind of agrarian society which gives birth to bandits, the kind of peasantry which nourishes them, and in doing so conclude its history. The nineteenth and twentieth centuries have been the great age of social banditry in many parts of the world, just as the sixteenth to eighteenth probably were in most parts of Europe. Yet it is now largely extinct, except in a few areas.

[...]

Insofar as bandits have a 'programme', it is the defence or restoration of the traditional order of things 'as it should be' (which in traditional societies means as it is believed to have been in some real or mythical past). They right wrongs, they correct and avenge cases of injustice, and in doing so apply a more general criterion of just and fair relations between men in general, and especially between the rich and the poor, the strong and the weak. This is a modest aim, which leaves the rich to exploit the poor (but no more than is traditionally accepted as 'fair'), the strong to oppress the weak (but within the limits of what is equitable, and mindful of their social and moral duties). [...] In this sense, social bandits are reformers, not revolutionaries.

However, reformist or revolutionary, banditry itself does not constitute a social *movement*. It may be a surrogate for it, as when peasants admire Robin Hoods as their champions, for want of any more positive activity by themselves. It may even be a substitute for it, as when banditry becomes institutionalized among some tough and combative section of the peasantry and actually inhibits the development of other means of struggle. Whether such cases occur has not been clearly established, but there is some evidence that they may. Thus in Peru, the pressure of the peasantry for land reform was (and in 1971 still remained) notably weaker in the departments of Huanuco and Apurimac, where agrarian problems were by no means less acute, but where there was (and is) a very deeply rooted tradition of cattle-rustling and brigandage. However, the question awaits serious investigation, like so many other aspects of banditry.

Two things may, however, turn this modest, if violent, social objective of bandits – and the peasantry to whom they belong – into genuine revolutionary movements. The first is, when it becomes the symbol, even the spearhead, of resistance by the whole of the traditional order against the forces which disrupt and destroy it. A social revolution is no less revolutionary because it takes place in the name of what the outside world considers 'reaction' against what it considers 'progress'. [. . .] The second reason why bandits become revolutionaries is inherent in peasant society. Even those who accept exploitation, oppression and subjection as the norm of human life dream of a world without them: a world of equality, brotherhood and freedom, a totally *new* world without evil. Rarely is this more than a dream. Rarely is it more than an apocalyptic expectation. [. . .] Yet there are moments when the apocalypse seems imminent; when the entire structure of the state and existing society whose total end the apocalypse symbolizes and predicts actually looks about to collapse in ruins, and the tiny light of hope turns into the light of a possible sunrise.

At such moments bandits are also swept away, like everyone

135

else. [...] Indeed, nothing is more striking than this subordinate coexistence of banditry with major peasant revolution, of which it thus often serves as a precursor. [...] The *sertão** of north-eastern Brazil, which was the classical home of the *cangaçeiros*, was also that of the *santos*, the rural messianic leaders. Both flourished together, but the saints were greater. The great bandit Lampião, in one of the innumerable ballads which celebrate his exploits,

Swore to be avenged on all
Saying in this world I'll respect
Father Cícero and no one else.[1]

And it was, as we shall see, from Father Cícero, the Messiah of Juazeiro, that public opinion derived Lampião's 'official' credentials. Social banditry and millenarianism – the most primitive forms of reform and revolution – go together historically. And when the great apocalyptic moments come, the brigand bands, their numbers swollen by the time of tribulation and expectation, may insensibly turn into something else. [...]

When banditry thus merges into a large movement, it becomes part of a force which can and does change society. Since the horizons of social bandits are narrow and circumscribed, like those of the peasantry itself, the results of their interventions into history may not be those they expected. They may be the opposite of what they expected. But this does not make banditry any less of a historical force.

Among the *cangaçeiros* of the Brazilian north-east there are those, like the great Antônio Silvino (1875–1944, *fl.* as bandit chief 1896–1914), who are mainly remembered for their good deeds,

* The back country of north-eastern Brazil beyond the frontiers of concentrated settlement.

and others, like Rio Preto, mainly for their cruelty. However, broadly speaking, the 'image' of the *cangaçeiro* combines both. Let us illustrate this by following the account of one of the backwoods bards of the most celebrated *cangaçeiro*, Virgulino Ferreira da Silva (?1898–1938), universally known as 'The Captain' or 'Lampião'.

He was born, so the legend goes (and it is the image rather than the reality which interests us for the moment), of respectable cattle-raising and farming parents at the foot of the mountains in the dry backlands of Pernambuco state 'in that time of the past when the back country was pretty prosperous', an intellectual – and therefore in the legend not a particularly powerful – boy. The weak must be able to identify with the great bandit. As the poet Zabele wrote:

Where Lampião lives
Worms become brave,
The monkey fights the jaguar,
The sheep stands his ground.

His uncle, Manoel Lopes, said this boy must become a doctor, which made people smile for

Never was seen a doctor
In that immense sertão*;*
There men knew only cowhands,
Bands of cangaçeiros
Or ballad-singers.

Anyway, young Virgulino did not want to be a doctor but a *vaqueiro* or cowpuncher, though he learned his letters and the 'Roman algorism' after only three months at school and was an expert poet. The Ferreiras were expelled by the Nogueiras from their farm when he was seventeen, being falsely accused of theft. That is how the feud began which was to make him into

an outlaw. 'Virgulino,' someone said, 'trust in the divine judge,'
but he answered: 'The good book says honour your father and
mother, and if I did not defend our name, I would lose my manhood.' So

He bought a rifle and dagger
In the town of São Francisco

and formed a band with his brothers and twenty-seven other
fighters (known to the poet as to their neighbours by nick-
names, often traditional to those who took up the career of the
bandit) to attack the Nogueiras in the Serra Vermelha. From
blood-feud to outlawry was a logical – in view of the superior
power of the Nogueiras a necessary – step. Lampião became a
roving bandit, more famous even than Antônio Silvino, whose
capture in 1914 had left a void in the backwoods pantheon:

He spared the skin
Neither of soldier or civilian,
His darling was the dagger
His gift was the gun ...
He left the rich as beggars,
The brave fell at his feet,
While others fled the country.

But during all the years (in fact *c.*1920–38) when he was the
terror of the north-east, he never ceased to deplore his fate, says
the poet, which had made him a robber instead of an honest
labourer, and destined him for certain death, tolerable only if
he had the luck to die in a fair fight.

He was and is a hero to the people, but an ambiguous one.
Normal caution might explain why the poet makes his bow to
formal morality and records the 'joy of the north' at the death
of the great bandit in 1938. (By no means all ballads take this
view.) The reaction of a backwoodsman in the township of

Mosquito is probably more typical. When the soldiers came by with their victims' heads in jars of kerosene, so as to convince all that Lampião was really dead, he said: 'They have killed the Captain, because strong prayer is no good in water.'[2] For his last refuge was in the dried bed of a stream, and how else except by the failure of his magic could his fall be explained? Nevertheless, though a hero, he was not a *good* hero.

It is true that he had made a pilgrimage to the famous Messiah of Juazeiro, Padre Cícero,* asking his blessing before turning bandit, and that the saint, though exhorting him vainly to give up the outlaw's life, had given him a document appointing him captain, and his two brothers lieutenants. However, the ballad from which I have taken most of this account does not mention any righting of wrongs (except those done to the band itself), no taking from the rich to give to the poor, no bringing of justice. It records battles, and wounds, raids on towns (or what passed for towns in the Brazilian backwoods), kidnappings, hold-ups of the rich, adventures with the soldiers, with women, with hunger and thirst, but nothing that recalls the Robin Hoods. On the contrary, it records 'horrors': how Lampião murdered a prisoner though his wife had ransomed him, how he massacred labourers, tortured an old woman who cursed him (not knowing whom she entertained) by making her dance naked with a cactus bush until she died, how he sadistically killed one of his men who had offended him by making him eat a litre of salt, and similar incidents. To be terrifying and pitiless is a more important attribute of this bandit than to be the friend of the poor.

[...]

The examples of genuinely unqualified cruelty, on the other hand, are not normally those of characteristic bandits. It is perhaps a mistake to classify as banditry the epidemic of blood-lust which swept the Peruvian department of Huanuco from about 1917 to the late 1920s, for though robbery formed part of it, its

---

* The effective political boss of the north-eastern state of Ceará.

motive is described as 'not exactly this, but rather hatred and blood-feud'. It was indeed, according to the evidence, a blood-feud situation which got out of hand, and produced that 'fever of death among men', which led them to 'burn, rape, kill, sack and destroy coldly' everywhere except in their native community or village. Even more obviously the ghastly phenomenon of the Colombian *Violencia* of the years after 1948 goes far beyond ordinary social banditry. Nowhere is the element of pathological violence for its own sake more startling than in this peasant revolution aborted into anarchy, though some of the most terrifying practices, such as that of chopping prisoners into tiny fragments 'in front of and for the entertainment of the fighting men crazed by barbarity' (later to be known as *picar a tamal*) are alleged to have occurred in earlier guerrilla campaigns in that bloodthirsty country. The point to note about these epidemics of cruelty and massacre is that they are immoral even by the standards of those who participate in them. If the massacre of entire bus-loads of harmless passengers or villagers is comprehensible in the context of savage civil warfare, such (well-attested) incidents as ripping the foetus out of a pregnant woman and substituting a cock can only be conscious 'sins'. And yet, some of the men who perpetrate these monstrosities are and remain 'heroes' to the local population.

Undoubtedly political consciousness can do much to change the character of bandits. The communist peasant guerrillas of Colombia contain some fighters (but almost certainly not more than a modest minority) who have transferred to them from the former freebooting brigand guerrillas of the *Violencia*. 'Cuando bandoleaba' (When I was a bandit) is a phrase that may be heard in the conversations and reminiscences that fill so much of a guerrilla's time. The phrase itself indicates the awareness of the difference between a man's past and his present. However, while individual bandits may be easily integrated into political units, collectively, in Colombia at least, they have proved rather unassimilable into left-wing guerrilla groups.

In any case as bandits their military potential was limited, their political potential even more so, as the brigand wars in southern Italy demonstrate. Their ideal unit was less than twenty men ... In the Colombian *Violencia* after 1948 the very large insurgent units were almost invariably communist rather than grassroots rebels ... Large forces were, as in Lampião's band, broken up into sub-units, or temporary coalitions of separate formations. Tactically this made sense, but it indicated a basic incapacity of most grassroots chiefs to equip and supply large units or to handle bodies of men beyond the direct control of a powerful personality. What is more, each chieftain jealously protected his sovereignty. Even Lampião's most loyal lieutenant, the 'blond devil' Corisco, though remaining sentimentally attached to his old chief, quarrelled with him and took his friends and followers away to form a separate band. [...]

Politically, bandits were, as we have seen, incapable of offering a real alternative to the peasants. Moreover, their traditionally ambiguous position between the men of power and the poor, as men of the people but contemptuous of the weak and the passive, as a force which in normal times operated within the existing social and political structure or on its margins, rather than against it, limited their revolutionary potential. They might dream of a free society of brothers, but the most obvious prospect of a successful bandit revolutionary was to become a landowner, like the gentry. Pancho Villa ended as a *hacendado*,* the natural reward of a Latin American aspirant *caudillo*,† though no doubt his background and manner made him more popular than the fine-skinned Creole aristocrats.

---

* Large landowner, owner of an estate (*hacienda*).

† Military chieftain establishing political power, a sadly familiar figure in Latin American history.

And in any case, the heroic and undisciplined robber life did not fit a man much for either the hard, dun-coloured organization-world of the revolutionary fighters or the legality of post-revolutionary life.

[...]

The bandits' contribution to modern revolutions was thus ambiguous, doubtful and short. That was their tragedy. As bandits they could at best, like Moses, discern the promised land. They could not reach it. [...] More than this. The Mexican Revolution contained two major peasant components: the typical bandit-based movement of Pancho Villa in the north, the mainly unbandit-like agrarian agitation of Zapata in Morelos. In military terms, Villa played an immeasurably more important part on the national scene, but neither the shape of Mexico nor even of Villa's own north-west was changed by it. Zapata's movement was entirely regional, its leader was killed in 1919, its military forces were of no great consequence. Yet this was the movement which injected the element of agrarian reform into the Mexican Revolution. The brigands produced a potential *caudillo* and a legend – not least, a legend of the only Mexican leader who tried to invade the land of the *gringos* in the twentieth century.[3] The peasant movement of Morelos produced a social revolution; one of the three which deserve the name in the history of Latin America.

[Let us] conclude with some reflections on three [countries] where the very different itinerary of the national bandit tradition can be compared: Mexico, Brazil and Colombia. All three are countries which became familiar with large-scale banditry in the course of their history.

All travellers along its roads agreed that, if any Latin American state was quintessentially bandit country, it was nineteenth-century

Mexico. Moreover, in the first sixty years of independence the breakdown of government and economy, war and civil war gave any body of armed men which lived by the gun considerable leverage, or at least the choice between joining the army or police force on government pay (which, then as later, did not exclude extortion) or sticking to simple brigandage. Benito Juarez's Liberals, in their civil wars, lacking more traditional patronage, used them extensively. However, the bandits around whom the popular myths formed were those of the stable era of Porfirio Díaz's dictatorship (1884–1911) which preceded the Mexican Revolution. These bandits could be seen, even at the time, as challengers of authority and the established order. Later, with sympathetic hindsight, they might appear as precursors of the Mexican Revolution. Thanks chiefly to Pancho Villa, the most eminent of all brigands turned revolutionaries, this has brought banditry a unique degree of legitimacy in Mexico, though not in the USA, where in those very years violent, cruel and greedy Mexican bandits became the standard villains of Hollywood, at least until 1922 when the Mexican government threatened to ban all films made by offending movie companies from the country.[4] Of the other bandits who became nationally famous in their lifetime – Jesus Arriaga (Chucho El Roto) in central Mexico, Heraclio Bernal in Sinaloa and Santana Rodriguez Palafox (Santanon) in Veracruz – at least the first two still enjoy popularity. Bernal, killed in 1889, who was in and out of politics, is probably the most famous in the age of the media, celebrated in thirteen songs, four poems and four movies, some adapted for television, but I suspect that the impudent Catholic but anti-clerical trickster Chucho (died 1885), who has also made it on to the TV screens, remains closer to the heart of the people.

Unlike Mexico, Brazil moved from colony to independent empire without disruption. It was the First Republic (1889–1930) which produced, at least in the grim hinterlands of the north-east, the social and political conditions for epidemic banditry: that is to say, transformed the groups of armed retainers tied to particular territories and elite families into independent operators roaming over the area of perhaps 100,000 square kilometres covering four or five states. The great *cangaçeiros* of the period 1890–1940 soon became regionally famous, their reputation spread orally and in chapbooks by local poets and singers.[5] Mass migration to the cities of the south and growing literacy were later to spread this literature to the shops and market stalls of the monster cities like São Paulo. The modern media brought the *cangaçeiros*, an obvious local equivalent to the Wild West, on to cinema and television screens, all the more readily as the most famous of them, Lampião, was actually the first great bandit to be filmed live in the field. Of the two most celebrated bandits, Silvino acquired a 'noble robber' myth in his lifetime, which was reinforced by journalists and others to contrast with the great but hardly benevolent reputation of Lampião, his successor as 'king of the backlands'.

Yet it is the political and intellectual co-option of the *cangaçeiros* into Brazilian national tradition that is interesting. They were very soon romanticized by north-eastern writers and, in any case, were easy to turn into demonstrations of the corruption and injustice of political authority. Insofar as Lampião was a potential factor in national politics, they attracted wider attention. The Communist International even thought of him as a possible revolutionary guerrilla leader, perhaps suggested by the leader of the Brazilian Communist Party, Luís Carlos Prestes, who in his earlier career as leader of the 'Long March' of military rebels came into contact with Lampião [in Ceará in 1926]. However, the bandits do not seem to have played a major part in the important attempt by the Brazilian intellectuals of the 1930s to build a concept of Brazil with popular and social as against elite and political bricks. It was in the 1960s and 1970s that a new generation of intellectuals transformed the *cangaçeiro* into a symbol of Brazilianness, of the fight for freedom and the power of the oppressed; in short, as 'a national symbol of resistance and even revolution'.[6] This in turn affects the way he is presented in the mass media, even though the popular chap-book/oral tradition was still alive among north-easterners, at least in the 1970s.

The Colombian tradition has followed a very different trajectory. It is, for obvious reasons, completely overshadowed by the bloodthirsty experience of the era after 1948 (or, as some historians prefer, 1946) known as *La Violencia* and its aftermath. This was essentially a conflict combining class warfare, regionalism and political partisanship of rural populations identifying themselves, as in the republics of the River Plate, with one or other of the country's traditional parties, in this case the Liberals and Conservatives, which turned into guerrilla war in several regions after 1948, and eventually (apart from the regions where the now powerful communist guerrilla movement developed in the 1960s) into a congeries of defeated, formerly political armed bands, relying on local alliances with men of power and peasant sympathy, both of which they eventually lost. They were wiped out in the 1960s. The memory they have left has been well described by the best experts on the subject:

> Perhaps, except for the idealized memory that the peasants still hold in their old zones of support, the 'social bandit' has also been defeated as a mythical character ... What took place in Colombia was the opposite process from that of the Brazilian *cangaço*. Over time the *cangaço* lost much of its characteristic ambiguity and developed towards the image of the ideal social bandit. The *cangaçeiro* ended up as a national symbol of native virtues and the embodiment of national independence ... In Colombia, on the contrary, the bandit personifies a cruel and inhuman monster or, in the best of cases, 'the son of the *Violencia*', frustrated, disoriented and manipulated by local leaders. This has been the image accepted by public opinion.[7]

Whatever the images of the FARC (Fuerzas Armadas Revolucionarias de Colombia), the chief guerrilla force in Colombia since 1964 – guerrillas, paramilitaries and drug-cartel gunmen – that will survive into the twenty-first century, they will no longer have anything in common with the old bandit myth.

1969

Notes

1   R. Rowland, 'Cantadores del nordeste brasileño', in *Aportes*, 3 January 1967, p. 138. For the real relations between this bandit and the holy man, which were rather more *nuancés*, cf. E. de Lima, *O mundo estranho dos cangaçeiros* (Salvador, Bahia, 1965), pp. 113–14, and O. Anselmo, *Padre Cícero* (1968).

2   Nertan Macedo, *Capitão Virgulino Ferreira da Silva: Lampião*, 2nd edn (1968), p. 183.

3   The most dramatic evidence of this comes from the village of San José de Gracia in the uplands of Michoacan, which – like so many Mexican villages – expressed its popular aspirations by mobilizing under the banner of Christ the King *against* the revolution (as part of the *Cristero* movement, best known through Graham Greene's *The Power and the Glory*). Its excellent historian points out that it naturally 'abhorred the great figures of the Revolution' with two exceptions: President Cardenas (1934–40) for distributing the land and ending the persecution of religion, and Pancho Villa. 'These have become popular idols.' Luis González, *Pueblo en vila* (1968), p. 251. Even in 1971 the general store in a very similar township of the same area, a place not visibly much given to literature, contained *The Memoirs of Pancho Villa*.

4   Allen L. Woll, 'Hollywood Bandits 1910–1981', in Richard W. Slatta (ed.), *Bandidos: The Varieties of Latin American Banditry* (1987), pp. 171–80.

5   Linda Lewin, 'Oral Tradition and Elite Myth: The Legend of Antônio Silvino in Brazilian Popular Culture', *Journal of Latin American Lore*, 5/2 (1979), pp. 57–204.

6   Gonzalo Sánchez, Prologue to Maria Isaura Pereira de Queiroz, *Os cangaçeiros: La epopeya zandolera del Nordeste de Brasil* (Bogotá, 1992), pp. 15–16.

7   Gonzalo Sánchez and Donny Meertens, *Bandoleros, gamonales y campesinos: El caso de la Violencia en Colombia* (1987), p. 168.

11

Peasant Insurrection

My title needs some defining. By 'peasants' I mean country-
men of not more than moderate wealth (by prevailing social
standards) who cultivate their land primarily with their own
and their families' labour, or who want land for this purpose;
and for whom this activity is not just a business but a way of life.
That is to say the term excludes, in addition to 'townsmen', (a)
landlords who have land cultivated for them primarily by other
people's labour; (b) rural proletarians who would not wish to
become peasants; (c) rural entrepreneurs for whom agriculture
is primarily a business.

There are a considerable number of borderline cases, but
this will do as a guideline. The term 'peasant society' means
the social organization of an agricultural economy in which
peasants play the predominant part; or the social organization
of that sector of such an economy in which they do – e.g. the
nineteenth-century Russian village minus the superstructure of
the gentry.

By 'peasant insurrection' I mean social movements in which
peasants seek to attain ends which are determined by their collective position as peasants. Thus the participation of peasants

147

in the civil wars of nineteenth- and twentieth-century Colombia does not automatically constitute a peasant movement, but the land agitations of the 1930s do. Any movement in which land, rights, rent or similar questions are at issue is automatically a peasant movement, if conducted by peasants or in a peasant society, but not all peasant insurrections or movements need be socio-economic in this strict sense. Beyond what point insurrections lacking this specific and concrete socio-economic content cease to be peasant movements is an interesting question, which we need not pursue too far here. Are rural millennial movements peasant movements? Pretty certainly, at least in many cases – e.g. when nobody except peasants or people of peasant origins are involved, as in Palma Sola (Dominican Republic, 1963). Are nativist movements such as the Race War in Yucatan [which began in 1847 and continued to the beginning of the twentieth century]? Probably. Are nationalist or xenophobic movements with strong peasant support but no specific peasant programmatic content, like the Iron Guard in Romania? They could be. The test is perhaps how much peasant participation there is, and how far their programme is *de facto* translated into terms of peasant interests by its peasant supporters.

[. . .]

'Insurrection' means any movements in which a significant number of peasants take part simultaneously, and in which they use physical coercion – or more generally, in which they refuse to play the socially subaltern role they are normally supposed to. Thus insurrection excludes (a) small marginal bands of outlaws, such as may exist at the most peaceful and passive times and (b) peasant movements such as the formation of rural co-operatives or others which do not imply a challenge to the prevailing social conventions. Insurrections can be both more modest and more impermanent than revolutions, successful or otherwise.

*

148

Let me begin with a big question. Why are peasant insurrections so much more common in some countries than in others? In China than in India, in Peru than in Brazil? Can we say that there is such a divergence at all? I think we can. Though the history of the peasants is so unknown in many countries that almost anything might still be discovered about it, the slightest scratching at its surface in, say, Peru, reveals a persistent tendency to such insurrection during the past two hundred years whereas in, say, Colombia before the twentieth century it does not seem to.

I cannot answer this question and refer you in passing to Barrington Moore [*Social Origins of Dictatorship and Democracy. Lord and Peasant in the Making of the Modern World*, 1967]. I merely wish to pose it, since all others with which this paper are concerned, are subordinate to it. Let me distinguish it, by the way, from the question about the *effectiveness* of peasant insurrections, which has no logical connection with it. Historically Chinese peasant insurrections have been extremely effective, and Peruvian peasants extremely ineffective in national terms; but we are not entitled from this to conclude that Chinese peasants were more likely to rebel than Peruvian peasants; though of course this may be so. Palermo holds the record for riotousness among European cities; St Petersburg neither lent itself to rioting nor appears to have much of a history of it before the Revolutions: the effects of the few Petersburg riots were far greater than those of the many Palermo insurrections for quite different reasons.

Perhaps it is worth making one point in passing. The answer is not to be found by singling out certain factors or 'variables', economic or otherwise, however convenient this may be to those who dream of turning history into a 'behavioural science'. Men always live in situations which are by definition unlike those in a laboratory, and while some factors can be eliminated by comparative analysis, and others stressed, they *always* act in common. Poverty itself is not a cause for rebellion in societies in which every peasant – or indeed everybody – is more or less poor, as in the *sertão* of north-east Brazil, and where no peasant expects to be anything else. And where (as on many Latin American frontiers in the nineteenth century) there is plenty of land to be settled, land hunger will hardly be a major factor in peasant discontent. But suppose squatters colonize this land in isolated nuclear families, as I have seen them do in the Chaco. Unless such a unit has two or three grown men's labour power, it will almost certainly not have enough to establish itself permanently. In such cases family structure inserts a mechanism for generating agrarian discontent into a situation of totally free colonization with unlimited land. Again, suppose we find that the open frontier attracts men who have to, or want to, get away from the settled world of lordship and subordination. Then the stimulus which can move them into action need only be much slighter than elsewhere. Here the socio-political structure in general counteracts the 'laboratory' effects of free land. There are plenty of cases in point, not only in Latin America but on the steppe frontier of Tsarist Russia, where all major peasant risings began in the seventeenth/eighteenth centuries. But suppose, yet again, that the settlers are a millennial religious community, which regards itself as separate from the unregenerate and is – as so often happens – unusually successful at pioneer agriculture. They may then be entirely quiet, unless the state tries to interfere with them; and they may even, in case of local peasant insurrections, take the side of the status quo. Here both the political structure and religio-cultural elements enter the scene. All we can do a priori is to construct a more or less abstract model, with low predictive capacity. Some of the German sectarians in Brazil have a history of insurrection. Have the Mennonites and others in Paraguay? I don't know, but I haven't heard of it.

Having mentioned the *big* question, let me be a little more concrete about a smaller, yet still fairly ambitious one. There are,

as a look at the Mexican Revolution will suggest, two quite different types of peasant insurrection, which I shall call the Villa
and the Zapata type. The Zapata type involves the entire local
peasantry. It is a mobilization of communities, even of regional
societies, through the structure, customs, etc. of the communities. Compare the way in which Zapata found himself at the
head of his community, and then by a process of osmosis – or
rather of tacitly mobilized consent – of his entire people: he was
leader *'por cariño'*. The Villa type is a mobilization of the marginal, the outlaws, the men who have little to lose and much
to gain: bandits, cowhands, footloose men, deserters, armed
bands.

This division is very general. I am told, for instance, that
the classical Chinese peasant movement is of the Villa rather
than the Zapata type: an expanded version of the outlaw
bands, swelled by the landless, the starving, the marginal.
The peasant movements with which I am more familiar, on
the other hand – for instance the Sicilian Fasci of the 1890s,
the anarchists in Spain – seem to me to belong to the Zapata
type. We should expect their local leaders to be men of local
standing, settled, married with families and kin (always allowing for the social divisions and political structure of their
area). Movements which begin by the formation of a peasant
league are of this type, I think. Movements of *comunidades* one
would expect almost by definition to be like that. This doesn't
mean that the marginal men are not involved – indeed they
are essential from a military point of view. But, as in the case
of the Zapata movement, all that is needed here is that the
leaders of the wider movement should have the respect of
the tough men – as Zapata had, because he was not merely
a farmer but a horse-breaker, a dandy, a good man with
women, etc.

Clearly the motives will be different in each case. But how?
Here is scope for research and thinking. Why will one movement take a Zapata form, another a Villa form? Obviously in

151

pastoral areas, in mountains, etc. a Villa is more likely, but only there? Like many questions, I must leave this one open.

What I have said has a bearing on certain theories of peasant revolt, notably that of Eric Wolf [*Peasants*, 1965 and *Peasant Wars of the Twentieth Century*, 1969], which seem to me to be slightly incomplete insofar as they leave the Zapata–Villa distinction on one side. Wolf's main thesis, with which I agree broadly speaking, is that the main force of peasant revolutions resides in what is culturally the most traditionalist sectors of peasant society, and economically or socially the 'middle peasantry', i.e. neither the rural poor and landless labourers nor the richer, commercially farming *kulaks*. It is indeed for him subjectively a movement to defend or restore the traditional economy and society against disruption – but a movement whose strength naturally lies among those who have not yet been definitively disrupted, or on the other hand, who have discovered that the new economy and society provide them with an inviting alternative. Of course if we accept this general view it does not mean that we deny the participation, even the initiative, of either the bottom or top strata of the village. The people at the bottom or the marginalized may provide ready mobilization [...] the top people may provide initiative and leadership, or their own specific discontents around which a wider movement can crystallize, as around the *arrendires* in La Convención, Peru.

One point on which I think there can be no serious argument concerns the rural proletarians. If modern large-scale commercial faming – 'agro-industrial enterprise' – establishes itself in the shape of plantations or suchlike, the permanent rural proletariat will stop being peasants. They will act like proletarians in a specific rural setting, through unions, political parties, etc. (This does not apply to temporary or seasonal migrants, who are, as it were, on leave from their existence as peasants.) [...]

So let me eliminate the rural proletariat (in the strict sense of the word) from the present discussion, if only because there are few plantations which do not impinge upon, or are impinged upon by, other sectors: (a) labourers not directly employed but through contractors (*padrones*), making the permanent labour force much weaker than in, for example, the Peruvian *haciendas*; (b) peasants – often squatters – providing the plantation with food; (c) Indians. It is not often that agro-industrial enterprises can be isolated from their peasant context.

Let us, however, leave them aside for our purposes and consider the likelihood of particular kinds of complexes of peasants rising in Latin America today. There have been few *general* peasant insurrections – apart from Peru in 1960–4 – so we should not be surprised to find the general scheme of Wolf not necessarily providing us with more concrete guidance. Looking at what I know of the area, I would say that the following groups have been most 'explosive' in different situations. I list them in no particular order; they sometimes overlap: (a) squatters and peasant colonists; (b) potential *kulaks* in agrarian conflicts arising out of the extension of cash crops; (c) *comunidades* (here landhunger plays a special role); (d) frontiersmen; (e) peasants in regions of traditional (mostly communist) agitation.

The role of the squatter is particularly explosive, since his conflicts arise essentially out of the challenge by the law of state and landowners to his *de facto* occupation of land which he knows to be unutilized and therefore 'morally' the tiller's. Also because it tends to occur in zones remote from authority. Hence the unusually high activity of this numerically quite small group. There is a squatter element in virtually all agrarian agitations: in frontier areas like La Convención or central Peru; in the famous independent banana-growers strike in conflict with the United Fruit Company in Santa Marta, Colombia in 1928; in Goiás (Brazil) in the early 1950s; throughout most Colombian agitations; and in pre-revolutionary Cuba. But it can also, I am sure, be discerned in the activities of the *colonos* on Peruvian *haciendas* who are, according to the Peruvian anthropologist Hugo Neira [*Los Andes: tierra o muerte*, 1968], the core of highland unionism; or for that matter in the disputes about land in the increasingly populous and land-poor *comunidades*.

The role of the cash-crop peasant is equally evident in the coffee areas of Colombia and La Convención, Peru, where there is a conflict between a type of agriculture essentially suitable to small and medium production and a pattern of land ownership essentially favourable to large estates.

The *comunidades* agitation seems to arise essentially from the squeeze produced by population growth on the one hand, the exhaustion of communal lands on the other – politically sharpened by the long process of often illegal appropriation by expanding *haciendas*.

The frontier situation is suitable for agitation because of the relative economic freedom of the pioneers engaged in subsistence agriculture – and the political and social factors which drive men on to the frontier and make them more combative.

A history of past agitation and organization is important because it provides both the catalyst and the forces of leadership, organization, sympathy by local literates, etc. which can turn discontent into action – and tie it on to wider movements.

Editor's note

A final section of this unpublished essay on the way in which peasant thinking affects peasant insurrections was left unfinished. But see 'Ideology and Peasant Movements', below.

12

Ideology and Peasant Movements

The term 'ideology' will be used in this paper in two senses: (a) a formulated and generally recognized system of beliefs about society (often with a recognized brand name, such as liberalism, nationalism, communism, etc.) from which programmes of social and political action can be or are derived; and (b) a similar system of beliefs, which is not formulated as much or consciously held, but which nevertheless forms the basis of social and political action of a given group of men. In other words, 'ideology', as used in this paper, includes not only the ideologies commonly recognized and labelled as such, whose significance may be confined to a minority sector of society (the literate or educated) but *all* systems of ideas about society which determine social and political action. The distinction is of operational importance in a continent such as South America, where ideologies of type (a), at least in their secular post-1789 form, may be politically effective among a restricted stratum (e.g. Comtist Positivists in Brazil or Mexico) but totally unknown or incomprehensible to the bulk of the population. Type (a) will be called socio-political theories, type (b) systems of action. It follows that theories, insofar as they are confined to elite or other politically influential minorities become effective by imposing a certain pattern of action on the masses, systems of action by mobilizing them.

[...]

The major political changes ('revolutions') of Colombian history, for example, have always owed a great deal to groups of the elite mobilized – at least at a crucial stage of their careers – by specific ideologies [conservatism and liberalism]. [...] Communism played an analogous role in the formation of the anti-elites of the 1920s, which subsequently became the transforming force of the Liberal Party in the 1930s and 1940s. Orlando Fals Borda argues in *La subversión en Colombia* (1967) that in the 1960s the time for another 'subversion' of this type had once again come, and discerns the outlines of the new anti-elite in Camilo Torres and the young Fidelist revolutionaries.

The extent to which ideologies not merely mobilized potential social changers, but determined the shape of the changes, is a more complex question. It is evident that revolutionary ideologies, whatever their specific programmatic content, would predispose their adherents to demand social and political changes more radical than those envisaged, or even believed to be possible, by those who operate within the status quo, whether as conservatives or piecemeal reformers. [...] But how far does the rise of ideological anti-elites simply reflect the widespread consciousness of new problems which require new and radical solutions? How far are the changes due to these ideological groups the result of their theories and programmes, and how far to mass movements of revolt which force certain kinds of political action on the national agenda? The question is complex. No doubt [...] in 1928–48 the force which transformed Colombian politics came from popular movements. No doubt the institutional changes which followed found a more suitable vehicle in the Liberal Party, for partly ideological reasons – because this party believed in 'progress', 'economic growth' and 'the people' rather than in 'order', 'tradition' and 'hierarchy'. No doubt the small groups of radical ideologues who provided the impetus of the change (in terms of politics and ideas) contributed something specific to the institutional changes. But what and how much?

The question becomes even more complex if we bear in mind two facts generally characteristic of Latin American ideology: (a) its evident debt to foreign models and (b) the striking divergence between what such foreign models mean in their countries of origin and in the real context of Latin American politics. The influence of – sometimes the tendency to copy – European ideologies such as utilitarianism, positivism, utopian socialism, Marxism, fascism, etc. is familiar. It is equally well known that in the Latin American situation the meaning of such ideological labels, and the practical consequences of adherence to an ideology, may surprise the European or North American, as witness the political activities of Latin American groups and men inspired by, or claiming to be influenced by, the European Fascism of the 1930s. In general all ideologies have, in the Latin American context, had one or more of three major objectives: (a) to transform backward countries into advanced ones; (b) to transform (formally or informally) dependent countries into genuinely independent ones; and (c) to construct a bridge between the small elites and the mass of the impoverished and backward population. [. . .]. The normal form [of Latin American ideologies] has been one taken over from among the most suitable, the most fashionable or the most prestigious ideologies of the 'advanced' worlds, insofar as these are not evidently incompatible with objectives (a), (b) or (c). The relatively few ideologies independently evolved in Latin America have had the same fundamental objectives. They are, characteristically, combinations of 'socialism' and '*indigenismo*' (though in Colombia such autochthonous ideologies have so far played only a very minor role).

In brief, most available ready-made ideologies were designed for purposes other than those which preoccupied educated Latin Americans, and therefore tended, when adapted to their purposes, to become unrecognizable or inconsistent. [...] Thus, in the case of Jorge Eliécer Gaitán in the 1930s and 1940s it was difficult to establish, as Raul Andrade has observed, 'where the sympathizer of Mussolini ended, the Liberal chief began, and the leftist leader had his roots'. It is possible that ideologies which are both variants of global models and specifically tailored for the circumstances of Latin America, may have begun to emerge since the 1950s, but it is probably too early for a firm judgement.

[...]

The social movements of the period since the 1920s in Colombia have been associated with ideological movements and groups which have sometimes provided the masses with a framework of organization, leadership, programmes and formulated aspirations. However, it is probable that these movements occurred in areas unaffected by left-wing agitation and organization as well as in areas where this was influential. Nevertheless, insofar as leadership or inspiration from outside the traditional environment of peasant action provided local movements with a more effective and lasting policy and framework than might otherwise have been expected, the role of ideology is significant – [as in, notably,] Cundinamarca, Tolima, among the Indians in Cauca, and in the banana zone of Magdalena. [However], the precise manner in which outside ideological movements penetrated the peasantry, and the extent to which they were effective mobilizers of action, is not clear.

[...]

The movements of the late 1920s and 1930s were undoubtedly – or increasingly came – under the leadership of the ideological left, partly communist, partly populist-liberal, partly (as perhaps in Sumapaz) grassroots peasant organizers influenced by socialist or communist ideologies. It is a curious fact that the Colombian Communist Party, officially formed in 1930, complained to the International in 1935 that its membership was insufficiently proletarian, being composed primarily of peasants and Indians, rather than workers. There can be no doubts that the institution of *local* land reforms – i.e. the forced sale of estates to the peasants cultivating them – in the early 1930s, as in parts of Cundinamarca and Valle, was largely due to such organized movements. [...] A glance at the map also demonstrates that the areas in which communist or other left-wing 'armed self-defence' was successfully organized in the 1950s are largely those in which the movement of the early 1930s had been strongest and best organized (e.g. Viotá, Sumapaz, Mariquita-Marquetalia), so that we have here a history of upwards of thirty years of peasant organization.

How far does this indicate the acceptance by peasants of ideologies of the modern type? The subject may be discussed under two headings: (a) liberalism, (b) communism.

There is no doubt that from the middle of the nineteenth century liberalism had mass roots, so that to speak of a peasant as liberal means that he recognized a personal political loyalty as well as clientship of a patron who happened to support the Liberal Party. At the same time there is no evidence that this loyalty had any direct ideological implication. It appears to be rather, in the word of Fals Borda, 'a collective defense mechanism' 'dictated by a desire for mutual defense during times of attack by outsiders', so that it is irrelevant – except for the historian – whether a *vereda* happened to be Liberal or Conservative, so long as it was one or the other collectively. And indeed politically equally divided neighbourhoods are rare. The major political aspirations of nineteenth century Liberalism appear to have been irrelevant.

In the second quarter of the twentieth century a new element entered, as a genuine political consciousness began to emerge among peasants. At this point a tendency to choose Liberalism as the party 'of the people' makes itself felt, encouraged by the development of socially conscious or 'New Deal' forces within the Liberal Party. Though *Gaitanismo* appealed more powerfully to the urban poor than in the countryside, there is some evidence that the great populist demagogue made a significant impact among the peasantry.

[...]

We are in a better position to say what communism meant to the peasants supporting it. It did (does?) *not* stand primarily for economic collectivism. In Viotá, long controlled by the Communist Party, not even co-operatives appear to have been instituted; in Sumapaz the only economic activity organized in common was the distribution of water, traditionally a collectively planned matter. The simplest definition of its *actual* significance is that it stands for:

a) a movement of men who demand their rights – not so much 'natural' or new rights as legal old rights;

b) the legitimization of an economy of independent peasants operating in the manner to which the local peasantry is accustomed, but where necessary with formal sanctions;

c) The establishment of a peasant autonomy at the subordinate level which peasants regard as proper to them. Thus in both Viotá and Sumapaz small crimes and disputes were settled in the community, serious ones were left – or handed over to official justice, except during periods of enforced independence (as when engaged in war against government forces) [...] Commercial and credit transactions were under the state system, and indeed the commercial centres to which peasants brought their produce were not in the grassroots communist system.

d) A formal structure of social organization through

160

membership of the Party to which the majority of adult men in Sumapaz belonged in the 1950s. It would seem that the Party undertakes the maintenance of good custom and morals, either directly or through local councils (cabildos) [...] Sumapaz discouraged fiestas, even for fund-raising purposes, as likely to lead to drinking and fighting, though Viotá was less puritanical.

e) An educational system – always a matter of major importance to politically conscious peasants. Political education for adults was practised in both Viotá and Sumapaz, independent schools were founded and the right to appoint suitable teachers in state schools was tenaciously demanded, and indeed informally accepted in long-autonomous peasant neighbourhoods.

We may conclude that, insofar as it is a grassroots movement of peasants, Colombian communism seeks to establish or re-establish the traditional norms and values of peasant society. It is a movement of modernization chiefly insofar as it established the possibility of effective and organized peasant action, links this with an ideology of modernization, provides a powerful impetus to and mechanism of education, and probably also a method by which potential leaders and cadres can be recruited, developed and trained from among the peasantry. We may conclude further, that, where left to themselves, the peasants select from the communism which reaches them from the outside those elements – and probably only those elements – which make sense to them in terms of their previously held aspirations. It does so almost irrespective of the Communist Party official views. Thus, according to Juan Friede (*Problemas sociales de los Araucos*, 1964), the general analysis of the situation of the Arauco Indians in the communist or communist-influenced literature circulated in the Sierra Nevada is extremely remote from their reality. The local labour organizations and the Liga de Indígenas have nevertheless maintained a permanent presence and occasional influence insofar as they have been the only organizations through which the Indians have been able to make their protest heard. Where, as in Viotá, that protest has at some point achieved its object under communist leadership, a more permanent relationship between the peasantry and the movement develops. The peasants 'become communist' and remain so. However, though sociologically and politically interesting, the communist peasant communities in Colombia are quantitatively of very limited importance.

[...]

1977

13

Peasant Land Occupations: The Case of Peru

Whoever studies peasant movements is familiar with the phenomenon of the mass invasion or occupation of land. The present
paper attempts to analyse this form of collective peasant militancy, mainly in the light of evidence from Peru, though also with
some reference to other countries.[1] Its object, however, is not to
study a specifically Peruvian phenomenon but to penetrate behind
the actions of peasants to the social and political assumptions and
the strategic thinking which underlie them. The purpose of this
paper is to throw light on the question of peasant revolutionary
activity. The extent to which the specific historic situation of Peru
and of comparable countries determines the nature and shape of
its land invasions will be considered incidentally.

I

There are three possible types of land occupation in Peru, as
elsewhere, depending on the legal situation of the land to be
occupied, both in terms of the prevailing official legal system
and the legal norms actually accepted by the peasantry. The
two do not necessarily coincide.

The land to be occupied may belong to the peasants, but they have been alienated, legally or otherwise, in a manner which they do not recognize as valid. Land invasion therefore equals the recuperation of their own land. Thus the peasants of Oyon (in the Andes, north-east of Lima) denied that they had invaded the land of the Sociedad Agricola y Ganadera Algolan in August 1963, since the land in dispute – some pastures at about 5000 metres altitude – was and had always been theirs.

Second, the land occupied may belong to nobody, or in legal terms to the government as public land. In this case the process of peasant colonization or squatting turns into an 'invasion' only when there is some dispute about legal title. The most usual case is one in which such land is simultaneously claimed by peasants and landlords, neither of whom may, or indeed in most cases will, have a valid property right under official law. This situation is common in the unsettled frontier regions of several South American states, though not particularly so in Peru, except on the subtropical Amazonian slopes of the Andes and sometimes in odd corners of the vast uncultivated stretches of land belonging to some large *hacienda* which tend to be regarded, understandably, as no-man's-land by the peasants.

The legal argument here is different, since there can be no appeal to title, or even custom and prescription. It is rather that the land belongs to him who cultivates it by means of his labour. This argument was accepted in Spanish colonial law, which adjudicated empty lands (*tierras baldías*) to those who cleared, sowed or otherwise cultivated them within a given time-limit, fixing the size of the holding according to the ability of the holder to cultivate it. The Civil Code of, for example, Colombia recognized this mode of possession among others, and Law 200 of 1936, passed in consequence of large-scale agrarian agitation, made this the primary criterion of the ownership of empty lands. The appeal here is not to a legal title or its equivalent (for example prescriptive right), but to a general principle. Thus in 1963, 350 squatters organized in an Asociación de Nuevos Colonos occupied two estates in the subtropical zone of Tingo María on the ground that 'they are unproductive, so we have a right to them'.

Thirdly, the land may unquestionably belong to someone other than the invaders, even by the legal doctrines and documents which they themselves accept, as when peasants expropriate landlords from their demesne holdings. This situation must be sharply distinguished from that in which peasant tenants, paying rent either in labour, money or kind, assert property rights as freeholders in the land they actually occupy and cultivate, for this does not in itself challenge the right of the landlord to the land he cultivates directly or with hired labour. Nor does it constitute an 'invasion', since the peasants are already on the holdings whose legal title they wish to change. Clearly expropriation is the most consciously revolutionary form of land occupation. In Peru, and more generally in Latin America, it is also the rarest (except, of course, in the historically common form of the expropriation of the weak by the strong). To be precise, it seems to occur rarely if at all among peasant movements which are not directly influenced by modern political ideologies.

The present paper will deal primarily with land invasions of the first type, which form the overwhelming bulk of recorded invasions in twentieth-century Peru.* The characteristic movement of this sort is the recuperation of lost common lands by peasant communities. [...] As Dr Saturnino Paredes put it, arguing against some deviationist members of the small (Maoist) Peruvian Communist Party of which he was then general secretary:

---

* One hundred and three *invasioines* were reported in the Lima press from 1959 to 1966, including seventy-seven in the period of maximum agrarian unrest, August–December 1963, the overwhelming majority being land recuperations. The reporting is, however, extremely defective.

In Peru the fact is that the peasantry living in communities ... is convinced that the lands now in possession of the latifundists belong to the peasants, because they have worked them, and because they hold title to them in some cases and because of the right of immemorial possession in some others.[2]

The right by labour is clearly implicit in all the other claims to possession, though (except in the case of newly settled land) it is not distinct from the right to immemorial possession, since this merely means that uncounted generations of peasants have tilled a particular piece of land or grazed their animals on it. Hence perhaps the fact that I have not come across any land invasion justified purely by the slogan 'the land to the tiller' except where modern political ideologies enter into the affair. This does not mean that it is insignificant. [...] For peasants, possession without labour is unthinkable, since what land they have must be used.

But if immemorial possession is title enough, such possession validated by actual documents is even better. Given the nature of the Spanish colonial system, there are plenty of Indian communities with such documents, and these are typically adduced to legitimize land invasions. [...] The young sectarians of the Maoist Communist Party regarded this as a petty-bourgeois aberration, arguing that the only thing to do with land titles of the feudal or bourgeois period, whoever they favoured, was to burn them; but, as Dr Paredes pointed out justifiably, and speaking from ample experience: 'All this reveals that the opportunist left liquidators have no experience of the peasant movement and have never had anything to do with any [peasant] community.'[3]

The entrenched legalism of peasant land invasions is a fact which both the student and the agitator neglect at their peril. To possess *papelitos* ('little pieces of paper') is very important for a Latin American peasant community. Whether real or forged they are cherished, preserved, hidden from possible robbers, because to lose them would in some way affect their rights, though one can hardly say that it would weaken their sense that they exist. John Womack has given a moving account of the preservation of the land titles of Anenecuilco, the *pueblo* of the great Emiliano Zapata.[4] There are even, I am told, cases of Bolivian villages which, having been given land by the agrarian reform, went to the former owner asking for a document of transfer to make it all legal. As we shall see, this legalism does not prevent such peasants from making revolutions. For one thing, they are inclined to reject as morally invalid and 'unnatural' laws, however constitutionally correct, which take away common lands.

At this point the peculiarities of the Latin American situation must be mentioned, since they turn legalism in the strictest sense into a potent, if also limited, social force among the peasantry. The Spanish conquest guaranteed legal recognition and communal lands to the Indian communities, under the control of the royal bureaucracy, while simultaneously attempting strict control of the conquistador settlers, though with little success. The *hacienda*, the large estate whose owners became the *de facto* holders of power, therefore developed side by side with the peasant communities, its territorial expansion legally limited by the rights both of the crown and of the Indians – legal limits which were not entirely abolished, though for practical purposes made inoperative, in the period of independence. Consequently their expansion took place largely by naked appropriation, especially in the late nineteenth and twentieth centuries, when large tracts of land formerly without much economic value became both potentially profitable and accessible to markets. The typical large *hacienda* of Latin America is therefore based not on legal ownership (by virtue of a 'new law' against an 'old law'), but simply on the fact that the power of the large landowner was greater than that of the state, where the two did not actually coincide in his person. An old lawyer and ex-politician in the

Peruvian central highlands has gone so far as to argue that land reform had been unnecessary, since all that was required to secure an effective redistribution of the land was to ask landowners – *any* landowner – to show title to their estates, and return the land held without good title to the peasants from whom it had originally been taken.[5]

Thus in Colombia, following an agrarian agitation, the titles of three latifundia belonging to J. Otero Torres and covering something like 300,000 hectares were officially investigated. The original title to the property in 1823 referred to 426 hectares. In the Peruvian central highlands the Hacienda Tucle in 1887 held title to some 12,000 hectares, though even this was not undisputed. By 1915 it had somehow acquired 103,000 hectares. [...] Since the owners who thus acquired stolen property did so in proper legal form, they expected, and normally got, the protection of the courts; and if they had no title at all, their ability to overawe the Indians and their political influence over local judges and policemen was normally quite sufficient to fend off challenges.

This is, of course, to oversimplify a complex situation. *Haciendas* might have legal titles to enormous territories, but actually use only a small part of them, leaving the rest to nobody or to the *de facto* occupation of the peasantry, which would naturally assume that actually working the land gave it the right of possession or property, at any rate better right than the inactive landlords. Communities might strengthen their moral claim to the land by forging or extending ancient titles. Moreover, as we shall see, rival legal claims to land opposed not only peasants to *haciendas* but also communities to other communities, especially when – as happened in the course of time – groups of peasants left the original settlement to establish themselves elsewhere in communal territory (normally, in Peru, by moving into another ecological niche higher or lower on the Andean slopes which stretch from the tundra at the top to the subtropics and tropics at the bottom).

They would then attempt to form separate communities carving out their own communal lands, whose boundaries were in dispute with the mother-settlement.

Nevertheless, Latin America in general and the areas of solid Indian settlement in particular provide an unusually large number of peasant communities with legal documents of communal ownership of land alienated by naked or barely disguised robbery. To this extent the problem of legitimizing peasant rights is unusually simple in theory. On the other hand, very frequently the demand for land, however objectively revolutionary, requires no ideological challenge to existing legality.

II

Let us now turn to some actual invasions of land. A land invasion is normally a rather standardized affair, decided and carried out by the whole community as a collective entity. This means that it is normally discussed in advance. [...] The intention to invade is therefore normally known to the landlords and the authorities, who are in a position to take countermeasures, if police, troops or their own armed men can be got to the disputed frontier, which may of course be rather remote and inaccessible. [...]

The invasion itself is a major ceremonial occasion. Such events 'take place amid great clamour. The leaders appear on horseback blowing horns' (Cuzco, 1964), 'to the sounds of horns and drums' (Cuzco), 'to the accompaniment of huzzas and horns' (Anta, Cuzco), 'singing and dancing to the tunes of regional music' (Paruro, Cuzco), 'sounding horns and firing off rockets' (Potaca, Junin). In recent years they seem to have been accompanied by large numbers of flags. [...] Peruvian flags were universal in the 1960s, but in the politically radicalized Cuzco department they were accompanied by Castroite slogans – 'Tierra o Muerte', 'Venceremos' and so on. [...] As in all great collective ceremonials it is also far from unlikely that

169

the participants are often rather drunk, though the evidence –
which comes overwhelmingly from landlords or officials – is
inclined to overstress this point.

The mobilization for an invasion normally takes place in the
evening, the actual operation, on sound military principles, at
dawn, though this is not invariable. A more or less large mass of
men, women and children – to the number of hundreds or even
thousands – accompanied by livestock, implements and building materials, occupies the disputed territory, tearing down
fences, walls and other boundary marks, and immediately proceeds to build simple huts or other structures, generally along
the line of the boundary claimed as legitimate. The families
immediately establish themselves there, start to pasture their
flocks (where necessary expelling the landlords' animals), and
to plough up and sow the land. In some instances a more cautious line is followed, a reconnaissance party being infiltrated
which, if there is no sign of massive opposition, is followed by
mass occupation. [. . .]

An important distinction between the classical communal land invasion and land occupations organized by more
modern political movements must, however, be pointed out.
The strategy and tactics of modern occupations, whether of
land or workplace ('sit-ins' or 'work-ins'), envisage them as
demonstrations or means of bringing pressure to bear on the
authorities, that is to say as a means to an end. Thus – to take
an example from an organized peasant movement – the movement led by Jacinto Lopez in the state of Sinaloa (Mexico) in
the 1950s used land invasions in this limited way. The peasant
congress of Los Mochis, Sinaloa, in 1957 threatened invasions
if the promises to provide a legal solution for the problems of
the petitioners were not soon kept. When nothing happened,
land occupations took place in early 1958, but the invasion
of 20,000 hectares of irrigated land by three thousand peasants was symbolical. 'In the cultivated parts it consisted of the
planting of the national banner in the middle of those lands,

while the main bulk of the peasantry stood or sat on the roads along those fields ... When army units came to dissolve the sit-ins, the intentionally unarmed peasants left peacefully.'[6] The mass land occupations organized in the spring of 1971 by the Asociación de Usuarios in Colombia were also deliberately short-lived. In brief, unless part of an actual agrarian revolution or insurrection, land occupation in modern politically organized peasant movements is an incident in a long-term campaign.

But for the classical communal movement it is campaign, battle and, with luck, final victory. It is not the means but the end itself. So far as the invaders are concerned, all would be well if the landlords, the state or other outside forces withdrew and left the community to live and work on the land they had now justly recuperated. As realists, the peasants may know that this is unlikely though (as we shall see) land invasions tend to be undertaken only when the situation looks favourable. However, even if they are expelled yet again by lord or government, they have at least reasserted both their right to possession by labour and their capacity to work the land they claim as their own – an important point, since their capacity to do so may be challenged. But the object of the operation is not tactical. It is to take the land back and stay there.

It will already have been observed that the classical land invasion is not specifically Peruvian, or even Indian. There are indeed plenty of exact equivalents elsewhere in Latin America. In Chile *all* the land invasions (*tomas de fundos*) by small cultivators up to 1968 were recuperations of alienated common lands by Mapuche Indians, though elsewhere they were undertaken by non-Indian peasants, as in Venezuela, where there were an estimated five hundred cases of invasions of expropriable lands at the beginning of the agrarian reform process in the late 1950s and early 1960s. The lands invaded were frequently those taken away from the peasants earlier. But European parallels are also to be found. [...] Something very like the classical communal land invasion can be found in circumstances very different from those of the Peruvian highlands. They belong to the history not of Peruvian Indians or Latin America, but of peasant communities.

III

To understand the nature of such invasions and the role they play in peasant action, it may be convenient to follow one particular such movement through at least some of its ramifications: that of the community of Huasicancha, a small and overwhelmingly pastoral Indian settlement in the central highlands of Peru, roughly near the point where the departments of Junin, Lima and Huancavelica meet. We are fortunately in a position to trace the struggle of this community for a particular area of common pasturelands back to the sixteenth century, a fairly rare example of continuous documentation.

[...]

Several points of interest emerge from [a] history of four centuries of struggle for Huasicancha's pastures. How did a community of illiterates maintain the exact memory of the lands it claimed, so precise that the 'ocular inspection' of 1963 confirmed in every particular the titles of 1607? For, though they had documents, for most of their history they obviously could not read them; indeed even the white lawyers whose business it was had sometimes to employ palaeographers for this purpose. In the 1960s an illiterate witness for the community, one Julian Paucarchuco Samaniego, fifty-nine years old, answered this question by saying that he had known the boundaries since 1922 because 'when he was a boy his father took him up and showed him the boundaries, and that is the reason he knows them'.[7] Presumably in every generation since the sixteenth century fathers had taken sons up to the high pastures to keep alive the memory of the lost lands in the same way.

Secondly, and perhaps more important, the Huasicancha story shows how misleading is the stereotype of the passive and subject Indian. For four centuries Huasicancha, small, remote, isolated and stubborn, never ceased to struggle for its right. Not being either Western liberals or student insurrectionaries, the peasants quite failed to make a choice in principle between peaceful and violent, legal and non-legal methods, 'physical' and 'moral' force, using either or both as occasion appeared to demand. But they never abandoned their claims.

Thirdly, it is clear that the belief that the peasant horizon is entirely circumscribed by local factors is mistaken. Huasicancha may have known little about Lima and nothing about Madrid, Rome or Egypt, but it was sensitive enough to changes in the wider world which seemed to shake the foundations of the local power structure. Nevertheless, the horizon was local, insofar as the unit of their action was the community, its setting the interlocking systems of estates and communities in their part of the highlands. They were [. . .] politically mobilized in national terms and produced cadres for national movements. And yet it seems that for the community this was either ancillary to its own struggles or a by-product of its development in a particular historical context. [. . .] Their ambition was not to change the system so much as to make the best of it when it was strong, to push it back when it looked like yielding.

IV

Nevertheless, peasant action and political change interacted in complex ways. Who organized and led land invasions? Since they were affairs of the community as a whole we must assume that in the classical form they were led by its leaders and officials, whose leadership so often (as in the Russian *obshchina*) required the ability to identify and express the consensus of 'the people', though conversely the readiness of the people to listen to men of wisdom and judgement, perhaps coming from

173

families with a record of leadership in the community, was a powerful element in formulating such a consensus. We must remember that communal democracy proceeds by 'the sense of the meeting' rather than by majority vote. But, in the period in which our documentation is best, community decision was a more complex affair than in the example described in the prologue of John Womack's brilliant book on Zapata.

In the first place, the 'Community' itself cannot always be regarded as ancient and traditional. As often as not it was new in two senses: because it had broken away from an older community for demographic or other reasons, and because it utilized a specific juridical device which might itself be novel, and which happened to be advantageous, for example from the 1920s the procedure of 'recognition'.* No doubt the ways in which bodies of new settlers organized and took collective decisions were the traditional ways of peasants with the age-old experience of communal action, but the element of novelty is not to be overlooked.

In the second place, each Peruvian community was itself being transformed by a process of internal class differentiation, and increasingly also by what may be called external differentiation, namely the formation of a (relatively more prosperous) emigrant group in the city or cities, a group from which the men whose opinions carry weight – not least because of their presumed political know-how – are often chosen. Paradoxically, the emigration of the kind of local notable whose family used to monopolize village offices may well leave the road to village political leadership open to others, even to newcomers.

---

* Since for the peasants such devices had no organic connection with the 'real' community, but belonged to the world of state, state law and politics, they could be treated quite pragmatically. Thus at the peak of the social agitation of the early 1960s many communities organized themselves as trade unions (*sindicatos*) because this appeared to be helpful in their struggles. I understand that at present (1973) some in central Peru are asking for the status of *pueblos jovenes* ('young settlements') which was devised by the military government for urban shanty towns, because this promises advantages in obtaining access to electricity, roads, etc.

The uneven progress of education also introduced a new element into village politics. In brief, modernization brought with it broader contacts with the outside world, initially for some, increasingly for many.

[...]

Its most obvious form was the help provided by union and political organization in the local cities (such as Cuzco) or politically committed local intellectuals – students and lawyers – whether on their own initiative or on that of the peasants, aware that such help was available. Too little is known of the political micro-history of communities to generalize, and even the more readily documented spread of peasant unions and federations of communities, such as were powerful for a time in the central highlands, is only known in a rather fragmentary way. However, the role of the political movements – APRA until its transformation, and later the various Marxist movements – is plainly important, as mobilizers of local cadres, as catalysts of peasant activity and perhaps above all as forces turning separate local agitations into a wider movement. Less obvious, but equally important, is the collapse of the belief in the permanence of the prevailing power structure, which liberated activist peasants who had previously chosen to serve the lords for new positions as popular leaders. [...]

The typical land invasion of recent years was therefore a rather complex affair. The official representatives of the community were almost always present, as they had to be; but by their side as often as not were 'instigators' or 'agitators'. Old and new social and power structures in the village intermingle, roles are transformed. This mixed character of the leadership may be illustrated from one of the rare detailed studies of village activism. In Marcantuna (Mantaro Valley) the fourteen men singled out as communal leaders in the mid-1960s included two in their twenties (a student and a book-keeper), one in his thirties (a farmer-cum-trader), four in their forties (white-collar worker, farmer-cum-truckdriver, famer/labourer, farmer), five in their fifties (three farmers-cum-artisans, two farmers), and two over sixty (both farmers). Seven of these men had incomplete or terminated primary education, five partial secondary education, one higher education, while the educational status of one is unknown. We can unfortunately not rely on the indications of their politics, since press reports tend to present all activists uniformly as bolsheviks.

V

Finally, what light do the invasions throw on the question of peasant revolutionism? It seems evident that *objectively* a mass process of land invasion can have revolutionary consequences independent of the subjective intentions of the invaders, if the proportion of usurped land in estates is large enough, and the population in the communities recuperating their ancient lands sufficiently numerous. Something like this occurred in large parts of Peru in the early 1960s. The nature of Peruvian statistics makes figures little more than figures of speech, indicating general orders of magnitude. But it seems not improbable that there were in 1961 (according to the census) something like 4500 '*comunidades parcializadas o ayllus*', that is peasant communities, of which 2337 had by 1969 got themselves officially 'recognized'. Their total membership in 1961 may have consisted of say four hundred thousand heads of families or say two million individuals out of a total rural population in highland Peru of about four million.[8] [. . .]

Of these communities at least half have disputes about boundaries – a figure based on a series of samples and regional surveys – and pretty certainly this figure is an absolute minimum. [. . .] It is obvious that, when all or most of such communities simultaneously claimed their rights, the structure of local latifundism automatically collapsed (unless restored by military force). That is what happened, broadly speaking, in the central highlands in the second half of 1963. Humpty Dumpty fell off the wall: after 1963 nobody could put him together again and the managements of the great estates – the Ganadera del Centro, the Division Ganadera of the Cerro de Pasco Corporation, Algolan, Corpacancha and the rest were perfectly aware of it. Just so, a year earlier, the structure of latifundism in the valleys of La Convención and Lares had collapsed under the mass refusal – which turned out to be permanent – of the serf-tenants to perform their labour services. For this time – for reasons which would take us beyond the scope of this paper – military force was not used to restore the old order.

At the same time we must ask ourselves whether *subjectively* this process amounts to a peasant revolution. This is very much less certain. Broadly speaking, in primitive rebellions the 'revolutionary' and the 'reformist' movements can normally be distinguished, though not necessarily by the amount of violence involved in either. The former have subjectively much greater ambitions, expressed either in millennial terms or perhaps in the attempt to restore some lost golden age of the past, that is in Peru the Inca Empire.[9] Henri Favre perceptively distinguishes – apropos the Maya of the Chiapas highlands in Mexico – between the two types of what he calls 'rebellion' and 'insurrection': the former both localized and limited in its objectives, to the restoration of the customary balance, temporarily disturbed, the latter an attempt at the total restructuring of the colonial situation.[10] [. . .]

There are peasant movements which quite evidently challenge not only the abuse of lordship, but the fact of lordship itself. [. . .] There is little evidence (apart from cases of known communist or Trotskyite leadership) of Peruvian peasants challenging lordship as such, for example the ownership of demesne lands, though there was a growing and effective reaction against labour services. The traditional patron–client relationship between lords who 'consider themselves protectors of the

Indians whom they call their children (*hijitos*)' still remained valid in many parts, the lords being more aware of impending changes than the peasants. The classical burning of big houses, murder of landlords and so on are virtually absent from the agitations of 1958–64, which are notably peaceful. What we have here is not the traditional *sublevación indígena* on a large scale, but a spontaneous mass assertion of legal rights, stimulated by, but not apparently – except in a few areas – imbued with a modern, or for that matter an ancient, revolutionary ideology. There are no signs of any mass conversion to some form of communism, even in Cuzco. Marxism remained the ideology of the cadres, though increasingly of peasant cadres, as APRA was, at any rate outside the 'solid North' where that party established itself as a mass movement.*

As has been pointed out, this is not incompatible with making what amounts to a social revolution, or even with a vague if growing sense that the old era is coming to and must come to an end. Nor is it in theory incompatible with the evolution of such peasant movements into conscious peasant revolution in a nationally revolutionary situation. On the other hand it must be pointed out that in several regions of Latin America the estate system itself is a fluctuating entity. In the course of post-colonial history *haciendas* have been formed, expanded, split up and reformed depending on political change and economic conjecture. The communities probably never benefited permanently from these fluctuations, but their permanent pressure, becoming relatively more effective in periods of recession for the large estates, need not imply the belief that any one such recession marks the final

* The nature and extent of APRA's mass support outside the working class remains obscure. It is now generally agreed that in the past twenty years or more its support among, and interest in, Indian peasants has been far smaller than party mythology has claimed. [...] But the history of APRA at the grass roots during the period when it was, or was seen as, a revolutionary movement, remains to be seriously investigated.

extinction of all *haciendas*. In brief, we must bear in mind both the strength and the limitations of traditional peasant movements.

These turn into peasant revolutions when the aggregate of the 'little worlds' is simultaneously set into motion, almost invariably by some event or development in the 'big world' over which the peasants have no control, but which moves them into action. (What factors were responsible for this mobilization in the Peru of 1958–64 cannot be discussed here.) They become *effective* peasant revolutions either when unified and mobilized in a sufficiently large number of politically crucial areas by modern organization and leadership, probably revolutionary, or when the national structure and crisis is such that strategically placed regional peasant movements can play a decisive part in its affairs. This happened in Mexico 1910–20 with Pancho Villa's northerners, because of their armed mobility, and with the followers of Zapata, the 'cock of the South', in Morelos, because that state is next door to the capital. Neither of these things happened in Peru, except faintly in the 1880s when Caceres, who sought the support of the Indians whom he had organized into anti-Chilean guerrillas during the War of the Pacific, marched the men from the central highlands into the capital, but hardly as a revolutionary leader and certainly without social-revolutionary consequences. In the early 1960s the land invasions were indeed sufficiently overwhelming in the central highlands and in Cuzco, sufficiently serious in other parts of the highlands, to cause the highland *hacienda* system to collapse. But, unlike Marx's proletariat, the spontaneous force of the peasantry, though capable of killing landlordism, was unable to dig its grave. It made agrarian reform inevitable. But it took an army coup, after several years of shilly-shallying, to bury the corpse of the highland *haciendas*.

1974

Notes

Some notes in the original essay have been omitted from the version that appears in this volume.

1 The main sources used, in addition to the press and a substantial number of Peruvian official and semi-official publications, are the documents held by Zone X of Agrarian Reform (Huancayo Office) and the 'Juzgado de Tierras', Huancayo, and the archives of several former estates, especially the former Sociedad Ganadera del Centro, Sociedad Ganadera Tucle and Compania Ganadera Antapongo. All these estates are in the Peruvian central highlands.

2 *En Torno a la Práctica Revolucionaria y la Lucha Interna II, Pleno del Comité Central del Partido Comunista Peruano. Informe Político* (Lima, 1970, mimeo), p. 12. Dr Paredes is a lawyer with long experience of peasant work.

3 Ibid.

4 John Womack, *Zapata and the Mexican Revolution* (1969), Epilogue, pp. 371ff.

5 Interview with Sr Oscar Bernuy Gómez, Huancayo, June 1971.

6 Gerrit Huizer, *Report on the Study of the Role of Peasant Organizations in the Process of Agrarian Reform in Latin America* (ILO-CIDA, Geneva, 1969, mimeo), pp. 241, 243.

7 Juzgado de Tierras, Huancayo, Exp. 69.831, fj 35.

8 Rodrigo Montoya Rojas, *A Proposito del Caracter Predominantemente Capitalista de la Economía Peruana Actual* (Lima, 1970), pp. 110–11.

9 Local insurrections to restore the Inca regime or expressing specific support for the Incas are not uncommon in nineteenth- and twentieth-century Peru, until the 1930s. For the Inca myth, see A. Flores Galindo, *Buscando un Inca: Identidad y Utopia en los Andes* (Havana, 1986).

10 Henri Favre, *Changement et continuité chez les Mayas du Mexique* (Paris, 1971), pp. 269ff.

14

A Peasant Movement in Peru

This paper seeks to describe and analyse the peasant unrest that occurred in the province of La Convención in the department of Cuzco, Peru [in the late 1950s and early 1960s].* There has to date [1965] been a great deal of talk about this persistent, widespread peasant movement, but it is yet to be the subject of serious study. My own research has been superficial, although I have added to local testimonies and observations a study of the Peruvian press, on a local and a national level, during the years 1961 and 1962. This is far from sufficient to make the study a

---

* ***Editor's note***. For a detailed description of the geography, agricultural development, system of landholding and labour relations in La Convención, see Chapter 9, 'A Case of Neo-Feudalism: La Convención, Peru', above.

In 1960 the total population of La Convención was estimated at sixty thousand. The province contained 174 *haciendas* (of a total of some 700 in the Cuzco department). There were around four thousand *arrendires*, settler-colonists from the *altiplano* who had received land (*arriendos*) in return for various labour and personal services (*condiciones, palla, maquipura, huata faena, semanero*, etc.) to the *hacendado*, and some twelve thousand *allegados* to whom the *arrendires* sublet plots of land and who were generally responsible for carrying out the duties of the *arrendires* on the owner's land. Beneath the *allegados* were the landless agricultural workers (*agregados, habilitados, peones*). There were only four *comunidades indígenas* in La Convención (out of more than two hundred in the Cuzco department).

181

serious one; Europe is so poorly informed about the agrarian movements in Latin America, however, that even an incomplete, preliminary report might have some value.

[...]

Despite clear signs of a potential class conflict within the peasantry in La Convención - some *arrendires* were said to be wealthier than the smaller *hacendados* - it would appear that the bulk of the *arrendires* considered their interests to be in opposition to those of the *hacendados*. Their self-interest in the conversion of a neo-feudal into a capitalist relationship with the *hacendados* and the creation of leasehold or independently owned peasant properties was the same as that of the *allegados*. *
A local campaign [in 1957–8] by a small group of peasants who were practically *kulaks* was converted into a solid peasant movement that encompassed the majority of the province's rural population. Towards the end of 1962, the provincial Federación Campesina had 110 affiliated unions (*sindicatos*), ranging from about twenty to six hundred members.

[...]

How was this possible? The first reason is simply that the divisions at the heart of the peasantry were largely neutralized by those factors that strengthened bonds of solidarity. Besides general poverty, the peasants of La Convención are countryfolk and not city-dwellers, Indians by origins and not Creoles. At the same time, the men's clothing (though not the women's) tends to be more modern than in the highlands and, although Quechua is the language used in meetings of the unions, the Spanish language is understood and even spoken. What is more, the majority of the *sindicatos* seem to have a nucleus of

* The main demands of the general strike of *arrendires* in 1961–2 were the following: the abolition of labour obligations owed to the landowner; the payment of rent in money; new leases of a minimum of six years; the right to plant 10 per cent of the land with food crops; the right for the *arrendires* and the *allegados* to buy land; the complete abolition of any obligation to sell their harvests to the *hacienda* and to buy their own provisions from the *hacienda*. *Crónica*, 30 April 1962.

militants who are literate. A great part of this modernization is clearly due to the influence of the communists, as we shall see.

What is most important is that all the peasants share a common condition, as feudal subjects or dependents, in situations of uncertainty and with no guarantees. Even the *arrendires* were not landowners as such; and what is more, they had good reason to believe that once they had improved the condition of the virgin lands on the *hacienda* that could be cultivated and were accessible, establishing crops there, the *hacendado* would expel them and take these improved lands into his own control. The common obligation to carry out labour and personal services for the landowner (whatever the form of contract or custom), the common absence of economic rights and the common subjection to the arbitrary power of the *hacendado*, connected the richest *kulak* to the poorest *peón*, uniting them in opposition to injustice. Some aspects of this injustice shocked some peasants more than others, while some – not necessarily the economic aspects – affected them all equally.* In turn, for the *jornaleros* and *braceros* who had no direct interest in the main demands of the *arrendires* and *allegados*, the fact that the peasants had their resistance movement against the landowners offered them the possibility of demanding their own rights effectively, even of the acknowledgement that they had rights at all. It provided them with an example to be followed, a movement to join. Their situation would improve just like that of all the other kinds of peasant.

And how was it possible that such a broad and powerful organization, especially one led by communists and by other kinds of Marxist revolutionaries, managed to establish itself in such a remote area? It is evidently due to the uncommon and traditional strength of the Communist Party in the Cuzco

---

* The most common grievance I came across against an important *hacendado* was that he had broken with tradition in not taking on the responsibility of providing education for the illegitimate children he had with the Indian women. This weighed against him as heavily as his 'murders and tortures'.

region, its principal stronghold, and in the town of Cuzco itself. In this part of Peru, the APRA [Alianza Popular Revolucionaria Americana] never extended its hold as much as it managed to do in the north, even though it addressed itself to the Indians in particular. The leader of APRA in La Convención, R. Sernaqué, originally an *odrúista* [supporter of President-dictator Manuel Odría 1948–56], was a notorious opponent of the peasant unions. (He was killed in 1962.) The communists reached La Convención in 1934 at the moment when a union of workers was being organized in Maranura, today [1965] still a stronghold of the orthodox Communist Party, though the union was later suppressed and seems to have disappeared temporarily during the Odría period. The Communist Party, its cadres and intellectuals, supplied assistance and organization to the Federación de Trabajadores de Cuzco (in whose buildings the Federación Campesina would later have its offices); the intellectuals of Quillabamba (principally, it would appear, lawyers, bank employees and teachers) supplied legal assistance among other things. If a peasants' organization was going to establish itself in La Convención, it could only do so by means of the train from Cuzco, that is to say, with the organizational support provided by the local Communist Party.

When the communists first arrived, they found especially favourable terrain amid the pioneers who had settled on the edge of the forest on under-populated pieces of land – independent, unruly, little inclined to tolerate the serfdom that was to be found in the highlands. A good example is André González, one of the leaders of the movement led by Hugo Blanco in Chaupimayo [in 1961–2]. González was born in 1928 in Izcuchaca in the province of Anta, between Cuzco and La Convención. When he was a child, he worked on the Sullupuchyo *hacienda*, which belonged to the Luna family; it is interesting to note that this *hacienda* was in a permanent state of conflict with a neighbouring *comunidade indígena* over the ownership of certain lands. It is said that he was whipped

184

for having neglected the cattle and allowing some sheep to be stolen – and that he had been confined to bed for eight days as a result, an indication of the extreme brutality of the treatment he received. To get his revenge – and this incident, too, is itself significant – he entered the *hacienda*, armed, and 'stole the legal title deeds', which he burned. He then fled into the *tierra de nadie* of La Convención, where he settled in Chaupimayo in 1946, raising a family of four, before 'setting up contacts with some politicians'. Such men – and there are a number of them in the frontier regions of the Amazon basin, since they are far away from masters and from government – were to become communists and the natural leaders of the peasant movements.

The movement in La Convención, whose origins – as we have seen – go back to the 1930s, was reinvigorated after the fall of the Odría dictatorship in 1956. It would appear that this process began with a rebellion against the Romainvilles of Huadquiña,* where a union was established, or rather, re-established, in 1957. It appears that the immediate cause was outrage at the whipping of Matías Villavicencio, the brother of Leónidas Carpio, a Chaupimayo leader. In addition to other misdeeds, the Romainvilles were accused of having usurped lands on the far side of the Yanacmayo river that did not legally belong to them, an accusation that could have been brought against plenty of other *hacendados*. From that moment on, a state of virtual war was established between the peasants and the Romainvilles, who abandoned the valley, leaving their properties in the hands of their administrators. It has been impossible

* The principal and most unpopular *hacendado* in La Convención was Alfredo de Romainville, head of a family whose original *hacienda*, acquired by Mariano Vargas in 1865 and estimated at 500,000 hectares, was later divided between members of the family into smaller units (though still of more than 100,000 hectares each), e.g. Carmen Vargas de Romainville (Hacienda Huadquiña), Maria Romainville de la Torre (Hacienda Huyro).

for them to return ever since. It is also by no means impossible that a fall in prices on the world market was linked to the growing militancy in the province. Around 1958 there were several unions (the number is estimated at 20 per cent of those that existed in 1962), including Maranura, Huyro, Santa Rosa, Quellouno, and a provincial peasant federation was set up, with eleven unions affiliated.

Not much is known about the development of the movement between 1958 and 1962 [. . .] In 1961 the *arrendires* organized a strike that seems to have been effective, since there are reports of problems with the harvesting of coffee, cocoa and fruit. Some sources claim that the *arrendires* remained on strike for more than a year. At the end of 1961 there were reports of forty-two unions with thirty thousand members on strike in La Convención.

A department-wide Federación de Campesinos y Comunidades del Cuzco was founded at that time, with 214 organizations affiliated, and at the start of 1962 the Federation organized a major gathering of peasants at Quillabamba. The government dealt with what was clearly by now a mass movement by officially abolishing by a decree dated 24 April 1962 'services performed for free or in exchange for usufruct of the land' in the valleys of La Convención, Urubamba and Calca.

Clearly this victory gave the movement a great deal of encouragement, and its demands became increasingly ambitious. A petition was launched asserting that the peasants had already 'paid for' their lands with the work they had carried out on them. Mass land occupations followed. [. . .] In Ipal, in the province of Calca, three hundred *comuneros* expelled the *hacendado* Adriel Núñez del Prado and his family from an estate that, they claimed, had been usurped from a community by a legal decision that was not justified. But this collective action was not typical of La Convención province since not many *comunidades* were to be found there (though two of the four that did exist were affiliated to the Cuzco Federation). In May, a group who came from Chaupimayo had prevented the workers at the Alcuzama *hacienda* from cutting the wood destined for making the sleepers for the railway line then being extended, and in August armed peasants from Quellomayo and Huacay-pampa expelled the woodcutters from the Santa Rosa *hacienda*, claiming that it no longer belonged to the Romainvilles. [...] Around mid-October, there was an announcement of disputes being settled in thirty-six *haciendas* [...] but the occupations soon started up again. Huadquiña, Pavayoc, Paltaybamba, San Lorenzo, Versalles, Echarate, Granja Misión were among the *haciendas* occupied. It was said that most of the *haciendas* in Lares and Calca had fallen to the peasants and that all or almost all the *hacendados* had left the valleys or were getting ready to go. The occupation of at least seventy *haciendas* would appear to be confirmed. On 20 October, the press published the text of an agrarian reform law recently promulgated.

The intensification of the peasant movement in the spring of 1962 coincided with the first cracks to open up within its ranks, principally between the orthodox communists and the other groups of revolutionaries who considered the communists too moderate and who supposedly favoured Castro-type uprisings. When the unrest was at its height, Luis de la Puente, leader of the Movimiento de Izquierda Revolucionaria (MIR), a break-away from APRA, appeared in Quillabamba at a meeting of thirty-six unions. He demanded the right to speak as a delegate for the federations of the provinces of Quillabamba and Lares, but given the weakness of APRA in this area it is not obvious nor indeed likely that any MIR leadership had previously been present.

The main dissidents were Trotskyites whose leader was Hugo Blanco, a young intellectual who had come into these valleys from his native town of Cuzco following the emergence of the peasant movement in 1958. The movement had attracted a number of intellectuals, some of them foreigners. Blanco had gone largely unnoticed until the spring of 1962, when the newspapers in Lima began to build him up as a kind of Peruvian Fidel Castro, drawing attention to his links to guerrilla groups and professional revolutionaries which were being formed elsewhere (although in those days Blanco, whose main hideout was in Chaupimayo, denied being a guerrilla leader).

The tension at the heart of the movement was quite apparent: in April, thirty-two of the seventy-two existing unions demanded Blanco's expulsion from La Convención [...] A split emerged in the valleys and in Cuzco between the pro-Blanco and anti-Blanco groups (the latter identifying themselves, subsequently, with the leadership of the official Communist Party) [...] It is clear that the pro-Blancos were supporters of more radical, more militant policies than the other Federation leaders, yet it is still not really possible to assert that they intended to establish a 'liberation zone' in La Convención with guerrilla support. Armed groups certainly were organized, though even in late 1962 no one in the valleys had ever claimed that they were anything other than defensive units. It may be that Blanco had in mind to carry out a guerrilla revolution, although after his arrest [on 30 May 1963, about twenty kilometres from Quillabamba] he claimed, apparently, that Peru was not yet ripe for a war of this kind. The objections of the moderates [...] were that this policy risked provoking the authorities to acts of repression.

It is hard to measure the extent of Blanco's influence on the peasant movement. It is clear that the success of the *arrendires'* strike in 1961–2 (which had no apparent revolutionary aims) was in itself enough to enlarge and radicalize the movement. The direction that it took, that is, the occupation of landed properties by force, and the expulsion of their owners, though not on the whole their administrators, owed much to Trotskyite initiative, even though land occupations were in accordance with orthodox communist tactics and also happened elsewhere without any influence from Trotskyism or the MIR. The organizing of armed units [...] was undoubtedly a result of Blanco's initiative. However, these units did not play an important role in La Convención, even though there was great admiration for 'the rebels' [...] And as far as it is possible to tell, they restricted their activities to defensive operations, acts of sabotage, attempts to free prisoners, though it is nonetheless not impossible that they may have carried out a number of raids, on police patrols, for example. In any case, the local population was not convinced. Blanco's arrest did not provoke any immediate reaction.

Systematic government repression might have provoked a true guerrilla movement, but the government took great care not to use such measures, particularly after the military junta took power in July 1962. [...] The new government seems to have accepted the inevitability of agrarian reform in La Convención and hoped to be able to calm people down by making concessions, while at the same time keeping order through the judicious deployment of force. In fact, considering the serious unrest, the local conditions, the nature of the soldiers and the Peruvian police, there were extremely few deaths to be deplored in the valleys: there were far more in the highlands of Cuzco and in Cuzco itself.

The peasant movement reached its peak in the closing months of 1962 with the general occupation of properties in La Convención. Its victory was tacitly acknowledged by the authorities who focused their efforts on pursuing Blanco's armed groups, which did not enjoy the unanimous support of the organized peasant movement, and on preventing the movement from gaining ground in the rest of the region, in more densely populated area with more 'explosive' social problems. In December and January there followed the systematic arrest of local militants and leaders (and including eighty leaders from ninety-six unions in the valleys), the declaration of a state of siege, etc. However, the promise of agrarian reform still held; general Oscar Arteta even specified that it would encompass the *haciendas* of Huadquiña, Echarate, Paltaybamba,

Maranura and Chaullay, and went so far as to cast some doubt on the legality of their owners' property rights. The local *hacendados* now considered the battle well and truly lost. Romainville announced a change in his tactics with a request to the government for the expropriation of his property, which was effectively a plea for compensation for the lands he had, in fact, already lost. The minister of agriculture met representatives of forty-five trades unions in Quillabamba, and 5 April saw the publication of a plan to expropriate twenty-three properties in La Convención, with fourteen thousand peasants as their beneficiaries.

[...] La Convención remained unsettled; but from then on, the objective was no longer to occupy land so much as to precipitate the implementation of the promised reforms, to study the terms according to which these would take place, and to secure the liberation of leaders and militants who had been arrested. The government of President Fernando Belaúnde Terry [elected in June 1963] looked favourably on the first two of these objectives, [...] but faced resistance in Congress from a combined APRA–Odríista opposition. In July, four hundred peasants were allocated 1545 hectares of land on Luis González Willys's El Potrero *hacienda* – neither this property nor its owner having played a leading role during the struggle – and there was immediate and probably legitimate criticism that non-unionized peasants were given priority treatment in the distribution of land. At the end of 1963, almost no other allocations had been carried out. Furthermore, the government had no apparent intention of releasing arrested peasant leaders and militants in advance of their scheduled date. [...] Renewed discontent, both political and economic, led to a general strike in December 1963 in Cuzco and La Convención [...] However, this was no longer a local problem in La Convención but a national problem, with repercussions in this particularly belligerent province.

*

To conclude, it is worth adding a few reflections about the peasant movement of La Convención at its peak, and about its profound significance.

At its heart, as we have seen, there were about a hundred *sindicatos* of varying size. They were expected to elect *juntas directivas* of fourteen or fifteen members, including seats allocated for female representation, although the majority of women participated only through their husbands acting as their intermediaries. The union members set the amount of their dues themselves: since most people were so poor, it was impossible to require a compulsory amount from them. They would gather once a fortnight or once a month, minutes being taken by whoever was literate, usually a young man, and each union regularly sent a delegate to an assembly of delegates held on Saturday evenings in Quillabamba. Mass gatherings (ten thousand people or more) sometimes took place in the capital, a remarkable number if one considers how challenging transport could be. At Chaupimayo, and perhaps elsewhere, too, the union began by building a primary school for eighty students from a number of villages, with a paid teacher, and planned to install electricity, the costs of which would be met through a tax raised from the families of two hundred of the *arrendires*. It is clear that the aim of the unions was not only economic improvement and modernization but also the provision of education. It is apparent that political awareness was increasingly strong, although some peasants seemed to think that Fidel Castro was a man fighting against the *gamonales* in another region of Peru, while others had never heard of him. What they did feel most sharply, without any doubt, was a hatred towards the *hacendados* and a determination never to put up with their abuses again.

The debate about Hugo Blanco, the role of Castroism, etc. has obscured the precise nature of the peasant movement. For an ordinary peasant in La Convención, the matter of knowing whether or not the union's methods were revolutionary was of hardly any importance. Their revolution was the expulsion of the *hacendados* and the occupation of land, and this was indeed accomplished, even though the threat from the rich and the presence of the police and army clearly showed that the victory might not last very long. What happened in the rest of Latin America, in Lima or even in Cuzco was less important for now. In certain places (such as Chaupimayo, Blanco's stronghold), there are clear indications of a revolutionary exaltation [...] I chatted with an 'evangelical' militant, who explained the social revolution to me in biblical terms ('Christ was on the side of the peasants, as is clear from reading the Scriptures'), and he claimed that many others thought the way he did. On the other hand, and I can base this only on chance observations, which are probably misleading, the atmosphere in December 1962 seems to have been one of excitement rather than exaltation.

What, in this situation, was the role of violence? There was astonishingly little. Occupying the *haciendas* was a symbolic gesture, followed quickly by the withdrawal of the occupiers [...] Apparently one *hacendado* was killed, before the main period of *hacienda* occupations, and there were two or three acts of revenge, but no co-ordinated attacks on the owners, nor on the *gamonales* or the police, even in the excitement of victory. In truth, taking account of the situation in the practically lawless frontier areas, the treatment the peasants had endured and their wretched living conditions, it is striking how few acts of violence did take place.

What, ultimately, was the significance of the movement in La Convención? It was independent of the peasant movements in the highlands of Cuzco and in the other regions of Peru. These were generally movements of Indian communities occupying what they considered common lands monopolized (for most of living memory) by feudal owners, but which were increasingly indispensable to Indian populations that were rapidly expanding on common land limited in size and exhausted. They were also a protest against the habitual demands of the *hacendados* and, in the final analysis, an assertion of basic human rights by men who up until that point had felt all their rights had been denied them. [. . .] The movement in La Convención was essentially a movement of a new frontier region. Peasant settlers from the *altiplano* who were individualistic and commercially minded and transformed the local economy in the direction of agriculture for export found themselves battling with a parasitic superstructure of neo-feudal land ownership that stripped them of what they considered the fruits of their labours.

There are other areas of this kind on the frontiers of the Amazon basin, in Peru and elsewhere, but they represent only an infinitesimally small part of South America's rural population, and for this reason one must not treat their problems as typical. They are nonetheless interesting on two grounds: first, they show the political potential of these non-traditional, modernizing elements among the peasants, including the purely Indian peasants of the Andes, and they also show the relative absence of initiatives on the part of the poorest and most oppressed: the class of agricultural workers possessing only a little land or none at all, a class that can be found elsewhere, too. The fact that this peasant movement found its expression through communist organization is due, in this case, to local factors. Nonetheless, it is no coincidence that it was receptive to communist doctrine, as was the case with similar movements in other frontier regions. In societies like those of South America, where a peasant is denied all rights, oppressed and barely treated as a human being, any movement that assures him he is indeed a human being and that he has rights is bound to succeed; this is what communism offers and for the most part it is the only kind of movement to do so. And if one were to ask peasants who have practically never heard of them what they are, these communists, they tend to reply that they are 'men who demand the rights that are theirs'.

The geographical position of La Convención, linked in a few hours by railway to an area of Peru that is important and experiencing increasing social ferment, at the heart of both the old Inca empire and of the Indian population of the Andes, naturally generated more publicity for the movement than is usual for outbreaks of social agitation in remote tropical frontier regions. It undoubtedly contributed to the explosion of unrest among the peasants, in the middle class and among students in Peru at the end of 1962. But this local movement serves only imperfectly to shed light on those peasant movements that are more typical of the South American continent.

1967

Translated from the French by Daniel Hahn; translation revised from the Spanish by the Editor

Notes in the original essay have been omitted from the version that appears in this volume.

Editor's note

In the discussion that followed the presentation of this paper at an international conference in Paris in October 1965, the principal points Eric made were the following:

When I say that La Convención isn't a typical case, I don't mean that it has no influence on peasant unrest in other parts of Peru. On the contrary, this influence is crucial, and it's quite evident that at a given moment, let's say 1962, for example, and perhaps since then, La Convención was something of an inspiration, not only for the peasant movements, but also for the general politicization of Peru that's so striking to anyone who visits this country. The fact that La Convención saw the organization of a powerful agrarian movement that achieved such significant successes had a great deal of influence on other regions. But in the *altiplano*, for instance, the unrest, the unions, the demands have not been the same. These are indigenous communities, peasants with different problems, and, all in all, it's possible to say that the majority of Peru's peasantry do not have the same problems as those in La Convención. [...]

Communism first and foremost represents a demand for human rights. That is important. And not only for human rights, but for legal rights, written down in black and white. Secondly, it represents practical lessons in organization. In my opinion, without the help of the working class in Cuzco and of the groups – even the intellectual ones – mobilized by communism (such as bank employees, primary and secondary school teachers, etc.) it is fairly certain that a movement with the scope, the strength, the tactical and strategic direction of La Convención's would not have come about. Thirdly, I would say that communism represents a world view, one which is primarily a view of the modern world, a way for man to fit into the world, and not simply into the small plot of land, into the small valley, that is the peasant's traditional horizon. [...]

[...] The different kinds of peasant movements, the student movements, the movements of workers' unions, the movements of people from the *barriadas*, fertilize one another [...] tend to reinforce one another ... Each of these sectors [makes] a contribution and in the case of La Convención ... a crucial contribution ... Time will tell whether popular forces [in Peru] will be able to win those rights to which they are fully entitled. We can but hope.

15

Peasant Movements in Colombia

I

The historiography of social movements in Colombia is perhaps even more unsatisfactory than that of most other Latin
American countries, and the student cannot but regret both the
absence of secondary works and the unreliability of statistical
and quantitative primary sources. For this reason a survey of
Colombian peasant movements must at present, at all events
until the late 1920s, rely on impression rather than established
facts, and it is entirely possible that serious historical research
might invalidate these impressions. Nevertheless, since we must
start somewhere, let it be with the following apparent paradox.
Colombia has relatively few records of powerful economic and
social movements of the peasantry *as a class* before the mid-
twentieth century. At the same time Colombia has a record
of armed action and violence by peasants (e.g. guerrilla war)
second perhaps only to Mexico. This is particularly evident
since the Second World War, but it may also apply to earlier
periods of civil war, e.g. in the last third of the nineteenth century. Our problem is to explain this curious combination of
facts.

The history of peasant agitation is so poorly known, that it is entirely possible for research to discover examples of important movements in the colonial period or the nineteenth century which we ignore at present. Nevertheless, whereas the most superficial acquaintance with the history of, say, Peru, Bolivia and Brazil, suggests the existence of endemic agrarian discontent and periodic local peasant insurrection in the first two, of characteristic movements of primitive rural agitation such as social banditry and millennialism in the third, Colombian history suggests no such tradition of unrest. Orlando Fals Borda (*La Subversión en Colombia*, 1967) goes so far as to build an entire theory of Colombian development on the assumption that a brief initial period of acute conflict (1537–41) was succeeded by an unusually complete acceptance of social subordination by the Indian, i.e. the rural population, an unusually successful Pax Hispana, a '*pas social casi sin precedents en la historia universal*'. It is true that the Comunero movement of 1781 appears to have had some echo among the peasantry of Choconta, the *only* break in political tranquillity since 1540, but a comparison with the contemporary movement of Tupac Amaru [in Peru] demonstrates its relatively modest character, and its failure ever to develop into a major movement for the restoration of the pre-colonial society.

The politico-economic changes of the nineteenth century [...] and, more generally, the disintegration of the traditional Indian society [...] produced social tensions. [...] Nevertheless, the action of the peasantry remained limited. Even in the revolutionary period 1847–53 the bands active in parts of the countryside, in the *sabana* of Bogotá, Cauca and the Valle del Cauca, seem to have come mainly from the towns (where mass organization among the urban poor was much more developed). [...]

On the other hand the armed mobilization of peasants on a non-class basis seems always to have been substantial. Considerable numbers of peasants followed their local *hacendados* and *gamonales* into the numerous and murderous civil wars of the nineteenth century, and in particular cases – e.g. the guerrilla war in Tolima 1898–1901 – provided the main, if not the only fighters. It is perhaps significant that the Tolima guerrillas and their leaders – with a few exceptions men of the people – came from the same areas which were later to provide both Liberal *guerrilleros* in the *Violencia* of 1948 – and communist self-defence forces – e.g. Ibagué, Sumapaz, Viotá. As for the armed mobilization during the *Violencia*, which was confined almost entirely to peasants, the figures are by any standards impressive.

[. . .]

II

Historically and agriculturally, Colombia is divided into three major zones, the Pacific Caribbean coastal belt, the central belt of mountains and the basins of the Cauca and Magdalena rivers, and the complex of eastern plain and *selva* draining into the Orinoco and Amazon valleys. Of these the central zone has always been the most important. The Magdalena river has been, historically speaking, the main axis of Colombia as colony and republic.

The coastal belt will not concern us much here. Much of it is still virtually undeveloped, thinly populated and outside the major currents of Colombian politics and social movements. A limited area around the mouth of the Magdalena and near the ports of Cartagena and Barranquilla was more intensively developed, mainly along the lines of the classic Caribbean plantation systems. But though this region has played an important part in the history of Colombian agrarian movements, if only as the scene of the great Santa Marta banana strike of 1928 against United Fruit, it has little in common with the rest of the country.

The eastern plains and *selvas* will also not concern us very much. The *selvas* were, until recently, virtual no-man's-land, inhabited only by Indians and a few free peasant squatters filtering or fleeing into this frontier region from the west, not counting the periodic incursions of adventurers and labourers in search of some temporary boom-product, such as indigo, quinine bark or rubber. The more northern Llanos Orientales, adjoining the similar region of what is now Venezuela, were and still are to some extent, a region of pastoral economy, semi-independent and semi-nomadic *llanero* cattlemen, and herdsmen-peasants tilling temporary subsistence plots in suitable spots. For most of its history this 'Wild West' has been thinly populated by a formidable body of armed riders and raiders, who provided Bolívar with his major military asset in the wars of independence, but have since tended to be left to their own devices. East of Villavicencio, the gateway to the plains, no Colombian or any other government has had much to say, and the economic use of this area for anything except a primitive pastoral economy has had to wait for the mid-twentieth century. The Colombian east has provided refuge for peasants wishing to evade the wars and lords of the centre, fighting men, and its own pattern of social struggle, ranging from banditry to guerrilla war against foreigners and large ranchers. Its connection with the rest of the country has been marginal.

The main central zone is both more important and more complex. It consists essentially of alternate strips of cordillera, table-lands and valleys running from south to north: western cordillera, Cauca valley, central cordillera, Magdalena valley, eastern cordillera. (The region of Colombia south of the point where the Magdalena–Cauca river system originates and the Andes divide, forms the department of Nariño, which always occupied a marginal position, closer to Ecuador than to the state to which it actually belongs.) The heartland of the central region lay in what now forms part of the departments of Cundinamarca, Boyacá and Santander. These were the high savannahs and table-lands between the Magdalena river and the eastern cordillera where the Chibcha Indians established their society and the Spanish conquistadors their capital and major settlements. This was an area of fairly dense Indian population practising subsistence agriculture. It remained the most populated and densely settled part of Colombia until the twentieth century.

West of this heartland there is the region of Antioquia, much more backward and thinly settled by the Indians, most of whom were quickly exterminated by the demands of mining, the activity which attracted white settlers of the lower class into this area in relatively large numbers. Antioquia therefore became a region sparsely populated by poor white subsistence farmers, prospectors and miners, until, with the exhaustion of the mines, the Antioqueños entered on their proverbially successful career of economic enterprise and internal migration in the nineteenth century. Leaving behind them a very backward subsistence agriculture over most of their homeland, a flourishing urban centre of business enterprise, and the basis for the modern coffee economy, their colonists headed south. Relative to the old Chibcha heartland, Antioquia has therefore tended to gain in population and wealth.

South of Antioquia and Cundinamarca (that is to say in the upper Magdalena and Cauca valleys and the neighbouring mountains), Spanish colonization meant little more than the division of the land into vast *haciendas* of lay or ecclesiastical seignors, the recognition of native *comunidades*, and the establishment of modest provincial towns like Popayan to serve as social and administrative centres for a huge and almost entirely unutilized region. Economically 'Cauca' [...] was a blank; as late as 1877 90 per cent of its territory consisted of *baldíos*, or unappropriated if not uncultivated lands. Demographically it remained largely Indian. From the middle of the nineteenth century the colonization of this space began mainly, as we have seen, from Antioquia. With the growth of the coffee economy

200

the Cauca valley (the present departments of Caldas and Valle) became relatively densely settled areas and in recent years the fastest-growing parts of the entire country.

In agricultural terms, virtually all of colonial Colombia was dominated by a subsistence economy, producing little more of a surplus than was needed to feed the few and modest towns – even Bogotá in 1851 had only about thirty thousand inhabitants – and the requirements of the caste of the white lords, proud, but by European or even Latin American standards not notably rich and luxurious. It was a society of exploitation and lordship. [...] On the other hand, there was no strong economic incentive to intensify exploitation, since transport difficulties virtually precluded the export of agricultural produce abroad (except from the immediate vicinity of some parts of the Caribbean coast) and there was little urbanization. Even today [1969] the traditional provincial centre in Colombia supplies its needs in food within a radius of a few dozen kilometres. The major subsistence crops were maize and wheat in the temperate highlands, bananas, yucca, etc. in the tropical lowlands. The Indian peasantry, though ready to adopt both new crops and other technological innovations, remained technically backward. Even in 1960, 65 per cent of all holdings (91.5 per cent in the Caribbean region) were cultivated without any power other than human muscle, the remainder mainly with wooden ploughs.

The agrarian changes which began to take shape from the middle of the nineteenth century can be grouped under five headings: (a) the adoption of market products produced by extensive methods, most notably *cattle*; (b) the spread of intensive cultivation on a smaller scale for the export markets – at first *tobacco*, later increasingly *coffee*; (c) the development of export plantation crops (notably *bananas*); (d) the development of food production for the growing urban market; (e) the spread of subsistence peasant colonization into hitherto unsettled and uncultivated areas.

201

With the exception of a) most of these developments took place since 1890. In territorial terms all except a) affected only relatively small areas. Thus in 1961–2 the main area under crops [maize, coffee, rice, wheat, cotton, potatoes, beans, manioc, bananas and tobacco] amounted to 2.25 million hectares out of a total of 114 million hectares, i.e. less than 2 per cent; or about 9 per cent of the area with any kind of agricultural or pastoral utilization. The most important economic crop, coffee, utilized a mere 0.5 per cent of the country's total area, though it produced 80 per cent of the value of Colombian exports and more output than any other coffee-producing region of the world except Brazil. It is important, in discussing the problem of the Colombian peasantry, to remind oneself of the general emptiness and under-utilization of this huge country [and] the relative share of agriculture and pastoral economy even today. Thus in 1962–3 13 per cent of the total area of the country, or more than 50 per cent of the area under any form of agricultural and pastoral utilization, consisted of pastures and earlier this proportion was substantially higher.

Such is the economic background to a study of Colombian peasant movements. However, before approaching the subject more closely, it is essential to note a number of non-economic factors. The first of these is the remarkable degree to which the indigenous Indian population has been assimilated to the '*mestizo*' pattern, the second, the unusual degree to which Colombian peasants have been actively involved in the political life of the country. The two phenomena may not be unconnected.

The 'racial' composition of the Colombian population in the 1950s was given as: whites 20 per cent, *mestizos* (white–Indian) 58 per cent, mulattos (white–negro) 14 per cent, negroes 4 per cent, zambos (Negro–Indian) 3 per cent and Indians 1 per cent, of which the negro, mulatto and zambo population is entirely confined to the coastal areas and the empty hinterlands of the northern departments. Yet in the central heartland and the south, Indians predominated as much as in the main

Andean countries and Mexico, though perhaps less densely settled, and in the central heartland white rural settlement was always small. In Saucio (a few dozen kilometres north-east of Bogotá on the main highway) the population considered itself Indian until the end of the eighteenth century. Even in the late nineteenth century 30 per cent of Boyacá, 15 per cent of Cundinamarca, 15 per cent of Cauca were still regarded as Indians, and even 8 per cent of Antioquia. In fact, and unlike Ecuador, Peru and Bolivia, the bulk of Colombia's Indians, after the dissolution of the *resguardos* and communities in the nineteenth century, have simply turned into social, if not biological *mestizos*. The Indian problem (including the land problem of Indian territories) remains a marginal problem of those indigenous communities which, in hitherto undeveloped or inaccessible areas, maintain their community structure and refuse to be absorbed into the white or *mestizo* economy. We shall consider it below, but this rapid and large-scale process of what in the Andean *altiplano* would be called *cholificación*, distinguishes Colombia from the other areas of dense Indian settlement.

The political structure of Colombia has also long – i.e. mainly since the mid-nineteenth century – been peculiar. The country has from the start been unusually immune to *caudillismo*, but has on the contrary been governed by an effective two-party system (Liberal and Conservative), peculiar inasmuch as its roots reach down to the village and the peasantry. Whatever the origins of this system, liberalism and conservatism became, from the mid-nineteenth century, hereditary loyalties not only of families, but of communities, accepted as such by all members of the *vereda* or neighbourhood. 'Most *veredas* in Colombia can be classified according to this political dichotomy,' writes Fals Borda in *Peasant Society in the Colombian Andes* (1955). 'Neighbourhoods with a balanced number of Conservatives and Liberals are hard to find. When rural families migrate, they tend to move to *veredas* of the same political affiliation, where they will not be harassed and where they can count on the solidarity of the whole group in case of emergencies.'

The frequency and savagery of Colombian civil wars, and the degree to which peasants and other common people could be mobilized not only into armies led by landlords but in independent guerrilla formations, are largely a reflection of this two-party division. It is to be noted that political conflicts provided an alternative to social conflicts: they tended to replace the vertical confrontation of the lower class against its ruler with the horizontal confrontation of Liberal communities against Conservative communities, and the occupation of the landlord's lands with that of the murdered or expelled neighbours of a different political allegiance.

III

Let us now turn to the social problems arising out of the agrarian changes sketched above.

Plantation agriculture

Since this is largely confined to the coast, isolated from the remainder of the country, it may be conveniently dealt with first. The production of bananas for export began in 1877 in Riofrio, in the hinterland of the port of Santa Marta, between the (largely Indian) Sierra Nevada de Santa Marta and the Magdalena estuary. The British-owned Santa Marta railway opened up this tropical lowland territory, reaching Riofrio in 1891 when systematic exportation began. From 1899 the plantations (American-owned) formed part of the gigantic United Fruit combine, which raised the area under bananas from 13,000 hectares (1900) to 82,000 hectares (1913). By 1932 there were 55,000 hectares under fully irrigated cultivation, dominated by United Fruit, but with Colombian estates and holdings producing 45 per cent of the output. Production rose from less than 300,000 bunches in 1900 to 6.3 million in 1913 and 10.3 million in the peak year of 1929 (when Colombia ranked third as a banana producer after Honduras with 28 million bunches and Jamaica with 22 million).

The Colombian banana zone differed from other such zones in the Caribbean area in three ways: (a) it formed only a tiny part of a very large state, and thus saved Colombia from becoming a 'banana republic' by limiting the political power of United Fruit; (b) a substantial part of production came from local growers, who developed their own conflicts with the United Fruit which dominated the zone; and (c) being in an area within reach of a fairly dense local population, the labour force on the plantations consisted of Colombians rather than, e.g., imported Caribbean Negroes. Hence while, for instance, the strikes in Costa Rica and Panama in 1918–19 were sometimes influenced by the ideology of the Negro nationalist 'Back to Africa' movement of the Jamaican Marcus Garvey, the early Colombian disputes were non-political or anarchist, the later ones led by Marxists.

Friction between local growers and United Fruit developed in the 1920s [...] and between plantation labourers and the company, on a number of the usual labour issues, but especially on sub-contract. For the bulk of the labourers were employed not directly by the company but by contractors (*padrones*), for whom the company disclaimed responsibility. [...] Agitation grew, encouraged both by the small Revolutionary Socialist Party (in which the Colombian communists were active before the formation of their own party in 1930) and by left-wing deputies like Jorge Eliécer Gaitán. The great strike of November 1928 was the result not so much of their agitation – the communists were, if anything, on the cautious side – as of the spontaneous militancy of the workers and the delaying tactics of the company. The demands were purely trade unionist, but the Unión Sindical de Trabajadores del Magdalena which led the strike had the support of all local opinion, including not

205

only the disgruntled Colombian growers but the chambers of commerce of Santa Marta and Barranquilla, and indeed of the soldiers, many of whom refused to fire on the strikers.

However, enough of them obeyed orders to produce a massacre which led to mass riots, which were suppressed by military force. The number estimated killed ranged from forty (a figure given by the military) to fifteen hundred (a figure given by the strike leader), but almost certainly ran into several hundreds. The strike was nevertheless successful, though it has been argued that the company settled on slightly less generous terms than it would have been prepared to grant before the military operations.

The great banana strike of 1928 had two kinds of consequences. First, and in terms of Colombian politics, it was systematically exploited by the Liberal opposition against the Conservative government, and played a significant part in the defeat of the Conservatives in 1930, which ended forty years of their political domination and opened the era of populist Liberalism which determined the fortunes of Colombia in the next twenty years. Second, it turned the banana zone and the adjoining areas into centres of strong labour (and indeed communist) activity, which extended beyond the plantation belt into the towns in the north and west, and the Indian mountains in the east, partly due to victimized strike-leaders who fled into the mountains and settled there, partly due to Indians who visited the banana zone. The strike movement did not die down [...] and a peasant movement developed under the wing of the workers. At the 1938 National Labour Congress several peasant leagues and a Liga de Indígenas de la Sierra Nevada were represented from this region. This tradition remained alive. However, the movements of the Santa Marta region are not comparable to those of the other parts of Colombia in which agrarian agitation becomes important, and no more needs to be said about them at present for this reason.

Extensive market production

By far the largest proportion of land in agricultural use is still, as we have seen, devoted to extensive cattle-ranching; according to the UN Economic Commission for Latin America estimate of the 1950s is something like 90 per cent of all exploited land. A very substantial proportion of the land is still in the hands of relatively few owners. According to the agricultural census of 1960 (the first of its kind) some 15,500 properties classified as 'multifamiliar grande' or 1.2 per cent of all holdings, averaging 727 hectares in size, cover 45 per cent of the total exploited surface, and 636 properties of over 2000 hectares, averaging some 11,000 hectares each, cover no less than 20.1 per cent of the total exploited surface. These latifundia are also the major units of cattle-ranching. [...]

One may add that they are also the units in which Colombian cattle-raising, inefficient and traditional to an extraordinary degree, is at its least intensive. Thus in the department of Cundinamarca, where the presence of the great city of Bogotá and some industrialization might, one would have thought, encourage the development of an efficient agriculture, something like 45 per cent of the agricultural exploited area consists of 'natural pastures'. [...]

Since little historical work has been done in this field, we cannot accurately trace the changing fortune of the Colombian latifundium. [...] We know that in the Republican period both church lands and *resguardos* were divided up, or encroached upon by neighbouring landlords or settlers. [...] It is quite clear that *haciendas* grew immensely by occupying *tierras baldías* without legal title. We may presume therefore that the latifundist sector increased, and may have become more concentrated. [...] We may also suppose that the rise of a market economy from the mid-nineteenth century led most *haciendas* to develop chiefly as cattle ranches, since this was the simplest and cheapest way of exploiting them, and one which, despite its inefficiency and low yield, produced substantial gross incomes for those who owned vast enough estates. There is some evidence of such a systematic turn to cattle-ranching.

However, whether or not there was concentration of landed property or an extension of the area of extensive cattle-ranching, the social effect of maintaining so vast an extension of territory outside agriculture was bound to be considerable. On the most conservative hypothesis, the increase in population was bound to lead to land-shortage among the peasants, thus forcing men either to migrate into undeveloped territory or, more likely, to crowd further on the broken land of the mountain slopes, which could not be used for ranching. If we assume an actual transfer of former peasant land to cattle ranges – which certainly took place in some regions – we must suppose that peasants were actually expelled from their holdings, to become peons on the *haciendas* to settle on the mountain sides or to migrate. The development of cash crops for the world market hardly affected this situation, since the most important of these (coffee) flourished best on land not suited to cattle-raising, and in any case, as we have seen, the area covered by such crops even today is relatively modest. [. . .]

The major effect of the predominance of the cattle-ranching economy has therefore been to intensify the social and economic problems of the peasantry in the remaining sectors of Colombian agriculture. It has not, on the whole, given rise to many social conflicts within the cattle-ranching area itself, except in the past twenty years in the Llanos Orientales, which are a special case.

Peasant colonization

Peasant migration was an obvious response to land-shortage in a country in which empty land is plentiful. It has taken place at all times, though more intensively at some times than at others – for instance during and after the murderous civil wars which always produced their *levée en masse* of refugees. Most of this migration today goes to the cities and is thus beyond the subject of this paper. Part of it is the mere geographical displacement of tenancies or titles of property. However, another part consists of simple occupation of empty land without legal title, or where legal ownership is disputed, and this has given rise to considerable social struggles, as might be expected.

The occupation of land is not, of course, confined to peasants. Much – indeed most of the utilized part – of the *tierras baldías* in the public domain have been occupied by more powerful, influential or wealthy men, and therefore do not concern us, except insofar as they may include energetic and enterprising potential *kulaks* or rural entrepreneurs, who are often a militant group in quasi-feudal environments. Unfortunately the statistics do not permit us to separate these two (or three) types of squatting clearly. [...] Nor, of course, do the census figures of 1960 give us any guide to past history. They merely indicate the extent of the phenomenon.

However, it is possible to distinguish the different colonizing situations and sources of conflict arising out of peasant squatting. They are as follows:

A. Pure squatters: peasants whose position is not challenged, perhaps because of the remoteness of their holding; peasants whose rights are challenged by neighbouring landowners, capitalists or politicians who covet the land they have brought under cultivation; peasants who squat on land which is under nominal private ownership, but unutilized or abandoned by its legal owners, who reassert their rights as soon as they observe that it has some value.

B. Semi squatters; i.e. peasants who are permitted (mostly by verbal contract) to bring empty land under cultivation in return for some kind of services to the landowner on the utilized part of this property. These may include

special forms of tenancy such as the roza of the Caribbean departments, in which peasants on the margins
of large cattle ranches clear forest or other land for the
hacienda, retaining the right to cultivate it on his own
account for a certain period (e.g. two years); other forms
of such pioneer tenancies; peasants cultivating land in
dispute, e.g. these subject to occasional inundations in
river-valleys, which they consider '*tierras de nadie*' while
the *haciendas* claim rights over them.

The history of the agrarian movements arising out of this
kind of peasant colonization cannot be written yet. We know too
little about this, about all other aspects of Colombian rural society. Still, two things are clear about it. First, and in spite of the
relatively small proportion of the peasantry represented by these
squatters, their agitations have played a leading part – perhaps,
with one exception, the leading part – in the social movements
of the non-Indian peasantry. Second, we would not expect such
movements to occur with any frequency except (a) in a period of
fairly extensive peasant colonization and (b) at points where the
land colonized by peasants had significant economic value for
landlords or those who claimed to be landlords.

There were, it seems, two periods of important peasant
colonization: in the third quarter of the eighteenth, and in the
last quarter of the nineteenth and early twentieth centuries. It
is improbable that there was any great competition for land in
the second half of the eighteenth century. On the other hand as
market production on the land developed – whether for cattle,
foodstuffs or cash crops – in the nineteenth and especially the
twentieth centuries, grounds for conflict began to multiply,
all the more so since in the course of the nineteenth century
private *hacendados* had clearly occupied vast areas of what was
legally state land (and what was almost certainly known to
the peasants as being neither owned nor used), which they
now claimed as private property. To give one example. When,

following a dispute between *colonos* and landowners in the area
where the departments of Cundinamarca and Tolima adjoin,
official inquiries were made into the latifundia of El Pilar,
Paquilo and La Cascada, belonging to Jenaro Otero Torres,
it was discovered that the original title to the property in 1923
covered 426 hectares; but by 1932 the latifundium extended
over 300,000 hectares.

The nature of these disputes might vary. Thus on the lands
claimed by United Fruit in the department of Magdalena, of
which only a relatively small part were used for banana production, a number of colonists had squatted, occupying – or so it
was claimed – upwards of 9000 out of 55,000 hectares, which
they used not for the production of bananas, but for subsistence
and increasingly to produce food for sale to the growing non-
agricultural sector of Santa Marta and the banana region.

Their major problem was lack of access to irrigation, which
was under the control of United Fruit, and in any case limited
to banana areas. By the early 1920s the problem was already
acute, that is to say within a generation of the effective start of
banana cultivation in the zone, and within a dozen years of the
major expansion of the United Fruit acreage. A government
commission on the allocation of *baldías* operated in the region
from 1924, and the discontent of the *colonos* merged with the
great strike agitations which we have already discussed.

Again, as we have seen above, extensive cattle ranches
encouraged peasant settlers to clear land which they eventually hoped to incorporate into the *hacienda*. Thus in Tolima we
know that cattle-ranching followed peasant colonization up the
mountain sides in the twentieth century. Inevitably conflicts
arose, especially when peasant settlers could establish coffee
production, a form of agriculture which, as we shall see, is
admirably suited to small cultivators. The intense conflicts in
the Sumapaz region, and especially in the *municipios* of Cunday
and Icononzo, stemmed largely from this. Much of the region
had been lately colonized – Icononzo was not founded until

Viva la Revolución

about 1900 – and in Cunday the area of cattle-raising was still expanding as late as the 1940s, while the *municipio* had by then the fourth-largest acreage under coffee in the department, a substantial production of yucca, not to mention one of the highest rates of population increase in the department.

As it happens, we have some information about the prehistory of the agitations in the Sumapaz region. In 1932, when the conflict came into the open, the peasants claimed to have been on their holdings for thirty years, i.e. virtually from the original settlement of the area. Disputes had been growing, especially in the great boom period of the 1920s, which saw the massive expansion of coffee production in the region. By 1928, as a result of these conflicts, the government was obliged formally to reassert its right over a large disputed area as a '*reserva territorial*', and the landlords entered on the course of systematic coercion and persecution of the settlers which was to lead to riot and deaths.

It would therefore seem that the problem of the colonists became acute in the 1920s. Whether it would have led to major agrarian movements without the major political change of 1930, which ended forty years of Conservative rule and began twenty years of populist Liberal government, we cannot say. Perhaps not, for under conditions of stable and traditional political relationships, the force of the state was virtually identical with that of the landowners; the police-post and what passed for the local jail were actually located in the main building of the *hacienda* of Sumapaz, and as the commission of enquiry makes clear, the local *alcaldes*, policemen and such representatives of higher authority as came into the region, identified themselves totally with the local men of power. At all events, after 1930 the peasants became more militant, organized and, to a considerable degree, they were victorious.

As we shall see, the *colonos*, in Sumapaz and elsewhere (as notably in the Hacienda El Soche, nearer to Bogotá, and El Chocho, Fusagasugá, old centres of struggle), were not the only factor in this change. Yet they were an important one, especially since the Sumapaz region was later, under its leader Jan de la Cruz Varela, to form a large part of that virtually 'liberated area' commonly known as the Republic of the Tequendama, which maintained both peace and independence during the *Violencia*, under communist or near-communist leadership and protected by its armed self-defence. It is particularly interesting, insofar as its organization and leadership seems to have become autochthonous, and, at least initially, not under the influence of the communists.

Peasant agriculture for export

If we leave aside the temporary boom in *tobacco* production, which has left behind a relatively modest survival, mainly in Santander, the characteristic export crop of Colombian agriculture is *coffee*. It began its vertiginous expansion after 1870, but made its most rapid progress after the First World War. In 1915 there appear to have been less than 50,000 hectares under coffee, by 1929 300,000, in 1950 about 650,000, in 1960 900,000 hectares. This cultivation was and is concentrated almost entirely in the Quindío, i.e. in Antioquia, the south of the old heartland (Cundinamarca) and the old undeveloped lands of the south: Caldas, Valle del Cauca, Tolima, Cauca. The coffee areas of the northern heartland, never of comparable importance, have tended to decline both relatively and absolutely.

Coffee is a traditional peasant crop. In 1960 over 75 per cent of the area cultivated with this crop was in units of less than 50 hectares (which constituted over 90 per cent of the number of all *explotaciones*). Smallholdings of up to 5 hectares formed 56 per cent of all holdings and cultivated about 20 per cent of the area under coffee. If the figures are comparable, this indicates a substantial decline in such minifundia, which are supposed to have formed 87 per cent of all coffee *exploitaciones* and to have

213

cultivated 49 per cent of the area in 1932. Economic concentration clearly took the form of the growth of medium-sized commercial farms, and not of large plantations which have no significant economic advantage. In 1960 there were only 205 coffee plantations of over 100 hectares and probably not one larger than 300. It is clear that the optimum unit of production remains small enough for family cultivation, supplemented by hired labour (largely from minifundists) during the harvests.

However, the structure of landownership differs from that of cultivation. Broadly speaking in Calda and Antoquia two-thirds of the minifundia (0–5 hectares) are owner-occupied, 30 per cent occupied by tenants – mainly on share-cropping terms – 1 per cent occupied without legal title and 2 per cent in other ways. 70–75 per cent of medium farms (5–50 hectares) are owner-occupied, 2 per cent held in miscellaneous ways, while the proportion of tenancies and squatters varies considerably: from 14 to 28 per cent and from 1 to 10 per cent respectively. The larger the holding, the less likely it is to be held without legal title; this correlation holds good up to 100 hectares. The figures are interesting because they suggest that medium peasants and substantial cultivators constitute a much larger proportion of *colonos* than poor peasants.

It is clear that substantial problems arise in the coffee economy, first, out of the relation between landowners and cultivating tenants or sharecroppers and, second, out of the relation between cultivators and hired harvest workers. The two cannot be clearly separated, since the typical minifundist cultivator, with an average yield of perhaps 250 kg for holdings of 1 hectare or less, must depend on other sources of income. We need hardly add that the coffee economy also gives rise to problems which affect all producers (e.g. the movement of prices) and to those which affect all poor peasants (e.g. their economic and political dependence on middlemen, townsmen and the rich in general, the difficulties of transport, credit, etc.).

As usual, we are poorly informed about the past history of

these problems. However, it seems that in several regions the original development of coffee production, like that of tobacco during the boom of 1850–70, took the form of large-scale plantations, perhaps financed by the new bourgeoisie. It is significant that where this happened, as in Viotá, Fusagasugá, El Colegio (in the border zone of Cundinamarca and Tolima, which we have already had occasion to observe), we find an unusually sharp confrontation between the increasingly parasitic large estates and the peasant cultivators who increasingly established themselves as the efficient and dominant units of production or other tenants who wished to engage in coffee production.

The case of Viotá, where coffee was pioneered in this manner from 1870, is particularly relevant, because this *municipio* has produced the most advanced of all peasant agitations. It would seem that tension between peasants and landlords mounted (as usual) during the 1920s, and reached breaking-point after 1930, when coffee prices collapsed. Under the leadership first of the revolutionary socialists and then of the Communist Party, the tenants refused to pay rent – they maintained their strike for several years – while attempts to meet the lower prices by wage-cuts led to a series of major strikes by the *peones*. Armed self-defence units were organized. As a result, by the middle of the 1930s the *haciendas* actually began to sell off their land to the embattled tenants and Viotá became, and has since remained, in effect an independent communist republic of peasant coffee cultivators.

How significant the agrarian movements in the coffee economy were is difficult to judge. In the Cuninamarca–Tolima–Caldas border zone, where they achieved their greatest successes, they are not easy to disentangle from such other phenomena as the grievances of the *colonos*. On the whole the peasant movement of the 1930s was distinctly weak in the main coffee departments – Caldas, Antioquia, Valle – and what there was, seemed largely to have consisted of *colonos*.

The problem of the Indians

Though the Indian population of Colombia was being rapidly absorbed into the non-Indian or scattered, with the distribution of the *resguardos*, it remained sufficiently self-contained in some parts of the country to present a specific agrarian problem. This arose, as in other parts of Indo-America, out of the struggle to maintain the native *comunidades* and their lands against encroachment and partition, and out of the increasing inadequacy of the communal lands, eroded, subdivided, etc. with the growth of population. The Indians' struggle was made more difficult by the necessity to fight on two fronts: against the encroachments of white or *mestizo* peasant settlers and townsmen as well as against those of the large *haciendas* or the new rural bourgeoisie. Fortunately, the Indian struggles of the past have been somewhat less neglected than those of other Colombian peasants, thanks to the devoted labours of historians such as Juan Friede, and their hopeless resistance is thus, in part at least, documented. Here we need merely note that at the time of the emergence of the modern peasant movements in Colombia, the Indians still formed significant sections of the population in the extreme north of the country (Guajira) and in the sparsely populated south-west of the Andean region (Cauca, Huila). As we shall see, they participated in the general movement.

IV

In the present stage of research it is not possible to write the history of Colombian peasant movements before the 1920s, except, as already observed, for the struggles of the Indians to preserve their communal lands. We have already suggested that this may indicate that there were few peasant movements of importance, and this is indeed not unlikely, but the question must be left open. From the 1920s on, indications of agrarian unrest multiply, and from 1928 on, or perhaps more exactly in the 1930s, a significant peasant movement emerges, and can be at least partly documented, even in the present defective state of our knowledge. Our main sources are the data on trade union organization and the reports emanating from the labour movement itself.

The *Reseña del movimiento sindical* 1909–37 records all [ninety] unions existing in 1937 (at the peak of the social unrest of the 1930s) and registered since 1909. [...] It confirms that the peasant movement had its greatest strength in Cundinamarca [thirty-one unions] and Tolima [sixteen unions], with a sizeable Indian movement in Cauca, and of course in the banana zone of Magdalena. However, it also suggests that the movement under left-wing leadership was weak in Antioquia, Valle, Santander and Norte de Santander, Huila, Bolívar, Atlantico and Caldas, and virtually negligible in Nariño and Boyacá.

This suggests that the actual peasant movement cannot be simply measured by the strength of formal peasant syndicates or leagues, let alone by that of left-wing organizations, who were, as we see, influential in certain zones. [...] Indeed this is so. The Colombian peasant movement of the period between the 1920s and the Violencia was unusually decentralized and unstructured. It was nevertheless extremely powerful.

The tension between *colonos* and *hacendados* over land rights had, as we saw above, been gradually increasing in the course of the great imperialist boom of the early twentieth century. By the middle 1920s, though there is little sign of formal peasant organization, it is evident that there was widespread litigation between peasants and landlords over claims to the public lands which both had occupied without title. The Supreme Court decision of 1926 that land must revert to the state if the owner could not produce the original documents of ownership was *de facto* a victory for the peasants. The mere fact such a decision was taken is the measure of the silent pressure in the countryside. It is against this background that the agitations of the late 1920s must be seen. It was at this point, moreover, that both

217

the young revolutionary socialist groups and populist-minded politicians like Jorge Eliécer Gaitán appeared on the agrarian scene.

The economic depression and the political triumph of the Liberal Party in 1930 intensified the [peasant] agitation, [and not only in] the areas of major political activity which have already been mentioned (in Cundinamarca, Tolima, etc.) [...] In the most advanced cases direct action – sometimes armed action – won something like a land reform. [...] A number of *haciendas* sold out to the peasants, others to the department. [...] In 1934 the situation had become so acute that the Supreme Court once again – but this time in an atmosphere of organized peasant agitation – returned to its 1926 decision. By this time the political situation had also changed. The 'New Deal' government of López Pumarejo (1934–8) entered upon a period of systematic social reform based on popular support.

The major result of this was the famous Law 200 of 1936, which in effect recognized the rights of the *colonos*. This law laid down that land which had not been economically exploited for ten years was to revert from private ownership to the state. The significance of this measure has been much debated. It has been considered as virtually ineffective and also as 'one of the biggest accomplishments that is often ignored' (Albert O. Hirschman) inasmuch as it amounted to a partial and unplanned distribution of land among at least a section of the peasantry, and a strong incentive for landowners to develop their estates. Probably both judgements are true. Where there was no peasant movement, it remained a dead letter; where there was such a movement, it encouraged both peasants and landlords. Certainly the occupation of land by *colonos* continued to grow in the 1930s and 1940s, though at the same time it encouraged landowners to evict peasants who might become *colonos*. There are no reliable statistics about its actual effects.

After 1938 the agrarian movement lost the support of the government. López, re-elected in 1942, found himself under increasing pressure from a coalition of landlords and businessmen, and was in any case now disposed to encourage the immediate increase of production by all means in order to take advantage of the wartime boom. Law 100 of 1944 reversed the policy of Law 200 of 1936, whose application it delayed by another five years. It forbade the planting of trees and other long-living plants by tenants or sharecroppers without the explicit permission of the landlord, in order to encourage landowners to take on tenants and sharecroppers without the fear that they might establish *colono* rights. A considerable radicalization of politics followed. Gaitán, who had established himself as the politician with most effective appeal to the poor, split the Liberal Party and won 45 per cent of its votes in the presidential election of 1946, but at the cost of letting the Conservative candidate win for the first time since 1930. Shortly after he became the official leader of the party, with the almost certain prospect of succeeding to the presidency and hence of a government reverting to a populist policy. His assassination in 1948 prevented this *dénouement* and ended a phase in Colombian history. Instead of a social revolution, or a populist regime, there was anarchy and civil war. The hopes of the left were buried in the *Violencia*.

The peasant movements have therefore since 1948 been overshadowed by this bloodthirsty, anarchic civil war, which affected the coffee region in central Colombia (Antioquia, Caldas, Cundinamarca, Huila, Tolima), the north of Cauca, parts of Boyacá, the two Santanders and some regions of the Llanos Orientales. Even two years after the official conclusion of the civil war [in 1953] it still covered 40 per cent of the country. Though not a social movement, the *Violencia* provided a surrogate for agrarian discontent, inasmuch as it enabled peasants to expel each other from their holdings; thus in Tolima (1958) thirty-five thousand *fincas* – or half of all holdings enumerated in the census of 1960 – had been abandoned. The liquidation of the cattle-economy – totally extirpated from the south and east of Tolima, partially from Huila, the north of Cauca and large regions of Antioquia – is also to be noted in this connection. In some areas of Tolima the relation with agrarian movements is even clearer. Here the peasant mobilization of the *Violencia* aimed at the occupation of *'tierra de nadie'* – i.e. of uncertain legal title, or took the form of armed peasant vengeance against landowners who had evicted tenants. The *Violencia* is in any case strongly correlated with peasant migration and colonization. It occurred very markedly in zones of colonization and has been most endemic in the departments in which the percentage of immigrants in the active agricultural population is by far the highest: Valle (54.4 per cent), Caldas (31.9 per cent) and Tolima (24.2 per cent).

The more strongly organized centres of the older peasant movement stood outside the *Violencia* and resisted it; from 1950, when armed self-defence began in Chaparral (Tolima), by military action were necessary. Communist-led guerrillas have been estimated at 10–15 per cent of the total. Mons. Germán Guzmán, our major source, lists three such units in Cauca (the old centre of Indian agitation), three in Cundinamarca, five in Tolima, and three in the empty frontier territories of Huila and Meta. In some areas this attempt to keep the *Violencia* at bay succeeded, and virtually autonomous zones of peasant administration were created and maintained, e.g. in Sumapaz and Viotá. The extent of local organization may be indicated by a cyclostyled document, convoking the eighteenth Regional Conference of the Communists in the Tequendama (December 1962). This provides for preparatory meetings in at least thirty-three different *municipios* and localities. It is significant that these contain the names of the places and forcibly expropriated *haciendas* familiar to the student of the agrarian agitation of 1929–34 in this part of Colombia. It is perhaps equally interesting that the first project of the unimpressive Agrarian Reform of 1961 was for an area equally familiar to the student of that now remote period: Cunday.

At this point we may conclude our survey of Colombian peasant agitations, leaving the movements of the 1960s, such as they are, for the attention of students of contemporary Colombian affairs. What conclusions – tentative and even speculative – can we draw from it?

First, the major wave of peasant movements in the history of the Republic seems to have been that of *c*.1925–48. It was a 'decentralized kind of initiative ... a decentralized violence' (Hirschman), but very significant in the limited, though substantial, regions in which it operated. In a number of places it was and has remained organized by politically conscious peasant cadres and communists, though these centres are not of great numerical size. In 1960, the peasant movement had not expanded significantly beyond the limits it had reached in the 1930s.

Second, the two major situations out of which peasant agitation developed were (a) the conflict of *colonos* and landowners over land to which neither had a clear legal claim, i.e. mainly in areas of new settlement and cultivation, and (b) the conflict of peasant-producers and estates over the right to cultivate profitable new cash crops, especially coffee. These two situations overlap in several areas, such as Tequendama-Sumapaz. Third, the *Violencia* of the years after 1948 may or may not have provided an alternative outlet for agrarian discontents, but it undoubtedly led to a recession of the peasant movements, which have not revived on anything like the old scale since 1970.

1969

16

Peasants and Politics

Let us consider whether there can be such a thing as a national peasant movement or a national peasant revolt or uprising. I very much doubt it. Local and regional action, which is the norm, turns into wider action only by external force – natural, economic, political or ideological – and only when a very large number of communities or villages are simultaneously moved in much the same direction. But even when such widespread general action occurs, it rarely coincides with the area of the state (as seen from above), even in quite small states, and it will be less a single general movement than a conglomerate of local and regional movements whose unity is momentary and fragile. The men from the coast and the men from the mountain may be too different from each other to meet more than briefly on the same ground.

The greatest peasant movements all appear to be regional, or coalitions of regional movements. Alternatively, if peasant movements develop all over a state's territory, unless sponsored or organized by the state's authorities, they are unlikely to be simultaneous or to have the same political characteristics or demands. In the worst case this composition of large peasant movements from a mosaic of small ones may create merely a series of scattered enclaves which do not affect the rest of the country. Thus in Colombia quite powerful agrarian movements, mostly organized by the Communist Party, developed in the 1920s and 1930s in certain types of zones – in the coffee-growing tracts, in Indian areas, which had their specific problems, in frontier or new settlement areas among squatters and colonists, and so on. Even the national co-ordination of the Communist Party produced not a single peasant movement, but a scattering of 'red' peasant areas often far distant from each other; nor has a nationwide movement developed from these scattered areas, though some have proved capable of spreading their influence regionally. Of course national political or guerrilla cadres may emerge from these isolated and often enduring little nuclei, but this is another matter.

In the best case, such peasant movements may occur in one or two strategically placed regions where their effect on national politics is crucial, or in areas capable of producing powerful mobile military forces. This was very much the case in the Mexican Revolution. The bulk of the peasantry in that country was not much involved in the revolution of 1910–20, though as a result of the revolution's victory several areas became organized. Still, the largest mobilization of the Mexican peasantry connected with the revolution was almost certainly, as it were, the wrong way round – the movement of the Cristeros in the 1920s which rose for Christ the King *against* the secular Agraristas. Subjectively, theirs was undoubtedly a peasant revolution, though both its timing and its ideology made it objectively counter-revolutionary. Nevertheless between 1910 and 1920 two regions happened to exercise enormous political effect. One was the frontier region of the north, with its footloose armed men – cowboys, prospectors, bandits and so on – which produced Pancho Villa's army with its mobility and capacity to range widely: a Mexican equivalent to the Cossacks. The other was the much more solidly based communal revolution of Emiliano Zapata in Morelos, which had purely local horizons but the enormous advantage of being situated next door to the capital city of Mexico. The political influence of Zapata's agrarian programme derives from the fact that his peasant levies were close enough to occupy the capital. Governments in large and loosely administered areas such as early twentieth-century Latin American republics are resigned to losing control of outlying provinces from time to time to local dissidents or insurrectionaries. What really worries them is insurrection in or in the backyard of the capital.

Where peasant revolutionaries do not have this advantage, their limitations are much more obvious. The great peasant movement in Peru in the early 1960s is a good example, being probably the biggest spontaneous mobilization of this kind in Latin America during that decade. There was at this period nationwide unrest, including unrest among the workers and the students. The agrarian movement was active both in the coastal plantations – which cannot be classified as belonging to the peasant economy but are better called by the local name of 'agro-industrial complexes' – and in the peasant highlands. Within the highlands, again, there were very extensive movements in both the southern and the central highlands and patchier outbreaks of land occupation, strikes, the organization of peasant unions and so on elsewhere. Two characteristics may be noted. First, though more or less simultaneous – the movement was at its height in 1962–4 and reached its peak in late 1963 in the centre and a little later in the south – the regional movements were not really linked with each other, or effectively with the non-peasant movements. Second, there were curious gaps. Thus the traditional area of 'native risings' in the south, the Department of Puno, was notably inactive. The traditional type of movement was no longer central or relevant, though as recently as 1910–21 it had been very active indeed. In Puno the peasant movement took the form of the establishment of a political machine by local *kulaks* and traders, which soon after showed remarkable political strength. Meanwhile, immediately to the north, in the department of Cuzco the direct action of peasants organizing unions and occupying the land, inspired by the success of the frontier peasantry in La Convención, was proceeding on a massive scale, though the men of La Convención themselves, having already achieved their main objectives, were militant chiefly in defence of their conquests. The widespread Peruvian peasant movement in 1962–4 produced unrest rather than revolution.

I am therefore inclined to think that the idea of a *general* peasant movement, unless inspired from outside or, even better, from above, is quite unrealistic. [. . .]

This is not to underestimate the strength of such conglomerate movements. If unified by some outside force – a national crisis and breakdown, a sympathetic reformist or revolutionary government, or a single nationally structured and effective party or organization, they may make the difference between success and failure for major revolutions. Even by themselves they may make an agrarian system or the structure of rule in the countryside unviable, as the 'Great Fear' of 1789 did in France and the Peruvian wave of land occupation did in 1962–4. There is good evidence that some time between June 1963 and February or March 1964 the bulk of the estate owners and lords in the central and southern highlands decided to cut their losses, faced with a general peasant mobilization, and began to liquidate their assets and think in terms of compensation for expropriation under some sort of agrarian reform. This did not make agrarian reform automatic. It took another five years and a military coup to impose it; but it merely buried the corpse of a highland landlord economy which had already been effectively killed by the peasant movement.

The potential power of a traditional peasantry is enormous, but its actual power and influence are much more limited. The first major reason for this is its constant, and in general quite realistic, sense of its weakness and inferiority. The inferiority is social and cultural, for instance as illiterates against the 'educated': hence the importance to peasant movements of locally resident and friendly intellectuals, especially the most formidable of village intellectuals, the primary schoolteacher. Their weakness is based not only on social inferiority, on the lack of effective armed force, but on the nature of the peasant economy. For instance, peasant agitations must stop for the harvest. However militant peasants are, the cycle of their labours shackles them to their fate. [...] But, at bottom, peasants are and feel themselves to be subaltern. With rare exceptions they envisage an adjustment in the social pyramid not its destruction, though its destruction is easy to conceive. Anarchism, that is, the dismantling of the superstructure of rule and exploitation, leaves the traditional village as a viable economy and society. But the times when this utopia can be conceived, let alone realized, are few.

In practice, of course, it may not make a great deal of difference whether the peasants are fighting for an entirely different and new society or for adjustment of the old, which normally means either the defence of the traditional society against some threat or the restoration of the old ways which, if sufficiently far in the past, may merely amount to a traditionalist formulation of revolutionary aspirations. Revolutions may be made *de facto* by peasants who do not deny the legitimacy of the existing power structure, law, the state and even the landlords. [...] A movement which only claims to 'recuperate' communal lands illegally alienated may be as revolutionary in practice as it may be legalist in theory. Nor is the line between legalist and revolutionary an easy one to draw. The Zapatista movement in Morelos began by opposing not *all haciendas*, but merely the new ones which had been introduced in Porfirio Díaz's time. [...]

The major difference lies not in the theoretical aspirations of the peasantry, but in the practical political conjuncture in which they operate. It is the difference between suspicion and

226

hope. For the normal strategy of the traditional peasantry is passivity. It is not an ineffective strategy, for it exploits the major assets of the peasantry, its numbers and the impossibility of making it do some things by force and for any length of time, and it also utilizes a favourable tactical situation, which rests on the fact that no change is what suits a traditional peasantry best. A communally organized traditional peasantry, reinforced by a functionally useful slowness, imperviousness and stupidity – apparent or real – is a formidable force. The refusal to understand is a form of class struggle, and both nineteenth-century Russian and twentieth-century Peruvian observers have described it in similar ways. To be subaltern is not to be powerless. The most submissive peasantry is capable not only of 'working the system' to its advantage – or rather to its minimum disadvantage – but also of resisting and, where appropriate, of counter-attack. The stereotype of the Russian *mujik* in the minds of educated Russians [...] is very similar to the stereotype of 'the Indian' in the minds of Andean whites [...] In fact there is a system in such behaviour.

Passivity is not, of course, universal. In areas where there are no lords or laws, or in frontier zones where all men go armed, the attitude of the peasantry may well be very different. So indeed it may be on the fringe of the unsubmissive. However, for most of the soil-bound peasants the problem is not whether to be normally passive or active but when to pass from one state to the other. This depends on an assessment of the political situation. Broadly speaking, passivity is advisable when the structure of power – local or national – is firm, stable and 'closed', activity when it appears to be in some sense changing, shifting or 'open'.

Peasants are perfectly well able to judge the local political situation, but their real difficulty lies in discerning the wider movements of politics which may determine it. What do they know of these? They are normally aware of belonging to some wider polity – a kingdom, an empire, a republic. Indeed the familiar peasant myth of the remote king or emperor who, if only he knew, would put matters right and establish or re-establish justice both reflects and to some extent creates a wider framework of political action. At the same time it reflects the normal remoteness of the national government from the local political structure which, whatever it may be in theory, in practice consists of state power and law exercised by and identified with the local men of power, their kin, clients or those whom they can bribe and overawe. What else they may know varies widely with the actual political system. Thus if national courts exist, which is by no means always the case, litigation may well bring even remote communities into some relation to the national centre, doubtless via a chain of intermediary urban lawyers. The Peruvian community of Huasicancha, some 4000 metres up in the mountains, could hardly be physically more remote – but, since it obtained its first judgement in the viceregal court at Lima against a usurping Spaniard in 1607, it has never ceased to be aware of at least some dimensions of the wider polity of which it is a distant part.

As we approach the present [1973], the details of national politics become increasingly important and known – for instance, when elections and parties enter the scene, or when the direct intervention of the state in the affairs of localities and individuals requires some knowledge of its institutions and their operation. Moreover, with mass emigration the village is likely to possess direct links with the centre in the form of colonies of its own people settled in the capital or elsewhere, who know city ways. But long before this happens peasants are aware of changes within the system, even if unable to describe or understand them precisely. War, civil war, defeat and conquest may involve the peasants directly and open new possibilities when they put the national rulers at risk and change the local ones. Even lesser events in the politics of the ruling class such as elections and *coups d'état*, which hardly affect them directly, may be rightly read as encouraging or discouraging. They may not know exactly what is happening in the capital, but if family A ceases to provide the local senator while its rival family B appears to be riding high, there will be considerable local reappraisals, doubtless first among the townsmen, but also eventually in the villages. The Mexican Revolution – even in Zapata's Morelos – began not so much as a revolution but as a breakdown of the long-established local political balance which in turn depended on the smooth operation and permanence of Don Porfirio's system of national government.

If any major national change may open new possibilities or close old ones, then a fortiori news of reform or otherwise favourable change mobilizes peasants. Thus when a reformist government supported by the APRA (Alianza Popular Revolucionaria Americana) party came into office in Lima in 1945, communities which had operated on the assumption of stability promptly changed their tactics. [...] It is as though the villages, always conscious of potential strength even within their subalternity, required only the assurance of goodwill or even mere toleration from the highest authorities to straighten their backs. Conversely, of course, any hint that power will once again stamp on them encourages them to retreat into their shells. As the 1945 reformist government led to a wave of agrarian unrest and organization, so the imposition of the military government in 1948 brought land invasions and peasant unions to a brusque stop – until under a new government after 1956 the peasants gradually become aware that the situation is once again rather more open.

This sense of constant potential or actual confrontation of force may perhaps derive from the very exclusion of the traditional peasantry from the official mechanism of politics or even law. Relations of force – either real trials of strength or ritualized ones – replace institutionalized relations. [...] If the peasants wanted to attract the notice of the authorities they had no effective way of doing so except by challenging authority through direct action, since there was no political machinery for making themselves heard. This was risky, since punishment was normally sure – but certainly peasants, and probably even lords and government, would calculate the dose of violence offered. In the invasions of 1947 it was the inexperienced communities who stayed and were massacred when the soldiers came. Huasicancha, with centuries of experience of alternating litigation and direct action, evacuated the occupied ground quietly when the troops came, and temporarily made the best of what law could achieve.

Confrontation could thus be quite non-revolutionary: it is an error to think of every incident of peasant challenge by force as a 'rising' or 'insurrection'. But it could also, because of the very nakedness of the political relation of force which it implied, lend itself to revolution. For what if it looked as though the definitive end of the rule of the gentry was at hand? At this point we are on the border between the territories of hard political assessment and apocalyptic hope. Few peasants would hope that their own region or village alone could achieve permanent liberation. They knew too much about it. But if the entire kingdom, indeed the entire world, was changing? The vast movement of the *trienio bolchevista* in Spain (1918–20) was due to the double impact of the news of the successive collapse of empires – the Russian, followed by the Central European ones – and of an actual *peasant* revolution. And yet the further the centres of decision were from the known and understood local power structure, the hazier the line between actual judgement, hope and myth (in both the colloquial and the Sorelian sense). The signs by means of which men foretold the coming of the millennium were, in one sense, empirical – like those by which they foretold the weather; but in another they were expressions of their feeling. Who could tell whether there was really 'a new law' or a rider carrying the Tsar's manifesto in letters of gold giving the land to the tillers, or whether there simply ought to be?

One might push the hypothesis a stage further and suppose that, conversely, the disappointment of hope within a concretely assessable situation would be less lasting than that of global or apocalyptic hopes. When the troops came and expelled the community from the lands it occupied, it would not be demoralized, but wait for the next suitable moment for action. But when the expected revolution failed, it would take much more to restore the peasants' morale.

1973

Notes in the original essay have been omitted from the version that appears in this volume.

17

Peasants and Rural Migrants in Politics

I

For the economic and social historian and the student of contemporary politics, the crucial dates in the history of Latin America do not occur in the first quarter of the nineteenth century, when most of the continent won independence from Spain or Portugal, for this did not substantially alter their economic and social structure. They occur in the late nineteenth century, when these countries entered the world economy in their now familiar roles as mass exporters of certain primary products, whose balances of payment depended in the main on such exports. This phase lasted until 1930, when the simple, hitherto expanding export monocultures collapsed and the societies based on them fell into crisis, though the basic orientation remained. In the middle of the 1930s all but three Latin American states (Mexico, Peru, Paraguay) relied for more than 50 per cent of their exports on one, or at most two, of the following commodities: coffee, bananas, sugar, cotton, meat, cereals, wool, copper, tin and oil. Eight relied on coffee and bananas, two more on coffee and sugar or cotton. [...]

Before the last decades of the nineteenth century a great part of the rural area of Latin America was not seriously orientated towards the world market, or often towards any but the purely local market. Another part relied on older and declining staples (like sugar in north-east Brazil), or on temporary 'boom' products. Large areas which we now associate with the characteristic products of their countries, such as the Cuban provinces of Oriente and Camagüey, had a quite different economic complexion. By modern standards most regions of Latin America were not even colonial or semi-colonial economies, but simply underdeveloped areas.

The rise of the export economy was bound to have the most far-reaching effects on the society and politics of the continent. However, so long as it took the form of a headlong, though fluctuating, expansion into apparently unlimited North American and European markets, the full extent of these effects was not widely realized, for they were largely absorbed and assimilated by the existing social and political systems of the Latin American republics, dominated by the traditional controllers of their politics, the owners of large estates and the vested interests of administration and the export–import trade of the capitals and ports. In the urban and non-agricultural sectors change was indeed visible, especially in the southern part of South America (Argentina, Chile, Uruguay, south Brazil) where economic development was most rapid. In central and south Mexico the effects for the new agrarian economy were already strong enough to create a revolutionary situation, for in these regions the new market-orientated *hacienda* was not merely an adaptation of an older pre-existent latifundist economy, but expanded at the direct expense of a dense Indian population living in autonomous village communities.* But, by and large, change remained below the political

* The Andean regions, in which estates and communities coexisted in a similar manner, were much slower to enter the economy of the world market except through the rather specialized products of mining.

and social surface. What precipitated it was the 1929 depression, i.e. the sudden and almost total collapse of the world markets on which Latin America had relied.

The immediate effect was to produce a continent-wide crisis in the finances of governments, and consequent political crises. In 1930–1 regimes toppled, peacefully or by military coup, in Argentina, Brazil, Chile, Ecuador, Peru, Bolivia, Colombia, the Dominican Republic, and shortly afterwards in Cuba. However, this short-term crisis would have been of little but local interest had it not indicated a more profound and long-term change in the affairs of the continent. It is true that neither the basis of so many Latin American economies – export monoculture – nor that of so much Latin American social structure and politics – the oligarchies based on large estates, import–export trade and government – were fundamentally altered as yet. But neither did they return to the old dispensation. The economy of massive primary exports and free capital and commodity imports no longer functioned automatically; the one had to be buttressed by manipulating the other, and behind the temporary walls of restriction and control new economic and political interests, notably those of Latin American industrialists essentially supplying the native market, grew up. [. . .] But, above all, the masses of ordinary Latin Americans began to enter – and in due course to dominate – the politics of their countries. [. . .]

II

The great bulk of these new entrants were countrymen, since in 1930 the city population formed only a modest minority in all countries except Argentina, Chile, Uruguay and Cuba. Those who took the most obvious part in politics were henceforth the millions who flooded into the cities, and especially into the handful of giant cities. They came overwhelmingly from the country, and remained, at least for a time, displaced peasants. The political changes in the rural areas were, and have in general remained, less striking than those in the cities. However, these are the main focus of this paper.

The economic structure of the Latin American countryside was one of export agriculture or subsistence farming, though the fantastic expansion of the cities from the 1930s added an increasingly important sector supplying the rapidly growing domestic urban market. Broadly speaking, we can say that it was dominated by the two phenomena of the transfer of land from subsistence or extensive light use to market production, and the increasingly precipitous flight of manpower from the land. The social or legal structure was overwhelmingly one of large estates, sometimes with the attendant 'minifundist' peasantry, or of a coexistence of large estates with independent village communities, as in areas of solid Indian settlement. The thinly populated frontier regions (mainly on the fringes of the Amazon basin) into which a growing population began to filter were no exception to this, for insofar as they were not beyond the range of all administration or even knowledge, they too were normally owned or claimed by some form of latifundist.

The transfer to a cash-crop economy put an inevitable strain on this latifundist structure; whether it took the form of the transformation of the old extensive latifundio into an *hacienda capitalista* (to use the convenient distinction of Colombian agrarian reformers) or plantation, development through various forms of tenant farmers or sharecroppers, the substitution of urban or foreign entrepreneurs for the old *hacendados*, or some other pattern. The change from an older to a newer staple product, or the diversification of production, had equally disruptive effects. The subsistence sector was less affected by such changes, but in its turn suffered the increasing pressure of a rapidly growing population on fixed – and deteriorating – land, or indeed often on land diminished by the encroachments of the estates.

The political structure of the Latin American countryside was (except for revolutionary Mexico) that of formal or informal power exercised by local families of estate owners – sometimes in rivalry with others of their kind – each at the apex of a local pyramid of power and patronage; controlling, or seeking to control against local rivals, both the local parts of government administration and the local influence in national government. There was [...] no government power in the countryside except by the agreement of such magnates and patrons. Insofar as political 'parties' existed, they were [...] merely labels tied on to local families and their clienteles, whose votes (if they had any) went, like their armed support and their loyalty in general, to their *patron* or lord.* So far as the mass of the peasantry was concerned, there was no such thing as 'national' politics, but only local politics which might or might not have national labels attached to the local persons of power.

This structure has persisted to a considerable extent, partly because of the persistence of its social base, partly because of the separation of town and country which is so characteristic of underdeveloped regions and which both excluded many country-men from the political process as conceived in the city and made the politics that came from the city appear incomprehensible, irrelevant or unacceptable. To take an example. In Brazil (and in several other countries) illiterates are excluded from the vote, i.e. in a region like the Brazilian north-east a minimum of 75 per cent of adults as late as 1950. The traditional parties hesitated to interfere between the politically influential *fazendeiros* (landowners) and 'their' people, so that for practical purposes nobody other than the extreme left asked the peasants for their opinions, and the constitution provided little scope for hearing their answers. This does not imply that the rural masses were uninterested in politics, or unprepared under certain circumstances

---

* We may, for the sake of simplicity, neglect the exceptions to this generalization which had already begun to develop by the 1950s, notably in the southern tip of the continent, but also in Colombia, where 'conservatism' and 'liberalism' had genuine, if quite 'unmodern', roots among the masses, in Peru, where APRA had begun to win independent mass support, and elsewhere.

to oppose the political status quo. However, their traditional movements often took forms incomprehensible to the urban politician, as in the messianic movements which found a fertile soil in the Brazilian north-east and parts of the south between 1890 and the 1930s, all the more so as these sometimes claimed to be monarchist. They were political, of course, even in the narrowly accepted sense of the word. The famous prophet Padre Cícero of Juazeiro became the virtual boss of the state of Ceará from 1914 to his death in 1934, and as a man of influence, received the same consideration from the federal government as any other grandee. Yet the movements which stood behind men of his kind, and were able to give them the equivalent of patronage and influence, were themselves unable either to enter official politics or to change its character.

Urban-based movements which did sometimes attempt to reach the peasant normally failed – or had only localized success – like the labour and socialist movements of European pattern. Why this was so is not altogether clear. The anarchists, whose capacity to mobilize rural masses is proved in Europe, appear to have had negligible success in their propagandist activities, except among the equivalent of urban and industrial workers (such as the Bolivian miners). The communists, lacking serious strength everywhere except in Chile, Cuba and Brazil, undoubtedly established pockets of agrarian strength here and there – as in parts of Cuba, or one or two places in Colombia – but remained essentially an urban or industrial workers' movement with a few attached intellectuals. The socialists, negligible except among immigrant European communities, seem hardly even to have tried. It may be that the cultural gap between city and countryside was too wide, or that the left failed to find the slogans which would move the peasants, or to formulate them in an acceptable way. It is certain that the left only slowly learned to search for the specific language accessible to peasants, and the specific forms of demand likely to mobilize them, and probably did not do so systematically until the 1950s.

There are evidently exceptions to this generalization. The peasant-based revolutions of Bolivia (1952) and Cuba (1959) are the most obvious ones. The first is less of an exception than it seems, for the Bolivian Revolution was made essentially by a combination of dissident officers, urban intellectuals, and one of the rare powerful industrial-labour movements (the Miners' Union), and the peasant movement as a whole emerged after its victory. (There was, however, a significant local movement in the valley of Cochabamba, among a rather less traditional and isolated peasantry, under Marxist influence and led by José Rojas, a local peasant who had seen something of the world.) The decisive step in the mobilization of the peasants lay rather with the non-peasant revolutionaries who (correctly) decided that agrarian reform and the granting of rights to the Indians were the indispensable conditions for maintaining a new regime.* The Cuban Revolution was much more obviously peasant-based, at least in its guerrilla phase, though curiously enough the movement found its centre not so much in the areas already partly mobilized in earlier communist agitations, but in the Sierra Maestra, where it was brought by the urban guerrillas.

Two less successful examples of peasant mobilization may also be mentioned: Peru and Colombia. There is little doubt that APRA's mass basis, especially in the northern departments of Peru which are its stronghold, reflects some success in appealing to rural strata, especially in the agriculturally proletarianized zone of sugar and cotton production. To what extent it does, cannot be said with certainty, for APRA's past successes at elections are irrelevant: the literacy qualification excluded from the vote the bulk of the Indian peasants, whose spokesman APRA claimed to be. Nevertheless, and though

---

* They were right. After 1952 Bolvia, which previously counted its military coups by the hundred, acquired a dozen years of unprecedented political stability before the regime was overthrown in November 1964.

both the structure and ethos of APRA in its days of glory were much more those of an urban or labour movement than a peasant movement, we may allow it a modest degree of peasant political mobilization in its time. The case of Colombia is more interesting, because there is nothing modest about the peasant mobilizations which, between 1948 and 1963, may have put a peak total of some 30,000 armed guerrillas and bandits – almost exclusively peasants – into the field, and which cost the lives of a number of Colombians estimated, upon the most conservative calculations, in six figures. [It was] the greatest of all Latin American agrarian movements outside the Mexican Revolution.

[...]

Broadly speaking, we may therefore say that, until the present [1967], the growing dissatisfaction and unrest of the Latin American peasantry has not found an expression commensurate with its importance; except perhaps in the headlong avalanche of rural migrants who have voted against the status quo with their feet by moving into the city slums. Nevertheless, and especially since the middle 1950s, signs of agrarian unrest and agrarian political mobilization have been multiplying, and it may be useful to survey them briefly. With the possible exception of Colombia, none of them has been organized by the traditional parties of the continent (which is not surprising), or to any extent by the populist movements which became so characteristic of the continent in the early 1950s.* Leadership and inspiration have come largely from the Marxist left (communist, socialist, Maoist, Trotskyist, Castroite, or whatever the label), and this may account for its comparative localization.

Four types of peasant have proved most susceptible to such agitation. The first, and least typical, consists of independent

---

* APRA's part in the very widespread Peruvian peasant unrest of 1961–3 was small and confined to its traditional northern fiefs.

peasant pioneers seeking to evade the advances of the market economy and the growing encroachments of lord and state by pushing into the unsettled and unknown frontier regions surrounding the Amazon basin. Communist nuclei of this sort are known to exist in inland Brazil (Goiás and Mato Grosso) and in the Amazonian regions of Colombia (Meta, Caquetá). Land is not normally a problem for such men, for there is plenty of it. Freedom is what drives them inland, freedom that they associate with the only ideology that comes to them with the message that peasants are men with rights. In numerical terms this frontier communism is negligible.

The second type, numerically far more important, consists of peasant (i.e. normally Indian) communities claiming, or rather reclaiming, their communal lands since the late 1950s, and often doing so by direct occupation. Such occupations of common lands are of importance in the Indian parts of Chile, in the Andean region in general, and especially in Peru, where they reached large and national proportions in 1961–3. Here again the object of the peasantry is to return as far as possible to the traditional subsistence agriculture of the community, though population growth and the deterioration of lands are likely to make this impossible even after the recovery of alienated common lands. However, it would be a mistake to regard such movements as simple traditionalism sailing under the red flag for want of any other. The mere fact of collective and positive peasant action is proof of political self-discovery and the desire for change. It is a revolutionary act of peasants, especially Indians, to behave as if such terms as right, freedom and justice applied to them just as to other men, even when it is a question of something as obvious as the legal right to specific pieces of land alienated within living memory by trickery or force. Moreover, there is evidence that this political self-discovery is also a burning desire for a share in *modernity*, which finds expression in the passionate and universal drive for education and enlightenment. Almost the first thing any peasant community does when it can is to build a school. (This has been very striking in Bolivia since the revolution of 1952.)*

The third type of restless peasantry is even more interesting. It consists of the most dynamic, modern-minded and market-orientated elements – one might almost say the future *kulaks* of Latin America. The peasant movements of the eastern slopes of the Peruvian Andes (which include the most militant and successful of the communist agitations, that of La Convención) are very good examples of this. They consist of Indian farmers who have individually migrated into hitherto unexploited territories now being rapidly opened up to cash-crop agriculture (coffee, tea, etc.). The movement of La Convención is essentially based on the agitation of a limited number of prosperous colonists (*arrendires*) for tenant rights against the latifundists, which at the peak of the agitation passed naturally into the demand for the expropriation of the *hacendados*. These *arrendires* are men who received insecure tenancies on vast estates for labour rents – so many days' work on the lord's demesne – which they in turn subcontracted to *allegados*, who in fact performed most of the labour service. It is fairly evident from areas where such colonization does not occur on land already parcelled out among latifundists, that it is likely to produce a stratified peasant society without a special tendency towards collective political radicalism, at least at present. What gives rise to an agrarian revolutionary movement is the oppressive rigidity of the latifundist straitjacket in which the new farmers find themselves constrained.

---

* A communist peasant organizer put it as follows: 'There are three things you have to do to get anywhere with peasants. The first is, you must live exactly as they do. If you can't stand the food, you can't organize peasants. Second, you have to talk to them not just about the land, but about this land, which used to belong to them in their grandfather's day but was taken over by the Hacienda X. Third, you must always be teaching them something. I'm not an intellectual, so I teach them football. But learn something they must – they insist on it.'

There remains a mass of less readily classifiable peasant occupiers and tenants in conflict with the latifundist system which dominates them and the unpredictable hazards of the new or the changing market economy.

It is neither possible nor necessary to analyse all the complexities of Latin American agrarian problems here, but a few general observations may be made. The first is that the actually landless group, the rural proletariat, is normally among the least politically dynamic or readily organizable agrarian groups, except perhaps in regions of advanced plantation labour, by the quasi-urban methods of trade unionism. It is the peasant – and not necessarily the peasant with insufficient land – who provides the most immediately explosive element. Second, mere minifundism or poverty is not sufficient to produce agrarian agitation. It is normally the juxtaposition of the peasant and the *hacienda* (especially the *hacienda* with changing economic functions and structure – e.g. shifting from extensive to intensive exploitation, or from direct plantation to exploitation by tenants or sharecroppers) which produces the politically inflammable mixture. Thus in Colombia, the Department of Boyacá, where small and medium holdings predominate, has remained politically conservative, whereas the Department of Valle del Cauca, where large and small properties coexist, has been notably more rebellious. Third, it is the increasing involvement in a monetary and market economy which, whatever its form, produces particular tensions found neither in the traditional subsistence economy nor in old-established and unchanging market economies.

All this provides an ample basis for the political awakening, or even the revolutionizing, of the Latin American countryside, and Mexican experience shows that the mere fact of past land reform is no bar to it, so long as the process of economic development in the countryside continues. It is delayed by the political and cultural lag of the country behind the city, its inaccessibility, and the usual inability of peasants to take more than local or traditional initiatives without outside leadership. Possibly in areas of mass emigration the lowering of economic pressure and the loss of the most dynamic peasant cadres may also maintain the social temperature below boiling-point. On the other hand the increasing absorption of the rural zones into national politics tends to work in the opposite direction.

III

Whatever the effect of rural emigration on the countryside, it is as nothing to its effect on the cities, which have been flooded – indeed drowned – by an influx of peasants without parallel in the demographic history of the world.

The growth [of the principal Latin American cities] is unprecedented and extraordinary [between 1940 and 1960, São Paulo, for example grew from 1.8 million to 4 million, Mexico City from 1.5 million to 4.5 million, Lima from 500,000 to 1.7 million]. And so is the general rate of urbanization. Around 1960 Argentina, Chile, Uruguay, Cuba and Venezuela already had an urban majority, and so possibly had Mexico. By 1970, on present trends, they will have been joined by Colombia, Peru, and even Brazil.

Inevitably such an influx was bound to destroy the older social and political structure of the cities. [...] The process of dilution and structural change can be illustrated by the example of São Paulo. [...] Foreign-born workers, a majority until the Second World War, fell to about 10 per cent of the labour force within twenty-five years. Their place was taken partly by the city-born (i.e. largely their own children), but mainly by internal immigrants, especially in the less skilled occupations. [...] It will be evident that this influx was likely not only to burst the bounds of any already existing labour movements but also to destroy much of the unity of background and style of the smaller and older proletariat. And this is indeed so. In São Paulo, as in Buenos Aires, the older unions were swamped by new government-sponsored and sometimes government-controlled bodies, while the traditional socialism, anarchism or communism of the early proletariat retreated into the higher ranks of skill or to the fringes of industry.

It may be – but there are no studies on this difficult subject – that the same process of dilution or depolitization affected also the unorganized activities of the labouring poor, such as riots. At all events, it is remarkable how few riots – even food riots – there have been in the great Latin American cities during a period when the mass of their impoverished and economically marginal inhabitants multiplied, and inflation as often as not was uncontrolled. Thus the last great riot of the unaided poor in Bogotá (student-initiated riots are another matter) occurred in 1948, since when the population of the city – and it is fair to say the body of misery it contains – has risen from less than 650,000 (1951) to over a million (1964). Or rather: there is unrest and violence. What is missing, unless the direction comes from students, from old nuclei of left-wing leadership (as in Niterói, opposite Rio de Janeiro), or from governments above, is the old-fashioned city 'mob' with a knowledge born of experience of what are the strategic and politically vital points of the city, where riot will have the maximum effect.

It need hardly be added that the rural influx also (and most directly) affects the pattern of political parties and votes. It may be argued that the characteristic populist leaders and parties of the 1940s and 1950s, whatever their claim to national and rural interest, represented primarily movements based on the urban poor, and hence increasingly on the new internal immigrants. This is particularly clear in the case of Argentina, where Perón deliberately made himself the spokesman of the new internal immigrants, the *cabecitas negras*, against the European and citified natives of Buenos Aires.

The political attitudes of the immigrants are naturally dictated by their poverty, the insecurity, the appalling living conditions, and the hatred of the rich of a gigantic and constantly expanding proletariat and sub-proletariat. Yet this is a population with no prior commitment – or even potential commitment – to any version of urban or national politics, or indeed any beliefs which could form the basis of such politics. Unlike most nineteenth-century transatlantic migrants, they lack even a potential nationalism, for they are not foreigners. Unlike the East and South European migrants of the early twentieth century, they lack a native tradition of socialist/anarchist or labour movements which could hold them together in the strange land. What they do possess, the habits and reactions of rural kinship and communal life, doubtless help them to make themselves a little more comfortable in the big city by settling in groups from the same village or province, by transferring peasant mutual aid to the building of slum shacks or modest houses, and in other ways; but it does not, as it were, reach up far enough socially to be a political guide. They understand personal leadership and patronage alone.* It alone provides a link between the political worlds of the hinterland and the city. Untouched by any other traditions, such as the anti-*caudillista* ones of liberalism or socialism, the new immigrants look naturally for the powerful champion, the saviour, the father of his people.

The politicians, with or without parties or movements, who have succeeded in gaining the support of the urban masses vary widely in their personalities or political attitudes. They might be old-fashioned oligarchs or generals, who gained a reputation

---

* It is often argued in Latin America that the new immigrants transferred the sort of loyalty they had given to their feudal superiors to any person of power and influence who could give them benefits in return for some support. This is a considerable oversimplification, though it has some truth in it. There are deeper reasons, both in the rural tradition of politics and the social situation of the urban masses, for a natural tendency towards *caudillismo*. Even in Europe it emerged clearly in early labour movements in the transformation of certain individuals into heroes and charismatic leaders; and this in spite of the deliberate discouragement of such a tendency by the early socialist parties, and the extremely poor natural equipment of some of the leader-figures with charisma.

for helping the people by lavish patronage, or the provision of work, or the right kind of building, or who were merely lucky enough to coincide with a period of exceptional prosperity. In Lima General Odría [...] has gained the largest body of support in the *barriadas* (shanty towns) against the competition of APRA, Acción Popular and the various Marxists. Vargas and Perón were old-fashioned political officers or oligarchic bosses who transferred to a deliberately populist programme; Batista in Cuba (whose early populism tends to be forgotten because of his later tyranny) was that somewhat rarer phenomenon, an actual man of the people – a sergeant, not an officer. All these, however, were leaders who established themselves by their action as rulers, past or present, i.e. by performance and not promise. This is also true of the revolutionary father-figures like Paz Estenssoro in Bolivia or the much greater Cárdenas in Mexico, whose reputation rested on their actual achievements. Governing is clearly by far the easiest way to become a populist leader in Latin America.

Cases of leaders who made their way from opposition to power for the first time by the support of the urban masses are much rarer, and not only because of the comparative rarity of governments coming to power by the votes of the masses or by their insurrections. Jorge Eliécer Gaitán of Colombia is the clearest example, though in fact his crucial step to the power that would have been his if he had not been assassinated was to capture the leadership of the Liberal Party, which implied the presidency. This is rather easier to do with a strong but minor following than the capture of national office directly.[*] The rise of Jânio Quadros in Brazil appears to be an even clearer case, for he owed nothing to any pre-existing machine, but since he rose not simply as a champion of the poor, but also (at least in

[*] Gaitán, a Liberal by origin, formed his own National Revolutionary Leftist Union in the 1930s, but had sense enough to return to work within his old party, demonstrating in 1946 that he could lose the party any presidential election by withholding his sizeable personal vote.

São Paulo) as the standard-bearer of 'clean government' in the interests of the rich and the middle classes, he was not quite the political barefooted boy that he seemed. [...]

Equally rare is the politically most mature form of populism, the combination of a leader with a strong and permanent movement or organization once again preceding power. Examples may be sought – with varying degrees of lack of success – in the Aprista types of party, in the Chilean Frente de Acción Popular (FRAP), perhaps in the new Christian Democratic parties, but not, curiously enough, in the communist parties, whose relative lack of success may well be partly due to their systematic refusal to accept this pattern of popular politics. Their leaders, throughout Latin America, have normally been functionaries or intellectuals; and the one obvious example to the contrary, Luís Carlos Prestes, proves the rule convincingly. For this gifted man, who spontaneously moved into the role of a Latin American revolutionary people's champion through his career as an insurrectionary officer and the myth-producing adventures of the 'Prestes Column' which traversed the hinterland in the 1920s, did his best, as soon as he actually became a communist, to conform to the stereotype of the party secretary as then established in the Communist International. He nevertheless retained a substantial charisma for the limited area of the working-class movement.

We may therefore conclude in general that the experience of populism reflects the relative passivity and lack of initiative of the urban masses, much more readily mobilized by an existing and sympathetic power from above (or by a former holder of power seeking to regain it) than capable of carrying a man or movement to the top. The only clear case to the contrary is that of Colombia, where Gaitán's assassination was followed by a formidable and entirely spontaneous rising of the Bogotá poor. But the situation which developed in Colombia between 1934 and 1948 was so clearly one of potential – and not merely urban – social revolution from below that normal criteria hardly apply to it.

The immaturity of the masses is also clearly reflected in the instability of the 'movements' which grew up around many of the populist leaders, whose essential relationship with their followers was that of the orator facing the people on the *plaza*. [...] Examples of solid and permanent popular movements are not unknown: APRA is one. Yet the most striking example of a populist movement which survived the disappearance of its leader is Peronism; and this because it transformed itself into a typical labour movement organized by and based on the (Perón-sponsored) trade unions. However, the industrial development which could provide the base for such a transfer is rare in Latin America.

A further factor diminishes the explosiveness of the rural immigration in the city: the obvious superiority of city life, even in the most purulent *favela* or *barriada*, to the countryside. This is not merely a matter of statistical fact: nowhere is the gap between the average income and consumption of city dwellers and country-men wider than in Latin America. According to ECLA, the UN Economic Commission for Latin America (1964), average incomes in Caracas, for instance, are ten times as high as in rural areas, a by no means unusual figure. Nor is this advantage merely that of the industrial or regularly employed workers, in the strict sense of the word, who tend to form an aristocracy among the poor which is not without its bearing on the political attitudes of their labour movements, socialist or otherwise. It affects the bulk of the migrants. Of the immigrants into Buenos Aires one-fifth say that they have sometimes regretted their decision to migrate, but two-thirds are satisfied with it.

[...] Nevertheless, the poverty, overcrowding, insecurity, social disorganization, and the other troubles of city life are such that the vast and inchoate masses who keep pouring into them cannot but remain a potentially explosive force. [...] The governments which operate from the presidential palaces in the midst of these growing rings of misery and hate do not look

248

out upon them with any sense of comfort. There have been few urban insurrections of late, but the events in the city of Santo Domingo in May 1965 prove that the urban masses may have lost nothing of their potential power.

We can now summarize this discussion of the impact of the rural and ex-rural masses on the politics of Latin America. At first sight it has been comparatively slight, though in the cities it has produced a new electorate and new clientele for political leaders and movements – often of the populist kind – which has transformed the official political scene in many of the republics. One might go so far as to suggest that, while in the early stages of the post-1930 social changes – say from 1930 to 1950 – it may have produced a radicalization of Latin American politics, reflected in various successful and abortive revolutions and changes of regime,* in the later stages it may well have led to an apparent lowering of the social temperature. That lowering is only apparent. The explosive potential of the countryside may be diminishing, because of its rapid relative depopulation, but not its possibilities as a base for guerrilla action. The explosive potential of the cities would be diminishing only if the industrialization of the republics were capable of providing employment at the rate of migration, or if alternative employment became available. Neither is so far the case.

The countries of Latin America are, socially speaking, a broad-based, rapidly tapering pyramid, exceptionally poor at the bottom, exceptionally rich at the top, and not very much in between. [...] It is improbable that this situation provides the foundation for stable social and political systems. It is more than probable that the comparative lull in the mass politics

* The Cuban Revolution of 1933, the revival of the Mexican Revolution in the 1930s, the Bolivian Revolution (whose roots go back to the period well before 1952), the remarkable advance of Colombia towards spontaneous combustion, the rise of Acción Democrática in Venezuela, of Getúlio Vargas in Brazil and Perón in Argentina are some examples; as are the 'Socialist Republic' of 1932 and the Popular Front government of 1938 in Chile.

249

of Latin America – a lull which even the Cuban Revolution did little to disturb – will prove temporary. When it ends, the observer may fervently hope that it will produce some sort of a solution, and not one of those relapses into anarchy which have been by no means unknown in Latin American history, and of which Colombia since 1948 provides so tragic an example.

1967

Notes in the original essay have been omitted from the version that appears in this volume.

IV

REVOLUTIONS AND REVOLUTIONARIES

18

The Mexican Revolution

The revolution that began in Mexico in 1910 attracted little foreign attention outside the United States, partly because diplomatically Central America was Washington's exclusive backyard ('Poor Mexico,' its overthrown dictator had exclaimed, 'so far from God, so near to the USA'), and because initially the implications of the revolution were entirely unclear. There seemed no immediately evident distinction between this and the 114 other violent changes of government in nineteenth-century Latin America which still form the largest class of events commonly known as 'revolutions'.[1] Moreover, by the time the Mexican Revolution had emerged as a major social upheaval, the first of its kind in a Third World peasant country, it was to be overshadowed by events in Russia.

And yet the Mexican Revolution is significant, because it was directly born of the contradictions within the world of empire, and because it was the first of the great revolutions in the colonial and dependent world in which the labouring masses played a major part. For while anti-imperialist and what would later be called colonial liberation movements were indeed developing within the old and new colonial empires of

253

the metropoles, as yet they did not seem seriously to threaten imperial rule.

[...]

Where global imperialism was at its most immediately vulnerable was in the grey zone of informal rather than formal empire, or what would after the Second World War be called 'neo-colonialism'. Mexico was certainly a country both economically and politically dependent on its great neighbour, but technically it was an independent sovereign state with its own institutions and political decisions. It was a state like Persia rather than a colony like India. Moreover, economic imperialism was not unacceptable to its native ruling classes, inasmuch as it was a potential modernizing force. For throughout Latin America the landowners, merchants, entrepreneurs and intellectuals who constituted the local ruling classes and elites dreamed only of achieving that progress which would give their countries, which they knew to be backward, feeble, unrespected and on the margins of the Western civilization of which they saw themselves an integral part, the chance to fulfil their historic destiny. Progress meant Britain, France and, increasingly clearly, the USA. The ruling classes of Mexico, especially in the north where the influence of the neighbouring US economy was strong, had no objection to integrating themselves into the world market and therefore into the world of progress and science, even when despising the ungentlemanly boorishness of gringo businessmen and politicians. In fact, after the revolution it was to be the 'Sonora gang', chieftains of the economically most advanced agrarian middle class of that most northern of Mexico's states, who emerged as the decisive political group in the country. Contrariwise, the great obstacle to modernization was the vast mass of the rural population, immobile and unmovable, wholly or partly Indian or black, plunged into ignorance, tradition and superstition. There were moments when the rulers and intellectuals of Latin America, like those of Japan, despaired of their people. Under the influence of the universal racism of the bourgeois world they dreamed of a bio-logical transformation of their populations which would make them amenable to progress: by the mass immigration of people of European stock in Brazil and in the southern cone of South America, by mass interbreeding with whites in Japan.

The Mexican rulers were not particularly attracted to the mass immigration of whites, who were only too likely to be North Americans, and their fight for independence against Spain had already sought legitimation in an appeal to an inde-pendent and largely fictitious pre-Hispanic past identified with the Aztecs. Mexican modernization therefore left biological dreaming to others and concentrated directly on profit, science and progress as mediated by foreign investment and the philoso-phy of Auguste Comte. The group of so-called *científicos* devoted itself single-mindedly to these objects. Its uncontested chief and the political boss since the 1870s, i.e. for the entire period since the great forward surge of the world imperialist economy, was President Porfirio Díaz. And, indeed, the economic develop-ment of Mexico under his presidency had been impressive, not to mention the wealth which some Mexicans derived from it, especially those who were in a position to play off rival groups of European entrepreneurs (such as the British oil and construc-tional tycoon Weetman Pearson) against each other and against the steadily more dominant North Americans.

Then, as now, the stability of regimes between the Rio Grande and Panama was jeopardized by the loss of goodwill in Washington, which was militantly imperialist and took the view 'that Mexico is no longer anything but a dependency of the American economy'.[2] Díaz's attempts to keep his country independent by playing off European against North American capital made him extremely unpopular north of the border. The country was rather too big for military intervention, which the USA practised with enthusiasm at this time in smaller states of Central America, but by 1910 Washington was not in a mood to discourage well-wishers (like Standard Oil, irritated by British influence in what was already one of the major oil-producing countries) who might wish to assist Díaz's overthrow. There is no doubt that Mexican revolutionaries benefited greatly from a friendly northern border; and Díaz was all the more vulnerable because, after winning power as a military leader, he had allowed the army to atrophy, since he understandably supposed that army coups were a greater danger than popular insurrections. It was his bad luck that he found himself faced by a major armed popular revolution which his army, unlike most Latin American forces, was quite unable to crush.

That he found himself faced with a revolution was due precisely to the striking economic developments over which he had presided so successfully. The regime had favoured business-minded estate owners (*hacendados*), all the more so since the global boom and substantial railway development turned formerly inaccessible stretches of land into potential treasure-chests. The free village communities mainly in the centre and south of the country which had been preserved under Spanish royal law, and probably reinforced in the first generations of independence, were systematically stripped of their lands for a generation. They were to be the core of the agrarian revolution which found a leader and spokesman in Emiliano Zapata. As it happened, two of the areas where agrarian unrest was most intense and readily mobilized , the states of Morelos and Guerrero, were within easy riding-distance of the capital, and therefore in a position to influence national affairs.

The second area of unrest was in the North, rapidly transformed (especially after the defeat of the Apache Indians in 1885) from an Indian frontier into an economically dynamic border region living in a sort of dependent symbiosis with the neighbouring areas of the USA. It contained plenty of potential malcontents, from former communities of Indian-fighting frontiersmen, now deprived of their land, Yaqui Indians resentful of their defeat, the new and growing middle class, and the considerable number of footloose and self-confident men often owning their guns and horses, who could be found in empty ranching and mining country. Pancho Villa, bandit, rustler and eventually revolutionary general, was typical of these. There were also groups of powerful and wealthy estate owners such as the Maderos – perhaps the richest family in Mexico – who competed for control of their states with the central government or its allies among the local *hacendados*.

Many of these potentially dissident groups were in fact beneficiaries of the Porfirian era of massive foreign investments and economic growth. What turned them into dissidents, or rather what turned a commonplace political struggle over the re-election or possible retirement of President Díaz into a revolution, was probably the growing integration of the Mexican economy into the world (or rather the US) economy. As it happened the American economic slump of 1907–8 had disastrous effects on Mexico: directly in the collapse of Mexico's own markets and the financial squeeze on Mexican enterprise, indirectly in the flood of penniless Mexican labourers returning home after losing their jobs in the USA. Modern and ancient crisis coincided: cyclical slump and ruined harvests with food prices soaring beyond the range of the poor.

It was in these circumstances that an electoral campaign turned into an earthquake. Díaz, having mistakenly allowed public campaigning by the opposition, easily 'won' the elections against the chief challenger, Francisco Madero, but the defeated candidate's routine insurrection turned, to everyone's surprise, into a social and political upheaval in the northern borderlands and the rebellious peasant centre which could no longer be controlled. Díaz fell. Madero took over, soon to be assassinated. The USA looked for but failed to find among the rival generals and politicians someone who was both sufficiently pliable or corrupt and able to establish a stable regime. Zapata redistributed land to his peasant followers in the south, Villa expropriated *haciendas* in the north when it suited him to pay his revolutionary army, and claimed, as a man sprung from the poor, to be looking after his own. By 1914 nobody had the faintest idea what was going to happen in Mexico, but there could be no doubt whatever that the country was convulsed by a social revolution. The shape of post-revolutionary Mexico was not to become clear until the end of the 1930s.*

1987

Notes

1 Edwin Lieuwen, *Arms and Politics in Latin America* (1961), p. 21.
2 Friedrich Katz, *The Secret War in Mexico: Europe, the United States and the Mexican Revolution* (1981), p. 22.

* **Editor's note**. In *Age of Extremes* (1994) Eric wrote: 'President Lázaro Cárdenas (1934–40) revived this original dynamism of the early Mexican Revolution, especially in the matter of agrarian reform ... The land reform closest to the peasant ideal was probably the Mexican one of the 1930s, which gave the common land inalienably to village communities to organize as they wished (*ejidos*) and assumed peasants were engaged in subsistence agriculture' (pp. 105, 307).

19

The Cuban Revolution and Its Aftermath

After 1945, for both the opponents of revolution and the revolutionaries, the primary form of revolutionary struggle in the Third World seemed to be guerrilla warfare. A 'chronology of major guerrilla wars' compiled in the middle 1970s listed thirty-two since the end of the Second World War. All but three (the Greek civil war of the late forties, the Cyprus struggle against Britain in the 1950s and Ulster 1969–) were outside Europe and North America.[1] The list could have been easily prolonged. [...]

In the third quarter of the twentieth century all eyes were on the guerrillas. Their tactics, moreover, were strongly propagated by ideologues on the radical left, critical of Soviet policy. Mao Tse-tung (after his split with the USSR) and, after 1959, Fidel Castro, or rather his comrade, the handsome and peripatetic Che Guevara (1928–67), inspired these activists.

The 1950s were full of Third World guerrilla struggles, practically all in those colonial countries in which, for one reason or another, the former colonial powers or local settlers resisted peaceful decolonization – Malaya, Kenya (the Mau Mau movement) and Cyprus in the dissolving British Empire;

the much more serious wars in Algeria and Vietnam in the dissolving French Empire. Oddly it was a relatively small movement, untypical but successful, which put the guerrilla strategy on the world's front pages: the revolution that took over the Caribbean island of Cuba on 1 January 1959. Fidel Castro was a not uncharacteristic figure in Latin American politics: a strong and charismatic young man of good landowning family, whose politics were hazy, but who was determined to demonstrate personal bravery and to be a hero of whatever cause of freedom against tyranny presented itself at a suitable moment. Even his slogans ('Fatherland or Death' – originally 'Victory or Death' – and 'We shall be victorious') belong to an older era of liberation: admirable but lacking in precision. After an obscure period among the pistol-packing gangs of Havana University student politics, he chose rebellion against the government of General Fulgencio Batista (a familiar and tortuous figure in Cuban politics since his debut in an army coup in 1933 as the then Sergeant Batista), who had taken power again in 1952 and abrogated the Constitution.

Fidel's approach was activist: an attack on an army barracks in 1953, jail, exile, and the invasion of Cuba by a guerrilla force which, on its second attempt, established itself in the mountains of the remotest province. The ill-prepared gamble paid off. In purely military terms the challenge was modest. Che Guevara, the Argentinian doctor and highly gifted guerrilla leader, set out to conquer the rest of Cuba with 148 men, rising to 300 by the time he had virtually done so. Fidel's own guerrillas only captured their first town of 1000 inhabitants in December 1958.[2] The most that he demonstrated by 1958 – though that was much – was that an irregular force could control a large 'liberated territory' and defend it against an offensive by an admittedly demoralized army.

Fidel won because the Batista regime was fragile, lacking all real support, except that motivated by convenience and self-interest, and led by a man grown lazy by long corruption. It collapsed as soon as the opposition of all political classes from the democratic bourgeoisie to the communists united against him and the dictator's own agents, soldiers, policemen and torturers concluded that his time had run out. Fidel proved that it had run out, and, naturally enough, his forces inherited the government. A bad regime which few supported had been overthrown. The victory of the rebel army was genuinely felt by most Cubans as a moment of liberation and infinite promise, embodied in its young commander. Probably no leader in the short twentieth century, an era full of charismatic figures on balconies and before microphones, idolized by the masses, had fewer sceptical or hostile listeners than this large, bearded, unpunctual man in crinkled battle-dress who spoke for hours at a time, sharing his rather unsystematic thoughts with the attentive and unquestioning multitudes (including me). For once revolution was experienced as a collective honeymoon. Where would it lead? It had to be somewhere better.

Latin American rebels in the 1950s inevitably found themselves drawing not only on the rhetoric of their historic liberators, from Bolívar to Cuba's own José Martí, but on the anti-imperialist and social revolutionary tradition of the post-1917 left. [...] Though radical, neither Fidel nor any of his comrades were communists nor (with two exceptions) even claimed to have Marxist sympathies of any kind. In fact, the Cuban Communist Party, the only such mass party in Latin America apart from the Chilean one, was notably unsympathetic until parts of it joined him rather late in his campaign. Relations between them were distinctly frosty. The US diplomats and policy advisers constantly debated whether the movement was or was not pro-communist – if it were, the CIA, which had already overthrown a reforming government in Guatemala in 1954, knew what to do – but clearly concluded that it was not.

However, everything was moving the Fidelist movement in the direction of communism, from the general

social-revolutionary ideology of those likely to undertake armed
guerrilla insurrections to the passionate anti-communism of the
USA in the decade of Senator McCarthy, which automatically
inclined the anti-imperialist Latin rebels to look more kindly
on Marx. The global Cold War did the rest. If the new regime
antagonized the USA, which it was almost certain to do, if
only by threatening American investments, it could rely on the
almost guaranteed sympathy and support of the USA's great
antagonist. Moreover, Fidel's form of government by informal
monologues before the millions, was not a way to run even a
small country or a revolution for any length of time. Even populism needs organization. The Communist Party was the only
body on the revolutionary side which could provide him with
it. The two needed one another and converged. However, by
March 1960, well before Fidel had discovered that Cuba was to
be socialist and he himself was a communist, though very much
in his own manner, the USA had decided to treat him as such,
and the CIA was authorized to arrange for his overthrow. In
1961 they tried by an invasion of exiles at the Bay of Pigs, and
failed. A communist Cuba survived seventy miles from Key
West, isolated by the US blockade and increasingly dependent
on the USSR.

No revolution could have been better designed to appeal to
the left of the western hemisphere and the developed countries,
at the end of a decade of global conservatism; or to give the
guerrilla strategy better publicity. The Cuban Revolution had
everything: romance, heroism in the mountains, ex-student
leaders with the selfless generosity of their youth – the eldest
were barely past thirty – a jubilant people, in a tropical tourist
paradise pulsing with rumba rhythms. What is more, it could
be hailed by all left revolutionaries.

In fact, it was more likely to be hailed by the critics of Moscow,
long dissatisfied with the Soviets' priority for peaceful coexistence
between it and capitalism. Fidel's example inspired the militant
intellectuals everywhere in Latin America, a continent of ready

trigger-fingers and a taste for unselfish bravery, especially in heroic postures. After a while Cuba came to encourage continental insurrection, urged on by Guevara, the champion of pan-Latin American revolution and the creation of 'two, three, many Vietnams'. A suitable ideology was provided by a brilliant young French leftist (Régis Debray) who systematized the idea that, in a continent ripe for revolution, all that was needed was the import of small groups of armed militants into suitable mountains to form 'focuses' (*focos*) for mass liberation struggle.[3]

All over Latin America enthusiastic groups of young men launched themselves into uniformly doomed guerrilla struggles under the banner of Fidel, or Trotsky or Mao Tse-tung. Except in Central America and Colombia, where there was an old base for peasant support for armed irregulars, most such enterprises collapsed almost immediately, leaving behind the corpses of the famous – Che Guevara himself in Bolivia; the equally handsome and charismatic priest-rebel Father Camilo Torres in Colombia – and the unknown. It was a spectacularly misconceived strategy, all the more so because, given the right conditions, effective and lasting guerrilla movements in many of these countries *were* possible, as the (official communist) FARC (Armed Forces of the Colombian Revolution) has proved in Colombia since 1964, and the (Maoist) Shining Path movement (*Sendero Luminoso*) proved in Peru in the 1980s.

1994

Notes

1   Walter Laqueur, *Guerrilla: a historical and critical study* (1977), p. 442.
2   Hugh Thomas, *Cuba or the Pursuit of Freedom* (1971), pp. 997, 1020, 1024.
3   Régis Debray, *La révolution dans la révolution* (1965).

20

A Hard Man: Che Guevara

Che Guevara has become a political legend more rapidly than any other revolutionary of our generation, with the possible exception of Patrice Lumumba, and almost certainly more spontaneously than anyone else. This was evident within a few days of his death. Such an unusually speedy apotheosis will no doubt give historians and sociologists plenty to think and research about, but whatever the reasons for it, one thing is already clear: the myth of Che has only limited points of contact with the reality. Everyone agrees that he was brave, handsome, relatively young, an intellectual and revolutionary who sacrificed his life for the liberation of the oppressed. However, beyond this point opinions diverge.

The image which appears to predominate among the politically conscious young is that of Che as the exemplary rebel, rejecting both bourgeois convention, old-fashioned communist doctrine and bureaucracy, abandoning routine for the guerrilla life, ministerial office for the jungle bivouac. Long hair and beard have even allowed the hippies to claim him, surrounding him with their art-nouveau fretwork and coloured lights. One might call this the image of Che as the hero of the post-Stalinist revolutionaries and dissidents, if this new left were not a conglomerate of so many entirely distinct ideological elements. Certainly Che appeals to all its components, but perhaps with special force to that romantic, libertarian, avant-garde sector which seems to form so large a part of this movement of middle-class youth.

The Guevara image is indeed largely romantic, not to say Byronic: Camiri is the Missolonghi of the 1960s. That is why it is wrong. Che was indeed a revolutionary, but his points of reference were not Byron, the students of Berkeley or even Bolívar, but Lenin.

We cannot yet trace the course of his conversion to, or convergence with, 'bolshevism': the word is intended to label a political approach which is at the opposite pole from the libertarian. In spite of the Marxist influences he may have absorbed in the Argentine university or, more probably, in the *trotskisant* milieu of his first marriage, he did not claim to have been much of a Marxist when he joined Fidel's expedition; nor is it likely that anyone deeply involved in any communist organization, orthodox or heterodox, would at that time have thrown himself with quite such a 'spontaneous and somewhat lyrical resolve' into what looked like a very half-baked adventure. However, he seems to have been somewhat more of a Marxist than most of his comrades, perhaps because of his Guatemalan contacts and experiences, and he certainly emerged from the Sierra Maestra convinced and clear, and developed his knowledge of Marxist literature in the reading circles which he attended so diligently as Minister of Industry. His convergence with bolshevism is all the more striking, since he was plainly not impressed by the various communist organizations with whom he had come in contact, and of whose revolutionary potential he had a low opinion. Perhaps the likeliest explanation is that it was the logic of being a systematic revolutionary which led to similar conclusions in Latin America as in Tsarist Russia or China.

The convergence was both a matter of strategy – here he found himself closer to Mao than to Lenin – and of what can best be described as *style*. The classic style of bolshevism was systematically anti-romantic and anti-rhetorical: or rather, it buried the 'great feeling of love' which Che considered to be the major motivation of the (intellectual) revolutionary, beneath the 'cool brain' and the ability to 'take painful decisions without moving a muscle' of the effective militant. Its ideal was the mobile professional revolutionary ('changing countries more often than shoes' as Brecht put it), for whom revolution was a vocational skill, the readiness to give his life part of his qualifications, and the point about fighting not the exaltation of heroism, but practical efficiency at the job. A frightened man simply has no business with guerrillas. The *Reminiscences* [Che Guevara, *Reminiscences of the Cuban Revolutionary War*] waste no time on the problem of fear. Conversely it was, as he implies, a weakness of the heroic Camilo Cienfuegos that 'he did not measure danger; it was a game for him, he played with it, handled it like a toreador the bull': 'his character killed him.' The *Reminiscences* say nothing about his own suicidal bravery, a concession to unreconstructed Latin American human nature: but he regrets that he never became sufficiently meticulous in the care of his arms.

Bolshevism was a hard style, and Guevara made himself into a hard man. Rebellion was useless without discipline, organization and leadership: the cadre of the revolutionary vanguard useless unless both efficient and prepared to recognize no limits to his duty, and no material rewards for his actions. The *Reminiscences* are primarily a set of variations on the theme that enthusiasm is not enough, and that guerrillas cannot subsist without discipline (the penalty for infraction being death), practical knowledge of the job and voluntary puritanism, though they are also an admission that these conflicted with the motives which actually brought most fighters into the Rebel Army.

Revolution was thus a full-time vocation, incompatible (except at rare moments of leisure) with the graces of life. Guevara the young Baudelairian made himself into a puritan, and narrowed his interests as an intellectual down to the requirements of the struggle. Perhaps excessively and demonstratively so, just because he was an intellectual, and one with both a first-rate brain and, when he would let himself go, a style of powerful, controlled emotion. He could write the prose of a classical poet. Yet his rare and lapidary opinions about culture and the arts show not the slightest sympathy for that identification of avant-garde art and avant-garde politics which sustains so many young rebel intellectuals, or for 'liberty' as an alternative to 'socialist realism', about which he was naturally contemptuous. At most he was prepared to admit that the 'relapse into the decadentism of the 20th century ... is not an excessively serious error, but we must overcome it, on pain of opening the gate wide to revisionism'.

To sum the matter up briefly, in the eternal debate which divides the revolutionary left into orthodox and antinomian, Calvinist and Anabaptist, Jacobin and sansculotte, Marxist and Bakuninite, Che was firmly on the side of the first and against the second. This is to some extent obscured, not only by the prevailing atmosphere of the movement of young rebels and dissidents who have chosen him as one of their symbols and which is largely antinomian and libertarian, but also by the specific strategy and tactic of revolution by volunteer guerrilla action with which his name is chiefly associated. Yet this also reinforces the parallel with bolshevism. It is no doubt true that a strong dose of voluntarism is characteristic of the libertarian tradition, anxious to unshackle the individual from the fetters of historic or other pre-determination. But it is also characteristic of Jacobin-style revolutionaries, who stress the role of initiative, organization, leadership and strategic sense against the action-paralysing certainties of historic inevitability; especially when, as before 1914 and today, historic inevitability does not seem to predict the imminent collapse of the enemy. Che was as firm a believer in historical materialism as Lenin, but Lenin was also criticized as one who favoured armed coups by volunteer elites.

It would be unnecessary to stress this affiliation of Che to the classical as opposed to the romantic school of revolution, if he had not been adopted as a symbol by the romantics. It is misleading to put an unusually and quite uncharacteristically rhetorical peroration by him on the dustcover of *Reminiscences*. The general tone of his writing – and talk – was a hard-headed, systematical, even pedagogic, clarity, which made good prose because of an admirable economy combined with the fortunate absence of jargon. The *Reminiscences* are unhappily not the best introduction to his works. They are not history, but a personal record of events, designed to encourage others to put down their experiences before memory faded and the available raw material for history was dissipated. Hence they lack the close and systematic reasoning which is the strength of his more fully worked-out writings.

These modest and fragmentary memoirs have been padded out by the publisher with a number of pieces of a different kind, more or less connected with the experience of the Cuban guerrilla struggle, all undated, and not always reliably translated. It is improbable that Che would have wished to publish a book which gave an account of the Cuban guerrilla so imperfect as to be actually misleading, but this is what has now appeared. It is regrettable that the editors of this collection did not establish some sort of perspective, either in an introduction or by reprinting one of Che's own synthetic articles – for example, the admirable 'Notes for the Study of the Ideology of the Cuban Revolution'.

However, imperfect as this book is, it does provide some clues to the puzzle why so able, clear-minded, practical and un-suicidal a revolutionary should have ended the way he did. The *Reminiscences* reveal an unusually easy situation for the Cuban rebels of the late 1950s: a system on the verge of collapse, and ready to accept *any* effective alternative government. For technical reasons best discussed in Guevara's *Guerrilla Warfare*, the cities with their much stronger organizations could not overthrow rulers who retained command of army and police. On the other hand it is clear that the few hundred guerrillas by themselves – for example, the two columns of eighty and 140 men who undertook the expedition to Las Villas – could not provide a decisive military threat to a stable regime. They provided a decisive *political* threat as soon as they had established themselves as the nucleus of an alternative government, with which everyone else hastened to come to terms before it was too late. Fidel quite rightly refused to negotiate terms, and left no option but capitulation; but the old state was ready to collapse into his arms, all the more so as – wrongly – he was not recognized as a social revolutionary. Under these circumstances the strategic and tactical choice of the revolutionaries could be narrowed down to that between urban insurrection and guerrilla war, negotiation and intransigence, and the objective of the guerrillas to establish themselves as *potential* winners, and to demonstrate that no other form of opposition, armed or peaceful, could so establish itself.

It did not follow that in different and more complex political conditions (even leaving aside the determination of the United States not to allow itself to be caught again), a guerrilla force of this type would be equally successful; though it did follow that many of the lessons of Fidel's movement were generally applicable. It did not even follow that the Cuban guerrilla pattern was the only one. It is, for instance (as Régis Debray has recognized), quite different from the Vietnamese. To give an example. It is at least arguable that in a country like Bolivia, where a guerrilla force may be essential for the achievement of a second revolution, its role is still likely to be subordinate to other foci of insurrection and consequently that the insistence on equating guerrilla and political high command is mistaken there. And, as Guevara himself observed, 'the only thing history will not admit is that the analysts and executors of the policy of the proletariat make mistakes'.

Fortunately, this posthumous achievement may be to prove his own statement wrong. It is true that the gambit-theory of revolution (by which the planned sacrifice of a Pearse or Connolly is what makes possible the liberation of Ireland) is generally an ex-post-facto rationalization of defeat. Nevertheless it is not always and altogether wrong, though there is no sign in Guevara's writings that he ever subscribed to it. Guevara dead remains a political force, though of a different and lesser kind than Guevara alive. He remains both an inspiring image and model, and a revolutionary fighter and thinker whose words and actions are worth serious study: which ought to mean, even for those most in sympathy with his cause, critical study. Unfortunately, in the aftermath of his death, there is a risk that the image will obscure the reality. It would be a pity if this happened.

April 1968

21

Guerrillas in Latin America

Latin American guerrilla warfare in the 1960s and the theories associated with the names of Régis Debray and Che Guevara is a vexed question. The subject is obscure and confused, and a few notes on it may be useful. They are formulated in a rather apodictic manner for the sake of brevity. One might call them: Twelve common errors about guerrilla warfare in Latin – or more exactly South – America, for I know too little about the Central American scene to discuss it profitably.

1. That the Latin American peasantry is 'passive'.

There is quite a lot of evidence to the contrary, though this does not imply that the poor agricultural population is or was uniformly and everywhere equally activist. Geographically, there is a tradition of endemic peasant rebellion in certain Mexican areas and in a large part of the region of dense Indian settlement in the Andes, notably Peru. Apart from exceptional episodes like the rising of Tupac Amaru in the late eighteenth century, most of these rebellions and insurrections are virtually unknown, but this reflects on the historiography of the Andean lands and not on their peasants. The most recent example of generalized (but decentralized) peasant activism in Peru is the early 1960s. However, it is probably true that certain types of peasantry are unusually prone to rebellion – e.g. (as Eric Wolf rightly holds) the traditionalist 'middle peasant', neither sufficiently involved in the new capitalist market economy as a *kulak* nor too poor, weak, oppressed and socially disorganized. Permanent landless wage or plantation labourers are the basis for rural trade unions rather than peasant rebellion. Traditional communal organizations threatened from outside tend to be potentially rather activist. So do individual frontier colonists and squatters. Mobile, active, and above all armed and combative cattlemen, bandit-types, etc. are of course far from passive, though ideologically rather indeterminate. All these cases are to be found in Latin America in large numbers.

2. That the guerrilla movement of Fidel Castro was an exceptional phenomenon.

It was exceptional insofar as it (a) succeeded and (b) inaugurated a social revolution. But *qua* guerrilla movement it was one of a long line of such movements in Latin American history and, quantitatively, one of the more modest. Even if we leave aside the wild horsemen who have frequently infused local wars and revolutions with a demotic component, and social banditry (the footslogging *cangaçeiros* of north-east Brazil were classified as a peasant guerrilla by the Communist International), there are still plenty of such movements. Many of them are obscure and forgotten, others have impinged directly on modern revolutionary or world politics, e.g. the systematic guerrilla warfare of the Mexicans in the 1860s, which defeated the French, the Zapatistas of the Mexican Revolution, the Prestes Column in Brazil in the middle 1920s. [...] Guerrilla war did not begin in the Sierra Maestra.

3. That Fidel Castro's guerrilla movement is a general model for Latin American revolution in general or guerrilla warfare in particular.

Its success was and remains an inspiration for revolutionaries, but its conditions were peculiar and not readily repeatable, (a) because Cuba is in many respects unlike most other parts of Latin America, (b) because the internal and international situation which, in the late 1950s, permitted a very heroic and intelligent, but rather small and ill-prepared, guerrilla force to overthrow the Batista regime is not likely to be duplicated, more especially because (c), chiefly as a consequence of Fidel's victory, the forces which are now mobilized against Latin American guerrillas are immeasurably more effective, determined and backed by the USA than was believed necessary before 1959.

4. That the 1960s saw a major outburst of guerrilla warfare in Latin America.

In 1960 there was, leaving aside some possibly surviving Peronist guerrillas in Argentina and the special case of the armed peasants' and miners' militias in Bolivia, one major example of armed action by rural revolutionaries: the mainly CP-led 'zones of armed self-defence' in various parts of Colombia, often misnamed 'independent republics'. The 1960s saw the development of two other movements, a significant, but rather marginal one in Venezuela, which never looked like being a politically decisive force, and a much more formidable one in Guatemala, which would almost certainly have won, if the certainty of all-out US hostility had not prevented the sort of general jumping-off-the-fence which so helped Fidel Castro. These three movements are still in existence. The Colombian one (now joined by a 'Fidelist' force, the ELN, and a Maoist one, the EPL) now operates a more classical guerrilla. The Venezuelan, abandoned first by the local CP, more recently (to judge by its leader Douglas Bravo's recent complaints) also by the Cubans, is now very much more restricted. The Guatemalan one is in existence, but its prospects are obscure.*

Broadly speaking, the situation today is comparable to what it was in 1960. Various other attempts to set up guerrilla operations, as in Peru and Bolivia, not to mention a few other areas, never really got off the ground.

5. That this relative failure indicates a lack of revolutionary potential in Latin America.

This view is becoming more popular as the result of the evident failure of the Cuban Revolution to be successfully followed up elsewhere. There is little warrant for it. Apart from the cases already mentioned under (4) above, the 1960s saw, among others, the largest peasant mobilization of probably the past 150 years in Peru (1960–3), a classical and entirely successful urban popular insurrection in Santo Domingo, stopped only by massive direct US intervention, an extremely interesting, though in the end unsuccessful populist-left process of radicalization in Brazil (1960–4), stopped by a military coup, urban insurrections in Argentina (1969) and a good many other phenomena not usually associated with social and political stability. What is at issue is not the existence of revolutionary social forces on this continent, but the exact form in which they find practical expression, their means of success or that of the alternative policies designed to dissipate them or to satisfy the needs which give rise to them.

---

* For reasons of brevity and convenience I have neglected various political divisions in these movements, and used such terms as 'Fidelist' and 'Maoist' in the colloquial sense, rather than enter into the acrimonious sectarian disputes about their meaning.

6. That the failure of the guerrilla attempts indicates the impracticability of such operations in Latin America today.

The survival in Colombia of effective armed peasant action over a period of (by now) anything up to twenty years, demonstrates that this is not so. The truth is that the politically motivated dismissal of the (CP-led) Colombian guerrillas by Régis Debray (who now admits that he had no first-hand acquaintance with them)[1] has created an unduly gloomy impression of guerrilla chances. Conversely, several of the guerrilla attempts which fitted better into the Debray thesis – notably the Peruvian ones of 1965 and Che Guevara's own Bolivian adventure – were doomed before they were started by sheer amateurism – e.g. ignorance of local Indian languages or local conditions, by strategic and tactical obsolescence – e.g. the failure to be aware of the new possibilities and forces of 'counter-insurgency', by a noble but ill-advised impatience but above all by fundamental political error. They assumed that because several of the objective conditions for revolution were present, therefore pure voluntarism, the decision of a few outsiders to start it would be decisive. Consequently small, in some cases numerically quite insufficient, groups remained isolated and fell relatively easy victims to their enemies: when a guerrilla lacks the social and political 'fish-in-the-water' basis which makes it into a guerrilla, it is after all no more than an ill-equipped, under-strength and probably undertrained Ranger unit without reserves and reinforcements. It can still succeed in very exceptional cases, but probably only if conditions over which it has no control at all are unusually favourable. But the *foco* theory of guerrilla war assumed (a) that these conditions could be influenced to a greater extent than is probable and (b) that a remote chance is reasonable odds. It is not. The Sierra Maestra does not justify the numerous other attempts to duplicate it, any more than Garibaldi's invasion of Sicily in

1860, which was successful, legitimized the various, uniformly unsuccessful and demoralizing, attempts at similar adventures organized by Mazzini in the 1850s. And the critique made by loyal Mazzinians in 1858 is equally applicable to Debray and Guevara:

> In our opinion it is seriously wrong: To impose action by a few on the inert and unprepared will of the many, whenever it suits you; To believe that a rebellion, which is easy to organize, can be rapidly turned into a large-scale insurrection; To import insurrection from without, before it has been properly prepared from within; To make immediate plans only for getting into action, while leaving the success of the action to look after itself.[2]

7. That 'armed self-defence' is incompatible with guerrilla war.

'Armed self-defence' is a tactic peculiar to situations of endemic civil war (as in Colombia after 1948), to post-revolutionary situations (as in Bolivia after 1952), and to regions where state power is intermittent or remote, and has no monopoly of arms, as in many South American frontier regions. It consists in effect in the setting-up of armed militias, normally combined with a fair degree of local autonomy, by communities or political movements in particular areas, almost always to defend themselves against incursions from outside, but possibly also to intervene in national affairs. The critique of this tactic, which is made most strongly in Debray's *Revolution in the Revolution*, holds that it was used for purely defensive purposes, which is correct, and that it was militarily ineffective, which is mistaken. The 'annihilation campaign' which the Colombian army waged in 1964–5 against the main 'armed self-defence' zones – we now have a splendid account of it from the guerrillas' side[3] – transformed it into ordinary guerrilla warfare, but did not eliminate it. At the present moment (or at least at the end of 1969) armed guerrillas under the same leadership were active in the same regions, including the very area in which the armed 'self-defence' units of Marquetalia had first awaited contact with government troops in 1964.

The critique of its (originally) purely defensive character confuses several things. It may be defensive (a) because the movements organizing it are uninterested in revolution, as many leftists thought the unorthodox CPs were; (b) because the general situation in the country is not revolutionary, as the orthodox CPs themselves claimed; or (c) because the peasants, unless and until attacked, are unwilling to launch themselves into guerrilla warfare or insurrection, or do not understand the need for it. The characteristic 'armed self-defence' area is one where the peasant (or as in Bolivia, the miners') movement has already achieved substantial local successes without civil war, which it is concerned to safeguard. The political problem is therefore real, and all who have actually organized such successful (local or regional) peasant movements, whether orthodox CP as in Colombia, or Trotskyist, as Hugo Blanco in La Convención (Peru), agree that in such circumstances defensive armed organization – which may pass into guerrilla warfare in response to outside attack – is the most practicable next step. Without it guerrilla war lacks an adequate basis. In Peru, Luis de la Puente discovered this to his cost when he chose 'purely mechanically', to quote Héctor Béjar,[4] to establish his main guerrilla base in La Convención and was left to fight and die in isolation.

The major and legitimate critique of 'armed self-defence' is that any grassroots peasant movement tends to have purely local perspectives, and must therefore be subordinated to a national strategy and embodied in a national guerrilla force with wider horizons. A revolutionary guerrilla must be more than the sum of its local components. But if it cannot rest content with building on the few ready-made local bases of armed action, it cannot sweep them aside either. What the masses are prepared to understand and do is a crucial consideration for any serious revolutionary; and especially what they are prepared to do in the places where they are already armed, self-confident and ready for action, and from which almost certainly a substantial proportion of the later fighters and leaders of the national guerrilla will be drawn.

8. That modern 'counter-insurgency' and US intervention have made effective guerrilla war impossible in Latin America.

Except for the Dominican Republic there has so far been no direct intervention by the US armed forces in the 1960s, though a good deal of direct and indirect support (finance, equipment, training, 'advisers', etc.) for the local Latin American state, or more rarely for freelance, forces which have conducted the anti-guerrilla struggles. What would happen if the US intervened is therefore a hypothetical question, though Vietnam provides at least one possible answer. We must therefore leave it aside.

On the other hand modern 'counter-insurgency' techniques have been tried with considerable effect. They have made the task of guerrillas much more difficult even in the most favourable political conditions, through innovations of both technological and strategic-tactical character. The helicopter is an obvious example of the first. The strategy of systematic encirclement and the separation of guerrillas from their supply and political base (e.g. by the forced removal of the peasants to concentration camps, 'strategic hamlets', etc.) is an obvious example of the second. By such means the major advantages of the guerrillas – mobility, invisibility, the merging into the local population, etc. – have been to a great extent offset. The object of effective counter-insurgency has thus been to isolate the guerrillas within a surrounded, preferably empty, space and then to reverse the traditional procedure by systematically tracking and harrying them with their specially trained and equipped counter-guerrillas (Rangers, etc.) until their units are broken up or cornered, when modern technology can bring up overwhelming reinforcements immediately against them.

It is evident that some of the guerrillas of the 1960s played directly into the hands of such a strategy, e.g. in Peru, where de la Puente not merely concentrated all his men and supplies on a remote and supposedly impregnable mountain massif, but actually advertised his intention to use it as his permanent base. It is also probable that the *foco* theory of guerrilla war, which envisages guerrilla units which are almost by definition a group of imported foreigners without a firm initial base among the local peasantry, suits counter-insurgency very well. It is also certain that even the best-prepared Latin American guerrillas were initially surprised by the new techniques and made serious mistakes – as the Colombian ones admit.

Nevertheless, the Colombian guerrillas have succeeded in maintaining their activity, in spite of their initial errors, in spite of the severe handicap of having to arrange for the evacuation, dispersion and resettlement of a civilian population, in spite of the strength and long anti-irregular experience of the Colombian army, and in spite of the deep political divisions in the countryside, which, after one and a half decades of civil war, provided far more potential local allies for the army than the solid anti-white Indian masses of the Peruvian Andes. They have succeeded not merely by tactical and technical adjustments, but above all by a profound understanding of the political base of guerrilla war.

Counter-insurgency makes this more rather than less crucial. To take two obvious points. By making the actual life of the guerrilla physically more taxing, it puts a premium on the ability to recruit *peasants* who can stand it more easily than imported intellectuals or even urban workers. All Latin American guerrillas which have maintained themselves have been predominantly composed of peasants – the Colombian

FARC (i.e. CP) almost entirely, a Colombian ELN unit about which we have information to over 90 per cent, Bravo's FALN units in Venezuela to 75 per cent.[5] Again, the extreme hazards to which the general peasant population is now exposed make it more crucial than ever to maintain links with them and, so far as possible, to protect them. Debray's view that 'in its action and military organization [the guerrilla] is independent of the civilian population; and therefore it is not called upon to undertake the direct defence of the peasant population'[6] is a recipe for suicide. It contrasts sharply with the Colombian experience and practice, which insists not only on the fundamental importance of maintaining a civilian organization, but on the most elaborate methods for safeguarding peasant supporters. This applies both to intelligence and operations. Thus it is (by Colombian experience) crucial to identify and screen all 'outsiders' in a region, especially those recently arrived – e.g. mulateers, traders and hawkers, small shopkeepers, travelling salesmen, healers and dentists, schoolteachers and other public officials, beggars, prostitutes or other 'foreign' women, etc. It is essential to have an apparatus of counter-propaganda to offset the promises of the counter-insurgent army or even the immediate tactics of friendship (free rides for children on helicopters and the like). It is essential to 'educate the people in a party spirit' in order to avoid the irresponsible or accidental behaviour which might aid the enemy. Even known supporters must never be exposed as such, i.e. they must always be instructed to give the army the *right* information about which way the guerrillas went, show them the *correct* amount of money they paid for supplies.

The test is in practice. Both the Bolivian and the Peruvian guerrillas were liquidated in a matter of months, with little difficulty. The 1964–5 campaign against Marquetalia (Colombia), conducted by sixteen thousand troops, lasted 533 days, and led to the setting-up of a national guerrilla force (the FARC) which remains active, as we have seen, in the same region in which the peasant militia were established before 1964.

9. That Latin American revolution depends essentially on rural guerrillas.

A rather simple-minded form of Maoism assumes that the countries concerned are overwhelmingly composed of countrymen. In Latin America this is now true only of a few small republics, and the rate of urbanization will soon make even the last major peasant countries – e.g. Brazil – predominantly urban. It is therefore clear that a strategy based on the village surrounding and then capturing the town is unrealistic. Serious guerrillas, such as Douglas Bravo in Venezuela, have no doubt that revolution to be successful must combine rural guerrilla and urban insurrection, not to mention dissident sections of the armed forces. Rural guerrillas have the advantage of operating in a social and sometimes geographical milieu which favours them, but the disadvantage that they may operate among what are minority groups of the population and – perhaps more seriously – in areas remote from the places where the actual decisions about the political future of the state are taken (e.g. in the capital and other great cities), or even in areas remote from the centre of gravity of the economy. No revolutionaries who fail to develop a programme or a perspective for capturing the capital cities are to be taken very seriously, especially in Latin America, where regimes have been used to losing political, or even military, control of outlying provinces for quite long periods without being seriously affected. Indeed, it is probable that but for US hysteria about Fidel, the Colombian government would have been in no hurry to 'annihilate' the 'armed self-defence' zones, which posed no major political problem at the time.

10. That urban guerrillas can replace either rural guerrillas or urban insurrection.

Urban guerrilla actions, or what can be plausibly called by such a name, have been in some ways as widely used in the

1960s as rural guerrillas, e.g. in Venezuela, Guatemala, Brazil and Uruguay. For reasons discussed in Guevara's book on guerrilla war, *La Guerra de guerrillas* (Havana, 1960), they are not comparable to rural guerrillas in military or political potential, and must be regarded as essentially preparatory or ancillary methods of revolutionary struggle. Nobody seriously argues otherwise. In Brazil they are regarded by their champions as a preliminary to the establishment of rural guerrillas, though also as a valuable agitational and propagandist medium. In Uruguay, whose population is overwhelmingly urban, the Tupamaros, most formidable of urban guerrillas on this continent, appear to see their function as one of sharpening the atmosphere of social and political tension rather than as the actual transfer of power, but it is difficult to judge. The urban equivalent of rural guerrilla war is the insurrection, a potentially decisive weapon (at least in the capital) but one with, as it were, a single shot at a time and an unconscionably and unpredictably long period of reloading. In the provinces it is less decisive, as demonstrated in the summer of 1969 in Argentina, where the failure of Buenos Aires to follow Córdoba, Rosario, etc. saved the regime. In the 1960s there has been one successful urban insurrection, in Santo Domingo in 1965, which was spontaneous, like most successful movements of this sort which do not take place when the question of state power has already been virtually decided, and one major unsuccessful organized attempt, in Venezuela in the early 1960s, in conjunction with both urban and rural guerrillas. It is improbable that at present many Latin Americans will underrate urban guerrilla action (or indeed the urban sector), but it is useful to distinguish between such actions which have a direct political purpose and those which arise from operational necessity, e.g. the very fashionable 'expropriations' of banks, etc. which supply urban guerrillas with the means of maintaining themselves. Though good for the morale of the guerrillas, they may not necessarily gain public support. It is also wise to remember a crucial political characteristic of such urban action in non-insurrectionary periods. While the rural guerrilla rests on the *connivance* of sections of the rural population, the urban guerrilla relies on the anonymity of the big city, i.e. the possibility of acting *without* the connivance of the people.

11. That there is any single recipe for Latin American revolution.

Reacting perhaps against the alleged passivity of local Communist parties, and certainly against mechanically applied international slogans about the 'peaceful road to socialism', many of the Latin American left adopted the opposite view that *only* armed insurrection in the form of guerrilla war was called for. This view, which neglected all the complexities of the situation, was never in fact fully applied in practice, except in ideological polemics. (The use of armed action is of course accepted by everyone on a continent where even ordinary government changes have commonly been achieved by arms. Few of even the most orthodox and moderate CPs have excluded it: some, as in Venezuela, Guatemala or Colombia have temporarily or permanently maintained guerrilla forces.) As an example, the Venezuelan left never overlooked the possibility of active support from dissident elements in the armed forces, and even the notably unrealistic Peruvian left was sometimes wise enough not to antagonize the army a priori by attacking, e.g. barracks.

Revolution in Latin America is likely to be a combined operation, either in a situation of internal political crisis within the established regime or, more rarely, of such permanent institutional instability that such a crisis can be precipitated. It is likely to combine social forces – peasants, workers, the marginal urban poor, students, sectors of the middle strata – institutional and political forces, e.g. dissidents in the armed forces and the

283

Church, geographical forces, e.g. regional interests in what
are normally very divided and heterogeneous republics, etc.
Unfortunately the most effective cement of such combinations,
the struggle against the foreigner, or more especially the foreign
ruler, is rarely applicable except in the small Central American
states, where the USA is in the habit of intervening directly –
but with potentially overwhelming forces – and perhaps, alas,
by local nationalisms directed against Latin American neighbours. Latin America has been economically colonial, but its
republics have been politically sovereign states for a very long
time.

Unfortunately also the Marxist left, never a major political
force outside a relatively few countries, is probably today too
weak and divided in most republics to provide either an effective national framework of action or a politically decisive force
of leadership. Indeed the net effect of the 1960s has been, for a
variety of reasons, to weaken and fragment it more than ever,
and to make its unification or even common action extremely
difficult. This does not exclude major social changes, even revolutionary ones, but makes it likely that the lead in these will be
taken, at least initially, by other forces.

12. That revolutionary movements can operate without political organizations.

Regimes can be overthrown without organization under certain
circumstances. Lenin predicted that Tsarism would fall under
the impact of some spontaneous movement, and it did, though
he did not therefore conclude that the party had no role to
play. When a prolonged struggle is envisaged (as in the classical
theory of revolutionary guerrillas) organization is more crucial
than ever and political analysis is indispensable. This applies at
all levels. Manuel Marulanda, writing as a Colombian peasant
guerrilla commander, has no doubts that organization, discussion and education are essential for the morale of the *guerrilleros*,

if only to keep them occupied between actions. ('That's why in camp we must have a political instructor at all costs. There has to be political training, military training, cleaning of arms and general tidying up.'[7]) Hugo Blanco, the Peruvian peasant leader, discovered that the major obstacle to transforming an impressive peasant union movement into 'armed self-defence' was his inability to build an adequate organized party structure out of the series of ad hoc mass actions and mass rallies.[8] At the opposite extreme, the rather casual choice of Bolivia as the zone of battle by Guevara – earlier, neighbouring regions of Argentina appear to have been envisaged – and the decision to go ahead without support from any significant Bolivian political force, demonstrate a serious underestimate of the importance of a political analysis of the conditions of such a struggle. It is possible under certain circumstances to assume that a population forms a single, relatively homogenous, explosive mass which has merely to be aroused to provide the conditions for revolutionary war. In fact, parts of the Peruvian Indian population did provide such conditions, and flocked to support the guerrillas of Lobaton and Béjar in 1965, being subsequently decimated for their pains by the army. The revolutionaries exposed and sacrificed them needlessly, being unable – from numerical weakness, plain ignorance and inexperience as well as lack of political analysis – to take the necessary precautions, or to provide an adequate organization and cadre and leadership which might have formed an effective peasant guerrilla, strengthened by the subsequent terror of the armed forces. But if these weaknesses were evident even in the simplest of local political situations, how much more important must they be in much more complex ones which are characteristic of Latin America, a very complex continent?

1970

Notes

Some notes in the original essay have been omitted from the version that appears in this volume.

1 Régis Debray reply to Paul Sweezy and Leo Hubermann, *Monthly Review*, edizione italiana, 11, 1–2, 1969.
2 Quoted in D. Mack Smith, *Il Risorgimento Italiano* (Bari, 1968), p. 426.
3 Jacobo Arenas, *Colombie, Guerrillas du Peuple* (Paris, 1969).
4 Héctor Béjar, *Les guerrillas péruviennes de 1965* (Paris, 1969), p. 71.
5 *Avec Douglas Bravo dans les maquis vénézuéliens* (Paris, 1968), p. 54.
6 R. Debray, *La révolution dans la revolution* (Paris, 1967), p. 40.
7 Arenas, op. cit., p. 118.
8 Hugo Blanco, *El camino de nuestra revolucíon* (Lima, 1964), p. 63.

22

Latin American Guerrillas: A Survey

In the history of Latin America the years after the Cuban Revolution will go down as those of the guerrilla dream. It was an odd period, for the disproportion between dream and reality was enormous. Though the dream was powerful enough to impose its image on the whole world through the *ikon* of Che Guevara (who was to inspire rural insurrections as far afield as Ceylon), by global standards the Latin American guerrillas were certainly not the most important and probably the least successful. Moreover, even within a Latin American context there was an odd unreality about them. In a continent which has a longer history of guerrilla warfare than most other parts of the world, little attention was paid to the actual wealth of home-grown historical experience. The most successful examples of actual guerrilla war in the area (and the ones which both preceded and survived the Guevarist era) were on the whole neither admired nor imitated, e.g. the Colombian Communist Party ones. Even the lessons of the one rather special case which was regarded as paradigmatic, the Sierra Maestra, were neglected by the very people who had formulated them.

While the dream lasted, comparatively little of real interest appeared about the guerrilla movements and attempts of the period 1960–7, except for some pieces of uncritical reportage, some governmental publications and those numerous polemical and programmatic writings which belong to the ideological rather than the practical history of the revolutionary left. This was natural enough, though it is greatly to be regretted that no Latin American guerrilla movement found an analytical reporter of the calibre of Basil Davidson, whose books on the guerrillas of Guiné and Angola, whom he accompanied, are worth the whole of the literature on the Latin American movements put together. Of course Davidson had the advantage of actually having fought in genuinely significant guerrilla movements during the Second World War.

After the failure of the Latin American guerrilla movement, both inquest and serious study began to come into their own. The inquests may be divided into two classes, which are not always clearly separated: the 'what went wrong' kind and the 'why it could never have worked' kind. The former question applies to the few examples where the rural guerrilla insurrection (alone or in conjunction with other forms of action) had a serious chance, or formed part of a rational political option, as in Guatemala and Venezuela; or perhaps in that home of indestructible armed peasant bands, Colombia. In Guatemala the guerrillas would pretty certainly have succeeded in the mid-sixties, but for the deep conviction of all senior officers and politicians in small Central American republics that God is far away and US intervention with overwhelming force is only too close at hand; a conviction which the events in the Dominican Republic in 1965 only strengthened.

In Venezuela, the call to arms was undertaken as part of a considered political strategy, and it was a close-run thing. In Colombia, there was almost certainly no comparably favourable situation in the 1960s, and what has to be explained – and can be explained in terms of the local situation – is simply the success of all but the most amateurish guerrillas, whether orthodox CP, Castroite or Maoist, in maintaining themselves in being in action for years rather than months, and, in the case of the orthodox communist FARC, virtually for a generation.

Nowhere else were rural insurrections undertaken in terms of a serious political analysis or with any real prospect of success. They were at best as heroically futile (and, one may add, as full of vague rhetoric) as in the various invasions of Italy by devoted and doomed groups of young Mazzinians in the 1850s, which had much in common with the Guevarist movements. Hence, there is no mystery about why they could not have succeeded. The general reasons are brought out in Luis Mercier Vega's somewhat disjointed book (with David Weissbort), *Guerrillas in Latin America: the technique of the counter-state* (1969), one of the many disillusioned anti-Guevarist tracts produced after the débâcle of the Bolivian insurrection in 1967. In brief, they failed because they contradicted everything that is known about rural guerrilla warfare, and most of what is known about how revolutions occur. They could have succeeded only by the merest fluke. Most of the organized Marxist groups – and by no means only the orthodox CPs – were at that stage opposed to them, recognizing both the superficiality of their appeals to Marx and Lenin, and their neglect of politics. Guevarism, as Mercier Vega points out, appealed primarily to middle-class intellectuals and (as he does not bring out so clearly) to young officers. It is a curious and not insignificant fact that some of the most militant guerrillas (Turcios Lima and Yon Sosa in Guatemala, Carlos Lamarca in Brazil) transferred from counter-insurgency to insurgency.

To analyse the reasons for failure is less difficult than to establish what actually happened. The most ambitious attempt to do so remains that of Richard Gott in *Guerrilla Movements in Latin America* (London, 1969). This book is still perhaps too close to its subject, both because the author sympathizes passionately with the Guevarists and because his was a pioneer

289

effort to collect the material and to put it into shape. Even so, it remains the basic narrative work in English, though inferior in analysis to *Diez Años de Insurrección en Améica Latina*, 2 vols (Santiago de Chile, 1971), a collection of studies edited by Vania Bambirra. Gott's work is no longer up-to-date about international policy (that is, the attitudes of Cuba, USSR, China, etc. to these movements), about the countries where guerrillas continue to be active, and about the literature published recently. It is silent about the urban guerrilla movement. Perhaps it might have contained some reference to the curious home-grown guerrillas in the lawless Mexican state of Guerrero, where, as the saying goes, economic prosperity means that men buy a new gun before they buy a radio. Genaro Vásquez (killed in 1972), a local schoolmaster, was already active in 1968, and a movement persists.[1] Still, the book is indispensable.

More interesting than the generally gloomy narrative history of the rural movements are the monographs about individual guerrillas which are increasingly emerging from within the movement, for these actually tell us something of real value not only about the technicalities of partisan fighting, but about the relations between the guerrilla and the rural population. Peru has produced some valuable works, notably Héctor Béjar's *Péru, 1965: Una Experiencia Libertadora en América* (Mexico, 1969), which is both sensitive and realistic.[2] Hugo Blanco's book *Land or Death: The Peasant Struggle in Peru* (New York, 1972) illustrated the failure of a mass peasant movement to develop effectively beyond a rudimentary form of armed self-defence – the basis of the Colombian guerrillas, so lightly dismissed by Debray – due, in his view, to the weakness of organization. Anything written by Blanco, a very able man, who has direct experience of what peasant movements in remote Latin American areas really are, must be read with attention. The most copious and interesting literature has, however, emerged from Colombia. The most valuable publications here are Germán Guzmán, *La Violencia en Colombia* (Cali, 1968) and Jacobo Arenas, *Colombie, Guerillas du Peuple* (Paris, 1969), which contains remarkable interviews with Manuel Marulanda, the peasant commander of the FARC (misdescribed by Robert Moss in *Urban Guerrillas*, London, 1972, as a 'notorious rural bandit').

With the collapse of the rural guerrilla phase, armed revolutionary action has increasingly shifted to the cities. The phrase 'urban guerrilla' for these movements can be misleading, for they rely not on the support or complicity of the population, as any viable rural guerrilla must, but on its opposite, the anonymity of the big towns. Operationally, they can therefore be self-sufficient, since all they need for supplies is money, normally obtained by 'expropriation' or ransom. Moreover, the classic Maoist or Vietnamese progression from partisan force to army, which eventually surrounds and captures the city, is here excluded. A clear distinction must therefore be drawn between urban guerrillas analogous to rural ones (e.g. the armed groups in the Catholic and Protestant areas of Ulster) and those who are, almost by definition, sealed off from the urban masses. Their political perspectives (insofar as they do not degenerate into an ideological cops-and-robbers conflict which is its own reward, or more likely penalty) therefore pose serious problems. The Brazilian ones – a reaction to defeat of the larger movement in 1964 – envisaged the eventual creation of a rural guerrilla, which never got off the ground. The Argentinian and Uruguayan ones, less tempted by the rural dream, appear to envisage a radicalization of the masses, in the general context of persistent economic and political crisis, both through politically dramatic and popular coups and the provocation of counter-repression which alienates the population. In Uruguay it is also likely that there was (is?) the perspective of provoking armed intervention from Argentina or Brazil, which would then form the basis of a wider people's war of liberation.

The weakness of these perspectives lies in an underestimation of the reserve powers of government, once it decides to mobilise itself fully against the armed groups, abandoning parliamentary and legal constraints. As events in Uruguay have shown, even the most powerful, deeply entrenched and politically sensible urban guerrilla is more vulnerable to this than at one time looked likely. Their strength lies in the endemic instability and economic crisis in which the armed groups of the River Plate lands operate. These, rather than the technicalities of urban guerrilla action and organization, are the basis of revolutionary hopes. It should be added that the armed groups of the 'southern cone', though sometimes (e.g. the Tupamaros) directly inspired by the Guevarist dream, have been realistic enough to recognize that they must operate in an environment of organized politics, and do not – at least in practice – seek to bypass or replace parties and the organized labour movement. They are therefore likely to have serious political significance, as indeed the Tupamaros have already shown. Whether they will be the main beneficiaries of the political changes they may have helped to precipitate is another question.

Robert Moss in *Urban Guerrillas* surveys the entire phenomenon from a hostile point of view. Much of what he says is sensible, though his observations about the rural guerrilla movements of the 1960s do not inspire the least confidence in his information. At any rate we may agree with him that mere military repression, however brutal and effective, as in Guatemala or Brazil, does not remove the bases of revolutionary agitation, where these exist, and also that, as in both these countries, the right-wing backlash may get out of control. There is, indeed, no serious doubt that in Brazil the urban movement of 1968–71 failed, and is unlikely to revive in anything like the same form. João Quartim's *Dictatorship and Armed Struggle in Brazil* (London, 1971) virtually admits this, though his insistence that 'armed struggle in Brazil is not the adventure of a handful of radicals' blurs the reasons for the failure. The bulk of the book consists of a concise and useful discussion of Brazilian developments between 1964 and 1969 from a left-wing point of view, though the reasons for the crucial failure of the early 1960s are not adequately discussed.*

Robert Moss admits that the Uruguayan Tupamaros are by far the most successful urban guerrilla movement up to the present, and the only one with serious political chances. Their success has led to a rash of journalistic publications, which have value chiefly as documents illustrating (generally from a favourable point of view) the technical mode of procedure in Tupamaro operations, and the attitude of Uruguayans towards them. They also make available various Tupamaro documents and statements. This is all that can be expected, since the success of the movement has been due largely to the rigidly maintained secrecy of its organization and to a discretion rare in Latin America. Maria Esther Gilio's *The Tupamaros* (London, 1972) is friendly reportage, *Nous les Tupamaros* (Paris, 1972) a Tupamaro-sponsored collection of operational reports, of considerable technical interest.[3]

It is presented by the ubiquitous Régis Debray, who obviously knows much more about the actual development of the movement from its beginnings in 1962 than Robert Moss, or than he is prepared (quite properly) to tell. M. Debray's long afterword lacks the brio, the self-confidence and the (alas, totally unrealistic) lucidity which made his *Revolution in the Revolution* so effective and disastrous as a manifesto of Guevarism. His attempts to prove that the Tupamaros have applied the Guevarist model need not detain us; the interesting thing about them is what they have changed, not what they have retained of their original ideas. His thesis that 'dual power' exists in Uruguay ('*sans métaphore ni hyperbole ni tromperie*') is wrong. It is difficult to believe that his account of the political democracy of the movement is realistic under conditions of deep clandestinity and repression though it is possible that, during the

---

* Ruy Mauro Marini's chapter in Vania Bambirra (ed.), *Diez Años de Insurrección* is outstandingly intelligent on this question.

period of virtual invulnerability and repression, this relatively small elite movement operating in a single city (Montevideo) might have organized congresses (but surely at some risk to security?). Much of what he discovers in the Tupamaros has been known to old-fashioned communists since at least 1917, but it is welcome that he is now prepared to recognize the value of 'the paradoxical fusion of a "mass line" and clandestine armed action' which is what makes the Tupamaros so effective. One doubts whether Lenin would have found the combination paradoxical.

By and large, the recent spate of writings on Latin American guerrillas remains journalistic and provisional. Its major value lies in the accumulation of historical raw material, and especially of first-hand participant descriptions of rural guerrilla experiences, which must be distinguished from propagandist interviews, open or disguised polemics by guerrilla leaders, etc.[4] That is why Richard Gott's book and a handful of brief memoirs from Colombia and Peru are likely to have the highest survival value. About the Tupamaros and similar movements, only interim reports can or ought to be written at present, on the basis of inadequate and selective information. As for the movements of the Guevarist period, a satisfactory analytical history has yet to be written. It probably will not be written for some time.

The existing literature provides plenty of material for political arguments and doubtless for compilations and recommendations for counter-insurgency purposes.[5] If anyone still requires proof, it demonstrates that the crucial factor in Latin American revolutions is not the readiness of groups of brave men and women to start armed actions, rural or urban, or even their technical competence, but the socio-economic and political situation in which it is conducted. As an ex-*guerrillero* from Colombia once put it to me: 'In this country anyone can start an armed band among peasants. The problem is what happens afterwards.' Nevertheless, this demonstration should not discourage revolutionaries. For, if the past ten years suggest that, in purely technical terms, the forces of government should be able to eliminate, control or side-track practically any irregular armed force, they also suggest that these governments have rarely even looked like being able to create the conditions of long-term economic, social, political and institutional stability. Revolutions are not, as Debray and Guevara thought, around the corner. But neither are they beyond the range of realistic policies: even, as the Tupamaros have shown, in what once used to be called the 'Switzerland of Latin America'.

1973

Notes

1 See Orlando Ortiz, *Genaro Vásquez* (Mexico, 1972).
2 Sara Beatriz Guardia, *Procesco a Campesinos de la Guerrilla 'Túpac Amaru'* (Lima, 1972), reprints the court proceedings against a number of peasants and rank-and-file militants in a 1969 trial. The record is tragic and illuminating.
3 See also Alain Labrousse, *Les Tupamaros* (Paris, 1972).
4 There are plenty of these. They sometimes contain incidental information of interest. Among those that have come to my notice are: *Avec Douglas Bravo dans les maquis vénézuéliens* (Paris, 1968); Ricardo Ramírez, *Autobiografia di una guerriglia, Guatemala, 1960–68* (Milan, 1969); Mario Menéndez, *Intervista con Fabio Vasquez, Capo Esercito de Liberazione Nazionale di Colombia* (Milan, 1968); Robinson Rojas, *Colombia, Surge el Primer Vietnam en la América Latina* (Montevideo, 1971) and numerous publications of the 1960s from Havana.
5 For a sample of these, see Jay Mallin (ed.), *Terror and Urban Guerrillas: A Study of Tactics and Documents* (Coral Gables, 1972).

23

US Imperialism and Revolution in Latin America

No empire in the twentieth century has been more power-ful and apparently unchallengeable than that of the US in Latin America, and no imperialists have pitched their claims higher – though for various reasons most North Americans have persistently disliked being labelled as such. The British long ago recognized the fragility, and eventual imperma-nence, of their Indian empire, the French the uncertainty of their African one. Both were only too well aware that, where the relationship with their dependents happened to be informal and economic, it called for a considerable degree of political flexibility. Only the US has not merely taken its per-manent supremacy south of the Rio Grande and Key West for a fact of nature, but formulated it in terms which exclude the slightest abrogation.

As Jerome Levinson and Juan de Onís point out in their lucid and valuable book, *The Alliance That Lost Its Way* (1970), the US security interest in Latin America, as traditionally con-ceived, consists of three propositions:

1. (dating from the Monroe doctrine in the early nineteenth century): The United States must keep potentially hostile extra-continental powers out of the hemisphere in order to deny them a geographically convenient basis from which to attack.

2. (dating from the days of Elihu Root in the early twentieth century): The United States, having become a capital surplus nation, must seek outlets for this surplus, generally abroad and particularly in Latin America. [...]

3. (dating from the onset of the Cold War in the late 1940s): The political apostasy of a Latin American country would cause the United States to lose face, weaken its influence in other parts of the world and undermine the confidence of important European countries in the ability of the United States to lead the 'free world' struggle against the monolithic communist bloc.

The dating, the rationale and the formulation of these propositions are open to challenge, but not their essential content, which implies that the US can not only keep any power out of the hemisphere but also prevent any Latin American government from doing anything Washington disapproves of. Both these assumptions rest on the overwhelming economic and politico-military domination of the hemisphere. The second predates the century. The first became a reality when US capital and enterprise replaced the British as the dominant factor in this part of the world, and has been steadily reinforced ever since. Everywhere else the US recognizes rivals, though perhaps weaker ones. In Latin America it does not, because none exists or is even visible.

Probably only Latin Americans are fully conscious of the effects of this assumption that the US is supreme, and they inferior, though it sometimes penetrates into the historical record.

'They don't think like us,' Thomas Mann, LBJ's State Department man on Latin America, is reported as saying. 'Their thought processes are different. You have to be firm with them.' Doubtless this public servant thought he was merely stating 'the obvious', just as his well-known support for US business in Latin America merely reflects the normal attitude of his countrymen. It looks different south of the Rio Grande.

However, what is perhaps even more significant and galling than both the persistent assumption that the US knows better and its persistent subordination of Latin interests to its own is the assumption that Latin America is not even worth bothering about, outside the occasional moments of panic that punctuate long periods of neglect. What makes this even more insulting to Latin Americans is the sense that these moments of panic are due less to their own actions than to the possible reactions of more important states about which the US government is really worried, and to the effect upon its situation in other parts of the globe, where the US is more vulnerable. The prestige of Cuba, Fidel Castro and Che Guevara surely owes much to their being Latin Americans of whom big brother really had to take notice.

The history of US 'aid' vividly illustrates this assumption that the US back yard can normally be left unattended. Two excellent books enable us to survey US policy in this area for the past forty years: David Green's study of the rise and fall of Roosevelt's 'Good Neighbor' policy, *The Containment of Latin America* (1971) and Levinson and de Onís's analysis of the Alliance for Progress (referred to above). Both record the constant tendency to subordinate Latin affairs to the wider interests of the US. During the 1930s and the war years the stimulus to action was Fascism. 'At the beginning of the thirties,' wrote the State Department political adviser Laurence Duggan, 'the United States government was doing even less than private organizations; it was doing nothing at all. By the end of the thirties it was white hot with enthusiasm, born of fear of the Nazis. And therein lay the weakness of its new policy.' In 1941 an allegedly

German-linked plot was discovered in Bolivia. Within a matter of weeks a military mission had been sent and a $25 million aid programme announced. The war also made the US willing to settle the dispute over the Mexican nationalization of oil, which had been dragging on since 1937. The war, claims Green, bailed out the faltering New Dealers, providing them with the argument that economic development in Latin America was essential to 'hemispheric defense' against the Nazis.

On the other hand, it became increasingly clear that where Latin development failed to contribute to the US war economy (i.e. did not serve the direct mobilization of the raw materials which the US had to acquire in the hemisphere), it was sacrificed, except insofar as the US used the opportunity to freeze out European – and especially British – business and to make the continent entirely dependent on the US market. The fact that most of us would at the time have agreed with Roosevelt's scale of global priorities, and would probably still do so, should not obscure the resentment of Latins, who did not feel themselves to be threatened by Germany and Japan, and who were in any case not asked. The only country which retained some freedom of manoeuvre, Argentina, took a very different view of its economic and political interests at the time.

The German danger was short-lived, and in any case the US claim to global empire, though anticipated by Henry Luce in 1941, was not yet formally established. Hence the 'Alliance for Progress' period demonstrates the subordination of the continent to Washington's world policy even more clearly. The Alliance was a response to Fidel Castro, the first Cuban statesman within living memory to resist the habitual economic blackmail from the north. Guevara, at the Punta del Este conference of 1961, pushed the US into committing itself to hard figures. Fidel got it to resign itself to the signature of the International Coffee Agreement of 1960, to halt the price slide of this commodity which put the governments of Brazil, Colombia and various Central American republics at risk.

Conversely, the Soviet retreat in the missile crisis of 1962 immediately made social reform, adventurous planning and the subordination of individual business interests to national interests less urgent. In the words of Levinson and Onís, 'the United States stopped feeling that it was one minute to midnight in Latin America'. From 1964 the businessmen were back in force, from 1965 Vietnam took priority. 'Take it out of the Alliance,' said the administrator of AID when asked by the Bureau of Budget where cuts should be made. By 1968 his view was that Latin America had always had more funds than it could effectively use. The truth is that, as an official joked in the early years of the Alliance:

> We all know that there are only three categories of loans in the Alliance for Progress: very high priority, hysterical, and if-you-don't-make-this-loan-the-communists-will-take-over-the-country.

After the initial shock of Castro had been absorbed, it never looked as though the communists would take over any country.

This is no doubt the reason why the sheer amount of US aid to Latin America remained relatively modest in monetary terms and very small in real ones. As the director of AID's Office of Programming and Planning pointed out in 1967, before 1960 the net flow of official funds there was less than half the per-capita level for other regions. The Alliance brought it almost – but not quite – up to this average, but in the view of Levinson and Onís this is 'a much smaller percentage of development expenditures than in other areas ... Since more than half of foreign long-term lending is offset by amortization of past loans, the net resource contribution of foreign capital to Latin America has been relatively small.' The Alliance has at best staved off economic disaster rather than stimulated economic development.

The US attitude to Latin America has therefore normally been based on the belief that, without the intervention of global factors, US power is virtually absolute, and Latin American forces alone are feeble to the point of being negligible. Yet a more careful analysis of hemispheric relations, and occasional bitter experience, suggest the opposite. US power is limited, and any attempt to exceed these limits leads to defeat or failure. To be more accurate, while the power of the US economy is overwhelming and remains decisive, its political (and military) power is not. Moreover, even the immense force of US capital is to some extent at the mercy of political forces which Washington cannot override.

Both the record of the 'Good Neighbor' policy and that of the Alliance for Progress demonstrate these limitations, the latter more dramatically than the former, because US political megalomania was so much greater in the era of JFK than in that of FDR. There is indeed, in spite of David Green's argument to the contrary, a sharp difference in *tone* between the two periods, although there is some continuity of personnel and ideology. We may grant that in both the US put its interests first, saw Latin development in the light of its own advantage, economic and political, and opposed 'militant revolutionary economic nationalism'. Yet there is a substantial difference between the New Frontiersmen of the 1960s and the New Dealers of the 1930s.

It is illustrated above all by Mexico. This was a test case, since the revival of revolutionary and anti-imperialist dynamism in that country under Cardenas coincided with the New Deal and, through the nationalization of the oil companies, came into flat conflict with American capital. The US might well have wielded the big stick, as it had done in 1933 over Cuba, and was to do again (with disappointing results) over Argentina, admittedly moved by the fear of Nazi victory. (Mr Green suggests that the anti-fascist arguments were not seriously held, but his material suggests otherwise.)

In fact, Washington handled the Mexican situation, by and large, with tact and a marked absence of hysteria. It is hard to avoid the impression that influential New Dealers, headed by FDR himself, felt that, whatever the dangers to the US position, they could hardly blame Latins for demanding for themselves what the New Deal was demanding for North Americans. The oil companies, wrote the US ambassador from Mexico to FDR, 'are as much against fair wages here as the economic royalists at home are against progressive legislation'. The President himself was to say, in tones which no doubt grated on Latin ears, but express a genuine, if paternalistic, goodwill: 'Give them a share. They think they are just as good as we are, and many of them are.'

The Kennedy policy was a reaction to an immediate threat, a supplement to military intervention. The 'Good Neighbor' policy (about whose actual origins Mr Green is uncommunicative) was not born of a comparable political threat, and its object was to liquidate and replace military intervention. In fact this is what it did. Consequently Roosevelt's policy was also less vulnerable to the political changes of the decade, to which, with the exceptions already noted, it was relatively indifferent. (The US government was not, of course, significantly worried about communism, partly because, as another ambassador wrote from Mexico in 1943, the US had 'such a tremendous advantage in many respects over Russia', partly perhaps because after 1935 local communist parties were not notably anti-North American.)

The failure of the 'Good Neighbor' was economic. What Latin development took place owed little to US action, except insofar as the wartime starvation of the market encouraged local industrialization to substitute home-produced goods for imports, while the accumulating dollar balances of the Latins, which had originally looked chiefly like 'a three billion dollar non-interest-bearing war loan', proved to be extremely useful to Latin countries after the war. The numerous plans to increase the capacity of the Latin market to absorb US goods by industrialization, raising local incomes, etc. did not get very far. From the US point of view the major consequence of the Roosevelt period was to eliminate other imperialisms from the hemisphere.

Thanks to the admirable clarity and lack of doubletalk of Levinson and Onís, the balance sheet of that 'decade of maximum effort' which JFK announced in 1961 – i.e. of the greatest concentration of Washington's forces on Latin affairs in history – can now be drawn up. During this period the US tried to provide a solution for the economic and social problems of Latin America, and failed. The results of the Alliance range from the modest and spotty to total failure. Thus there has been 'an actual slow-down in job openings during the Alliance period; only about 60 per cent of job-seekers gained employment during the 1960s compared with 62.5 per cent during the 1950s'. Substantial industrialization has provided no significant new jobs. Even if we include the jobs generated by the bureaucracy, that well-known system of relief works for the unemployed educated strata in underdeveloped countries, the rate of employment in this sector has increased only from 23.5 per cent to 24.8 per cent of the total. It may be noted that, as 'the US corporate system includes more than a million local employees of US-owned companies and a huge structure of subcontractors, distributors and service-agents', or 20 per cent of all Latin American industrial workers, direct North American responsibility in this area is not negligible. The annual take-out is between 12 and 15 per cent of investments which amount to 12 per cent of all Latin export earnings. To put it in one sentence, Latin America is today further from providing a living for the mass of its citizens than it was before the Alliance.

The US also tried to provide a framework of political and institutional stability for the hemisphere. The ideologues of empire, i.e. the Americans for Democratic Action-New Frontier liberals, put their money, socially speaking, on those 'middle classes' which were, as in old-fashioned history books, always rising, and, politically speaking, on a supposed 'democratic non-communist left'. Its firmest pillars were presumed to be Rómulo Betancourt in Venezuela, the Peruvian APRA, and for good measure José Figueres in little Costa Rica; supplemented, since 1964, by Frei's Christian Democrats in Chile.

The less ideological imperialists were in theory (according to the 'Mann doctrine' of the LBJ era) content with anyone who would foster economic growth, protect US private investments and oppose communism, irrespective of their attitude to social reform. In fact, they tended to put their money on something like a coalition of hard-nosed technocrats, preferably deflationary, with the military, which would assure political stability for their operations. Brazil and Argentina, with their respective generals' regimes, were the models for this school of thought. The new pragmatism comforted itself with the belief that economic stability and growth would solve the social problems automatically, while a military paid for, trained and inspired by the US must be in some metaphysical sense 'constitutional', if not actually democratic.

Both failed. All that is left today as an effective political force of the 'democratic left' – we hear much less about the rising liberal middle classes – is Venezuela, whose vast oil revenues make certain kinds of reform uniquely practicable. We need not here discuss how democratic or left that country is. As for the 'democratic military', the pragmatic imperialists might have survived the discovery that the 'constitutional' Brazilian generals introduced systematic torture on a scale which even the Nixon administration could not entirely overlook, and did not introduce even a token agrarian reform. They found it much harder to survive the Peruvian demonstration that not even the local military is politically 'reliable' any more. To put it briefly, as summed up by Levinson and Onís, 'Entering office in January 1969, the Nixon administration found a small heap of discredited approaches to the dilemmas of Latin American development.' It has continued to look for a policy, but it has hardly as yet found one.

Levinson and Onís seem tempted to argue – though they never quite commit themselves to this thesis – that these failures were avoidable. To what extent were they due to errors, miscalculation, a refusal to concentrate the US effort consistently on the Latin task, the temptation to grab short-term advantages, to give in to business pressure, to the power mania of the military, etc.? It is easy enough to give examples of all these, and sometimes they are indeed flagrant, as in the case of Peru. What would have happened if the US had not virtually withheld aid from that country between 1962 and 1968 – it received only $74.5 million, as compared with $500 million for Chile, $450 million for Colombia – in order to force the Peruvians to settle with Standard Oil over the La Brea-Pariñas oil dispute and to buy American instead of French jet planes? If – as the authors do not stress – the old ADA mafia had not maintained its fondness for that political non-starter, Haya de la Torre's APRA, and rooted as strongly for Belaúnde?

Levinson and Onís have no doubt that US policy thus helped to bring the generals to power on a straight national-reforming platform. Perhaps so. But quite apart from the fact that all the alleged US errors and miscalculations are systematic, tending in one direction, the question remains whether US policy was capable of achieving the results it wanted even in the best case. Experience suggests that it was not. Chile, which received almost ten times as much aid per capita as Peru, and (under Frei) enjoyed almost unlimited goodwill in Washington, is today governed by the Popular Front of President Allende. The fact is that, as Levinson and Onís themselves recognize, what happens in Latin America is something 'that the United States may influence in minor ways but cannot begin to dominate or direct':

Unquestionably the readjustment process will affect the United States in both its political relationships and its property holdings in Latin America. These effects are inevitable, in part simply because the United States has such ties to a region undergoing basic change, and in part because Latin American societies, deeply divided in so many ways, often find a degree of unity – real or spurious – in aggressive nationalism. [...] The lesson that the Alliance has taught in this critical area is that the United States must learn to live with and expect change, and that its response should be flexible and measured, rather than excessively rigid and tough.

It is a lesson of failure and defeat, and the visible commitment of the writers of this passage to the primacy of US interests makes their admission particularly impressive.

On the other hand, the continued and growing economic influence of the US in Latin America deprives that admission of some of its bitterness. For the truth is that, while US *policy* has failed in a fairly spectacular manner, the US economic hold has been strengthened. In the 1960s Latin America 'ranked second only to Canada as a market for the United States', and after the brief post-Castro panic, private investment resumed its southward flow to the point where a 'shift in investment emphasis from Canada and Western Europe to Latin America' can be noted.

It is unwise to suppose that empire is unattractive or insignificant to American corporate enterprise. Indeed the results of US investment have been more helpful to the US than to Latin America. Between 1961 and 1968 $3.3 billion was invested and reinvested there, while $7.1 billion flowed northward in profits and earnings, and during the same period the share of world trade held by Latin American exports declined from 7.5 per cent to 5.6 per cent. Whatever the political developments, it is extremely improbable that relations with the US will not remain the dominant economic factor for most Latin countries. Still, it is increasingly evident that US capital will be subject to strict political controls and limitations. It will be able to do plenty, but not whatever it wants.

If it is now clear that the US cannot impose its own ideas of the future on Latin America, even if it knew how to set about it, where the continent is actually going is by no means obvious. Its tendencies of development have been further obscured by writers of the radical left, who have indulged in their own versions of political maximalism, a sort of mirror image of Washington's own. Hence the unjustified despondency of a good deal of their writing. Paradoxically, both right and left look back on the 1960s without pleasure.

This criticism is applicable even to so good a book as James Petras's collection of studies on *Politics and Social Structure in Latin America* (1970). It provides convenient, concise and informed surveys of a variety of important topics, such as class and politics, the middle class, guerrilla movements and revolutionary movements, based on a wide acquaintance with the area and the literature, and first-hand research, especially in Chile, which is dealt with in greater detail in the author's *Politics and Social Forces in Chilean Development* (1969). Yet the tone, though not unhopeful, seems unduly negative. The impression a reading of this book creates is that 'a new political equilibrium' has been established in the area, and that, but for a possible 'new urban and rural insurgency', the 'delicate bargaining arrangements which have prevented some of the larger Latin American countries from experiencing thoroughgoing social and political change' are likely to continue in operation.

There seem to be two reasons for this note of disenchantment. The radical left has tended to dismiss any change other than those visibly bringing closer some more Cuban-type revolutions, and (at least until the election of Allende in Chile) any political tactic other than armed insurgency. (This does not imply agreement with any specific recipe for insurgency, such

as that of Régis Debray, which Petras demolishes fairly con-
clusively.) But the Cuban Revolution remains isolated, and is
clearly – in spite of marvellous achievements – struggling with
great domestic problems. The tactic of armed insurgency has,
on the whole, failed.

In *Down There* (1970) José Yglesias, who has looked for the
revolutionary left in Brazil, Peru and (pre-Allende) Chile,
records its bravery, determination and devotion, but also –
unwillingly – its isolation and lack of effectiveness at the time
of his journey. The most he can claim, quite correctly, is that
revolutionary activity and sentiments are alive, in spite of setbacks, and that Cuba remains an inspiration for the Latin left,
for reasons which his interesting chapter, 'Cuba Under Twenty-
Five', helps us to understand. Insofar as the left is exclusively
committed to a maximum programme, anything less than this
must be failure.

However, the disappointment of the left is also due to what
may prove to be a methodological error. It has looked for a
guaranteed revolutionary force, one that cannot be corrupted,
assimilated or absorbed into a going non-revolutionary system,
and it has done so by running through the list of the various
classes and other social or institutional groups, eliminating
those that do not qualify: i.e. all. Petras thus dismisses the peasantry, the industrial working class (a favoured minority stratum
easily turned into reformist ways), and the middle classes, business and bureaucratic. They are, as he is not the first to point
out, not a 'national bourgeoisie', for they oppose neither the
agrarian oligarchy, which they seek to join, nor US imperialism, to which they look for protection against social revolution
and for jobs in the dependencies of the US corporations. They
are by no means committed to economic development and
'modernization'. Of course this still leaves discontented groups,
but it is to be feared that these may also prove to be disappointing, since none of them can be regarded as consistently
revolutionary.

But in actual politics (which are not those of the macro-analysis of social change conducted on a very high level of generality, as by Marx), no class is permanently and under all circumstances 'revolutionary' in this sense. To look for such a one is to write pessimistic conclusions into one's premises. The important question is not about particular groups or institutions within a society, but about historic situations. Are they, to take the broad view, potentially revolutionary, as were those of, say, Eastern Europe at the end of the nineteenth century, or are they not, as those in Western Europe were not at the same period? If they are not, then the forces of revolution, however powerful, self-conscious and organized, are likely (unless fleeting occasions are seized successfully) to be absorbed into a going non-revolutionary system in some form, if only as institutionalized outgroups; or diverted from their course. Even revolts may then *de facto* resemble those 'rituals of rebellion' of the anthropologists, though this does not imply that the situation of basic stability must remain permanent. If they are revolutionary, the opposite tends to be the case.

Most of Western Europe since the 1840s has been non-revolutionary in this sense. The capitalist mechanism of growth functioned, though it had from time to time to be modified substantially, and therefore suffered not merely the short-term fluctuations built into it, but periods of major adjustment. At one point (1929–33) it actually looked briefly as though it was breaking down. The social and institutional framework was firm and stable enough to survive even the huge shocks to which it was periodically exposed, such as the world wars. Consequently the history of the revolutionary left has been one of persistent disappointment (as it saw the mass parties of Marx and later those of Lenin turning into reformist or abstentionist movements in practice), of self-delusion, or of a desperate search for some type of realistic strategy opening or preserving revolutionary possibilities in non-revolutionary situations.

There have been moments of hope, as after the October

Revolution and at the peak of the armed anti-fascist resistance, which actually produced the nearest thing Western Europe has known to revolution since 1848. There may be hope again, as capitalism enters a new phase of structural change, of which the outcome is difficult to foresee. But even in 1971 it requires a considerable suspension of disbelief to see communism on the immediate agenda in, say, Italy.

On the other hand, the situation in regions like Latin America is potentially revolutionary, because even fairly dynamic 'underdevelopment' has visibly not provided a mechanism for solving the continent's economic and social problems. These are, on the contrary, becoming somewhat more acute, as an analysis of the nature of 'underdevelopment' would lead us to suppose. Its social structures, strained and changing, have not so far found a general mould or pattern comparable to those of the 'developed' capitalist countries. Its political structures and institutions are labile, sensitive to such relatively slight stimuli as a run of boom years or a price slump in the international commodity markets.

In such regions, as in earthquake zones, the ground may collapse almost anywhere. It is pointless to look for guaranteed forces of 'stability' or 'revolution'. Everyone is aware that all existing solutions are provisional. Everyone is convinced of the inevitability of fundamental changes, most people of their necessity, though not always of their desirability. What is more, all possible solutions imply anti-imperialism, since the nature of the problems of the underdeveloped world derives from its relations to the developed world, in this instance overwhelmingly the US. None of them suggests that simple 'modernization', i.e. trying to become like the developed economies of the West, with their assistance, is an adequate, or even in most cases a feasible, programme.

Under these conditions, aside from the diminishing forces of genuinely traditionalist conservatism, revolutionary change may emerge from the least likely quarters. The Peruvian military, whose original ideological equipment seems to have been drawn from a mixture of pre-conciliar Catholicism and the counter-insurgency policies developed by French officers in the course of the Indochinese and Algerian wars, have emerged as reformers with a programme a great deal more acceptable to Fidel Castro and Allende than to Washington. An old-fashioned electoral popular front, of the kind that certainly produced no major changes in France in the 1930s, and is passionately rejected by young European leftists today as the high road to co-option, appears to release revolutionary developments in Chile; as it once did in Spain, another country with revolutionary conditions. The Latin Church itself, long notorious for its almost medieval conservatism, now breeds not only active revolutionaries in some quantity, but sections of its hierarchy and organization intervene actively in favour of fundamental change in several countries. If it comes to that, nobody would have predicted or indeed did predict in 1958 that Fidel Castro himself would turn into a Marxist–Leninist.

Such developments may not satisfy revolutionary Marxists, especially if, as is plainly the case in Peru, the reforming governments are suspicious of mass mobilization and strongly opposed to 'communism', at least at home. But, quite apart from the fact that the character of social and political changes cannot be judged by the badges which its leaders pin to their lapels (least of all in Latin America), major transformations cannot be dismissed as insignificant because they do not immediately bring about the movements and politics we favour. Nor can they be rejected simply because it is not quite certain whether one political force rather than another will finally benefit from them.

Such uncertainty is the occupational risk of politics. If the October Revolution had not occurred – and Lenin knew perfectly well that it was not 'inevitable' – the Bolsheviks might today be blamed by revolutionary critics for having agreed to support their enemy Kerensky against the insurrection of General

Kornilov in September 1917. Admittedly the risk of this alliance benefiting the tottering Kerensky government by that time was small; the prospect of its strengthening the Bolsheviks, who already held the initiative, was substantial. But the Marxist left in Latin America has never been in a position to place its bets on the favourite. In all but one or two countries its forces and mass support have been relatively insignificant, and it has rarely, even in revolutionary situations, been able to establish initiative, let alone hegemony, as an organized movement.

It has therefore generally been forced to choose between keeping itself pure and not very effective, and joining major political movements in which it did not take the lead, and whose shape it could only incompletely determine. Whether, during the past half-century, it made the best of its chances, is an interesting question, by now an academic one. That it was, and is, rarely in a position to call the shots cannot be in serious doubt.

The Marxist left in Latin America therefore is obliged to make the best of unfavourable and unpredictable situations. Its consolation is negative, but substantial. Latin America today is not, foreseeably, like Western Europe after 1848. It has not found its way. It remains a revolutionary continent.

Its future cannot be confidently predicted. That it should take the form of a series of copies of stable Western capitalisms is in the highest degree unlikely. That it will take the form of a multiplication of Marxist or communist regimes on the Russian, Chinese, Cuban, Vietnamese, or any other model is also improbable; but then this was never a perspective that looked very serious. Nobody knows where between these two possibilities the combination of mass discontent and militancy, anti-imperialism, nationalist movements for reform and development, and a Marxist intelligentsia will lead. To assume that it cannot lead to any position that might be satisfactory to the radical left is to push scepticism to excessive length. On the other hand, it is of course equally illegitimate to assume that it will or must.

In fact, the 1960s, which brought the US more setbacks than the 1950s, hardly authorize such scepticism. Naturally, it is unwise to judge Latin American developments by a particular moment of the fluctuating politics of this part of the world. [...] But even if we accept that the balance sheet in 1981 may look rather different, we cannot deny that in 1971 it indicates a radicalization of the hemisphere. Most of its republics have not shifted much, politically, apart from minor substitutions of unrepresentative generals for unrepresentative civilians or the other way round. One major country has certainly shifted to the right (Brazil), but several (Cuba, Chile, Peru, Bolivia) have veered to the left; in most cases further to the left than ever before in their history. Observers in Washington are aware of this. The left might take more notice of their sense of failure than it has.

The lesson that the 1960s taught the US government in Latin America (as they did more dramatically in Vietnam) is that there are severe limits to the power of even the biggest, richest and most mega-tonned imperial ruler. This should have been obvious, but one can understand how, in the intoxication of world power, it got to be temporarily overlooked. The lesson that this decade ought to have taught the left is even more obvious, and should never have required learning. It is that in potentially revolutionary conditions there is more than one way forward; fortunately, because the decade also demonstrated that revolutions cannot be made at will.

But the price of education has been high. It has been bought at the cost of the lives of many brave men and women, and of the fission and consequent weakening of the organized forces of the left in most of the hemisphere. Unfortunately it is by no means certain that the full price has yet been paid. The prospects facing the left in the 1970s are encouraging. Will it be in a better position to seize its opportunities than it was ten years ago? Nobody knows.

March 1971

V

MILITARY
REVOLUTIONARIES
IN PERU

24

Generals as Revolutionaries

In 1965 the Peruvian army razed a number of villages, and massacred a substantial number of peasants who had supported the guerrillas because they promised land reform. Nobody quite knows how many, since statistics in the Peruvian hinterland are, to put it mildly, approximate; but the country is not one in which peasant lives have been of much account. Nobody was surprised. But then, this summer – to be precise on 24 June [1969] – the military government which took over Peru late in 1968 suddenly announced what appeared to be the most radical land reform in Latin America after Fidel Castro's.

The news naturally startled most people concerned with Latin American affairs. Not that programmes of agrarian reform are rare. There is probably no government in Latin America which has not affirmed its theoretical devotion to them. Just as everybody in mid-nineteenth-century Europe, including landlords, knew that what remained of serfdom was doomed, so the rural oligarchies which still dominate so much of the Americas have few defenders in theory, and know that their very considerable political power can only postpone the end.

But it has been quite unusual for *military* governments to
initiate even phoney land reforms, or indeed for any Latin
American government to initiate any such reforms except as
part of a revolution, or under the immediate pressure of acute
agrarian unrest or some kind of left-wing mass movement. In
Peru there has been no great pressure from below since the
mass rebellion of the peasants subsided after its peak in 1963
and the revolutionary left in politics is negligible off the various
university campuses.

Yet there can be no doubt that the present reform is meant
seriously. It began with the expropriation of nine giant *haciendas*
in the fertile oases of the coast; in other words, most of Peru's
sugar production. The reform is just due to reach the highlands,
where the bulk of Peruvian peasants live. In some regions it is
not due to start until 1972 or 1973, because of the absence of
adequate maps, or because of particularly intractable problems
such as the fragmentation of petty peasant holdings – the worst
headache of any land reform anywhere.

However, it is to be complete in all parts of the country by
1976 (or five years after the start of the scheme). The land is to
be owned by small or middle peasants, by co-operatives or, of
course, communally by the upwards of two thousand (mostly
Indian) 'communities'.

These are very far-reaching changes – sufficiently serious to
have been welcomed by Fidel Castro himself. But what actually
happens in such a situation? Who carries out the reform? How
is it carried out? What do the people most directly affected
think and do about it? A few weeks ago I was in Peru and I
thought I would find out in the region of Chiclayo, about four
hundred miles to the north of Lima.

Agrarian reform in this part means the four giant sugar
estates of Tumán, Pomalca, Pucalá and Cayaltí, the largest of
which has a gross acreage of about 160,000, owned by native
or Peruvianized families. These huge estates have practically nothing in common with peasant agriculture. They are

extremely advanced, mechanized and efficient agro-industrial enterprises, each employing between 2100 and 3300 regular wage-workers, not counting up to a thousand seasonal labourers hired temporarily through contractors. (Nobody counts these. Their number tends to be persistently underestimated by people on the estate, and they are so far unaffected by the reform.) The closest parallel is with old-fashioned isolated mines running their own company towns, though the attitude of the estate owners to their *hacienda* combined the characteristics of the nineteenth-century industrialist and the feudal landed magnate.

The estates ranged from the total, if benevolent, paternalism of Tumán, the most efficient and prosperous, and the one with easily the best conditions, to the militant tropical squalor of Cayaltí, a sort of hot rural Rhondda, held together by the age-old hostility of a militant and all-pervasive union to an inefficient and intransigent management.

The estates provide wages, subsidized housing, subsidized food, shops, markets, cinemas and schools, and are the effective universe of most of their inhabitants.

So far very little has changed materially in that universe. Tumán has had a wage rise. Cayaltí has got back some of the men about whose redundancy it fought the last strike of its embattled history as a private enterprise. (The authorities don't like to think about the fairly general over-staffing produced by the combination of continuous mechanization and militant union resistance.)

There are new 'administrators', carefully trying both to destroy the old image of a feudal hierarchy and to keep their technologists and managers happy. Cayaltí demanded – and got – the dismissal of some technical people, 'because their presence constitutes a reminder of the old regime', but the Pomalca administrator congratulates himself on the fact that the owners used to manage their own *hacienda*, thus diverting the hostility of the people away from their engineers.

There have been democratic gestures – repainting and renaming the company's streets; repainting of the company houses; and a lot of speeches, discussions, elections of the committees which will organize the estates into co-operatives, with the help of the only grassroots organization concerned with the human side of the reform, the Office for Developing Co-operatives.

The Office was founded for much more modest objects, and filled with devoted, overworked and underqualified urban intellectuals doing their best. The managers know about the unions, and congratulate themselves cautiously on the fact that the anti-government APRA party seems to have lost them. But nobody knows what to make of the future co-operatives or the apparatus for organizing them, least of all the future co-operators, whose long and inconclusive meeting I attended in Cayaltí. They aren't yet *there*, like that 'community' of peasant squatters who immediately reoccupied the land they had 'invaded' ten years ago in Talambo, down the coast, who have their delegates on the *hacienda*'s 'special committee' and who are handled with great caution, not to say fear, by the authorities. In fact, everybody is playing it by ear, which is probably the way it is in the early stages of all revolutions.

But is this a revolution? Yes – insofar as it is sudden, virtually unplanned and potentially very far-reaching, at least for the rural society. No – inasmuch as it has been imposed from above on a (so far) passive population by generals who certainly don't want any uncontrolled, or probably any, mobilization of the masses. What has got through to the people of the *haciendas* is that there is soon going to be dramatic change for the better 'when the co-operative comes'.

They are sure that something really big will happen soon. There is immense faith in the government. This is so even in Tumán, where the old people were, and are, firmly behind the old master. The gap between hope and prospective reality is very wide.

There is a great readiness to make demands: vague and utopian in Tumán, where the disappearance of paternalism has simply left an aggregate of poor and ignorant men and women; precise in Cayaltí and the other places where the union has long given people a voice, a mind and a sense of being a community. The visiting sociologists with their questionnaires shake their heads, because when workers are asked their opinion, they say, 'Ask the union.' But a knowledgeable man who has spent fourteen years on industrial relations in the sugar and rice *haciendas* takes a different view. 'In Lima they think Tumán will be the prize exhibit as a co-operative. I don't think so. You can't run that kind of operation without the participation of the people, and in Tumán they have no experience of acting for themselves. They have always been like children.'

Where would the co-operative work best? 'In Pomalca. They have an active union, and sense enough to see that a majority of the organizing committee for the co-op are workers – even one woman. Not just white-collar and staff, like in the other estates. Wait six months and see.'

I don't know whether he's right, and it does not really matter to anyone outside Peru whether he is. But the fundamental point is valid, and it applies everywhere. Great social changes can't simply be imposed from the top. The people for whom they are undertaken must make them their own.

An agrarian or any other reform that is to work must be a political and not only a technical and administrative operation. The Peruvian government generals are not the only ones who still have to learn this fundamental lesson.

November 1969

321

25

What's New in Peru

During the 1960s writing about Latin America was one of the growth industries of literature. The immediate stimulus for this growth was Fidel Castro, who transformed the traditional *gringo* view of what a Latin American revolution was supposed to be, and with it also the conventional European view that what happened south of the Rio Grande was politically negligible to the rest of the world. Latin America ceased to be an object of history and became a subject. As it did not immediately erupt into general social revolution, and no longer posed significant problems of constitutional decolonization – most of it has long been politically independent though economically colonial – there has recently been a tendency to assume that it was all a false alarm. John Mander calls his new book *The Unrevolutionary Society: The power of Latin American conservatism in a changing world* (1969). Carlos A. Astiz concludes his study *Pressure Groups and Power Elites in Peruvian Politics* (1969) with the statement that

. . . the present distribution of power in Peru shows a remarkable tendency to remain essentially as it is and has been for a long time ... Neither revolution from above nor revolution from below seems to be around the corner.

A view he does not modify in a hurried postscript about the present military junta.

Such are the pitfalls of writing history on the journalist's (or the diplomat's, the visiting expert's, the intelligence officer's, the social science Ph.D.'s) time scale. Matters that determine the future of a continent do not oscillate at the same rate as our changing short-term hopes, fears and political assessments. Whatever may actually happen in Latin America, a number of facts about it are undeniable. Most of it is changing with great rapidity. More especially, its rates of population growth and urbanization are higher than those of any comparable area of the world. Unless something unexpected occurs, its rate of economic growth is lower, or at least no higher, than that of its population growth. Compared to the developed countries it is for the most part becoming relatively poorer and more backward, though probably in this respect its lag is somewhat less dramatic than that of other parts of the Third World. Finally, its political superstructures remain notoriously unstable. All this does not look like the setting for a scenario of unchanging conservative stability.

[...]

But ought we to talk about 'Latin America' as such anyway? Historically, of course, it makes a good deal of sense, allowing for the obvious limits of wide generalizations; more sense than talking about 'Europe'. [...] The continent was, after all, with the exception of Brazil, colonized by a single power for three centuries, and linguistically, culturally, and in religion and some other institutions, unified as no region of the same size had ever been before. Thereafter Latin America became (including Brazil) the economic colony of another single power – Britain – for another century, and has since been in a similar relationship to yet another, the US. To this day pan-Latin Americanism, based on this common past and reinforced within the Spanish area by common language, is a stronger ideological force in this area than similar beliefs anywhere else, except among the 'Arabs'. [. . .]

On the other hand it may be time to give Latin America as a unit a temporary rest, except for purposes of global economic analysis. Politically independent Latin America never was a unit nor did it even look like becoming one. Apart from the common fact of 'underdevelopment', which affects different parts of it in widely varying ways, the unity which Latin America has and had is one imposed from outside. At present it is, for the Latins, the common fear of and dislike for the domination of the US, and conversely, for the US, the habit of considering all these republics collectively as its imperial back yard. The rest of the world is where even a world power negotiates, draws lines of demarcation, compromises, or even fights local wars, because there are other interests to be considered. Latin America is where nobody else has any political or military business and the US merely 'intervenes', when not scaring outsiders off by the threat of nuclear war. As every politician between California and Patagonia knows, God, Russia and China (not to mention Britain, France, Germany and Japan) are far away. Only the US is near.

[. . .]

Nevertheless, common victimization does not exhaust the characteristics of a continent and a half. Fortunately there are signs that, for a variety of reasons, general discussions of Latin America are being increasingly supplemented by books on particular Latin American countries. It happens to be a convenient accident that several of the volumes under review deal with Peru, though all of them were written before the coup of 1968, which has, to everyone's surprise, placed that country in the centre of political interest.

In many respects Peru is a classic example of informal empire (or in modern terms, neo-colonialism), that is to say, of the symbiosis of local exploitation and foreign capital. The local exploitation, since the 1920s, has come from the 'oligarchy', a combination of coastal estate operators, *compradors*, and other racketeers involved in international business, grafted upon an older stock of quasi-feudal landowners such as still maintain themselves in power in the highlands, and hence assimilated to the social and political status of landed patricians. The foreign capital is now predominantly North American. Politically and economically the country divides into a relatively modernized coastal strip and the vast Indian hinterland of the mountains, with their *haciendas*, serfs, *comunidades*, mines, poverty and backwardness.

Alone among Latin American ruling classes the Peruvian oligarchy retained its passionate attachment to free trade and no government interference in economic matters, which expressed not only its acute reluctance to pay taxes but its conviction that the domination of foreign capital was a fact of nature, like the Humboldt current. (Even the early and revolutionary APRA party planned to replace the older quasi-feudalism by a modernized state capitalism *through* and not *against* American investment.) In no country has it been more pointless to seek for a 'national bourgeoisie', or even a significant sector of native manufactures. The foreigners bought Peru's primary products, built and ran the installations for their operation. The foreigners increasingly exploited the domestic market for manufactured goods. In return a few hundred Creole families received the large incomes which they traditionally spent in Paris, and the right to oppress their Indians any way they liked or, if on the coast, to run the country any way they liked. A rather larger middle stratum on the coastal strip received their more modest slices of pork out of the barrel.

The results of more than a century of this collaboration were until recently unimpressive, though they managed to keep central Lima largely intact as a colonial capital, until it was systematically destroyed in the property boom of the 1960s. It produced a few spectacular mountain railroads, monuments to Victorian British engineering, a number of extremely efficient cotton and sugar estates on coastal oases, a relatively modest percentage of the world output of some metals, a lot of fishmeal, and for its size and population the most backward country in Latin America. Except for a few mines, the foreigners took no serious interest in the Indian highlands, which contained two-thirds of the population, but even the coastal population was no great advertisement for the benefits of economic development through foreign investment. Peru was a country whose social injustice and plain misery made the blood run cold. If ever a country needed, and needs, a revolution, it was this. But none seemed likely.

Indignation, contempt for the Peruvian ruling class, and pessimism have shaped the book of Carlos Astiz, an intelligent Argentinian. Like other observers, he is equally struck by the country's vast potentialities, the modesty of its achievements, its dependence on the US, and the apparent impossibility of achieving any major political change. Where is it to come from? From the feeble middle strata, content to ape the foreigners and the oligarchs on whom they depend, not least for jobs in the swelling civil and military bureaucracy which, as in all underdeveloped countries, exists to provide jobs for them? From the favoured minority of organized plantation and industrial workers, who can bargain within the system? From the APRA, long a part of the political racket and sold to the US? From the weak, isolated and increasingly fissiparous revolutionary left?

Yet his pessimism is patently mistaken, for since 1968 there have been dramatic changes which this book would not have allowed us to predict or even to expect. They are no doubt, so far, changes of *style* rather than of substance. It is too early to hail the achievements, as distinct from the intentions, of the agrarian reform, though also (sceptics should be reminded) too early to write off the anti-imperialism of the generals. Still, there have been some startling changes. Who would have expected any Peruvian administration to provoke a confrontation with the US, even if its purpose was only to make a better bargain? (Carlos Astiz, for instance, has been unable to discover a *single* issue of foreign policy in the twentieth century on which Lima disagreed with Washington.) Who would have expected the Peruvian army to expropriate the sugar estates, not only of Grace and Gildemeister, but of the great oligarchic families themselves? In Peruvian politics the takeover of Hacienda Tumán was as extraordinary a step as the nationalization of the Schenectady works of General Electric would be in US politics. Who would have expected a Peruvian government to hand over newspapers to co-operatives and seriously to consider, as this one is doing, giving votes to illiterates?

The new factor in Peru's politics is not simply the conversion of army leaders to anti-imperialist nationalism and *desarrollismo*, for this is no longer uncommon among Latin American officers, a middle-class group which is today far from the old stereotypes of the aristocrat or the roughneck aspirant *caudillo*. It is the emergence of the forgotten majority of Peruvians – the Indian peasantry, at home or in emigration – into politics. Their actual role in national life was potentially always decisive, though in practice it was generally negligible. The weak point of the regime always lay in the instability of its domination over the sullen, powerless, unreconciled Indian masses, whose frequent rebellions are virtually unrecorded by historians. Like Tsarist Russia, oligarchic Peru lived on a volcano. Only the lack of leaders, and the localization, brevity and political irrelevance of the peasant revolts, kept it secure.

Conversely, the left knew the importance of the Indians, though it failed to mobilize them effectively. The first major shift in the Peruvian colonial economy – the victory of the coastal, American-oriented sector over the highland, quasi-feudal and British-oriented sector under Augusto B. Leguía (1919–30) – produced the first appearance of the masses as a serious factor in Peruvian politics. It was sufficient to stimulate two unique phenomena in Latin America: the home-grown (though Italian-influenced) Marxism of José Maria Mariategui, the most original socialist thinker of the continent, and the first genuine left-wing mass party, Haya de la Torre's APRA. But neither APRA nor Mariategui's much smaller Communist Party succeeded in breaking into the highland Indian masses, though the CP established a few bridgeheads in the south (especially in that bastion of Indian tradition, Cuzco) which were to be the bases of a later and wider peasant movement. The Indians remained outside the nation, outside citizenship – people not merely forgotten, but politically almost invisible.

The social earthquakes of the 1950s and 1960s have provided a firmer basis for their political mobilization. For the first time in history the highland society was breaking up, as demonstrated most vividly by the mass migration of Indians to the coastal cities. In Lima the number of inhabitants living in the shantytowns increased, between 1956 and 1961, from *c*.120,000 (10 per cent) to *c*.400,000 (26 per cent). The crucial phenomenon of this period was the mass insurrection of the highland peasants, mainly through a series of decentralized 'invasions of land', which began at the end of the 1950s and reached their peak in 1963–4. At this stage something like 300,000 peasants in all but one of the highland departments were involved in it.

Less dramatic, but politically no less significant, was the emergence of the *cholos*, an Indian petty-bourgeoisie distinct from the traditional ruling class of *mestizos* and the rare whites, which for the first time provided a cadre of political leaders (or political bosses) for the local peasantry. Edward Dew's *Politics in the Altiplano: The dynamics of change in rural Peru* (1969) is a remarkably interesting study of the rise of this stratum in the much researched department of Puno, and especially of the career of the Caceres brothers, whose Frente Sindical Campesino swept the municipal elections in most provinces of this department. Mr Dew's book has no high ambitions, but he has been lucky to observe the grassroots politics of an important region of dense Indian settlement at the moment of social awakening, and we can benefit from his observation.

With the emergence of the Indians into political visibility in the 1960s, the parameters of Peruvian politics changed. For the first time the rumblings of the social volcano had to be taken seriously: it had shown that it could erupt. At the same time, the possibility of bypassing the political system now existed, and with it the possibility of hauling Peru out of its state of backward dependence, an aim with which all except the oligarchy sympathized. The Belaúnde regime (1962–8) failed, largely because it allowed itself to be paralysed by a system of which it was a part. The army, which had installed it, eventually took over. There was nobody else to do so.

Unlike the Brazilian generals' coup of 1964, the Peruvian takeover was not the response to an immediate revolutionary danger, real or imagined. The army was certainly not afraid of the APRA, that thinnest of paper tigers, which so often threatened to win elections and invariably yielded to the army veto. It was not frightened by the revolutionary left, which had demonstrated its impotence outside the universities. In 1958–64 the left had been unable to do more than detonate peasant movements, which it had not the resources to control, and in 1965 it had utterly failed to launch an effective rural guerrilla movement, as Héctor Béjar's little book *Peru 1965. Notes on a guerrilla experience* (1970) tragically demonstrates. Mr Béjar, the leader of a small guerrilla movement which took part in the abortive risings of 1965, has had the leisure while in jail (where he still is) to reflect on the failure of the 1965 experience, and to provide an invaluable account of his own group's unhappy experiences in one region of the Andes. His book is a precious addition to the still exiguous literature about the concrete guerrilla experiences of his continent in the 1960s, though we need to remind ourselves (preferably by publishing an English translation of Jacobo Arenas's recent *Colombie, Guerrillas du Peuple*, Paris, 1969) that not all such movements have been as amateurish or unsuccessful as the Peruvian ones.

The Peruvian generals were and are afraid of a social revolution which might one day be led by the left, for – as Béjar also shows – the potential peasant support for insurrection was substantial. But they had and have time to cut the ground from under such a revolution by agrarian reform, which, as every Peruvian intellectual since Mariategui and Haya de la Torre knows, would also destroy the political power of the oligarchy.

The generals came to power at a time of political calm. They still enjoy this tranquillity, perhaps fortunately for their political cohesion, less fortunately for their prospects. Even progressive generals tend to be happier if the civilians keep quiet, but progressive generals may well be saved from reactionary ones by the readiness of the civilians to come out on the streets on their behalf. Only very recently have the workers of the great American mining corporation of Cerro de Pasco begun to mobilize en masse with consequences which cannot yet be foreseen.

What are the generals trying to do? One of them has explained their aims in *Le Monde* (20 February 1970):

We discovered the deeper reasons for the guerrilla insurrection of 1965: poverty, the scandalous exploitation of the masses, the social injustice of archaic structures ... Communism is no solution for Peru. So our objective is clear: we must fight against foreign dependence, which is at the root of underdevelopment. This implies that we must confront the foreign interests, mainly North American, which do not bother about Peru's interests. This again implies that we must fight against the local oligarchy, which is closely linked with the foreigners.

In other words, their negative aim is to avoid a social explosion by well-timed reform, and more immediately and superficially, to break up their old antagonist, the APRA; their positive aim, to develop the country's resources by a planned state capitalism, acquiring foreign aid on more favourable terms, and for purposes more directly useful to the Peruvian economy than in the past.

Whether they or anyone else have a clear idea of how to achieve these aims is another question. Politically they have played a strong hand well inside Peru, a weak hand carefully in international relations. At home, since there is no effective opposition or alternative, their main problem is how far they can go without mobilizing their potential mass support, which they have so far not attempted to do either by building up any leader's charisma (which might cause trouble among his colleagues) or by organizing any mass movement or party (which might create enemies by creating friends). Internationally, they are extremely vulnerable to US pressure, e.g. the withdrawal of the sugar quota, all the more so as they are naturally reluctant to face economic disruption. But they probably would face it, if pressed too far, and the threat to move sharply to the left is their major diplomatic asset.

The US does not want big trouble in a country remote from the area of quick and cheap military interventions, especially as plenty of Latin Americans are already looking to Lima for the demonstration effect of militant anti-imperialism, including influential officers in various countries, whose political views look no more incendiary today than the Peruvians' did three years ago. Who can forget where Castro and Nasser went when pushed too hard? Hence Washington and the junta are both cautious. They are playing for time. Both would be happy to find a formula which avoided conflict.

Is such a formula possible? In theory it is. The US is prepared to write off the present oligarchy and the backward agrarian system of the highlands. The Peruvian generals are patently in favour of North American investment and technical development, on terms which, as the Cuajone copper deal shows, are not unacceptable to US investors. Nobody will plan to send in the marines just because *any* American property is taken over, especially as sending the marines is not so easy. If the Kennedy policy (which failed) was to encourage anticommunist but 'economically realistic' democratic reformers such as APRA-type leaders and Christian Democrats, why should not the Nixon policy be to encourage reforming military governments, which is at any rate better for publicity than backing the Brazilian torturers?

The prospect may be acceptable to Washington. The trouble about it is that it offers no immediate answers to the economic, social and political problems of Peruvian backwardness, which are unusually acute. It offers time, which is valuable to a regime which is still (and inevitably) improvising and feeling its way. It offers agrarian reform (or rather the break-up of the large highland *haciendas*, the transfer of ownership of the agro-industrial plantations on the coast), but this in itself, however welcome, is not an adequate solution to the problems of Indian Peru.

The agrarian problem is no longer the only significant problem of the country, nor can it be isolated nowadays from the other problems of Peruvian society with which it is intertwined. For these the formula would merely offer yet another, updated, version of the theory that somehow imperialism can be the first stage of a national capitalism in an underdeveloped country. The history of Peru does not encourage confidence in this theory. It suggests rather that the combination of economic liberalism and foreign dependence must be broken, if relative underdevelopment is not to be perpetually regenerated.

Peruvian reformers, in and out of uniform, know this perfectly well. US interests and Peruvian interests do not coincide. However tactfully the confrontation is conducted on both sides – and if the generals carry out their programme, it is likely to generate an internal dynamic which will get in the way of mutual politeness – it will have to be a confrontation. If it is not, President Velasco and his colleagues will fail to achieve what they have set out to achieve. And Peru will still need and cry out for that social revolution, peaceful or violent, which is long overdue.

May 1970

26

Peru: The Peculiar 'Revolution'

I

While the Marxist government of Chile is cautious about what it has so far achieved, if not about its intentions, the military government of Peru has no doubt about what it is doing. It is making the Peruvian Revolution. The Peruvian government will not settle for less and resents any suggestion that it is just reformist. When on a recent visit I asked a group of officers from the COAP – the government's brain trust – how much further they hoped to push the process of change, the answer was: until every aspect of the nation has been fundamentally transformed.

Insofar as revolutions can be defined as transformations in the economic, social and institutional structure, a case can be made for this view. The generals have already changed Peru more profoundly than, say, the Nazis changed Germany or Perón Argentina. (These parallels are not supposed to suggest any similarity between these regimes; on the contrary, they throw doubt on the facile predictions that the Peruvian generals are 'moving in the direction of fascism', whatever that may mean.) On the other hand, insofar as revolutions are movements of masses, the Peruvian process clearly does not belong with them. It is not even a 'revolution from above' like Stalin's collectivization or Mao's Cultural Revolution. It involves no mass mobilization of popular forces by the government, no struggle against mass resistance or entrenched adversaries. The masses are simply outside the transformation that has taken place.

The Peruvian military regime has, for most of its three years in power, operated in a political vacuum. Representing an organized consortium of officers whose exact nature is obscure, but which clearly represented the armed forces, the regime took power in October 1968, without fuss or trouble, because there was no one else, and to the relief of the population. The reformist administration of Fernando Belaúnde Terry, whom the army had put into power in 1962–3 and would have preferred to support, had rapidly subsided into impotence and ineffectiveness. The major political party, Haya de la Torre's APRA, was no alternative, even had the armed forces not been feuding with it for many years. It was also bankrupt, a fact now recognized even by the Kennedy-type US liberals who supported it for so long.[1] The Marxist or Castroite left was negligible as a revolutionary force, as the guerrilla insurrection of 1965 proved, and relatively unimportant even as a minority working-class pressure group.

Changes had to be made, and since there was literally no other willing or capable force, the generals took over. They abolished parliament, elections and the superstructure of party politics, though not the parties themselves. Few Peruvians regret the passing of a system that was largely regarded as differing from military government mainly in being notoriously more corrupt. Political opposition simply faded away and barely exists as a serious factor. The APRA has retired to its usual position of semi-submerged *attentisme*, waiting for better times, confident – like the old German Social Democratic Party which it somewhat resembles – that it will retain plenty of loyal supporters, but in the meanwhile doing nothing and incapable of doing much.

The sects of the ultra-left remain politically negligible though perhaps a shade less inclined to be at one another's throats than before. The (Muscovite) Communist Party is the only political organization that maintains a serious independent presence, thanks largely to its influence in the Peruvian General Confederation of Workers (CGTP), not to be confused with the possibly declining Confederation of Peruvian Workers (CTP) of APRA. But the CP supports the generals and would in any case be incapable of providing a realistic alternative. In fact, so long as the armed forces remain united, there is no foreseeable prospect of the military regime being replaced.

This helps to explain one of the most unexpected characteristics of a military government that is itself very surprising: the unusual degree of civil liberties it maintains. The generals appear to be genuinely attached to these and proud of their liberalism. Not only have far fewer people been killed or jailed so far than in civilian Peru, but the present situation compares favourably with most other governments in Latin America. It would be too much to expect a perfectly clean record. There are a few old and new political prisoners, an exile or two, and though there is no censorship, the non-government press, though less tongue-tied than in, say, Mexico, undoubtedly picks its way with great care, except for the picture magazine *Carretas* which combines girls, fashions, and fairly uninhibited political commentary.

Any talk about Peru in 1971 being a repressive state is nonsense. Of course it may become so at any moment. There is nothing to prevent it. Indeed, some general or other may be arguing even now that the country could still maintain its liberal reputation even if a few more troublesome union men or ultra-left activists were put behind bars for a while. But so far the record is astoundingly good.

But if there is no opposition, there is no real support either. The generals have been joined by some civilians from the old parties, by numerous cadres from smaller groups like the Social Progressives, by a handful of left-wing intellectuals including, as is almost inevitable, ex-Trotskyites evolving yet another theoretical position, and by one of the leaders of the 1965 guerrillas, Héctor Béjar. On the whole, however, the Marxist left remains in opposition, with the major exception of the CP whose combination of critical support and organizational independence does not make it welcome to the government. The less sectarian student activists who poured into some agrarian reform organizations two years ago have tended to drift away in disillusion. The politically uncommitted masses, rural and urban, may well consider this government as better than its predecessors, and accept it as the only one there is likely to be for a good while, but probably there is today less hopeful expectation than there was during the first months of agrarian reform two years ago.

This is not very surprising in the big cities, particularly in Lima where 20 per cent of Peruvians live. On the eve of the military takeover something like 40 per cent of Lima's population was underemployed or unemployed, and something like the same percentage lived in anything from matting shelters to adobe shacks.[2] Since then, as the mass migration from the country has continued, unemployment has continued to rise while real wages almost certainly have not. Lately a few hangups in food supply have not made life easier. The housing situation, which appears to have been getting worse during the 1960s, is appalling and, as continued mass invasions of urban building sites show, explosive. The nearest thing to political trouble the government encountered in 1971 arose out of a squatting incident, which led to the brief arrest of a social activist bishop by the muscle-flexing Minister of the Interior (who very soon lost his job) and to the immediate and amply publicized provision of building land, roads, public utilities, and presidential visits for the new urban settlement of El Salvador.

That the peasantry remains passive – perhaps even less expectant and positive than two years ago, though with Peruvian Indians it is hard to tell – is less surprising than it seems. The agrarian reform is indeed genuine and profound, and advancing steadily toward the expropriation of all large estates by 1975. Though on balance less drastic than in Chile,[3] it is certainly no less radical and enthusiastic in its attack upon the landowning oligarchy as a class, which has already been swept away as a social and political force from the greater part of the countryside. This is undoubtedly a major change in rural life, as is the substitution of various kinds of co-operatives for the former *haciendas* in the highlands and on the coast.

Three reasons may be suggested for the lack of enthusiasm of the peasants. In the first place, most of them have not yet got any land. The 44,000 families who have benefited since 1969, though much more numerous than the 30,000 who got land in the six years of Chile's 'Revolution in Liberty', are only a small fraction of the 800,000 or so who are theoretically entitled to claim land under the reform. Second, what peasants mean by agrarian reform is essentially parcelling land, but this is not the view of the authorities, whose policy of setting up co-operatives arouses more suspicion than joy. Peasants are inclined to keep as far away from any government as they can, and co-operatives are identified with government.

Last, for the people on the expropriated estates to be bossed by technocrats who depend on the government, or even in theory on some annual meeting of co-operator/shareholders, does not seem any different from being bossed by technocrats who depend on an absentee landowner. The boss is still Ingeniero Somebody; if not the one who ran the *hacienda* before, very likely one who ran some other *hacienda* before. I asked a *servidor* of a large cattle ranch about the co-operative of which he is now a member. 'What co-operative?' he answered. And on

338

the same Sociedad Agricola de Interes Social (SAIS),* rightly regarded as a showplace of reform, the attitude of the former ranch hands is, 'Well, they say we're the bosses now. But we're bosses who take orders and don't give any.'

More unexpected is the passivity of the class that is perhaps the clearest beneficiary of the present regime, though it did well enough under Belaúnde: the urbanized and modernized Indian middle stratum of the *cholos*.† The sons of Indian *kulaks* and village entrepreneurs fill the big universities, whose students have multiplied perhaps fifteen-fold since the 1940s, providing the social base for the ultra-radical but short-lived Maoism of students who rapidly turn into respectable citizens after graduating. The country clubs, which have multiplied outside Lima on the model of the institutions of the old Creole middle class and the expatriate foreign executives, are filled with such families, pouring out of overloaded autos to pass a Sunday in a style which is still in many ways demotic, like the Impressionists' restaurants on the Marne: small businessmen, professionals, perhaps above all bureaucrats.

Unlike earlier generations of their kind, the new *cholos* do not seem to despise or sever their links with Indian origins. Probably most of the adults continue to speak Quechua as well as Spanish, and they certainly appreciate 'down home'

* The SAIS is a special form of co-operative which transfers the land of very large former estates or groups of estates not merely to their former tenants or hired hands (who may be very few, as on vast cattle ranches) but also to neighbouring communities of peasants, thus 'compensating the socio-economic inequalities of an area and distributing the profits of the collective enterprise in accordance with the developmental needs of each of the groups of peasants who are its co-proprietors'.

† François Bourricaud, who has built an entire sociological interpretation of Peru on the concept of *cholification*, defines *cholos* as 'those whose origins place them in the indigenous class, but who possess some social and cultural attributes which enable them to "better themselves" and attain higher status'. *Power and Society in Contemporary Peru* (1970), p. 22. This intelligent book, originally published in 1967, sums up the situation in the 1960s and thus illustrates the dramatic changes which have taken place since.

music and dancing, which remain the basis of Peruvian popular show business. The 'shade of contempt and condescension' which François Bourricaud noticed in the use of the word *cholo* in the 1960s is rapidly disappearing. The military regime is aggressively pro-Indian (though there is only one Indian in the top levels of agrarian reform). It is as much given to idealizing the Incas as official Mexico is the Aztecs, but with better reason, and lucky enough to possess a suitable culture hero in the great rebel Tupac Amaru. It is even planning bilingual schooling.

The *cholo* middle stratum lacks any obvious enthusiasm for the Peruvian Revolution, probably because the regime has not so far notably improved the possibilities of 'bettering themselves' that the *cholos* already enjoyed, except for very limited groups of technically qualified professionals. The bulk of them, in Lima at least, continue to live a life of struggle against low salaries, large families, high prices, poor living conditions, endless journeys to and from work, and occasionally uncertain supplies. Like most Peruvians (except the hostile students) they are not against the government, but neither are they actively for it.

The generals are increasingly troubled about the political void that surrounds them. It is not merely that a government that is sincerely devoted to making life human for all Peruvians and is, to say the least, the best administration the country has had within anyone's memory would naturally welcome more appreciation. They know that lack of popular commitment makes their task more difficult. Can a revolution, even 'The Peruvian Revolution', really be carried out simply by taking the vehicle of the state and pointing it in the desired direction? In Peru, an orderly, peaceful advance of bureaucrats flanked by lawyers and technicians will be blessed by historians for the ample and systematic documentation they generated. But, the observer asks himself as he works his way through the serried and ordered files of a Zonal Office of Agrarian Reform, is this really how revolutions are made?

In fact, the military government knows it is not. The very lack of any genuine impetus from below, or obvious social basis, has already pushed the armed forces into the virtually unique role of not just telling the civilians what to do, but actually being the government and administration. Not only are all ministers senior officers but down to subaltern functions decisions are made by uniformed colonels, captains or lieutenants. They have to be, inasmuch as the routine forces of administration, however loyal and efficient, cannot be relied upon to infuse themselves with the required dynamism.

One might say that in Peru the modern army, an increasingly bureaucratic organization, has accepted its destiny and actually become a bureaucracy. But it did not want to. The officers of the COAP say emphatically that the criteria of recruitment and promotion and the training of officers will not be modified to qualify them for the administrative tasks that they will have to carry out until they can hand them over to the civilians again and get back to the military hardware. That this is what they want I have no doubt. But it does not look as though they will be able to do so for a long time.

Even so, they need the people, and after months of difficult backstage discussion a plan for 'social mobilization' was finally announced – details to be filled in later – in the summer of 1971. The scheme will give scope to the various left-wing civilians who have thrown in their lot with the government, though it will be headed by a general, Leonidas Rodríguez, a handsome officer of whom, it is safe to predict, more will be heard since he combines his new functions with the command of the Armoured Division. No military coup has much chance of winning against this division. How exactly the mobilization of the people will work, nobody quite knows. It will not be a party or a 'movement'.

It will certainly not operate through any existing party, parties, or independent organizations, labour unions, peasant unions, or the like. Lacking any civilian organization and cadres of its own, the government is unwilling to hand over 'social mobilization' to forces out of its control, and more especially to the enemies it fears, such as APRA, the nearest thing to a mass party in Peru, or the supporters it distrusts, such as the CP. (It was notably cool toward the Committees for the Defence of the Revolution which the CP encouraged at one point and which have since faded from sight.)

Official statements and commentaries so far are remarkably vague ('A long and difficult process in the course of which multiple and complex problems will arise ... '; 'to contribute to the creation of conditions which will stimulate the emergence of autonomous popular organizations', etc.). Presumably 'mobilization' will operate through the organisms created or encouraged by the government, such as co-operatives, 'industrial communities', community organizations of the shanty towns now called 'young towns', etc. In fact, nobody knows. Something, it is hoped, will evolve.

II

What will or might evolve depends on the nature of the government and its 'Peruvian Revolution', a matter much discussed by the left, which has, with the exceptions of Fidel Castro and the old-style communists, taken a rather negative view of the generals. The left regards them as bourgeois reformers who have now (the date of self-revelation varies with the commentators) revealed that they will not evolve into left-wing progressive nationalists, but are seeking a new kind of dependent niche in a new version of a global imperialism. Such arguments are put forward in a very simple-minded way or in more sophisticated but still circular versions by sympathizers of the Peruvian ultra-left.[4] They are also put forward with admirable lucidity and intelligence by Anibal Quijano in his *Nationalism and Capitalism in Peru: a Study in Neo-Imperialism* (1972), the best statement of the opposition case which analyses the regime's economic policy up to the spring of 1971.

All these arguments tend to assume (a) that the Peruvian military must be for capitalism because they refuse to be for socialism, (b) that the international situation of Peru to which they aspire can only be described as 'neo-imperialism', and (c) that there is a serious possibility of a Peruvian economy based on a (dependent) domestic bourgeoisie. These assumptions somewhat oversimplify a very complex and ambiguous situation.

The complexity of the situation is indicated by the very existence of the arguments and uncertainties of the left. The Peruvian military are undeniably genuine reformers. It is [at the same time] also almost impossible to believe in their programme. Still, *they* believe in it, and have stuck to it with remarkable consistency, allowing for a good deal of tactical flexibility. Those who claim to have detected in them a decisive turn to the right (or, much more rarely, to the left) have tended to confuse tactical zigzags with changes of direction. But the road is sufficiently well marked for it to be clear where the military regime wishes to go.

The argument of President Juan Velasco Alvarado's regime is simply summarized.* Until 1968 Peru was capitalist, and it was dependent, underdeveloped, poor and backward because capitalism generates these things. Hence the regime is anti-capitalist and revolutionary, because it would make no sense simply to 'modernize', thus prolonging the system that generates all these evils. The mechanism that kept Peru down was a

* Virtually every public speech repeats it with variations, but I have followed more especially the Presidential Address on Independence Day, 1970, and the Second Anniversary of Agrarian Reform in 1971.

343

combination of local oligarchy and foreign imperialism. ('Is it not true that Peru was always under the rule of a small group of Peruvians who grew rich on the backs of our people and mortgaged the national wealth to the foreigner?') The regime opposes the oligarchy with an obviously sincere passion, not because it is economically inefficient but because it is the crucial link in the chain of imperialist exploitation.

The novelty of its agrarian reform was not technical but political. The reform of Belaúnde, apart from remaining on paper, had specifically excepted the modern efficient sugar estates of the chief domestic and foreign oligarchs on the coast. The generals began their reform by expropriating these *because* they represented the most efficient, hence danger-ous, oligarchs. On the other hand, the new Peru is certainly not to be communist, for the usual anti-totalitarian reasons. Moreover, neither system is at present a very attractive model: 'Both today show unequivocal symptoms of enfeeblement and crisis.'

The military answer is less easy to describe briefly, except in the meaningless phrase 'neither capitalism nor communism'. It has in it much that is reminiscent of the social Catholicism of the generals' interwar youth. There is the dream of harmoniz-ing capital and labour as mutually dependent and functionally necessary parts of the social organism, and consequently a deep distrust of organs of the class struggle or sectional pressure groups. There is the search for forms of economic organiza-tion that eliminate or modify the crude employer/worker relationship, especially in big business. Hence the enthusiasm for 'co-operative organization', a slogan that suggests all these things, but is vague and ambiguous enough to cover everything from *de facto* technocratic management to a kibbutz.

However, the anti-technological traditionalism that in the past often accompanied this type of ideology is quite absent. 'Peruvianism' lies not in any appeal to continuity and the com-munity of the past, in which little is to be found that inspires the

regime except perhaps the oppressed, exploited, but also struggling (Indian) people of Peru. Its populist sympathies, however,
do not extend to the traditionalism of the peasantry.

This positive programme is either too vague or utopian. Hence
the question is not so much what the regime wants to happen,
but what is likely to emerge from its efforts, which will inevitably be somewhat different. Moreover, there is no automatic
congruence, but a probable contradiction between the aims of
a Peru liberated from imperialism and underdevelopment and
of a harmonious social organism. Critics on the left assume that
since the regime is not socialist or communist – though actual
disclaimers of socialism are not easy to find – it cannot develop
except through some form of capitalism and must perpetuate
imperialist dependence in some shape. Its more naïve spokesmen, against all the evidence, regard the declared aims of the
government as so much window dressing, designed to make
the new version of dependent capitalism more palatable to the
masses.

Left-wing supporters somewhat more cautiously take the
view that the anti-imperialism is genuine, the reforms so far
'progressive' or at least not incompatible with what a progressive government might have done, and that the logic of their
position may push the regime to the left. Of course it is equally
possible that at the fork of the road the generals may take the
wrong turn, but that fork has not yet been reached.

Such arguments illustrate the difficulty of categorizing a regime
that refuses to fit into any of the familiar analytical slots, perhaps because the slots are not present. The truth is that the
regime attempts to fill a vacuum. It could hardly represent or
act for a Peruvian bourgeoisie even if that were its intention:
it would have to take its place because there is no national
bourgeoisie in Peru. There is nothing like the recognizable
social phenomenon of revolution in Peru, but still less is there

a counter-revolution or even an attempt to forestall revolution by well-judged reform, though this was in the minds of some of the generals.

The regime is there *instead* of the revolution that did not occur in 1960–3 but left behind it a necessity to ratify and systematize certain changes, which nobody else could do. The peasant risings of the early 1960s amounted politically to no more than an accumulation of localized unrest. Economically and socially they killed the traditional latifundism of the highlands, as the owners realized perfectly well. But the peasants themselves were unable to bury its rotting corpse. The military had to substitute for a bankrupt political system, totally incapable of anything except responding to the pressures of foreign enterprise and the local oligarchy. They had even, as we have seen, to take the place of the state machine. About the only thing the officers really 'represent' is people like themselves, i.e. professional men of generally modest provincial middle-class background making their careers in the public service. But this in itself does not get us far.

The only forces the army does not replace, because they are already socially present, are those of the working class and the labour movement; which are also the only ones (apart from the students) to maintain independent institutions under the new regime. Hence the government's suspicion of both APRA and the CP, both essentially proletarian-based – the organized peasant movements of the 1960s have disintegrated – and especially its deep suspicion of labour unions. Politically the small Peruvian working class is not a serious problem. Unlike its counterpart in Chile, it does not provide the basis for an alternative government. Its strongest components, the miners and the workers on the 'agro-industrial' estates of the coast, are labour aristocrats totalling perhaps 50,000 and 30,000 adult men respectively. Unlike the peasants, however, they constitute not merely a force of nature, but, through the unions, an organized and structured force. At the very least they have leaders who can be blamed.

The military rulers of Peru, as their conversation makes very clear, do not understand unions and wish they were not there. Their relations with them illustrate a major weakness of the Peruvian Revolution and explain, though they do not justify, some of the left-wing hostility to it. The government has made big mistakes in labour policy where it has controlled the situation directly, i.e. in sugar estate co-operatives, and will probably make similar mistakes with industrial labour, if its uneasiness about the way unions are going tempts it into direct control there.

Though the military rulers persistently refuse to believe it, union leaders are not secretly trying to sabotage the Peruvian Revolution or to turn it communist, if we except the scattered locals where the influence of the ultra-left is generally temporary. ('They can rarely maintain it,' a union leader told me. 'The university style of action is not the working-class style.') The APRA's federation, like its parent body, is politically quiescent. The rising CGTP shares the CP's attitude toward the regime, though actively organizing and campaigning for changes in the largely unreconstructed Ministry of Labour. It would certainly prefer not to embarrass the government it actively supports.

On the other hand, especially with an eye to its rivals, it must take account of the militancy of its members. In the cities they are for action because real wages are drifting lower, while in the mines the government's own anti-imperialism has encouraged the permanent hostility of the miners to their foreign employers, and their bargaining strength is greater than ever.* Leaders of genuine labour movements cannot coerce their members and

* According to its able General Secretary, Gustavo Espinosa, the CGTP is worried by the tendency of strong labour aristocrats like miners and oil workers to pull increasingly far ahead of the weaker majority; on the other hand this is where its strength lies. The other two major problems about which it is worried are organizational weakness and the low ideological level of the membership (July 1971).

must to some extent follow them, especially today. They are quite unlike army officers, though this is difficult for military men to understand.

On the sugar estates the failure to understand the unions has been particularly counterproductive. These strongholds of a militant, because fairly young, unionism – several did not win recognition until the early 1960s – were also strongholds of APRA in its main bastion, the 'solid North'. The government frankly hoped that the new co-operatives would also replace the unions. What did the workers need unions for if they actually owned the firm? More than this. Presumably in order to prevent the co-operatives from being taken over by APRA supporters not only was their electoral system made too complex and manipulable, but party and union functionaries and ex-functionaries are ineligible as delegates or functionaries of the co-operative. This would be rather like banning registered Democrats and United Automobile Workers activists from taking part in the running of a collectivized Chrysler plant. There have even been attempts to deprive union leaders of co-operative membership, met by strikes for their reinstatement.

A strong and recognized union, irrespective of political affiliation, has to negotiate with management, irrespective of its character; and, as the old managers of the *haciendas* learned, the other way round. Left to themselves the old unions and the new managers would have done the same, leaving the complex problem of the members' dual interests as co-owners and employees to settle itself by practice. That is what seemed to be happening in the first months after expropriation, when, incidentally, APRA influence in the unions was receding rapidly, at least in the region I then visited.

The result of the government's policy has been the precise opposite of its intention. Management (i.e. the technicians and white-collar workers who are the co-operative officials) is as separate from the workers as before; the unions have been pushed back and have become marginal and consequently militant; the APRA influence has revived; and the militants of the ultra-left are attracted from all over the country by the magnet of endemic industrial friction. The past year has seen strikes, semi-riotous demonstrations, resignations of managers and committees, and even the sentencing of strike leaders to light jail sentences and heavy fines for 'sabotage of the agrarian reform'. These are awkward developments in what were intended to be the showcases of the Peruvian revolution. They have been met by increasingly direct intervention by military functionaries and policemen in the management of the co-operatives.

III

Where then are the generals going? The simplest to predict are their international relations, for here the conflict between intention and result is least acute. The regime aims to make Peru independent, but since the country is poor, weak and backward, it is realistic enough to know that it cannot do without some foreign assistance. To be more precise, it believes that the costs of going it alone are prohibitive, as indeed they probably are. The major objective is to break the monopoly of US power without falling into dependence on any other single state. What would suit the government best is enough world rivalry between numerous powers – US, USSR, perhaps the Common Market, perhaps China – for little countries to diversify their dependence and have maximum room for manoeuvre.

Peru also hopes rather than expects that united action by Third World states will give each weak country a little more strength. At the moment, with the US in political and economic recession, prospects look promising, and Peru is negotiating for trade, technical assistance and investment with everybody from China to Japan and West Germany, as well as the US and the USSR. What if US power recovers? The officers, who discuss all these matters with a most agreeable frankness and lack of humbug, shrug their shoulders. A weak and backward country has to make the best of the world as it finds it.

The weakness of this position is that a weak country known to be unwilling to risk all has less bargaining power than it might have. There are people, including foreign businessmen, who think that Peru has been giving somewhat better terms than necessary to investors. Indeed, by current international standards the recent oil and copper contracts with foreign corporations are not ungenerous, while the Mining Law of 1971 is quite acceptable to them. Still, an argument about the percentage of royalties or repatriable profits must not be confused with one about fundamentals. To describe Peruvian policy as 'without hesitation ... pro-imperialist', as does Ricardo Letts, is to devalue language. In mining Peru has deliberately opted not for nationalization (though the state company will be very big) but for a state monopoly of marketing and most of the refining, which is a tenable point of view. In oil it has opted for what amounts to a service contract rather than a concession. The generals' policies are not in any way socialist, but since they do not claim to be socialists this observation is tautology rather than criticism. On the other hand their intention is plainly anti-imperialist.

So, undoubtedly, is their effect. The US corporations will doubtless resign themselves here as elsewhere to doing business under drastically less favourable conditions than in the past and will discover that money can still be made in the new way and indeed, given the troubles of the US economy, must be so made. Conversely, they can console themselves with the reflection that, if even the USSR calls on Western corporations to build plants, Peru will still find it advantageous to do business with them. So long as the capitalist industrial states remain richer and technologically more advanced than the socialist ones and the Third World, this will be the case, unless socialist regimes return to the ancient aim of a just austerity, denying themselves the products of technology of richer nations; which few of them seem inclined to do, and none can, except at the price of rigid isolation. But to say that US corporations will survive in Peru does not imply that nothing has changed. One has only to look at Peru's northern neighbour Ecuador, the greatest banana republic of them all, to observe the difference.

However, the generals' policies are not intended to be anti-business, in spite of putting all the basic industries into the public sector. They are certainly in favour of indigenous capitalist development, doubtless under the control of a commanding state sector, but also benefiting from its activities. Such a symbiosis is today normal, and in Latin America even the dynamic local capitalisms of Brazil and Mexico rely largely on it. But Peru is not Brazil or Mexico. There is no effective national bourgeoisie, and military decisions are unlikely to create what several centuries of history have denied the country.

What is most likely to happen is that the extreme weakness of domestic private enterprise and the restrictions on the participation in it of foreign capital will make the public sector grow far beyond the original intentions of the government. It will have to, unless Peru is to relapse into its old pattern of dependence. This will raise acute questions, analogous to those in Eastern Europe, about the suitability of large state bureaucracies in backward countries as economic entrepreneurs, about the role of incentives, technocrats, etc. However, unless we regard, say, Bulgaria or Romania as capitalist, these problems alone are not enough to characterize a state as 'bourgeois-reformist'. Nor, of course, enough to characterize it as socialist.

The Peruvian strategy of development is thus debatable, but cannot so far be regarded as 'pro-imperialist' or 'pro-capitalist'. The main danger that Peru may one day revert to type lies in the fact that its transformation is so controlled and orderly, the regime's fear of disruption and chaos so great, and the hope

351

of getting by without a critical confrontation with the US so attractive that it will undoubtedly tempt the government into concessions. The alternative would be to risk plunging into one of those iron ages which have been a normal part of the history of revolutions. The generals' real weakness may be that they want to combine revolutionary change with peace and quiet, thus making themselves vulnerable to blackmail from outside. But it is absurd to deny that they mean what they say or that they are not passionately determined to secure the independence of their country.

One has much more serious doubts about the social than about the economic aspect of the regime. There are two weaknesses here. In the first place planners and administrators tend to concentrate on 'hard' economic matters that produce measurable results, while paying little more than lip service to the social objectives of the government. One would not guess from their documents about 'the agrarian sector' that there is a major agrarian reform with specific and non-economic objectives and problems. The natural desire to keep production growing, or at least undisrupted, favours giving it overriding priority and keeping the management structure the way it is.

Socially, the biggest problem of the countryside is that the reform will – and if it provides workable family units must – leave vast numbers without land: up to 80 per cent according to one estimate.[5] But farm administrators are more preoccupied with the inefficiencies and high labour costs of overstaffed units, and tend to hope that the landless will just migrate somewhere. Technically it is easier to get quick and good results from the reform on the coast. So the hard, expensive, but essential job of creating the basis of efficient peasant farming in the Sierra is postponed.

Second, the government's own social plans, e.g. for 'communities' in industry, mining, fisheries, etc., are inadequate. These are essentially devices to promote workers' co-partnership and profit sharing within each enterprise as well as (through the Community of Compensation of the Mining Law) to make equal the shares in enterprises of varying profitability. The financial details need not detain us. Participation in management is also envisaged, but on a more modest scale than in the West German *Mittbestimmungsrecht*, and excluding union leaders. This is obviously insufficient to change the character of management. The government has high hopes for the 'communities', including no doubt the hope that they will supersede unions. This is improbable. Since they are still largely on paper, little can be said concretely about their functioning. An authoritative union view is that they will do no more than give some workers a useful insight into management. The prevailing business view is that they will diminish the profit incentive but could probably be circumvented.

The generals' intentions are not in doubt. To make life better and more humane for most Peruvians and to bring the people, whom previous regimes treated as little better than cattle, into the affairs of their nation are the goals to which they give at least theoretical priority.[6] There has been a lot of hard thought, as about educational reform, the present system having largely failed, in spite of the apparently large if unbalanced expansion of the 1960s. The average period of school attendance for all Peruvians is three years; 88 per cent drop out of high school, and there has been no diminution in the basic core of illiteracy, which is officially (and optimistically) given as 4 million or about 30 per cent of the population.[7]

There are also some sensible ideas about the development of the 610 do-it-yourself settlements in which perhaps 40 per cent of urban Peruvians live, but what they have done so far is inadequate for both the economic and social objectives of the regime. To take a single example. It will take more than has so far been done to turn the bottom 20 per cent of Lima's population, which received in 1967 just 1.3 per cent of the city's total income – in Mexico the corresponding figure was about 6 per cent – into genuine citizens, or even into a market for Peruvian industry. Thirty-seven per cent of Limenos receive less than fifty dollars a month in Latin America's most expensive city. The government has borrowed from José Maria Mariategui, the founder of the Peruvian Communist Party, the splendid slogan: 'Let us peruvianize Peru.' For people such as these it is still far from realized.[8]

IV

'If you were a Peruvian, what would you do?' The visitor is likely to be asked this question by young intellectuals not already totally committed to some political sect, and the answer is almost impossible to know. In the first place, the Peruvian military regime is one of those phenomena on which the views of the native and foreign left tend to differ, though international tact and loyalties may attempt to conceal the divergences. It is easy to think of Peruvian regimes of which socialists would approve more enthusiastically, but none that looks remotely probable, even after the end of the present one, which seems at the moment an unlikely contingency.

In the second place, the attitude that seems most reasonable, a critical support of the regime for the time being, is not one for which the military themselves have any sympathy, partly because they do not really trust any civilians, mainly because they do not trust anyone who is not totally committed to them. Like most governments, what they want is unqualified support, but unlike politicians' governments, they are not accustomed or resigned to the kind of supporter who from time to time turns critic.

On the other hand, however much one may sympathize with the personal difficulties of Peruvian intellectuals, they are not among the country's major problems, which are enormous, under the best of circumstances. Its agriculture consists of a

few patches of oasis, a few ribbons of mountain valley dotted
with handkerchief-sized Indian fields, a few strips between
the high sierra and the Amazonian jungle, and endless rough
grazing with a few marginal potato patches on the high *puna*.
Nobody since the Incas has managed to cultivate the highlands
effectively.

Peru has no industry that could stand up even to the competition of industry in Chile or Colombia. Its vast and booming
fisheries depend, like their predecessor, the briefly successful
guano industry of the nineteenth century, on the farming of
the developed world, or more exactly on the Western broiler
chicks and hogs which feed on fish-meal until some cheaper
food comes along. It has mineral wealth in large variety, but
this is the kind of resource that requires the sort of investments
and technology that tend to put Peru at the mercy of foreign
enterprise. About the only advantage the country has over
other underdeveloped economies is that it does not depend on
any single export commodity.

Peru may not be, in the nineteenth-century phrase, 'a
beggar sitting on a heap of gold', but its people remain poor
and desperately backward. The Incas are gone for good, but
their descendants are repossessing their country. From the
highlands squat, big-chested, earth-coloured men and women
flood into the coast and into the subtropical valleys, filling the
shanty towns with the curiously baroque Christian names, the
Quechua surnames of the sierra. Four hundred and fifty years
of subjection have taught this people of *muzhiks* in ponchos
nothing except how to endure, to survive in their tight but now
disintegrating peasant communities, to distrust and not to show
their thoughts to their rulers. These are not good qualifications
for life in the 1970s, in spite of the passion for learning and
progress which has been filling the highlands with primary
schools and the cities with families seeking a better education
for their children.

What are their prospects? If we leave aside the 'strong and sober' who become the *cholo* lower middle class (inevitably the parallels with Tsarist Russia come to the minds of students of Peru), they are social disruption, underemployment and poverty. The flight from the land, the uncontrollable growth of a megalopolitan slum zone, which are taking place in Peru today on a huge scale, are extreme versions of the social changes familiar in later nineteenth-century Europe, but in those days (and for those countries) capitalism worked, at least inasmuch as it created enough employment to absorb the new immigrants at a modestly rising standard of living. Hence, outside periods of acute and lasting depression, it seemed plausible enough to concentrate on the rate of economic growth, with employment (and the distribution of the new wealth) by and large left to take care of itself.

But today this will not work, least of all in such countries as Peru. It will merely produce a permanently unsolved social-agrarian problem in the mountains, without the massive remittances from emigrants to Birmingham and Turin which keep analogous areas in Ireland and southern Italy afloat today, and a flood of new townsmen with which neither the economy nor the social administration can cope.

The military regime is not to be blamed for its inability to solve the problem of providing work for the people, which implies fundamental social reconstruction, for (with the possible exception of China) no other regime in an underdeveloped country, socialist or otherwise, seems to have given social reorganization deliberate priority over economic growth, and whether even the Chinese are succeeding is obscure, like so much else about that country. But it would be highly unwise for the rulers of Peru to overlook the urgency of their country's situation. As it happens, the boom years of the 1960s and the collapse of the old rural quasi-federalism have given them a breathing space and an opportunity.

At the moment Peru is not on the verge of a social explosion, as it seemed to be between 1958 and 1963. But there is no reason to believe that tension will remain slack permanently. Agrarian pressure may well revive in the highlands, social discontent is certain to grow in the giant urban jungles, as it has in Bogotá and Caracas, where it has been reviving the political fortunes of even such discredited political contenders as the ex-dictators Rojas Pinilla and Pérez Jiménez. (But not, one may add for the benefit of optimists on the extreme left, those of the local Marxist movements.) The Peruvian military have so far been fortunate enough to plan and act without constraints, other than those of their country's weakness and backwardness. The time for them to consider whether their policies are adequate to achieve their objectives is now.

It would be both unfair and unprofitable to write off the military rulers of Peru summarily, as many on the left are inclined to do. Unfair, because they are serious and devoted men genuinely trying to revolutionize their country and make it independent, however reasonably we may disagree with them. They measure themselves against the major social revolutions of Latin America: not against the capitalist Mexico of the past thirty years, but against the aspirations of the Mexican Revolution. They deserve the compliment of being taken at their word.

Unprofitable, because they are for the politically foreseeable future Peru's best chance. They may fall victim to dissension within the armed forces, under the pressure of economic difficulties or social tensions, but their most likely successor would be a Brazilian-type military regime, which would be distinctly worse. They may not achieve their objectives, and it is important to point out in what ways their ideology and the nature and limitations of their policies make it difficult, if not impossible, for them to do what they say they want to do. But there is no one else in view who at present stands a realistic chance of achieving them, still less the more advanced objectives of a socialist Peru. The vacuum in Peru remains. There is still no one else to fill it.

The case of the left which rejects the generals is not only that they have turned or are likely to turn the wrong way (the latter is perfectly arguable) but that an alternative exists: a hegemonic Marxist mass movement is an immediate or at least imminent possibility. Unfortunately, there is no good reason to expect this. The history of Latin America is full of substitutes for the genuinely popular social revolutionary left that has so rarely been strong enough to determine the shape of its countries' histories.

The history of the Latin American left is (with rare exceptions such as Cuba and Chile) one of having to choose between an ineffective sectarian purity and making the best of various kinds of bad jobs: civilian or military populists, national bourgeoisies, or whatever else. It is also, quite often, a history of the left regretting its failure to come to terms with such governments and movements before they were replaced by something worse. Today, most of the Argentine left recognizes that it must work with and through the Peronists, who are the labour movement. Twenty years ago hardly any of them did. The Peruvian generals, a rather special variety of such a substitute phenomenon, may fall, fail or change the character of their regime. If they do any of these things, it will not be an occasion for self-congratulation.

December 1971

Notes

Some notes in the original essay have been omitted from the version that appears in this volume.

1   See Grant Hilliker, *The Politics of Reform in Peru* (Baltimore, 1971). The author demonstrates both the limits of APRA influence and its failure in recent years.

2 Jaime Gianella, *Marginalidad en Lima Metropolitana (Una investigación exploratoria)* (Lima, 1970, mimeo). The data of this very full sample survey were collected in 1967.

3 The maximum holding retainable by expropriated owners is probably larger, though the provisions of both reforms are too complex for simple comparison. For details see Luis Dongo Denegri, *Compendio Agrario: comentario, legislación, jurisprudencia*, 2 vols (Lima, 1971), which records changes up to mid-February 1971.

4 For an example of the first, G. Lessink, *Le cas du Pérou, Politique Aujourd'hui* (Paris, 1971); and of the second, Ricardo Letts, *Peru: Revolución Socialista o caricatura de revolución?* (Mexico, 1971, mimeo).

5 Cf. *Aspectos Sociales y Financieros de un Programa de Reforma Agraria 1968–1975* (Lima, 1970, mimeo).

6 Cf. items 1 to 4 of the Long Range Goals, as defined by President Velasco Alvarado in the Message of 5 December 1968. They are reprinted in R. R. Marett, *Peru* (1969), pp. 275–6.

7 *Reforma de la Educación Peruana: Informe General* (Lima, 1970), p. 16.

8 A translation of Mariátegui's *Siete Ensayos* (*Seven Interpretive Essays on Peruvian Reality*, Austin, 1971) has been published with an Introduction by the dean of Peruvian historians, Jorge Basadre. This is a welcome introduction to the work of the most original Marxist thinker produced up to the present in Latin America.

Editor's note

In reply to a long letter to the editors of the *New York Review of Books* from 'An Anthropologist' (name withheld) who argued that none of the reforms of the so-called revolutionary government in Peru, 'the latest in a long list of colonialist administrations', attempted to return any power the Indians, the Native American people of the Andean highlands and the Upper Amazon lowlands, principally speakers of Quechua and Aymara, 60 to 70 per cent of the population, Eric replied (*New York Review of Books*, 15 June 1972):

The writer of this letter and I clearly do not talk the same language [...] I cannot understand his use of the term 'Indian' which veers from one possible criterion to another: in the widest sense (i.e. that used to define black North Americans) probably more than his 60 to 70 per cent of Peruvians are Indian; in the sense of those living under 'indigenous institutions' such as the 'peasant [formerly 'indigenous'] communities' probably less than 20 per cent were even ten years ago [...] Let us try to establish a common universe of discourse. First, about the policy of the Peruvian government, which is propagating the glories of the Inca past, of Indian rebels like Tupac Amaru, and of Indian virtues with great enthusiasm, and actually planning schooling in the Quechua language. Whatever the gap between rhetoric and reality and between plans and realizations, what it is clearly *not* trying to do is to abolish the Indians as Indians.

[...] I do not myself believe that a policy of treating Indians as men and citizens just like anyone else is in some way a neo-colonialist plot, though it may have other drawbacks; but the Peruvian policy cannot be adequately described as assimilationism in this sense.

Second, about the prospects of the Indians' traditional way of life, which is incidentally, to speak economically and socially, very much more comparable to that of non-Indian communally organized peasants than this writer seems to think. It clearly retains far more strength in Peru than in, say, Mexico, and it would be deplorable if the future development of the country, and especially the highlands, were to bypass and destroy it rather than to build upon it. All the more deplorable as simple urbanization is not a satisfactory solution for the problems of the Third World.

But the fact is that this way of life has been changing and breaking down rapidly, perhaps in many regions irreversibly, and that the majority of Peruvians will soon be or are already urban. The traditional highland way of peasant life is not an adequate guide to what is *already* Peruvian reality, and simple preservation or reversal is not an adequate program. However powerful the cultural influence of the Indians in the future Peru, and however effective the blending of their characteristic and traditional way of life with the new social environment, it will not re-create the past. [...]

However, I agree with this writer – and have said so – that 'the mad dash to develop' will not solve the Indian problem, that this problem remains to be solved, and that, until the Peruvian people, whether communally organized Indians or not, take an active part in the transformation of their country, we cannot speak of the Peruvian Revolution as having taken place.

VI

THE CHILEAN ROAD
TO SOCIALISM

27

Chile: Year One

I

That constitutional transfer of power and a peaceful transition to socialism are possible has been theoretically admitted by Marxists ever since Marx put it on record in 1872. The prospect for this transition, however, remains shadowy. Marxist writing about it remains scarce and abstract rather than concrete, probably because practical experience relevant to such discussion is almost completely lacking. So far no socialist economy has come into existence other than by violent or non-constitutional transfers of power.

This makes the case of Chile today pretty well unique. Until November 1970, when Salvador Allende took office as President, the cases that might claim to be legal transitions to socialism belonged to three types, all equally useless as precedents. First, there were plenty of examples of transfers of power, peaceful or otherwise, to social-democratic or 'labour' governments. Unfortunately none of them made any attempt to introduce socialism and most did not even want to do so.

Second, we have the popular fronts of the 1930s, which are

at first sight rather similar to the Chilean Popular Unity, being essentially united fronts of socialists and communists within a wider electoral alliance of the left-of-centre. This alliance implied a theory of non-insurrectionary roads to socialism, at least among the communists, but in practice this perspective was academic.

In fact the immediate political aims of such governments were defensive – to turn back the tide of fascism – and they rarely had the chance to get beyond this point. In any case, the configuration of political forces was such that communists and serious socialists were generally in no position to dominate the alliance, and could therefore not have got much further, even if the policy of the USSR and the Comintern had encouraged them to try, which it did not. Such was the case of the Chilean Popular Front of 1938, in which the middle-class Radicals remained the decisive force.

Third, there were the governments of anti-fascist union which emerged out of the struggle against Germany at the end of the Second World War in a number of European countries. These might be considered the logical extension of the popular front strategy, and there is little doubt that a gradual and peaceful transition to socialism was in the minds of the communists and many resistance socialists who took part in them. The discussions on the nature of 'people's democracy' in 1943–7 make this fairly evident.

However, even if we overlook the armed struggle out of which these regimes actually emerged, the rapid breakdown of the national and international anti-fascist fronts very quickly put an end to this perspective. In the West the dominant political forces were entirely unprepared to allow such a peaceful transition, while in the East 'people's democracy' became a mere euphemism for orthodox communist rule on the Soviet model: in theoretical jargon, it was redefined as just another version of the 'dictatorship of the proletariat'. For practical purposes the peaceful road to socialism was blocked by the middle of 1947. This post Second World War episode provides little guidance for future attempts to open such roads.

The situation in Allende's Chile is thus unprecedented. There can be no doubt that the object of the Popular Unity government is socialism. Allende is in no sense like Léon Blum, Clement Attlee or Harold Wilson. The UP (Unidad Popular) is dominated by the two major working-class parties, both of which claim to be revolutionary Marxists. The only other party of substance in the coalition, the Radicals, was weak anyway and was so reduced in the municipal elections of April 1971 as no longer to be a serious brake on the Marxists.

On the other hand it is equally clear that the UP means to achieve its object gradually ('the progressive construction of a new power structure' is the phrase used in Allende's first Message to Congress, 21 May 1971)[1] and constitutionally. The 'Chilean Way' is contrasted with the dictatorship of the proletariat as a 'pluralist way, anticipated by the classics of Marxism, but never hitherto carried out concretely'.

This pluralist way is not to be identified with bourgeois democracy. Its legality will not necessarily remain that of the present which 'reflects the requirements of a capitalist system. In the regime of transition to socialism, the juridical norms will reflect the requirements of a people straining to build a new society. But there will be legality.' The institutional system will be modified by existing constitutional means, e.g. by substituting a unicameral for a bicameral Congress. Nevertheless:

> This is no mere formal compromise, but the explicit recognition that the principle of legality and the institutional order are consubstantial with the socialist regime, in spite of the difficulties they imply for the period of transition. We accept the political liberties of the opposition and continue our

political activities within the boundaries of our institutions. Political liberties are an achievement of Chilean society as a whole, insofar as it constitutes a state.

There is more than political calculation to Allende's attachment to the 'Chilean Way'. Unlike the ultra-left opposition outside the UP, and some elements within his own party, the President does not regard the existing situation as a mere interim, but potentially as the setting for long-term transformation. Internal or external counter-revolutionary violence is possible, but if it does not occur, legality and pluralist politics will continue. In other words, Chile is the first country in the world that is seriously attempting an alternative road to socialism.

This is a thrilling prospect and a politically valuable one. There is nothing countries, especially small countries, like better than to set an example to the whole world. In this instance the claim is probably true.

> As Russia did (in 1917) so now Chile faces the need to initiate a new way of building the socialist society ... Social thinkers had supposed that more developed nations, probably Italy and France with their powerful Marxist class parties, would be the first to do so. However, once again history allows us to break with the past and to construct a new model of society, not where it was theoretically to be most plausibly expected, but where the most favourable conditions for its realization come into being. Chile is today the first nation on earth called upon to realize the second model of transition to socialist society.

The Chilean experience is thus far more than a piece of political exotica for observers from developed countries. Socialism will never come to, say, Western Europe in the Chinese or

Vietnamese way, but it is at least possible to recognize in Chile the lineaments of political situations that might occur in industrialized societies, and the strategies that might apply there, as well as the problems and difficulties of the 'pluralist way'. This does not mean that the way must fail, and certainly not that it must not be tried.

Even the most serious and rigorous part of the Chilean insurrectionary left, the MIR (Movement of the Revolutionary Left), has now turned itself into a pressure group on the left of the Unidad Popular, attempting to radicalize its policy by grassroots mass action, but essentially supporting Allende's efforts, though it maintains its well-organized apparatus and foresees a future armed confrontation. The MIR does not appear to share the suicidal tendency of the lunatic fringe left to 'sharpen the class struggle' so as to produce such a confrontation as soon as possible, after which there would be good old-fashioned revolution or (more likely) total defeat and plenty of heroic martyrdom.[2]

But the natural sympathy that we feel for the Allende government and the passionate hope for its success should not blind us to the complexities of its situation. Just because Chile may actually be a model for other countries, we must look coldly and realistically at its experience.

II

The tourist-connoisseur of revolutions who arrives in Santiago these days misses the atmosphere, difficult to define but easy to recognize, of great popular liberations. Apart from some armed students, who do not impinge on the street scene, there are hardly any visible signs of upheaval except on the newsstands. There is none of that familiar explosion of pamphlets, leaflets and little journals: the contents of the ultra-left bookshop are austere compared to their equivalents in Paris or the US. The unofficial land occupations, though much has been made of them in the press, are negligible, at least in the numbers involved. Usually they are sit-ins of between ten and twenty people. There is no visible outbreak of official posters, portraiture and banners, and no more than the usual quantity of unofficial political graffiti. In fact, Chile at first sight looks much as it did in, say, 1969. The official explanation that Chileans are undemonstrative carries little conviction. They may not be Caribbean in their ebullience, but when they feel like it, they don't sit on their hands either.

The nearest thing to the Chilean mood, as it can be sensed by the casual visitor, is the mood of the early months (but not the first weeks) after the French Popular Front victory in 1936 or after the Labour victory in Britain in 1945. It is one of solid satisfaction among the organized left, quiet and unmessianic expectation among the unorganized poor, and hysteria among the rich and the spokesmen of the right. The immediate emotion of victory has subsided, the phase of troubles and loss of morale, though predictable and predicted, has not yet arrived. Things are better for the poor: so far the UP government has paid off and they know it.

On the other hand, except perhaps in some of the highly organized and politically conscious factories, mines and country settlements, life remains pretty much as it was. The former ruling class knows that it no longer rules, however, and it projects its fears of annihilation into those predictions of totalitarianism and slavery that are no more than the rhetorical small change of a country where parliamentary electioneering and political discussion are a popular sport of the middle class, as golf is elsewhere. On the extreme fringe of the right – and it is highly visible on the news-stands – this rhetoric reaches paranoiac heights of scurrility and lunatic accusation: terror already stalks the land, the police are supporting groups of left-wing assassins, and so on.

But what has actually happened?

The first thing to note is that the UP came into office under two grave political handicaps. It barely won a plurality – indeed it polled about 3 per cent fewer votes than in the lost election of 1964 – and therefore found itself with insufficient popular backing as well as with a Congress controlled by its opponents, not to mention armed forces only just held in check by the unquestionable legality and constitutionality of the UP's status. It has to operate exclusively with the powers and laws of its predecessors. It could and can pass new laws only with opposition agreement or when they cannot be opposed, like the nationalization of copper, against which no Chilean politician would go on public record any more than he would publicly vote for polygamy.

Indeed, in some respects the government's hands are more tied than before, by the Constitutional Amendment of January 1971, which is the price it paid the Christian Democrats for being allowed to take office. This episode is clearly described in the most useful book on the antecedents of the Allende victory, Eduardo Labarca Goddard's *Al Chile Rojo* (1971).[3] The existing powers admittedly include the possibility of asking for a plebiscite to override Congressional opposition, but the slim plurality of the Allende government – even though the municipal elections of 1971 show it to have been transformed into the slimmest of majorities – makes this a somewhat unpredictable device.

Such a situation happens to suit the gifts of Salvador Allende, who is, among other things, a brilliant and sophisticated politician of the orthodox kind, entirely at home with all the strategies and tactics of the possible in party caucus and Congress. Moreover, he has the immense and quite justified self-confidence of the man who has made it against all probability and prediction – nobody believed he could win and his own party at one point tried to drop him as a candidate. For such a man it is nothing to come to office with both hands tied behind his back – one by the opposition which controls Congress and the judiciary, the other by the elaborate formulas of his own mutually suspicious and divergent coalition. Much can be done within the limits of existing powers.

Constitutionality and legality provide Chilean presidents with a remarkable amount of scope, including some seventeen thousand valid laws among which legal ingenuity can discover much that is useful. Thus the UP has relied extensively on a decree, never repealed, of the two-week-long 'Socialist Republic' of 1932, a brief left-wing interlude during the worst part of the Great Depression led by the remarkably named Col. Marmaduke Grove.* This statute permits the government to take over any factory or industry that 'fails to supply the people' with its goods and services. The decree has been used to nationalize large sectors of industry where necessary, after the workers have occupied the relevant factories thus ensuring that they could not 'supply the people'. Even without legal authority, 'the resources of civilization are not exhausted' (as the British premier Gladstone is reported to have said when finding means of putting the Irish leader Parnell in jail).

Most of the banking system not already under public control has been nationalized by the simple device, apparently unexpected by the opposition, of the government's buying up a majority of shares at market prices and then running the banks as their new proprietor. (This device has aroused an entirely irrational fury among businessmen, who consider tactics they use themselves as somehow unfair when practised by a socialist government.) In one way or another the UP has therefore

---

* The role of the relatively small immigrant-descended community in Chilean public life is quite out of proportion to its size. Hence the frequency of un-Spanish names in Chilean public affairs, starting with the liberator O'Higgins: Frei, Tomic, Perez Zujovic in the DC, Allende Gossens, Toha among the Socialists, Chonchol in MAPU, Teitelboim in the CP, Schneider and Viaux in the army. The absence of xenophobia is one of the many agreeable characteristics of the country.

pushed ahead rapidly with its programme without as yet having
to rely on the goodwill of the opposition.

Such rapid progress would of course have been impossible but
for the policy of the Christian Democrats in 1964–70. It is an
error to suppose that the UP found itself faced with either 'feudalism' or a simple economy of competitive private enterprise,
or that any progressive government in any country, and especially an underdeveloped one, is likely today to do so. Chile was
already a country theoretically dominated by its public sector,
which provided some 70 per cent of all investment, employed
a large proportion of the population directly, and was engaged
upon fairly drastic interference with domestic and foreign private property.

The road to any kind of economic development in Latin
America leads through radical social reforms, a growing
importance of government in the economy, and some control
over foreign capital, which do not in themselves imply socialism. Thus the UP did not need to pass an agrarian reform law,
but could merely accelerate the rather hesitant progress of the
existing law. The UP possesses not merely a supply of general
powers, but has at its disposal many specific laws and institutions which can be adapted to suit its purpose. It can establish
and maintain a good rhythm of action, avoiding – at least for
the crucial first year or so – the jaws of the opposition which
controls Congress and the courts.

The second political handicap of the UP is intimately connected with the first. In addition to insufficient support it has
inadequate reserves of political loyalty. Numerically it may
now count on about half the voters, a distinct improvement
on September 1970, but still slim backing for the crises of
revolutionary constitutional politics. It has one solid core of
supporters: the industrial and urban proletariat, especially
the miners, and the organized and now unified labour unions.
Here alone – in spite of the existence of a few moderate and

business-unionist groups that raise economic rather than political problems, as among the copper miners – can Allende call
upon those reserves of long-term commitment that carry parties
and governments across the bad patches of their careers. The
classical proletariat of this type is larger and better organized
in Chile than in most other Latin American countries, large
enough indeed to provide a base for government; but it is a
minority of the population.

The support of the other three decisive sectors of the population is either conditional, unreliable or absent. The *countryside*
(about 30 per cent of the people) remains predominantly anti-
Allendist, in spite of substantial gains by the left in recent years,
especially among rural proletarians. The political effect of
rapid agrarian reform will almost certainly be to deepen the
divisions within this sector. However, the government could
probably get along without it.

The rather large *middle strata*, consisting mostly of white-
collar workers, many in public employment – perhaps 12
per cent of the Chileans work in government – would accept
a socialist government as much as any other. They have no
overwhelming commitment to a society of private enterprise,
though probably some strong anti-communist prejudices exist
among them, and no sense of identity with those who are
poorer. On the other hand they have to be convinced that
socialist power will last, or at least that it will recur as often as
non-socialist governments. They are not yet convinced of this.

The major body of unmobilized support for the left consists
of those miscellaneous and unclassifiable *labouring poor* who
are being generated in ever growing numbers by a process
of economic growth and social change that fails to provide
enough corresponding employment. Politico-social jargon
tends to define them as 'semi-proletarians' (sometimes even
as 'Lumpenproletarians'), or by referring to the shanty
towns and do-it-yourself settlements in which so many of

them live (*pobladores*), or just negatively as 'the marginal population'. They are not marginal but central to Latin American society, even in Chile. This stratum puzzles the traditional left, since it is plainly not being absorbed by any spontaneous historic process into a classical 'proletariat': it is not organizable by the familiar methods of, e.g., labour unions or held together by some ideology of class consciousness like Marxism.

Unions are of marginal importance to such people, because their conditions of work do not make them easy to organize, and hence they do not belong to the aristocracy of relatively well-paid, unionized and militantly radical proletarians such as the miners (that 4 to 5 per cent of the working population whose role in Chilean left politics is so disproportionately important). Their own embryonically political populism, radical but – except in local community organization – not democratic, has in the past been most easily mobilized into a mass movement by demagogic presidents or ex-presidents, preferably military. It is a mistake to think of their politics as purely operational, but there is no doubt that a leader with patronage and the ability to deliver roads and water for shanty towns or welfare payments for their inhabitants, speedily and with some *éclat*, attracts them more than one who can't.

But whatever the difficulty of mobilizing them by means of the traditional labour and socialist movement, these people are a natural constituency of the left, because they are poor and they work.* What is more, now that the peasantry is a rapidly shrinking force, they are increasingly the decisive sector of the Latin American masses. The Christian Democrats managed to make some appeal to them. To judge by

* Moreover, if other Latin experience is a guide, they are increasingly attracted by the slogans of the left. The largest of their mass movements at present, the ANAPO in Colombia, is being fed left-wing rhetoric in large quantities – Che Guevara, Camilo Torres and all – by leaders who would undoubtedly have preferred to stick to demagogic generalities if they had not sensed the mood of their followers.

375

the municipal elections of 1971, the UP has not yet converted them en masse.

III

What has the Allende government achieved so far? What has it been trying to do? It has been and is acutely aware of the narrow limits of time. Consequently the government concentrates practically all its thinking on that period of between six months and three years within which, according to various assessments, its fate will be decided. There is not yet much concrete thinking beyond this point, which is a pity.

In the first place, short-range policy is based on the agreed programme of the six parties of the UP, an elaborate platform negotiated with great difficulty before the election but now binding. Nobody knows what would emerge from the next stage of argument, and sensible politicians try to postpone it. Admittedly two of the six parties in the UP are now negligible, while the Radicals, down to 8 per cent of the vote, are reduced and in disarray. But the left-wing ex-Christian Democrat element in the coalition is by no means insignificant, in spite of the electoral weakness of its representatives in the UP, if only because it represents many votes that must be captured. Moreover, while Allende probably sees eye to eye on major questions with the powerful CP, the core of the UP and by far its most effective and rational component, divergences among various sectors of his Socialist Party and between them and the communists are substantial.

In the second place, the government knows perfectly well that the unusually favourable political situation within Chile and internationally, which allowed it to come to office and has largely paralysed its opponents in the US ever since, will probably not last long. So far the armies have manoeuvred for position. Sooner or later the government will come to confrontation and battle, though not necessarily in the naïve form

376

anticipated by ultra-left apocalyptics – e.g. a military coup against mass resistance, or a foreign armed invasion.* The short run is within range of prediction; even the medium run is not.

Third, but of course most urgent, the economic problems of Chile will be at their most acute during the next two years. These problems derive from two characteristics of semi-colonial countries that unfortunately exist in an exaggerated form in Chile: its dependence on a single export commodity and the inefficiency of agriculture, which makes it (like other South American countries) an increasingly large importer of basic foodstuffs. Eighty per cent of Chile's foreign income depends on the price of copper. About a third of its imports (in value) consist of food, and since Chileans under the UP eat spectacularly better than before, this quantity will rise.

There is virtually nothing that Chile can do in the short run about the price of copper, which has to stay well above forty cents if the calculations of the planners are to come out right. A great many things, including the end of the Vietnam War, could cause the market to drop for a sufficiently long time to be catastrophic. However, even if the market holds, there will certainly be an acute balance-of-payments crisis in 1972, which for various reasons, however, is expected to be less acute in 1973.

Unfortunately the two obvious ways of minimizing this crisis, exporting more copper and cutting imports, are very difficult.

---

* At the time this article goes to press, it looks as though a confrontation with the US may be on the way, over the issue of compensation for the nationalized copper mines. Both sides are under some pressure to stand up and fight: Washington, because a lot of money is involved and a dangerous precedent set by confiscation; Santiago because it would help the Chilean balance of payments considerably not to pay out all those dollars. Also 'no compensation' is a popular slogan, and the confrontation between a little people and the giant of US imperialism has distinct political advantages for the UP. On the other hand both sides also have good reasons for avoiding an open clash. Given the key role of copper both in the Chilean economy and in US–Chilean relations, some kind of crisis will be hard to avoid, but its repercussions, beyond a purely economic warfare between the two countries, are as yet impossible to predict.

Copper production will not expand as much as is desirable or planned. Farm production will be lucky to remain stable. The boom in domestic spending will raise the demand for industrial raw materials, which is the other large item in the import trade. Chilean leaders are fairly optimistic about overcoming the transitional difficulties in copper and agricultural production, which are the most pressing of their economic problems. Even cautious politicians reckon that this shouldn't take more than three years. But those three years will be difficult and crucial, and will keep their minds fully occupied.

IV

In this situation the government has pursued four objectives:

First, it has aimed to introduce irreversible 'structural changes' in the economy within its first year. The theory behind this appears to be a rather simple economic determinism. As one minister put it: 'If we deprive the bourgeoisie of its economic base, it will not be able to return.' The method has been essentially the expropriation and, outside agriculture, nationalization of key economic activities. The UP is by its programme committed to a three-part structure of the economy: a dominant public sector, a mixed public-private sector, mostly in the areas where technical progress and heavy investment in equipment and know-how (including those from abroad) are essential, and a private sector of, it is hoped, dynamic small and medium business. By now copper, nitrates, coal, iron, banking, cement, a good part of textiles, and a number of other firms have been taken over in one way or another, and foreign trade will presumably have to be nationalized.

Second, the Allende government has aimed to stimulate production and therefore employment, and at the same time raise the standard of living, by stimulating demand, i.e. by combining a sharp increase in money wages with a price freeze. The government assumed, on the whole correctly, that Chilean industry was working with a sufficiently large unused capacity to make this possible without immediate new investment, which private business was obviously not going to undertake. Giving more money to the poor, it was argued, would stimulate employment disproportionately, since they were in the market for commodities with a more labour-intensive production than the more sophisticated hardware of the middle-class market. It must never be forgotten that no more than 300,000 of the 9 million Chileans were the effective customers for industry.

This plan was risky, and during the first few dramatic months after 4 September, when bourgeois hysteria led to mass flights of capital and a temporary collapse of production, it did not look promising. However, by the spring of 1971 the policy worked, to the enormous relief of the government and surprise of foreign observers, not to mention the striking benefit of the Chilean people. Unemployment was lower than it had been for ten years and, except for some serious planning troubles that delayed the revival of the construction industries, would have been even lower. The standard of living of the poor rose dramatically. Even the consumption of flour (i.e. bread) rose by 15 per cent. The critics point out that with the increase in production Chile's endemic inflation also revived. It used to run at 25 to 30 per cent a year, and during Frei's last year at 35 per cent. Still, this year it will be no more than half of this. Domestic economic policy has so far been the most significant success of the Allende regime.

To demonstrate the material advantage of a popular government is indispensable for the UP since it must present itself at free elections. Allende cannot, even if he wanted to, impose the material sacrifices on his people that the Cubans have made for the past several years. This sets very narrow limits to government policy, though some of its followers are unwilling to admit this. The communists, being the most realistic, take the view that during this presidency rapid heavy industrialization must be subordinated to light and consumer goods. Allende probably agrees, but the matter continues to be debated. Whether raising the standard of living alone will provide a government of legal revolutionaries with adequate support is another question.

The third objective follows from this calculation. The government must raise output, especially of copper and farm produce, in order to at least maintain the supply of food and consumer goods. Here again Allende and the CP see eye to eye. Since rationing or an uncontrolled sharp cutback in imports would be political suicide, the 'battle for production' is the first priority. However, copper and agriculture pose rather different problems.

Most Chilean copper comes from three great mines formerly owned by US companies – El Teniente, Chuquicamata and Salvador. Since last September output has been poor, which is a serious matter, and costs have risen steeply, which is less serious.* To what degree this situation is caused by sabotage by Kennecott and Anaconda, or, more plausibly, by their attempts to cream off the easy and profitable deposits in anticipation of expropriation, is a matter of argument. Certainly it is a consequence of widespread non-cooperation by executives and supervisory personnel – about 300 are said by the opposition to have resigned – especially those who used to be paid in US dollars, which they then exchanged on the free and now black market for increasingly astronomic quantities of escudos. Inevitably the effect of stopping these dollar payments to Chileans has been to lower the real income of such people, in spite of the government's unenthusiastic readiness to pay them almost any salaries in escudos. (In the summer of 1971 the unofficial exchange rate was already over three times the pegged official rate.)

---

* In principle, since the costs are in local currency and receipts in dollars, valuable foreign exchange will continue to be earned so long as enough copper is sold at an adequate price.

But the difficulties also arise from the collective self-interest of the small labour aristocracy of copper miners, who did well enough out of the enclave economy of the US corporations and are not likely to do relatively as well in the future. Whether or not they actually supported Eduardo Frei Montalva's Christian Democrat government (and in Chuquicamata the UP failed to poll a majority in the presidential election), the spontaneous syndicalism of such groups tends to operate easily at the expense of the wider popular interest. The strikes of workers and technicians that broke out during the past summer reflect both factors.

The problem of farm output is much more complex. The Christian Democrat government had generally subordinated the rate of agrarian reform to the raising of output, which it did with substantial success. Only thirty thousand families out of the quarter of a million of the landless and minifundists received land. Consequently by the end of Frei's presidency the accumulating agrarian discontent was already exploding in a burst of land occupations and other rural conflicts. Even if Allende had not won, either land reform would have had to be speeded up or major trouble would have developed in the countryside. The UP has accelerated land reform, but at an immediate cost to output, as is usual in such cases.

The extent of the disruption in output is hard to judge, partly because it cannot be disentangled from the effects of some dramatic natural catastrophes during the first half of 1971, partly because these things are a matter of guesswork anyway. The disruption was due to sabotage or to realization of capital by those fearing expropriation – especially during the fall of 1970 when a lot of dairy and breeding stock was sold off for meat – to the uncertainty of the middle peasants about their prospects, and to the demoralization of peasants in the sector where land reform took place. This in turn was caused by the UP's failure to apply any single or clear policy. When any meeting of agrarian reform officials is likely to turn into an ideological-programmatic argument over rival tendencies, peasants are likely to feel that the old government may have been slow, but at least a man knew who made the decisions and what they were.

The more suicidal or utopian elements in the UP have even exaggerated the extent of this disruption, talking wildly, and not only implausibly but without evidence, of a 50 per cent drop in output in the reformed sector that, they argue, will be more than compensated by the progress of rural class struggle. The best estimate is that there may be some decline in output, though the official view is that the sowing this spring (our fall) will compensate for the drop in the last fall (our spring) sowing, which may be around 10 per cent. The government reaction has been to slow down the initially very rapid expropriation of land, in order to get the seven hundred or so estates that were effectively taken over (out of the nine hundred or so expropriated) into production. Official expropriations have been stopped until after April 1972. As for unofficial ones, the government's view is that of Allende's Message to Congress:

> The indiscriminate occupations of estates and farms are unnecessary and prejudicial. What we have said and done should be enough to make people have confidence in us. Hence the plans of the government and their implementation should be respected.

On this point Allende (supported by the CP) clashes with the left opposition of the MIR and also with elements in the left wing of his own party.

Allende's view assumes that the occupations are controllable. Probably they are, for they are only to a small extent the product of unmanageable grassroots unrest. Of the 150 or so occupations recorded on a day chosen at random in the summer of 1971[4] about 25 or 30 per cent were attempts by Mapuche Indians to recuperate lost communal lands, which is certainly the most spontaneous part of agrarian agitation now, but even so not – or no longer – a mass movement. These sit-ins involved perhaps seven to eight hundred individuals in all, and only three of them mobilized more than a hundred, which is peanuts by the usual Latin American standards of peasant land occupation.

The others were partly occupations by landless peasants demanding expropriations for their benefit, but mainly incidents in rural labour disputes in which landownership was not at issue. No more than a handful of people is involved in an occupation of either type. The *tomas de fundos* make foreign headlines, because they suggest riot and anarchy and because some fairly colourful figures on the uncontrollable fringes of the ultra-left are active in them, but at present Chile is a long way from rural insurrection.

The fourth objective of the government is not to be overthrown. The danger of a military coup, though present, does not seem immediate. The main reason for this is not the army's sense of constitutional propriety, which exists, but the knowledge that it would lead to civil war. It is one thing to occupy some streets and buildings quietly and bundle the president onto the next plane abroad, but quite another to start an unpredictable armed conflict.

Here lies perhaps the main advantage of a legal *Marxist* government, as distinct from that of ordinary civilian populist reformers, whose actual short-term policy may not be very different. Such populists have tended to abdicate when the logical but unintended confrontation with the right followed: in Brazil Getúlio Vargas committed suicide [in 1954], Jânio Quadros retired [in 1961], João Goulart fled [following a military coup in 1964]. Marxist reformers know that social transformation will face such challenges, are prepared to face them – at least we must hope so – and consequently they diminish the risk of such coups.

There is not much the UP can do about the armed forces, except to put the police under politically reliable control and to surround the President with a strong bodyguard recruited from political cadres (mostly former MIRists) which could gain a few precious hours while the masses were being mobilized. Both these measures have been greeted with hysterical abuse by the right. Whether the UP could win a civil war if it came to that point is another question, but in the short run its obvious determination discourages militarist adventures.

The right would therefore prefer not to return to power by armed insurgency; certainly this is the Christian Democrat view. The Chilean rulers have benefited too long from a stable and peaceful constitutionalism to throw it light-heartedly out of the window. As it happens there is at present a promising alternative strategy: to reunite the anti-Marxist forces, whose split gave Allende the election, and to vote the formidable Frei back into the presidency in 1976. The prospect is realistic. If the UP cannot substantially increase its solid support, and especially if its marginal support is eroded by the predictable economic troubles of 1972–3, then the right could win a straight electoral fight in 1973, thus perpetuating its control of Congress and its power of delay and sabotage. In other words, all the opposition has to do according to this analysis is to wait for the UP to run out of steam. It is the classical strategy for ruining popular fronts, and it has worked before.

The immediate objective would therefore be an anti-left victory in 1973, followed by a long lame-duck presidency. This, rather than short-term confrontation, is what realists in the UP are worried about, although nobody overlooks the threat of straight counter-revolution. There is cause for worry, even if the right overestimates the probability of economic breakdown, as it has consistently overestimated the government's economic troubles since 1970, and been disagreeably surprised by its substantial successes. What can Allende do about the threat from the right? More than is being done now.

V

Many of the problems of the UP are beyond its effective control, but there are three things that are not.

The first is its tempo. Revolutionary transformations depend on establishing and maintaining *initiative*. Constitutional revolutions are no different from any others in this respect. They must, merely, like chess offensives, maintain initiative within a given set of rules. It seems to me that the UP has not yet established this tempo. The election campaign generated its own impetus, which was reinforced by the enormous and unexpected satisfaction of victory and the failure of the attempts to stop Allende from taking office. Conversely, unexpected defeat and a genuine terror of revolution demoralized and temporarily paralysed the Chilean right. For a few months it had no effective strategy at all, and did little but run for cover. Again, the UP had a programme and the need to push it ahead in its first year carried it along for a while, at least until the difficulties of application began to emerge.

So far the UP has rolled along under this initial, and in a sense extrinsic, impetus. As it exhausts itself, it must be replaced by intrinsic strategic initiative. Any reforming government tends to start, at least potentially, with such a burst of speed. Non-revolutionary administrations cannot easily replace it once it is exhausted, and some, like the British Labour government of 1964, throw it away. Failing to generate this impetus, such governments find themselves pressed onto the defensive by domestic and foreign adversaries and the hazards of the world, such as balance-of-payments crises. Then they are lost. They will fade away, like so many of the old popular fronts, amid growing internal bickering; or will provide the conditions for their overthrow. In 1970 and 1971 the UP did not need to generate its moving force, but from now on it must.

*

This is made difficult by the fact that the UP is a coalition: its second serious weakness. To put it bluntly, the UP is a vehicle better designed for braking than for movement. In order to prevent any party (read: the CP) from establishing exclusive control over any part of government, all jobs were distributed on a rigid quota system, so that no official has an immediate superior or immediate subordinate from his own party. In order to prevent any party (once again, read: the CP) from dominating policy, 'the action of the President and the parties and movements forming the government will be co-ordinated by a Political Committee of all these forces', which will be responsible for considering 'the practicability and application [*operatividad*] of the government's economic and social measures and those concerning public order and international policy, as well as more especially the means by which they are realized'.[5]

What this means is that each department and agency of state consists of intertwined rival party machines. Each official gives his primary loyalty to one of these, through which he seeks to operate, bypassing the others where possible, neutralizing them where this is impossible. Disputes must be solved by interparty negotiation and major ones tend to go to the top. It also means incidentally (a) that the relatively few non-party ministers or officials must attach themselves to one machine or another to get things done, and (b) that it is extremely difficult to fire the numerous political appointees who turn out to be no good at their jobs, but are protected by the need to maintain the balance of the quota system.

Above all, it means that anything not specifically provided for in the pre-election pact is hard and slow to get formulated, and that quick and unambiguous decisions are almost impossible to make. The effect of this paralysis is disastrous, notably in agricultural reform. Any government that cannot make decisions rapidly is in trouble, but a revolutionary government that cannot is in very bad trouble.

Admittedly mutual trust between the parties is today much

greater than it was before the election. Even the MIR has come to terms and established a working relationship with both the Socialists and the CP – a relationship, however, that is better with one [the Communist Party] than with the other [the Socialist Party], since in MIR opinion (which is obvious truth), 'it is possible to have organic-relations with the CP leading to rational agreements'. Such relations are not easy to establish with the Socialists, a party which is little more than a complex of rival groups, patronage systems and political baronies, virtually incapable of acting as a party. Its main problem today lies on its left wing. Unlike the MIR, few of the clans on the Socialist Party left are serious revolutionaries, in spite of Guevarist and ultra-left rhetoric. Some would say – I quote a disillusioned nonpartisan progressive – that 'they are people who can't get used to the idea of being the government, since it was so much simpler to be in opposition'. Some less sympathetic observers would add that leftism is an easy way out for people who find they are no good at their new government jobs.

How important the left is within the Socialist Party is difficult to estimate. The left certainly elected the new General Secretary earlier this year, though Carlos Altamirano, who clearly aims to be the next presidential candidate of the UP (no Chilean president can serve two successive terms), is unlikely to identify himself with any one section of the party. The Socialist left is likely to be strengthened by the desire to compete with the CP, which can most easily be outflanked on that side, and by a familiar form of reaction to the disappointments and uncertainties of popular government. If the left, or any of its groups, were to gain genuine control of the party, this would be at least one solution to the perennial problem of the party's disunity. This is unlikely, and so the best hope lies in Allende, whose position (if only as the real vote getter) gives him considerable leverage in his party. Unfortunately he has so far been extremely slow to use this leverage.

387

In brief, the UP suffers from the familiar weaknesses of party alliances and coalitions in a parliamentary democracy. It is organizationally unsuited to the tasks it has accepted. The 'Chilean road to socialism' does not necessarily imply a single, still less a monolithic, party of the left, and anyway this is not a realistic possibility. But it does imply giving the existing alliance greater unity of decision and action.

Third, the UP has so far failed to mobilize the masses adequately in its support. It has, once again, reflected the weaknesses of its historical parents, bourgeois parliamentary democracy and the classical socialist labour movement. Parliamentary politicians think of mass mobilization essentially as getting votes. Traditional working-class leaders think of the union or party pulling the fellows out of mines and plants on to the streets. (One might add that the historical complement of both is a kind of leftism that rejects both elections and mobilization through 'bureaucratic' organizations and proposes instead to multiply grassroots mass action irrespective of circumstances.)

None of these is adequate for revolutionary purposes, least of all in countries where national elections may not be part of popular political culture or where the organized industrial proletariat is not the typical form of the labouring poor. All the traditions emerging out of liberalism and the classical socialist labour movement have, moreover, been suspicious of the charismatic style, the personalized politics, the face-to-crowd rapport, not to mention the freewheeling demagogy, which have normally accompanied the effective mobilization of 'the marginal'.

In the UP there is a lot of talk about how to get more votes in future elections or how to formulate a plebiscite that will win a majority; there is even a tendency to take otherwise minor electoral contests more seriously than they deserve. There is much planning about how to mobilize organized workers through the unions, about the best way to set up peasant councils or various factory committees. Conversely, on the left there is a rather simple belief that all will be well if only 'the struggle is transferred fundamentally to the factories, the estates, the slum settlements, the high schools and universities'.

But the fact is that the unorganized poor between elections are not as yet constantly *involved* with the government, that government is not constantly *present* for them. There is no equivalent of Fidel Castro's perpetual if one-sided dialogue with his people, or of FDR's regular fireside talks over the radio. This is not merely a matter of rhetorical style. A rabble-rousing technique is not necessary, and may not even be desirable, for the maintenance of such permanent conversation between a popular government and its people. What is at issue is a style of politics rather than of oratory or campaigning.

This is a problem that concerns President Allende as an individual more than the UP, although the suspicions of excessive presidentialism among his comrades and coalition partners may have to be overcome. (They might recall that the masses who became Democrats in the US because of FDR did not stop being Democrats after his death: personalized politics can precipitate permanent organizational changes of allegiance.)

The unorganized labouring poor will listen to Allende, because he has the prestige, power and paternal function of any president, and because he represents a government that is demonstrably on their side. They can be mobilized most readily as a national force by him, and they can be turned into a permanent and decisive national force, which is what Perón achieved in Argentina. He may have to choose a rather different personal style from his friend Fidel, but he should not forget one of the few lessons of the Cuban Revolution that are applicable in Chile, namely, that a leader capable of speaking directly to the most remote and least political of his poor fellow citizens is a major asset for any revolution, and probably indispensable for one that cannot coerce people but must persuade them.

VI

How can one sum up the first year of the Chilean Way? It has demonstrated what hardly required proof, namely, that a left-wing alliance can be voted into office. It has demonstrated something more important, namely, that it can thereafter act with some speed and decision in spite of lacking control of the armed forces and crucial parts of the constitutional machinery. It has demonstrated a determination to proceed with the construction of socialism, though its first year has not taken it beyond the boundaries of non-socialist reform.

So far what it has done is not *qualitatively* very different from what several other Latin American governments have done, are doing, or could well make up their minds to do. But unlike other reforming governments, it is based firmly on the working-class movement, and its primary inspiration is not nationalism or 'modernization' but the emancipation of the exploited, the oppressed, the weak and the poor. It has demonstrated considerable intelligence and political skill. Finally, its achievements, especially in the economic field, are substantial.

These things do not guarantee its success. It is plainly, like most under- or rather mis-developed semi-colonial countries, at the mercy of forces beyond its control, e.g. the copper market, to which it is all the more sensitive because Chile is after all, by the standards of the Third World, a highly urbanized and industrialized country with a complex social structure and modern consumption patterns. We do not yet know whether it is capable of overcoming the peculiar economic stagnation (combined in this case with permanent high inflation) that it shares with the rest of the 'southern cone' of Latin America, and for that matter with Britain, on whose economy this area was dependent for so long. Experience shows that such long-term weaknesses are more difficult to remedy than policy makers think. Nor do we yet know how the Chilean Way can overcome the major problem of underdeveloped economies, the lag of jobs behind population. The short-term difficulties of production, while serious, are not in themselves decisive.

Politically, the Chilean Way has not yet shown that a popular front, however dynamic and well-intentioned, is a revolution, however constitutional. It remains fettered not only by outside forces but by the nature of the political system and situation out of which it has emerged and the political forces which have combined to form it. No doubt it is too early to judge it. It has not yet been tested in serious crisis and by genuine challenge, and the UP's capacity to overcome its present weaknesses of style, organization and policy should not be underestimated. The next year may shake it, and may also transform it. But it will not be transformed spontaneously.

[...] Can the UP overcome [these crises and challenges]? Its opponents, including almost certainly the US government, are convinced that it cannot. Chilean government leaders and political figures are cautiously optimistic or, perhaps better, not pessimistic, even in private. So are some very able and politically uninvolved Chileans I talked to. A betting man who allowed his natural sympathy for Allende to bias his judgement a little would perhaps offer odds of six to four against, which is not discouraging. If he kept his sympathies entirely out of the transaction, he might perhaps offer two to one against. Even that is a great deal more than anyone would have offered to bet on the Bolsheviks after the October Revolution. Or, for that matter, on Salvador Allende's victory thirteen months ago.

September 1971

Notes

Some notes in the original essay have been omitted from the version that appears in this volume.

1 *La Via Chilena, del primer mensaje del President Allende al Congreso Pleno, 21 de Mayo 1971* (Santiago, 1971).

2 Cf. the MIR statement disavowing the assassination of the former Christian Democrat Minister of the Interior by the VOP, a small terrorist group. *Punto Final*, 22 June 1971.

3 Labarca, a journalist on the communist *El Siglo*, has been criticized for his treatment of the ultra-left (see Manuel Cabieses Donoso, 'Puntualizando la Historia', *Punto Final*, 25 May 1971), but the book is full of valuable information about the formation of the UP, the military plots, and other matters. Broadly, a carefully elaborated pre-election pact between Allende and the (left-wing) Christian Democrat candidate [Radomiro Tomic] was to govern their relations after the election. It provided that (a) if the right-wing candidate [former president Jorge Alessandri] were to come in third, UP and DC would accept whichever candidate won the plurality as the winner, provided that the margin of difference exceeded thirty thousand votes; (b) if Alessandri won, both UP and DC would accept his victory within twenty-four hours provided his plurality was greater than one hundred thousand; (c) if Alessandri came in second, whichever candidate came in third – in the event it was Tomic – would concede victory immediately, provided the winner had a plurality of at least five thousand votes over Alessandri. (In fact Allende's plurality was 39,000.) However, the DC leadership after the election, under the influence of ex-President Frei who, incidentally, appears not to have discouraged the military plots of which he was aware, made the support of Congress for Allende conditional on the promise of a constitutional amendment that would formally guarantee 'the survival of the democratic regime'. After some negotiation and modification such an amendment was subsequently passed. See Fernando Silva Sanchez, *Primeras Reformas Constitucionales del Presidente Allende* (Valparaiso, 1971).

4 My source is the confidential daily police report on these matters, which I was kindly allowed to consult.

5 Labarca Goddard, *Al Chile Rojo*, p. 235.

28

The Murder of Chile

The murder of Chile has been so long expected, and the agony of Allende's last months was therefore reported frequently enough in the press, for all those who live by getting their names in the media to offer public obituaries – except for Washington, which has (as I write) kept an eloquent silence. Even the British Labour Party, which took about as little interest in Chilean social democracy during its lifetime as it normally does in the affairs of Afghanistan, has greeted its death with some official tears. This is temporarily embarrassing to the murderers, whose model was a rather less well-publicized counter-revolution, which incidentally produced the greatest massacre on post-war record – the Indonesian one of 1965.

The young reactionaries had painted 'Djakarta' on the walls of Santiago before the coup; and the Chilean military is even now telling television viewers how successful Indonesia has been since in attracting foreign investment. There won't be any problem about foreign investment. Nobody will even know how many Chileans will fall victims to the vengeance of their middle class, since most of the victims will be the kind of Chileans about whom nobody has ever heard outside their factory, shanty town or village. After all, a hundred years after the end of the Paris Commune, we still don't know precisely how many were massacred after its suppression.

The chief trouble about the obituaries is that few of them have been very interested in Chile. The tragedy of this small and remote country is that, like Spain in the 1930s, its politics were of global significance, exemplary and, unfortunately, unprotected. It became a test case. The Americans knew perfectly well that it was a test case of something much simpler than whether socialism can come without violent insurrection or civil war. The issue for them was, and remains, the maintenance of imperial supremacy in Latin America. This had begun to be eroded in the past five years by a variety of political regimes not only in Chile but also in Peru, Panama, Mexico and, most recently, with Perón's triumph, Argentina. Perón rather than Allende probably finally tipped the scale towards encouraging a military coup. The United States had, with some confidence, relied on slow economic strangulation to finish off Chile – always a country with a staggering foreign debt, a rapidly rising import bill, and a single commodity to sell (copper), whose price collapsed in 1970 and stayed down for the next two years. But the Americans now felt they could no longer wait. In any case, the continued arms deliveries to the Chilean forces showed that the United States always kept the possibility of a coup in mind.

For the rest of the world, Chile was a more theoretical test case of the future of socialism. The right and ultra-left were both concerned to prove to their own satisfaction that a democratic socialism could not work. Their obituaries have been chiefly concerned to demonstrate how right they were. For both, it was Allende's fault.

The weaknesses and failures of Allende's Popular Unity were indeed serious. All the same, before the various mythologies get fixed in permanent moulds, it is as well to get three things clear.

The first, and most obvious, is that the Allende government did not commit suicide but was murdered. What finished it was not political or economic mistakes and financial crisis but guns and bombs. And to those commentators on the right, who ask what other choice remained open to Allende's opponents but a coup, the simple answer is: not to make a coup.

The second is that the Allende government was not a test of democratic socialism, but at most of the willingness of the bourgeoisie to abide by legality when legality and constitution-alism no longer work to its advantage. The Popular Unity did not have the sort of constitutional power which elected British Labour governments have had, and wasted. It had a president legally elected on a minority vote, faced with a hostile judiciary and a parliament controlled by its enemies, which prevented it from passing *any* legislation except by permission of the opposition. Allende operated not with constitutional power, but merely with such resources as ingenuity could extract from his position as the legal (if constitutionally crippled) president. Short of winning control at this year's parliamentary elections, there was no way of getting much further by constitutional means. And he did not win control.

But what of the unconstitutional means? Here the third point to note is that the choice of 'revolution', rather than 'legality', was not on. Neither in military nor in political terms was the Popular Unity in a position to win a trial of physical strength. Certainly Allende hated civil war, as any adult with histori-cal experience must, however convinced that it is sometimes necessary. But if Allende did all he could to avoid it, it was because he believed that his side would lose a civil war; and he was undoubtedly right. It was the other side which attempted to provoke a trial of strength – incidentally, by using the tradi-tional methods of the working class to devastating effect. And the national strikes of transport firms were designed not simply to paralyse the economy, but to face the government with the choice between coercion and abdication, and therefore to lever the armed forces out of their posture of political neutrality. For the reactionaries knew that if the armed forces had to choose between identifying themselves with the left or with the right, they would choose the right. The strikes failed last autumn, but succeeded this summer.

Against this, Allende had merely the threat of resistance. In effect, he asked the other side whether they were prepared for the awful and, in the long run, uncontrollable option of civil war. Probably he miscalculated the reluctance of the Chilean bourgeoisie to plunge into it. The left has generally underestimated the fear and hatred of the right, the ease with which well-dressed men and women acquire a taste for blood. But, as the event has shown, resistance from the left was organized. Only time will show whether it was organized sufficiently well. Perhaps not. But, unlike the Brazilian left in 1964, the Chilean left is going down fighting. And if the country is now entering a period of darkness, nobody can be in any doubt about who switched off the lights.

What could Allende have done? It is a difficult moment in which to conduct inquests into the possible mistakes of brave men and women, many of whom are or soon will be dead. One does not in any case wish to join those who are at present posing on Allende's grave with posters inscribed, in suitably differing ways, 'I told you so.' It is not even very easy, at this time, to distinguish between what was error and what was not, between things beyond the control of Chileans (like the copper market); things which might theoretically have been otherwise but were in practice not modifiable (for example, the paralysis of policies due to rivalries within the Popular Unity); and policies which could have been effectively different. There is no doubt that the economic gamble of the Allende regime – and it was always a gamble against the odds – failed.

I do not myself think that there was much Allende could have done after (say) early 1972 except to play out time, secure the irreversibility of the great changes already achieved, and with luck maintain a political system which could give the Popular Unity a second chance later. He neither could nor did offer to construct socialism during a single presidency. For the last several months, it is fairly certain that there was practically nothing he could do. However tragic the news of the coup, it had been expected and predicted. It surprised nobody.

September 1973

Editor's note

The final part of this article was severely cut before publication in *New Society*. In a letter to the editor in the following week's issue (27 September 1973) Eric summarized the points made in it 'for the sake of the balance of the argument':

1. The Popular Unity failed to maintain the support of the lower middle class and small farmers and businessmen, though it succeeded in extending its support among the workers and the poor. This failure was fatal. Both Allende and the Communist Party were aware of how important it would prove.
2. Thanks to the continued armed resistance of the Chilean movement not all has been or will be lost: unlike Brazil in 1964.
3. A return to the old Chilean democracy is unlikely. The future pattern is most likely to follow (with modifications) the now favoured Brazilian line: ultra-right-wing guerrillas, technocrats and plenty of foreign capital. The next victim may well be the 'Nasserite' wing of the Peruvian military.
4. In ten years from now the USA will probably feel less happy about Latin America than it does now.

VII

LATE REFLECTIONS

29

Murderous Colombia

About the only thing that most non-Colombians know about
the third largest country in Latin America, and virtually the
least known, is that it supplies cocaine and the novels of Gabriel
García Márquez. García Márquez is indeed a marvellous guide
to his extraordinary country, but not a good introduction to it.
Only those who have been there know how much of what reads
like fantasy is actually close to Colombian reality. The drug
traffic is also, unfortunately, an important element in it, though
one that authoritative Colombians are not anxious to discuss
much. It must also be admitted that they are a good deal more
relaxed about it than their North American opposite numbers.
This is probably because, authoritative or not, Colombians
today are chiefly worried about the rising tide of murder.

The country has long been known for an altogether exceptional proclivity to homicide. The excellent Americas Watch
report of September 1986 on human rights there points out that
homicide was the leading cause of death for males between the
ages of fifteen and forty-four, and the fourth-ranking cause of
death for all ages. Violent death is not simply one way in which
life can end in this country. It is, to quote a superb and chilling

recent exercise in oral history by Alfredo Molina, *Los Años del tropel: Relatos de la violencia* (Bogotá, 1985), 'an omnipresent personage'. But what Colombians fear is not simply death, but a renewed drift into one of those pandemics of violence that have occasionally flooded across the country, most notably during the twenty years from 1946 to 1966, which are known simply as *La Violencia*. This grim era has recently been seriously studied by an excellent group of younger local historians, among whom Carlos Ortiz's study of the coffee region of the Quindío in the 1950s, *Estado y subversión en Colombia*, is remarkable for showing what can be achieved by a combination of archival research, oral history and local knowledge. Among systematic attempts to link the *Violencia* years with the present, the book edited by Gonzalo Sánchez and Ricardo Peñaranda, *Pasado y presente de la Violencia en Colombia* (Bogotá, 1985), and Arturo Alape's *El Bogotazo: la paz, la violencia* (Bogotá, 1983), an important compilation of *hechos* and *testimonios*, should be mentioned.

Fear of a new high tide of murder – the last one killed some two hundred thousand – is both political and social. (The figure of three hundred thousand, quoted in the Americas Watch report, is not based on evidence, and is almost certainly too high.*) Colombia was for most of its history, and still is to a surprising extent, a land for pioneer settlers ('the classic *colono* with his axe, gun and hunting dog', to quote a description of the 1970s). National government and law still make only occasional incursions into much of the countryside from the cities, which in turn are only vaguely under the control of the capital. Even the

---

* ***Editor's note***. Following a letter from Aryeh Neier of Americas Watch published in the 26 February 1987 issue of the *New York Review of Books*, Eric apologized for wrongly assigning to Americas Watch in its report 'Human Rights in Colombia as President Barca Begins', September 1986, the figure of three hundred thousand deaths during *La Violencia* from another source. A previous report 'The Central-Americanization of Colombia', January 1986, had referred to 'more than two hundred thousand deaths' during *La Violencia*.

most ancient and powerful national institution – the Catholic Church – has only a skeleton organization. [. . .]

It was, and still to some extent is, something like a combination of the Wild West, twentieth-century Latin American urbanization and eighteenth-century England, in which a constitutional oligarchy of established rich families, divided into two rival parties (Liberals and Conservatives), constituted what government there was. Colombia had a national party system before it had a national state. The cohesion of this oligarchy and its genuine attachment to an electoral constitution have ensured that the country has practically never fallen victim to the usual Latin American dictatorships or military juntas, but the price has been endemic, and sometimes epidemic, bloodshed. For here arms are nobody's monopoly, and, for reasons that have so far eluded historians, the common people at some time in the nineteenth century adopted the Liberal and Conservative parties as rival forms of grassroots religion. As Alfredo Molano's book demonstrates, nothing can be more lethal than that.

[The transformation of Colombian society during the past sixty years] has put the traditional social and political order under enormous strain, and has occasionally ruptured it. How effectively it continues to exist today is a very big and open question.

Initially the pressure came from below, as the urban and rural masses were mobilized for struggle against the oligarchy, most notably by the extraordinary populist leader Jorge Eliécer Gaitán, whose assassination on a street in Bogotá in 1948 set off, within hours, a spontaneous insurrection of the capital, joined by the police, and propagated in numerous provincial cities through equally spontaneous assumptions of power by local revolutionary committees. Whether Gaitán was killed by the oligarchy, as the common people automatically assumed, cannot be known. That they had reason to fear this man, who had captured the Liberal Party and was about to become president, is certain. After all, single-handed he set off the only

403

known nationwide revolution by spontaneous combustion. [. . .] What should have been a social revolution ended as *La Violencia* because, perhaps for the last time, the oligarchical system managed to contain and take over the social insurrection by turning it into a party contest. But that battle escaped from control, and became an avalanche of blood, because the armed struggle of Liberals against Conservatives now carried an additional charge of social hatred and fear: the fear of Conservative oligarchs that their party would be a permanent minority against a Liberal Party which looked like capturing the newly aroused masses; and poor men's hatred of the other side not just as hereditary adversaries but as oppressors of the poor or as people who were better at making a little money.

The most murderous phase of the conflict (between 1948 and 1953) reconciled the establishment briefly to one of Colombia's rare military dictatorships, under General Rojas Pinilla, between 1953 and 1957. However, after his fall, threatened with loss of control both from soldiers and from social revolution, the oligarchy decided to close ranks. Under the National Front – which in effect is only ending in 1986 – the parties suspended their struggle, took turns to provide the presidency, and shared out the jobs equitably among themselves. The *Violencia* tailed off into politicized banditry, more or less liquidated in the mid-1960s, a phase analysed with much perception by in Gonzalo Sánchez and Donny Meertens in *Bandoleros, gamonales y campesinos: el caso de la Violencia in Colombia* (Bogotá, 1983). For a little while it looked as though the modern state might actually be coming to Colombia.

In fact, the pace and impetus of social change was, once again, too much for the social system; especially one ossified by a ruling class whose sense of the urgency of social reform has been atrophied by long success in killing off or driving out any undesirable elements. In the twenty-five years after 1950 Colombia changed from a two-thirds rural population to a 70 per cent urban one, while the *Violencia* set off yet another major wave of men and women who, by force, fear or choice, made tracks for one or other of the many places where a man and his wife could clear some ground and grow enough for their needs, far away from government and the powerful rich. New industry came to Colombia, which now makes French and Japanese cars, US trucks and Soviet jeeps. New primary products came, notably marijuana and cocaine, and so did tourism. New kinds of wealth and influence undermined the old oligarchy. Since 1970 several men who were not born into the old dynasties have made it to the top in Colombian politics: Misael Pastrana, César Turbay, Belisario Betancur. The social tensions which once burst into spontaneous revolution are still as tense as ever.

In the countryside they account for the steady expansion until 1984 of the guerrilla movement, which began in the mid-1960s with a few armed communist self-defence groups, driven into remote and inaccessible areas, but which the army failed to liquidate. They formed the original nucleus of the major armed movement of the past twenty years, the Colombian Communist Party's Colombian Revolutionary Armed Forces (FARC) which, at the time of the 1984 armistice, had twenty-seven 'fronts' or regional units. (The FARC's chief political commissar, Jacobo Arenas, has now published *Cese el fuego* (Bogotá, 1985), 'a political history' of the guerrilla force.) Basically it is a peasant movement of frontier settlers. For the essence of the 'agrarian problem' in a country with any amount of land to spare is not land hunger. It is, to put it simply, the defence of squatter rights against landlords with equally vague or uncertain legal claims to the ownership of vast and underutilized territories, but with more political and (until the arrival of the guerrillas) military power.*

*

* The standard cause of peasant rebellion elsewhere, the fight to regain alienated common lands, is, in Colombia, confined to former or surviving Indian communities, which form a special case. The first Communist mayor legally appointed in the country (1986) administers Coyaima, a typical Indian *'resguardo'* – and one long politicized for this reason.

The FARC was long underestimated by all except the army, because its members operated in the far hinterlands, and because city intellectuals didn't take those 'little peasants' (*campesinitos*) seriously. It never stopped growing, and numbered about three-quarters of all the guerrillas.[1] After 1965 they were joined by smaller rival and hostile groups. The Cuban-inspired National Liberation Army (ELN) was doomed by the lunacy of the Che Guevara–Régis Debray '*foco*' theory – of launching, from the outside, a guerrilla force in the hinterland – which it was to exemplify. The ELN attracted priests and students, but its pointlessness and lack of political objectives were soon evident. It has probably killed more of its own members and ex-members as 'traitors' than it ever killed soldiers. Virtually ineradicable, like all Colombian guerrilla movements, it refuses to sign any truce, and has few supporters at present but, thanks to its shaking down international oil companies, a lot of money.

A middle-class breakaway from the CP also formed the Maoist Popular Army of Liberation (EPL). The last and most widely publicized guerrilla movement, the M-19, was formed in 1974, and purported to be a response to the stealing of the 1970 presidential election from General Rojas, the ex-dictator, who launched a successful comeback as a Colombian Perón, or rather neo-Gaitán, appealing to the vast urban marginal population on a radical populist programme, and with enormous success. He undoubtedly won the 1970 election. But though the new guerrillas contained some former followers of Rojas, the M-19 was really formed by that characteristic Latin American phenomenon, the sons – and a few daughters – of good families for whom the Communist Party is not revolutionary enough.[2] Its chief leaders had been in the FARC. M-19 inhabited the social world of the Colombian upper middle classes and its leaders took the techniques of modern publicity for granted. In this world parents are neither surprised nor shocked that brave young men show the natural idealism of youth by revolutionary activity, and prove their manhood by what a local wit has called *machismo-leninismo* [...] Until it demonstrated its political bankruptcy between 1984 and 1986 the M-19 enjoyed enormous sympathies in these quarters.

The multiplication of guerrilla movements was a sign of frustration. Given the Colombian people's social ferment and the potential for armed struggle, why did the social revolution seem so remote? However, if the guerrillas posed no real threat to the system – General Rojas's short-lived mobilization of the urban masses had been much more dangerous – neither could they be eliminated by the (surprisingly small) Colombian army of about sixty thousand. They seemed a permanent part of a landscape in which groups of armed men belong just as naturally as rivers. But while army and guerrillas fought each other to a sort of draw in various rural zones, the social and political problems of which guerrillas were one symptom became steadily more explosive. The only explosion envisaged by both guerrillas and army (cheered on by the US Army which had trained so many of its officers) was a communist revolution. But, as other Colombians know better than anyone else, there are more dangerous – because unfocused and negative – forms of social explosion.

Belisario Betancur (1982–6) was the first president to recognize that the solution of Colombia's problems required major changes in Colombian affairs, and, as a precondition, an end to the endemic and pointless state of sub-civil war. He set out to achieve this against military resistance from both sides. A civilized Catholic intellectual, a maverick Conservative appealing deliberately to the growing body of his countrymen who no longer identify by blood with one of the two parties, he set out to open a new era in Colombian history. He achieved a peak of public success in 1984 when he fired a military minister and was thus able to sign a truce with all major guerrilla groups except the ultras of the ELN. By the end of his presidency, however, most of his initiatives seemed to be crumbling and his administration to be foundering in blood.

All the guerrillas (except the FARC) were once again fighting; the US had wrecked the possibilities for peace in Central America; the Cartagena Front of the Latin American debtor states – another of Betancur's favourite initiatives – proved to be only a brief headline story, while the drug mafia killed his minister of justice (one of fifty-seven judges assassinated during his term of office). The M-19's seizure of the supreme court, a publicity coup gone wrong, ended in the massacre of a hundred people, mostly judges and other civilians, discrediting army, guerrillas and the president himself.

Nevertheless, Betancur may still have opened a new era in Colombia. The country, long the most solid and loyal backer of US world policy, has shifted into non-alignment for the first time. Virgilio Barco, the new president, is a Liberal who overwhelmed an ultra-right-wing Conservative contender. He deliberately maintains Betancur's policies, even though the Conservatives are now a non-cooperating opposition. The FARC still maintains the truce and has turned from guns to votes with more success than expected, through the new left-wing party it formed, the Patriotic Union (UP). Paradoxically for a movement sponsored by the party of the proletariat, its strength is overwhelmingly rural. It is probably the first peasant party in Colombian history. (Conversely, its strength in the big cities is absurdly low, though larger than in the past: forty-four thousand among the four million residents of Bogotá, thirty-four thousand among the 2.5 million of Medellín.) President Barco is entirely committed to recognizing the new political pluralism, and especially the right of the Patriotic Union to state and municipal office. Under a quiet but explosive piece of democratic reform, mayors – who are now appointed by the regional governors – are soon to be actually elected. This and other recent reforms are undramatic but really quite major changes in Colombian politics.

*

These changes and the uncertainties about the future, not to mention the period of transition between presidencies, have produced a mood of tension, fear and dark expectations, stimulated by a sharp rise in political homicide and, more worrying because more novel, in 'disappearances'. It is impossible to say whether non-political killings, poorly covered by the press, are increasing, but there is no reason to suppose that the cocaine industry, which has got past the stage of (literal) cut-throat competition, has need of much murder, except of judges who might apply the 1979 extradition treaty with the US. Wild frontiers of free competition such as illicit emerald mining are more lethal – some three hundred corpses so far in 1986 – but they always are.[3] The real growth sector is right-wing terror.

This takes the form of threats against and murders of labour leaders and activists of the UP, who during September 1986 were falling at the rate of about one a day – an apparent rise in the rate of attacks on the left, which is said to have lost about three hundred during the last two years of the Betancur era. Even more sinister are 'unknown' death squads which, in defence of morality and social order, have taken to making weekend forays through cities like Cali and Medellín, killing 'antisocial' elements such as petty criminals, homosexuals, prostitutes or just plain beggars and bums indiscriminately. The 1986 figures for these massacres in Cali (Colombia's third largest city) speak for themselves: eighty dead in January, eighty-two in February, eighty-four in March, ninety-one in April, ninety-eight in May, 114 in June, one hundred in July, 102 in August, and seventy-nine in the first eighteen days of September. (The total for 1985 was 763.)[4]

The systematic nationwide campaign of assassination against left-wing leaders, especially those elected to office, suggests some co-ordination, but nobody has been able to come up with hard evidence of this. On the other hand nobody doubts that local army commanders and police forces are in close touch with paramilitary forces and death squads, which enjoy the enthusiastic support of local landowners (who include many ex-officers) and industrialists, not to mention the sort of radical right that draws no sharp lines between muggers, [frequenters of] gay bars, union organizers and the communist world conspiracy. It is also claimed, mainly in army quarters, that ultra-left guerrillas are responsible for such attacks.

Whoever they are, whoever organizes them, and whatever exactly the number of the 'disappeared' to date, the central fact about death squads and paramilitaries is that nobody, least of all persons associated with the armed forces, has been arrested, prosecuted, let alone convicted.[5] As a well-informed journalist put it to me: 'The only national co-ordination which has been clearly established consists in the decision not to do anything about these killings.' The extreme caution with which even brave politicians in a country with a long tradition of civilian supremacy treat the armed establishment is much the most worrying symptom of Colombia's present state.

Why should there be a wild rightist backlash? On its face, the immediate situation hardly calls for hysteria. The economy is expected to grow. The poor are no poorer than usual, and take as much pride as ever in being able to stand anything, having recently discovered the kind of popular heroes whose characteristic is toughness to the limits of the unendurable, namely mountain cyclists. Colombians, thanks to their heroes' participation in the Tour de France, now know more Alpine than Andean geography.

On any reckoning, the guerrilla situation is better. The six thousand or so in arms under the FARC doggedly maintain the truce against considerable provocation. They freely invite journalists to their remote headquarters, with excellent results for the image of their hard-bitten elderly chieftain, the legendary Manuel Marulanda, surrounded by equally tough men whose very *noms de guerre* are a reminder of the hopes of their youth: Timochenko, Ivan, Fidel Labrador.[6] The right complains that

410

public media like television should not give publicity to rebels, but rational politicians must welcome this exchange of ambushes for photo opportunities. In any case the most likely future for the UP, as for the pre-1914 socialist parties in European parliamentary countries, is not the revolutionary seizure of power, but a radical farmer-labour party with a solid base in the frontier territories, which gives it the chance to negotiate deals with the Liberals or, with luck, to hold a political balance in their favour.

As for the one thousand or so guerrillas – no estimate runs as high as two thousand – who are still or once again fighting, now united in the so-called National Guerrilla Co-ordination, their political bankruptcy has been underlined by the FARC's success in seizing its political opportunities. Their strategic bankruptcy is shown by the fission of various groups, by the M-19's loss of virtually all its top leaders in the desperate recent coups, and by the Cambodian-style activities of the Ricardo Franco group, an anti-truce student breakaway from the FARC, which massacred 160 of its own members – in fact, most of them – as traitors and police infiltrators.

It is hard to believe that in 1984 the guerrillas, according to (unpublished) opinion polls, enjoyed a 75 per cent favourable rating, and the M-19 were the darlings of the middle class. The chief admirers are now found in the shanty towns and slums where brave children dream of becoming heroes. If there is any strategy behind the wild guerrilla lunges of recent months, it is probably to raise insurrection in these areas, which the military could only control by indiscriminate bombing. At bottom the M-19 calculations were always those of stimulating a potentially insurrectionary situation into actual revolution by some dramatic military operation.[7] This is no more likely to happen now than when the army was fighting four times as many guerrillas. Militarily the guerrillas could not win then, and they can't win now, however satisfactory it was for them to prove that the army couldn't win either.

411

Why, then, the nervousness of the right? Perhaps it is because the disintegration of party system and state (except for the army) has once again shifted the centre of gravity from the capital to the regions, where various tense local situations do not look any better because the national situation is calm; and because those who feel threatened today are not so much the old oligarchic families who have stood off worse challenges without losing their cool, or the really super rich, but medium-size estate owners, entrepreneurs and politicos, on their way up. These people feel abandoned, as the guerrillas, fighting or non-fighting, remain in arms in the countryside, and as they themselves cross the red lights in their locked cars in the empty night-time streets of Bogotá or Cali, for fear that their throats will be cut if they stop. The presidents of the Chamber of Commerce, of the Rotary Club, Kiwanis and Lions' clubs, and the Association of Accountants (to cite some of the signers of an embittered anti-FARC manifesto from an outlying department):[8] for these the only good subversives and antisocials may well be dead ones; and in Colombia there are plenty of men and even a few women who can be hired to kill if the price is right.

Under the circumstances the most optimistic judgements one is likely to hear in Colombia are that nothing much is going to change. The more pessimistic range from an Argentinization of the country to its Salvadorization: military terror or civil war. Or perhaps the extension of what is already the case in Cali or Medellín, a three- or four-way chaos of violence by official forces, vigilante gangs, guerrilla supporters and plain criminals. Probably the darker of these are too gloomy. Colombia has an encouragingly long record of violent immobility. But President Barco is taking over in a distinctly worried country.

Where, in all this, do Colombians see the drug traffic? It depends from where you look at it. From the point of view of the frontier peasants, about whom much the most original book

412

on the subject has been written by three unassuming researchers from the National University, Jaime Jaramillo, Leonidas Mora, and Fernando Cubides, *Colonización, coca y guerrilla*, coca is in the first place a speculative but uncertain crop that has no competition as a profit maker, or for the wages one can earn picking it. Costs rise, mainly because the soldiers who are there nominally to fight the FARC, which acts as the local government, keep raising their demands for payoffs to ever more Andean heights, and in the early eighties the price slumped. Fortunately for the coca growers, the national government gave the narcotraffic a hard time after 1984, so prices are again high and stable. On the frontier the problem of a drug mafia does not exist, since anyone engaged in any business in those parts does so on terms acceptable to local authority. The real problem is that of the social disorganization which any backwoods bonanza brings – the children dropping out of school to earn unheard-of sums like five or ten dollars a day, the tough single men joining the coca rush from everywhere, for whose benefit townships of five hundred huts fill with four hundred prostitutes and the kinds of disorder familiar to every fictional sheriff. Perhaps most serious of all is the erosion of the simple pioneer values which both settlers and guerrillas lived by. Who will ever again believe that the good life is a patch of cleared land in the forest, a hunting dog, and a bit of yucca and bananas?

Seen from a higher observation post, the narcotraffic is considerably more alarming, though not – so far – because of addiction, about which Colombians remain cool. Nobody has made headlines of the fact that over the past six months the Bogotá police have seized precisely five hundred grams of cocaine ('as much as there is in this building right now, or in any other office of this size', to quote an informant in Bogotá). The real worry is the universal corruption spread by an industry that now provides Colombia with more export earnings than coffee[9] and, because the numbers of people involved are so small, produces by far the richest men in the country.

(Since new money and new art go together, its purchases are also said to have transformed the local market for contemporary painting.) Corruption of the judges, faced with the choice of becoming rich or dead. Corruption of the army, up to the level of some generals, as honest officers will bitterly admit; for nothing is more useful to the *narcotrafico* than the armed forces' system of road and air transportation. Corruption, obviously, of the police and, less obviously, of the guerrillas. Paradoxically, the only part of Colombian life that has refused to make room for the drug barons is politics. During the Turbay presidency (1978–82) there were signs that the drug barons, desperately keen to join the old establishment, were moving into national politics; but while candidates still take money where they find it, known representatives of the industry are kept out.

The national life is so permeated by this corruption that the legalization of the drug trade is widely and seriously suggested as the only way to eliminate the superprofits and the incentive to graft. Cocaine is seen as just one more crop in the history of tropical countries producing such crops, from sugar to tobacco through coffee. Exporting it is a business like any other, and in this instance one that exists simply because the US insists on snorting or smoking the stuff in ever more astronomic quantities. Left to themselves and the principles of Adam Smith, the consortia of Medellín investors would no more see themselves as criminals than did the Dutch or English venturers into the Indies trade (including opium), who organized their speculative cargoes in much the same way. The trade rightly resents being called a mafia. It is quite unlike the Italian or Italo-American mafias either structurally or sociologically.

It is basically an ordinary business that has been criminalized – as Colombians see it – by a US which cannot manage its own affairs. On two occasions during the past two years, the biggest names in the trade have offered to pay the country's national debt and retire from cocaine in return for amnesty and legitimacy. Some of the biggest operators, in any case, are by now out of trading and into cargo insurance. And if cocaine were as legal as coffee, with which, by the way, drug traders have business connections, the next generation of operators would not make their pile as the first ones did. And in any case – it is a note often heard – if the gringos were as serious about the drug danger as they claim, why don't they dose the Mendocino County marijuana fields with paraquat as they do in Guajira and send troops through Georgia as they do in Bolivia? President Barco spoke for virtually all Colombians, including those solidly in favour of US foreign policy, when he announced that under no conceivable circumstances would US troops be allowed on Colombian soil.

However, drugs are not uppermost in most Colombians' minds. They are quite prepared to leave the more lurid aspects of the subject to foreign authors like Charles Nicholl in *The Fruit Palace* (London, 1986), an old-fashioned Fleet Street exposé pretending to be a *Rolling Stone* rhapsody. They have more troubling things to think about, as President Barco passes his first hundred days, than 'an odyssey through Colombia's cocaine underworld'. And if we were in their shoes, so would we.

November 1986

Notes

Some notes in the original essay have been omitted from the version that appears in this volume.

1 Enrique Santos Calderón, *La Guerra por la paz* (Bogotá, 1985), p. 108.
2 However, during the brief period of the truce, in 1984 and 1985, M-19 recruited women in significant numbers – about 30 per cent according to Laura Restrepo, *Colombia: historia de una traición* (Bogotá, 1986), p. 233.
3 *El Tiempo*, 28 September 1986.
4 *El Espectador*, 20 September 1986.

5   The distinguished journalist Antonio Caballero, writing about the three hundred murdered UP activists: 'None of these cases have been investigated, or if they have, we do not know with what results. Not a single person is under arrest. Not a single person has been convicted' (*El Espectador*, 28 September 1986). The number of soldiers convicted for homicide or assault over the past six years is precisely eighteen.

6   See Santos Calderón, *La Guerra por la paz*, p. 303. It is true that not all 'fronts' of the FARC are equally disciplined. However, the 336 men of the XI Front (Middle Magdalena) are probably typical. They are described by a defector as spending their time (1) taxing farmers and landlords to raise funds, (2) punishing drug dealers and cattle rustlers, and (3) organizing the peasants, hopefully for a future takeover of power (*El Tiempo*, 19 September 1986).

7   For a useful analysis of what used to be M-19 perspectives (by the brother of one of its commanders) see Eduardo Pizarro's 'La Guerrilla revolucionaria en Colombia', in Gonzalo Sánchez and Ricardo Peñaranda (eds), *Pasado y presente de la Violencia en Colombia*, pp. 391–411.

8   'Clima de inseguridad azota el departamento del Huila' (*La Republica*, 25 September 1986).

9   Mario Arango and Jorge Child, *Narcotráfico: império de la cocaina* (Medellín, 1987), the best-informed Colombian treatment of the subject, contains useful calculations.

30

Nationalism and Nationality in Latin America

Nationalism is a topic of urgent academic interest in many parts of the world, because it is also a subject of urgent political interest. This essay deals with a part of the world which, in both respects, is somewhat anomalous: Latin America. This is strange, at first sight, since it has been seriously suggested by Benedict Anderson in *Imagined Communities* that the real global pioneers of modern nationalism were the Creole cities of eighteenth-century Spanish America. Yet the nationalism of elite minorities should not be confused with nationalism which possesses or develops a mass basis among the people in the form of national consciousness or an attachment to the symbols and institutions of nationhood, although there may be historical links between the two. Still less must it be identified with the characteristic ethnic/religious or otherwise exclusivist forms of national consciousness. In both these respects Latin America developed late. Indeed, it has remained largely immune to modern ethnic-cultural nationalism to this day.

Let me pass briefly over the colonial and early independence period. Tension between colonists and the metropolis and its inhabitants were growing, as was the demand for settler autonomy in the later eighteenth century, in the Spanish as in the British empires. It is not impossible to detect potentially nationalist elements in some spokesmen for Creole elite autonomy, particularly where it was possible, as in New Spain, to elaborate the myth that the local Creoles and *mestizos* represented, in some sense, a non-Hispanic and autochthonous tradition, though of course a Christianized one, namely a continuity with the pre-Columbian empires. The strongly Aztec flavour of modern Mexican nationalism is the result of this Creole 'invention of tradition' in the seventeenth and eighteenth centuries. Yet this potential nationalism was limited by the Creoles' acute distrust of the American masses, and fear of their social revolutions which were dramatically exemplified by Tupac Amaru in the 1780s and Toussaint Louverture in the 1790s. Indeed, as Anderson shows, Creole nationalism was largely directed against the apparently pro-indigenous policy of the Spanish crown, and Latin American independence was held at bay by the support of the indigenous communities for Spanish colonial power. Moreover, the real ideology of emancipation, in Latin as in British America, was that of the Enlightenment, for which the 'nation' was in no sense a Herderian or sociological and cultural concept. In throwing off its chains and choosing liberty, 'the people' constituted itself 'the nation', irrespective of its prior composition. A nation, according to the Abbé Sieyes, was simply 'the totality of individuals, united, living under a common law, and represented by the same legislative assembly'. In the classical cases of the USA and France, it had no other limits. 'The nation' was an open invitation to join it. In any case, the decision to rebel against Spain did not necessarily imply a rejection of Spanishness. [. . .]

But this brings me to a crucial question about Latin American, or at least Spanish American independence (the separation of Portugal from Brazil was quite different). Why did a North American nation undoubtedly emerge very rapidly between the Declaration of 1776, which was that of thirteen separate if allied colonies, and the end of the century, whereas nothing of the kind happened in Spanish America? Is it enough to say that the Spanish empire was so vast and heterogeneous that unanimous and co-ordinated rebellion like that of the thirteen colonies was impossible? Is it enough to point out that important areas within the empire were against independence – an opposition far more effective than any in the future USA? Is it enough to remind ourselves that the white population of the thirteen colonies, modest though it was in 1790 – somewhat under four million – was almost certainly larger, absolutely, and far larger relatively, than the total white population in the entire area between California and Cape Horn? This has been estimated at less than 3.5 million at the end of the colonial period (1825). Moreover, it should not be forgotten that the chief Latin American cities were much larger than their US equivalents. At the time of the first US census (1790) no North American city was larger than 42,000 (Philadelphia), whereas Mexico City was on the way to 120,000, Lima to 53,000 and even Caracas was approaching 40,000.[1] But independence brought the political decline of the Latin American urban elite and the rise of the rural landed proprietors and their soldiery. Hence, it might be argued, the natural constituency of the 'political nation' in Spanish America was weakened, for in an independence dominated by *hacendados* local and regional interests were more likely to prevail. All this is true. Nevertheless, it remains a fact that in the thirteen colonies the idea of a separate nation constituted by the totality of their (white and free) inhabitants was already part of consciousness even before the declaration of independence – perhaps more among the common people than among the elite – and the sense of unity among them was undeniable. It is difficult to detect such a sense in Latin America except in Brazil, where the totality of the Portuguese empire seceded as a single state. As we know, even the attempts to form greater regional units (Gran Colombia etc.) failed.

419

It follows that the Latin (or at least the Spanish) American states which emerged from the wars of independence were not 'nations' or 'nation-states' in any realistic sense, nor were they the results of movements of *national* liberation. In a large part of the area even the colonial administrative divisions, which were to provide (as in post-colonial Africa) so much of the framework for the new states, were comparatively new. They were the products of colonial reorganization by the Spanish monarchy in the eighteenth, sometimes the late eighteenth, century. Within each of these countries, with the probable exception of Chile (singled out for successful national existence by Bolívar himself), local and regional rivalries were far more obvious than what even their elites had in common. Hence the persistent history of civil or intra-regional wars in the early decades of independence, even in geographically coherent zones like the La Plata basin. Hence also the persistent tendency for Latin American states to form official or unofficial federations, until central state power began to establish serious control over the state's territory, mainly in the course of the twentieth century. *De facto*, not even the elites of the new states had much homogeneity or perspective. They lived in states whose very names were often post-independence inventions. They were national only insofar as the institutions of these new states, and particularly their nominally liberal representative constitution, provided them with a national stage on which to act out their combinations and conflicts. Perhaps the only bodies with a genuine interest in these states as 'national' units were the armies that established them or whose *caudillos* seized power in them. Once the existence of a new state was no longer in question, and regional secession was excluded from its politics (after 1830 it occurred only occasionally and under outside influence, as in Acre or Panama), the armies, however frequently their chieftains changed, were virtually the only institutions identified with the entire territory of the republic. The power to which any *caudillo* aspired was national. Considering how rarely soldiers of one American republic have shed the blood of soldiers of another country in the last 150 years (with the notable exceptions of the War of the Triple Alliance, 1864–70, the War of the Pacific, 1879–84, and the Chaco War, 1932–5), military glory plays an altogether disproportionate role in the national myths of South America.

We can, by common consent, eliminate the common people as vectors of the new national consciousness, with the exception perhaps of Paraguay and of Artigas' Uruguay, where independence was won and defended less against the old colonial power than against Buenos Aires and Brazil. Something like a genuine popular consciousness certainly developed in parts of Mexico around the Virgin of Guadeloupe, successor to the pre-Columbian divinity Tonantzin. Men rose under her banner in the days of Hidalgo and Morelos. However, while *guadalupismo* has undoubtedly merged with national consciousness among the Mexican masses, the black Virgin in the days of Hidalgo was less a symbol of *nationality* than the patroness and protectress of the *poor*, who were or are national only because they are Mexican. Andean popular ideology, in the form of Inca millennialism, well analysed by A. Flores Galindo in *Buscando un Inca. Identidad y utopia en los Andes* (1986), had no connection at all with the new republics until the 1920s.

Nor is there any reason why we should expect the common people to have had much interest in the nation or even any concept of it. The makers of national ideology in their states were either not interested in the bulk of the continent's inhabitants or, more likely, considered them as the main obstacle to national or any other progress. Antônio Cândido has perceptively compared Domingo Faustino Sarmiento, struggling against the backwoods tyranny of Rosas in Argentina with Euclídes da Cunha, trying to come to terms, some sixty years later, with the phenomenon of the inhabitants of the Bahia *sertão* in Brazil. The subtitle of Sarmiento's *Facundo* (1845), '*civilización o barbarie*', could equally well be the subtitle of da Cunha's *Os Sertões*

(1902).[2] On the one hand there was, to quote the Argentinian Esteban Echevarría (1829), the principle of progress, free association and liberty, represented for Sarmiento by the cities, on the other 'the antisocial anarchic principle of the status quo, ignorance and tyranny', represented by the countryside. And the city, in Sarmiento's day, though no longer in da Cunha's, was not only a minority, but politically marginalized.

In short, progressives required to generate a national sentiment to replace the ancient, and powerful, collectivities and corporations – local, occupational, religious, ethnic, etc. – which were such patient obstacles to progress. But this implied a frontal attack against everything the mass of the common people of Latin America held dear. No wonder local elites were attracted by an international ideology like Comtism, ideally suited to the situation of a determined modernizing elite with state power, confronted by the mass of immobile and hostile popular forces. Brazil's national ideology became Comtian and, but for the revolution, perhaps Mexico's might also have become so.

The despair about whether these masses could ever be got to move was such that, as we know, many of the believers in progress saw mass immigration by 'superior' races, i.e. Europeans, and the marginalization of Indians and Negroes, or even the local Creoles corrupted by the surrounding barbarism, as the only solution. Only Mexico showed no enthusiasm for it, since the influx of *gringos* was understandably associated with the transfer of large parts of nineteenth-century Mexico to the USA. However, in other respects their economic and cultural impact was welcomed, as was that of the British. Nineteenth-century progressivism and middle-class nationalism were not directed against foreign imperialism. Their ready welcome for foreign enterprise and immigration was entirely compatible with their kind of nationalism. There is no reason to doubt that the Chilean political ruling class felt and feels itself to be Chilean, even though virtually all of its members whose names come to mind – except for some of the omnipresent Basques – have names of patently foreign origin: Edwards, Pinochet, Frei, Allende Gossens, Alessandri, Marmaduke Grove, Foxley, etc. On the other hand this nationalism excluded the appeal to what might be called ethnic or historic populist nationalism. Let us recall Martín Fierro in José Hernández's *gaucho* epic poem of that name, who sang:

The gaucho just has to grin and bear it
until death comes to swallow him up
or we get a criollo chap to rule
this land in the gaucho way[3]

This sentiment of provincial resentment was what a new phase of nationalism under Perón learned to mobilize so successfully: the hostility of the 'real Argentina' against both the *porteños* of Buenos Aires and the foreigners. In fact, the reality of Peronism was quite different. In Perón's army more than half the generals were sons of immigrants, indicating a readiness to assimilate and a speed of assimilation without parallel in the world outside Latin America.

So, until the twentieth century, we have roughly two phases of Latin American nationalism: the post-independence phase when, in spite of French revolutionary rhetoric and military flag-waving, it was not very significant; and the era when it virtually coincided with anti-traditionalism. The 'nation' was identified with progress, i.e. economic development and the establishment of effective state power over the whole national territory. Only those committed to progress or who at least accepted it, could be seen as the true members of the nation.

The third phase begins essentially with the Mexican Revolution and the echoes of the Russian Revolution. It was characterized not only by the active and positive participation of popular movements in their country's politics on a national scale, but also by the recognition, among intellectuals and politicians, that the nation consisted of the people – *all the people* except perhaps the Indians of the *selva*. Three examples may illustrate this. The first is the student movement which, beginning in Córdoba (Argentina) in 1918, spread rapidly across Latin America to Peru, Uruguay, Chile, Colombia, Venezuela, Mexico and Cuba, and clearly inspired new populist-democratic and nationalist movements like the future APRA in Peru, and perhaps the future PRI in Mexico, MNR in Bolivia, Acción Democrática in Venezuela, and others. These movements were nationalist in the sense of being, for the first time, fundamentally anti-imperialist and establishing 'the people' as the basic objective of intellectuals' political action. The second example is the Peru of the 1920s, in which *indigenismo*, i.e. the recognition that Indians constitute the core of the Peruvian people, became central to Peruvian national consciousness. This found expression not only through oppositional intellectuals, like Mariategui and Haya de la Torre, but even in official government politics under Leguía, Prado and Sánchez Cerro. The third example is Brazil after 1930. The three books of that decade which formed the modern intellectuals' concept of Brazil and Brazilianness were surely Gilberto Freyre's *Casa Grande e Senzala*, Sérgio Buarque de Holanda's *Raúzes do Brasil* and Caio Prado's *Formação do Brasil Contemporâneo*. What all three have in common is a denunciation of race prejudice, an integration of the Indian, the Negro and the descendants of miscegenation into the 'nation' hitherto identified primarily with native or immigrant whites. In short, what they had in common was the extension of the concept of the 'nation' to the masses of its inhabitants.

What made this extension easier than before, at least for revolutionary intellectuals, was that the masses themselves now seemed ready for revolutionary action – and it was taken for granted that revolution aimed at creating precisely that society devoted to science, progress and enlightenment, in which the masses had hitherto shown so little interest. Haya de la Torre was at least as passionate a modernizer as Sarmiento, and so was Mariategui. 'The Andean peasant awaits a Lenin' wrote [Luís Eduardo] Valcárcel, [the Peruvian historian and anthropologist].[4] The Mexican Revolution had proved that he could at least produce a Zapata and a Villa. Moreover, however misleading the assumption that all the rural masses were only waiting for their Lenin, it was henceforth undeniable that *some* important sections of them could be mobilized by the left. In any case mass movements of the left could now come into existence not only, as in the Cono Sur, among the largely immigrant working classes, but also, as in Peru, among the non-white proletariat. APRA became a mass party of labour, even if its impact on the Indian heartlands was only marginal. From the Mexican Revolution on, all national ideologies in the Americas included the masses.

But let us not overlook the other aspect of the new nationalism, its anti-imperialism or xenophobia. It made the – novel – assumption that the major task of the nation, namely modernization through economic development, had to be carried out *against* Europe and the USA, and not essentially *through* foreign investment, primary exports and symbiosis with foreign enterprise in general. For obvious reasons anti-imperialist nationalism, though it had existed earlier, particularly in the regions exposed to Washington's gunboat diplomacy, came into its own with the World Depression. We are not talking simply of a new popular nationalist consciousness, which readily took the form of a simple hatred of foreigners or outsiders, as in Mexico, where it apparently led to a rise in the murder of foreigners – curiously enough, Orientals and *turcos* rather than *gringos* – which at least one author, F. C. Turner, *The Dynamics of Mexican Nationalism* (1968), has used as an actual index of the development of popular nationalism. I am thinking rather of the kinds of *desenvolvista/desarrollista* ideology which we find in Brazil among writers like Hélio Jaguaribe, who did not disclaim the label of 'national bourgeoisie'. For such people 'the nation' was, as in nineteenth-century European thought, a unit of economic development, based on 'the existence of a continuous territory [that] stimulates economic integration, which takes place all the more readily in proportion to its already existing cultural unity'. However, the fact that Brazil had developed as a dependent, primary-exporting economy of Europe, stood in the way of such integration. Until recently, Jaguaribe argued in *O nacionalismo na atualidade brasileira* (1958), this had deprived Brazil both of the conditions and the incentives to achieve it. However, what had recently developed was a cultural nationalism, linked to the modernist movement in the arts and other innovatory currents, followed by an economic nationalism, demanding state development of mineral resources, and a political nationalism identified with democracy, social justice and the strengthening of both central and local power against the power of the states.

'Developmentalist', anti-imperialist – i.e. anti-US, popular and concerned with the condition of the mass of the people, and politically leaning to the left: such has been the main current of Latin American nationalism since the 1930s. During that decade it looked for a moment as if a right-wing current, inspired by European fascism, might compete with it, but the end of Hitler and Mussolini eliminated this alternative. In any case, the social bases of these fascist-modelled movements in Latin America were often quite different from those of the European originals. The major antagonist of this progressive nationalist current today is, once again, *desarrollismo* through economic neo-liberalism, whether under civilian or military auspices. At present the 'national bourgeois' tendency, *desarrollista* state capitalism and socialist tendencies are in retreat, although these ideologies are probably still stronger in Latin America than in any other global region.

Two other questions may be raised in conclusion. What has happened to *mass* national consciousness and what is the prospect for Latin American nationalism in the current world revival of nationalist tendencies?

When did the mass of ordinary Mexicans come to see themselves as Mexicans, or Hondurans as Hondurans? These are no easy questions. It is not enough for men and women to be counted or registered or taxed by a government to feel a primary, or any, identification with the country which that government claims to represent. If they enjoy citizen rights, e.g. in a system of democratic politics, they are more likely to identify with their country, especially if democratic pressures bring about social reforms or other advantages which plainly benefit them. We can almost certainly assume a national consciousness in Uruguay since Batlle, in Argentina since Sáenz Peña. Again, large bodies of immigrants, treated as members of a particular nation abroad, will develop a national consciousness even if it is absent at home. [. . .] Equally, if people are mobilized by a force that preaches nationalism they will identify with 'the nation' through it: all APRistas will be aware of their *Peruanidad*, all Perónists are likely to feel strongly Argentinian.

However, it has been suggested that, in Latin America at least, the identification with the nation through admiration for a *person* who stands for the nation is more important than other forms of political identification. There is not much doubt that Getúlio Vargas inspired more poor Brazilians to feel Brazilian than anyone before or since. To this extent the ancient tradition of *caudillismo* has sometimes led towards the modern concept of nationalism, as *caudillos* have mutated into revolutionary or populist leaders – even such unpromising candidates as the generals Odría (Peru) and Rojas Pinilla (Colombia).

Nonetheless, the most decisive force for creating national consciousness was undoubtedly the development of modern mass culture, especially as reinforced by technology. Since the inception of the World Cup it is absolutely certain that every inhabitant of a country within reach of a radio or TV set – and who has not been since the 1960s? – has developed one form of patriotism; at least if the country possesses a serious football team. The World Cup dates back to 1930 when, as everyone should know, Uruguay beat Argentina in the final. Indeed, Latin America is no doubt the only continent in which football partisanship has led to, or at least contributed to, actual war – in the 'soccer war' of 1969 between El Salvador and Honduras. The development of radio has been equally crucial – more than that of TV because it has made certain kinds of music, or even certain tunes – and we are not talking about national anthems – into generally understood symbols of their countries, both inside and outside their frontiers, and because it has brought news of national affairs into remote areas and within reach of illiterates. Unlike print culture, the new high-tech oral and visual culture knows no educational limits.

Moreover, the very spread of literacy, i.e. of schooling, inevitably generates some national consciousness, since so much of school everywhere is devoted to inculcating it. A comparison of two Peruvian departments studies by Howard Handelman illustrates this. Even twenty-five years ago only 8 per cent of the adults in the Cuzco communities had radios, less than 30 per cent of children went to school, adult literacy was below 20 per cent and only 13 per cent travelled to nearby cities. However, in Junín more than half of the children went to school, 45 per cent of adults had radios and 30 per cent were literate. In 60 per cent of the communities all or most members could speak Spanish, whereas in Cuzco the majority of the people spoke no Spanish, and there were virtually no bilingual communities.[5] Without pursuing too far Karl Deutsch's thesis of nationalism as a function of communication, we should expect rural politics in Junin to be far more 'national', and this is indeed the case. As early as 1930 in the militant community of Huasicancha, rightly described by Gavin Smith as a particularly remote settlement, discussions about the national political situation 'were now part of daily village discourse'.[6] Yet we must never forget that even the consciousness that their struggle had a national dimension does not mean that Peru as such loomed large in the minds of the Huasican-chinos, compared to their really important problem, the conflict over land with the neighbouring Hacienda Tucle. However, by the 1960s there is no doubt at all that Peruvian flags, the standard symbol of the nation, were universally carried in peasant land invasions, so much so that in one place it was actually reported that peasants were making flags *for the purpose* of invasions. To the best of my knowledge this has not been so in the preceding bout of agrarian unrest in 1946–8. We cannot but conclude that in the interval there had been a substantial development of some form of national consciousness among the masses; most likely as a by-product of the massive emigration from the highlands in the 1950s which intensified the contacts between villagers and the urban world. Probably today very few, even among remote rural men and women in Latin America, lack some sense of national identification with their republic or country of origin, though it is far from clear what, if anything, this means in concrete political terms.

One thing, however, is clear. Revolutions that are seen as popular revolutions, governments seen as having genuine popular legitimacy, encourage a positive attachment to the nation, as Almond and Verba's comparison of Italian and Mexican attitudes in 1960 illustrates.[7] Both were then semi-developed states of Catholic background. In Italy only 3 per cent of respondents expressed pride in some political aspect of their nation, but in Mexico 30 per cent. Moreover, almost two-thirds of the Mexican sample said they could name some of the ideals and goals of the Mexican Revolution and did so: democracy, political liberty, equality, agrarian reform and – significantly – national freedom.

But what of the future? The current phase of nationalism in other parts of the world has three characteristics: (1) it is strongly ethnic-linguistic and/or religious in its justification; (2) it is largely separatist, insofar as it envisages the break-up of larger states, as in Canada, Spain or Britain; and (3) it is strongly historicist inasmuch as it uses the past, religious or cultural or political, as a point of reference, and in extreme cases, to define a programme for the future, mostly one of territorial expansion, as among the Israeli extremists. One might also say that (4) it is largely directed against *internal* enemies (a central government, immigrants, other minorities, etc.) rather than against other states.

This illustrates the anomaly of Latin America. Linguistically most of the area has Spanish or Portuguese as the common written language, and while other indigenous idioms are used, and have been increasingly given official recognition, following the example of Guaraní in Paraguay, *de facto* they are not regarded at present as potential alternatives to Spanish and Portuguese even by their speakers. The religious background of all continental states is Catholic, and while both nativist and syncretic cults exist, no country with the probable exception of Haiti regards these as essential to its identity, though it is not inconceivable that this might one day happen in Brazil. The mass immigrations from across the oceans have been extraordinarily well-integrated in the areas where they were significant (Argentina, Uruguay, southern Brazil), except perhaps for the large Jewish community in Argentina, both excluded and self-isolating for a generation or two. Curiously enough, the Arab immigrants have been more readily accepted and have advanced to the highest positions in a number of the republics (Menem in Argentina, Malouf in Brazil, Turbay in Colombia, and others in Bolivia, Ecuador, etc.).

There has been friction here and there arising out of cross-border labour migrations, as between Salvador and Honduras, and more recently Colombia and Venezuela, but on the whole major migratory currents such as those from Bolivia and Paraguay into the La Plata region, do not appear to have caused much trouble – certainly far less than similar migrations in Europe and North America. In any case, ethnic homogeneity, real or imaginary, has not been part of Latin American national consciousness since it belonged entirely to the upper-class Creoles. As for history, it unites rather than divides large parts of the continent, as is indicated by the persistent tendency both among regional intellectuals and outsiders, to treat the continent as a single unit. Even Brazilian intellectuals can be heard to talk about '*o pensamento latino-americano*'. Europe has no comparable sense of unity, in spite of Brussels' efforts. A career like Che Guevara's, which took him from Argentina via Mexico and Cuba to Bolivia, is hard to imagine in Europe, if only for linguistic reasons. But not only for linguistic ones. In Fidel's discourse we hear an echo of an earlier all-continental liberator, and it is symbolic that, in the twilight of Fidel's dream, García Márquez should write about the failure and death of Bolívar.[8]

Finally, separatism is plainly of negligible significance compared to the Old World, although we cannot exclude the possibility that it might one day develop. Still, while it cannot be overlooked in the island universe of the Caribbean, the rare, and so far temporary examples on the continent – Santa Cruz in Bolivia, Rio Grande do Sul in Brazil – have little to do with nationalism. Perhaps the traditional popularity of federal constitutions, and the sheer weakness and ineffectiveness of central state machinery have left far more scope than in Europe for effective local autonomy.

It is impossible to predict future trends. While there is probably more scope for traditional army-based disputes between national armies, as witness the periodic conflicts over ill-defined frontier zones, mainly around the Amazon basin, actual wars between the republics are not very likely. National appeals will no doubt serve in domestic politics to reinforce domestic demagogues and populist leaders, but given the low profile of labour migrations in the area, the pervasive popular xenophobia of Western Europe and North America appears to be lacking. Can we expect the melting-pot of Latin American nations to break up into mutually hostile communities on the basis of race, language or whatever? This is not unthinkable in Andean states with strong indigenous populations, where there is an undoubted substratum of Indian resentment against Creoles and *cholos*, as witness the 45 per cent of votes which the non-white (Japanese) candidate Alberto Fujimori, got against the novelist Mario Vargas Llosa, some of them no doubt because 'el Chinito' visibly was *not* white. Similar tendencies may exist in parts of Mexico. But these are speculations. In most other parts of the world, and certainly in Eurasia, the rise of nationalist movements is an immediate reality. In Latin America it is the subject of conjecture. For the time being, lucky Latin America.

1995

Notes

Some notes in the original essay have been omitted from the version that appears in this volume.

1 See W. D. Harris Jr., *The Growth of Latin American Cities* (1971); P. Bairoch, *De Jéricho à Mexico. Villes et économie dans l'histoire* (1985).
2 A. Cândido, Introduction to Sérgio Buarque de Holanda, *Raízes do Brasil*, 20th edn, 1988, p. xliii.
3 Quoted in J. L. Romero, *A History of Argentine Political Thought* (1963), p. 163.
4 Quoted in F. Bourricaud, *Power and Society in Contemporary Peru* (1970), pp. 146–8.
5 See H. Handelman, *Struggle in the Andes. Peasant Political Mobilization in Peru* (1975).
6 G. Smith, *Livelihood and Resistance. Peasants and the Politics of Land in Peru* (1989), p. 174.
7 S. Verba and G. A. Almond, 'National Revolutions and Political Commitment', in H. Eckstein (ed.), *Internal War* (1964).
8 Gabriel García Márquez, *El General en su laberinto* (1989).

31

A Forty-Year Relationship with Latin America

When I first went [to Latin America] in 1962,* the continent
was in one of its periodic moods of expansive economic confidence, articulated by the Economic Commission for Latin
America in the UN, an all-continental brains trust located
in Santiago de Chile under an Argentine banker, which rec-
ommended a policy of planned, state-sponsored and largely
state-owned industrialization and economic growth through
import substitution. It seemed to work, at least for giant,
inflation-plagued but booming Brazil. This was the time when
Juscelino Kubitschek, a president of Czech origin, had launched
the conquest of Brazil's vast interior by building a new capital
in it, designed largely by the country's most eminent architect,
Oscar Niemeyer, a known member of the powerful but illegal
Communist Party who, he told me, designed it with Engels in
mind.

Its main countries were also in one of the continent's occasional phases of constitutional civilian government which was
soon to end. However, the *caudillo* of the old type was already

* ***Editor's note.*** Mainland Latin America. Eric had visited Cuba in 1960.

on the way out – at least outside the Caribbean. The regimes of
the torturers were to be collectives of faceless and mostly colourless officers. In South America the only country under military
dictatorship at that time was the unusually old-fashioned Paraguay under the eternal General Stroessner, a nasty regime, kind
to expatriate Nazis, in a disarmingly attractive and charming
country, which lived largely by smuggling. Graham Greene's
touching *The Honorary Consul* is an excellent introduction to it.

[...]

What was most immediately obvious about [South American]
countries was not so much spectacular economic inequality,
which has not ceased to increase since, as the enormous gap
between the ruling and intellectual classes with which visiting
academics had contact, and the common people. The intellectuals, mostly from comfortable or 'good' – overwhelmingly
white – families, were sophisticated, widely travelled, and spoke
English and (still) French. As so often in the Third World (to
which the Argentines vociferously refused to belong), they formed
the thinnest continent-wide social layer. [...] If they were in
politics, they almost certainly had a spell as exiles in another
Latin American country or a common trip to Castro's Cuba; if
academics, a spell as members of some multinational establishment in Santiago, Rio or Mexico City. Since they were thin on
the ground, they knew each other or knew about each other.
[...] But the very fact that such people moved in a world equally
familiar with Paris, New York and five or six Latin capitals separated them from the world in which most darker-skinned and less
well-connected Latin Americans lived.

Outside the already urbanized 'southern cone' (Argentina,
Uruguay and Chile) these people were flooding from the countryside into the shanty towns of the exploding cities, bringing
their rural ways with them. São Paulo had doubled in size in
the ten years before I got there. They squatted on city hillsides
as in the country they had dug up unoccupied corners of the
big estates and built shelters and shacks, eventually to become

proper houses, the way it was done in the village, by mutual help of neighbours and kin, rewarded with a party. On the street markets of São Paulo, overshadowed by the new high-rise buildings, the masses from the parched hinterlands of the north-east bought shirts and jeans on instalment payments and the cheap illustrated booklets of verse ballads about the great bandits of their region. In Lima, Peru, there were radio stations broadcasting in Quechua to the Indian immigrants from the mountains, now numerous enough to constitute a market, in spite of their poverty. The great writer, folklorist and Indianist José Maria Arguedas took me to one of the music halls where, on Sunday mornings, the highland people came to listen to songs and jokes about 'down home'. ('Anyone here from Ancash? Let's hear it for the lads and lasses from Huanuco!') In 1962 it seemed almost unthinkable that thirty years later I would supervise the son of one of them for a doctorate at the New School in New York. It is an extraordinary experience to have lived with the first generation in recorded history in which a poor boy with an illiterate wife from a Quechua-speaking village in the high Andes could become a unionized hospital driver by picking up the skills of driving a truck and thus open the globe to his children. [. . .]

The people who came to the city were at least visible on the streets. The people in the countryside were doubly remote from the middle classes, including their revolutionaries such as Che Guevara, by geographical and social distance. Even those with the greatest interest in having the closest contacts with them found the differences in lifestyle, not to mention expected living standards, a forbidding obstacle. Few outside experts actually lived among the peasantry, though many had fairly good contacts in the countryside, including, as usual, the omnipresent researchers of various international organizations connected with the United Nations.

[. . .] When I first went to South America the major 'peasant' story, insofar as there was one, was about the Peasant Leagues

in Brazil, a movement established in 1955 under the leadership of Francisco Julião, a lawyer and local politician from the
north-east, who had attracted the attention of US journalists
by expressions of support for Fidel Castro and Mao. (I met him
ten years later, a small, sad, disoriented exile from the Brazilian military regime, living under the protection of the dramatic
Central European ideologue Ivan Illich in Cuernavaca,
Mexico.) A few hours at their offices in Rio in late 1962 showed
that the movement had little national presence, and that it was
clearly already past its peak. On the other hand, the two major
South American peasant or rural upheavals which no observer
with open eyes could fail to discover within a few days of arriv-
ing in their countries were virtually undocumented, and indeed
virtually unknown to the outside world at the end of 1962.
These were the great peasant movements in highland and frontier Perú and the 'state of disorganization, civil war and local
anarchy' into which Colombia had fallen since the implosion of
what had been, in effect, a potential social revolution by spontaneous combustion set off, in 1948, by the assassination of a
nationally famous tribune of the people, Jorge Eliécer Gaitán.

And yet, these things were not always utterly remote from
the outside world. The vast movement of peasant land occupations was at its height in Cuzco, where even tourists who did not
read local newspapers could, when walking around the Inca
blocks in the cold thin air of the highland evenings, observe
the endless, silent columns of Indian men and women outside
the offices of the Peasant Federation. The most dramatic case
of a successful peasant revolt at the time, in the valleys of La
Convención, occurred downriver from the marvels of Machu
Picchu, known to all tourists in South America even then. Only
a few dozen kilometres' train ride from the great Inca site to
the end of the railway line and a few more hours on the back
of a truck took one to the provincial capital, Quillabamba. I
wrote one of the first outside accounts of it.[1] For a historian
who kept his eyes open, especially a social historian, even

these first, almost casual impressions were a sudden revelation. [...] How could one not explore this unknown but historically familiar planet? My conversion was completed, a week or two later, among the endless slopes of stalls manned by squat, heavy-braided, bowler-hatted Aymara peasant women in the enormous street-markets of Bolivia. [...]

Colombia was a country of whose very existence hardly anyone outside Latin America seemed to be aware. This was my second great discovery. On paper a model of representative two-party constitutional democracy, almost completely immune to military coups and dictatorship, in practice after 1948 it became the killing field of South America. At this period Colombia reached a crude rate of homicide of over fifty per hundred thousand, although even this pales beside the Colombian zeal for killing at the end of the twentieth century.[2] [...] Colombian journalists used the term *genocidio* (genocide) to describe the small massacres in farm settlements and of bus passengers – sixteen dead here, eighteen there, twenty-four somewhere else. Who were the killers and the killed? 'A spokesman for the War Ministry said no categorical information about the perpetrators could be given, because the districts (*veredas*) of that zone [of Santander] were pretty regularly affected by a series of "vendettas" between the partisans of traditional political affiliations,' namely the Liberal and Conservative parties in one of which, as readers of García Márquez know, every Colombian baby belongs by family and local loyalty. The wave of civil war known as *La Violencia* that had begun in 1948, long officially ended, had still killed almost nineteen thousand persons in that 'quiet year'. Colombia was, and continues to be, proof that gradual reform in the framework of liberal democracy is not the only, or even the most plausible, alternative to social and political revolutions, including the ones that fail or are aborted. I discovered a country in which the failure to make a social revolution had made violence the constant, universal, omnipresent core of public life.

What exactly the *Violencia* was or had been about was far from clear, although I was lucky enough to arrive just at the time when the first major study of it was coming out, to one of whose authors, my friend the sociologist Orlando Fals Borda, I owe my first introduction to Colombian problems. I might have paid more attention at the time to the fact that the chief student of the *Violencia* was a Catholic Monsignor [Germán Guzmán], and that some pioneer research on its social fallout had just been published by a spectacularly handsome young priest from one of the country's founding clans, a great breaker of hearts, it was said, among young women of the oligarchy, Father Camilo Torres. It was not an accident that the conference of Latin American bishops which initiated the socially radical Theology of Liberation a few years later was held in the hilly Colombian city of Medellín, then still known for entrepreneurs in textiles and not yet in drugs. I had some conversations with Camilo and, to judge by my notes at the time, took his arguments very seriously, but he was still a long way from the social radicalism that led him three years later to join the new *Fidelista* guerrillas of the Army of the National Liberation which still survives.

Amid the *Violencia* the Communist Party had formed 'armed self-defence' zones or 'independent republics', as places of refuge for peasants who wanted or had to stay out of the way of the Conservative, or sometimes also the Liberal bands of killers. Eventually they became the bases of the formidable guerrilla movement of the FARC (Armed Forces of the Colombian Revolution). The best-known 'liberated' areas of this kind, Tequendama and Sumapaz, were surprisingly close to Bogotá as the crow flies, but, being mountain country, a long and difficult way by horse and mule. Viotá, a district of coffee *haciendas* expropriated by the peasants in the reforming 1930s, and from which the landowners had withdrawn, did not need to fight at all. Even the soldiers kept away, while it ran all its affairs under the eye of the political cadre sent there by the Party, a former brewery worker, and sold its coffee peacefully on the world market through the usual traders. The mountains of Sumapaz, frontier terrain for free men and women, were under the rule of a home-grown rural leader, one of those rare peasant talents who escaped the fate patronized by the poet Gray in his famous elegy, that of being 'some mute inglorious Milton ... some Cromwell guiltless of his country's blood'. For Juan de la Cruz Varela was far from mute or peaceable. In the course of his varied career as chief of Sumapaz, he was prominent as a Liberal, follower of Gaitán, communist, head of his own agrarian movement and Revolutionary Liberal, but always firmly on the side of the people. Discovered by one of those wonderful village teachers who were the real agents of emancipation for most of the human race in the nineteenth and twentieth centuries, he had become both a reader and practical thinker [...] He acquired his political education from Victor Hugo's *Les Misérables*, which he carried with him everywhere, marking the passages which seemed to him particularly apposite to his own or the political situation of the time. He acquired his Marxism, or what there was of it, rather later via the writings of a now forgotten English clerical enthusiast from the USSR, the late Hewlett Johnson, Dean of Canterbury, which he appears to have got from Colombian communists, whose belief in agrarian revolution appealed to him. Long accepted as a person of power and influence, whose region was beyond the reach of government troops, he sat for it in Congress [...] The first negotiations for an armistice between the Colombian government and the FARC were to be held on the hinterland of his territory.

The FARC itself, which was to become the most formidable and long-lasting of the Latin American guerrilla movements, had not yet been founded when I first came to Colombia, although its long-time military leader Pedro Antonio Marin ('Manuel Marulanda'), another home-grown countryman, was already active in the mountains adjoining the old stronghold of communist agitation and self-defence in South Tolima. It was only born when the Colombian government, trying out against the communists the new anti-guerrilla techniques pioneered by the US military experts, drove the fighters out of their stronghold in Marquetalia. Several years later, in the mid-eighties, I was to spend some days in the birthplace of communist guerrilla activity in the coffee-growing *municipio* of Chaparral, in the house of my friend Pierre Gilhodes, who had married into the locality. The FARC, stronger than ever, were still in the mountains above the township. [. . .]

Colombia, as I wrote after my return [in 1963], was experiencing 'the greatest armed mobilization of peasants (as guerrillas, brigands or self-defence groups) in the recent history of the western hemisphere, with the possible exception of some periods during the Mexican Revolution'.[3] Curiously, this fact was either unnoticed or played down by the contemporary ultra-left in and outside South America (all of whose Guevarist attempts at guerrilla insurrection were spectacular failures) on the ostensible grounds that it was linked to an orthodox Communist Party, but in fact because those inspired by the Cuban Revolution neither understood nor wanted to understand what actually might move Latin American peasants to take up arms.

It was not hard to become a Latin American expert in the early 1960s. Fidel's triumph created enormous interest in the region, which was poorly covered by press and universities outside the USA. I had not intended to take a specialist interest in the region, although I also found myself lecturing and writing about it in the 1960s and early 1970s in the *New York Review of Books* and elsewhere [. . .] [And] I continued to go there several times in each decade. [. . .]

Nevertheless, I never tried to become or saw myself as a Latin Americanist. As for the biologist Darwin, for me as a historian the revelation of Latin America was not regional but general. It was a laboratory of historical change, mostly different from what might have been expected, a continent made to undermine conventional truths. It was a region where

440

historical evolution occurred at express speed and could actually be observed happening within half a lifetime of a single person, from the first clearing of forests for farm or ranch to the death of the peasantry, from the rise and fall of export crops for the world market to the explosion of giant super-cities such as the megalopolis of São Paulo, where one could find a mixture of immigrant populations more implausible even than in New York – Japanese and Okinawans, Calabrians, Syrians, Argentine psychoanalysts and a restaurant proudly labelled 'CHURRASCO TIPICO NORCOREANO' (Typical North Korean Barbecue). It was a place where ten years doubled the size of Mexico City, and transformed the street-scene of Cuzco from one dominated by Indians in traditional costume to people wearing modern ('*cholo*') clothes.

Inevitably it changed my perspective on the history of the rest of the globe, if only by dissolving the border between the 'developed' and the 'Third' worlds, the present and the historic past. [. . .] It forced one to make sense of what was at first sight implausible. It provided what 'counterfactual' speculations can never do, namely a genuine range of alternative outcomes to historical situations: right-wing chieftains who become the inspiration of labour movements (Argentina, Brazil), fascist ideologists who join with a left-wing miners' union to make a revolution that gives the land to the peasants (Bolivia), the only state in the world that has actually abolished its army (Costa Rica), a single-party state of notorious corruption whose Institutional Revolutionary Party (the PRI) recruits its personnel systematically from the most revolutionary among its university students (Mexico), a region where first-generation immigrants from the Third World can become presidents and Arabs ('*Turcos*') tend to be more successful than Jews.

What made this extraordinary continent so much more accessible for Europeans was an unexpected air of familiarity, like the wild strawberries to be found on the path behind Machu Picchu. It was not simply that anyone of my age who

441

knew the Mediterranean could recognize the populations round the limitless dun-coloured surface of the River Plate estuary as Italians fed for two or three generations on huge pieces of beef, and was familiar from Europe with the prevailing Creole values of macho honour, shame, courage and loyalty to friends, as well as with oligarchic societies. (Not until the battles between young elite revolutionaries and military governments in the 1970s was the basic social distinction, so clearly formulated in Graham Greene's *Our Man in Havana*, abandoned, at least in several countries, namely that between the 'torturable' lower and the 'non-torturable' upper classes.) For Europeans those aspects of the continent most remote from our own experience were embedded in, and interwoven with, institutions familiar to historians, such as the Catholic Church, the Spanish colonial system or such nineteenth-century ideologies as utopian socialism and Auguste Comte's Religion of Humanity. This somehow emphasized, even dramatized, both the peculiarity of their Latin American transmutations and what they had in common with other parts of the world. Latin America was a dream for comparative historians.

When I first discovered the continent, it was about to enter the darkest period of its twentieth-century history, the era of military dictatorship, state terror and torture. [...] The generals took over in Brazil in 1964 and by the mid-seventies the military ruled all over South America, except for the states bordering the Caribbean. The Central American republics, apart from Mexico and Cuba, had been kept safe from democracy by the CIA and the threat or reality of US intervention ever since the 1950s. A diaspora of Latin American political refugees concentrated in the few countries of the hemisphere providing refuge – Mexico and, until 1973, Chile – and scattered across North America and Europe: the Brazilians to France and Britain, the Argentinians to Spain, the Chileans everywhere. (Although many Latin American intellectuals continued to visit Cuba, very few actually chose it as their place of exile.) Essentially the 'era of the gorillas' (to use the Argentine phrase) was the product of a triple encounter. The local ruling oligarchies did not know what to do about the threat from their increasingly mobilized lower orders in town and country and the populist radical politicians who appealed to them with evident success. The young middle-class left, inspired by the example of Fidel Castro, thought the continent was ripe for revolution precipitated by armed guerrilla action. And Washington's obsessive fear of communism, confirmed by the Cuban Revolution, was intensified by the international setbacks of the USA in the seventies: the Vietnam defeat, the oil crises, the African revolutions that turned towards the USSR.

I found myself involved in these affairs as an intermittent Marxist visitor to the continent, sympathetic to its revolutionaries – after all, unlike in Europe, revolutions were both needed and possible – but critical of much of its ultra-left. Utterly critical of the hopeless Cuba-inspired guerrilla dreams of 1960–7,[4] I found myself defending the second-best against the criticisms of campus insurrectionaries. [. . .] I was thinking of the junta of the reformist militarists under General Velasco Alvarado in Peru (1969–76) who proclaimed the 'Peruvian Revolution' on which I reported sympathetically but sceptically.[5] It nationalized the country's great *haciendas* and was also the first Peruvian regime to recognize the mass of Peruvians, the Quechua-speaking Indians from the high Andes now flooding into coast, city and modernity, as potential citizens. Everyone else in that pitifully poor and helpless country had failed, not least the peasants themselves, whose massive land occupation in 1958–63 had dug the grave of the oligarchy of landowners. They had not known how to bury them. The Peruvian generals acted because nobody else wanted to or could. (I am bound to add, they also failed, though their successors have been worse.)

It was not a popular note to strike, inside or outside Latin America, at a time when the suicidal Guevara dream of bringing about the revolution by the action of small groups in tropical frontier areas was still very much alive. It may help to explain why my appearance before the students of San Marcos University in Lima [. . .] did not go down at all well. For Maoism in one or other of its numerous sub-varieties was the ideology of the sons and daughters of the new *cholo* (hispanized Indian) middle class of highland immigrants, at least until they graduated.

But was there not hope in Chile? [. . .] I had been in Chile in 1971, on a side trip from Peru to report on the first year of the first socialist government democratically elected to everyone's surprise, including Allende's.[6] In spite of my passionate wish that it might succeed, I had not been able to conceal from myself that the odds were against it. Keeping my 'sympathies entirely out of the transaction' I had put them at two to one against.

[. . .]

Debates about the Latin American left became academic in the 1970s with the triumph of the torturers, even more academic in the 1980s with the era of US-backed civil war in Central America and the retreat of army rule in South America and entirely unrealistic with the decline of the Communist parties and the end of the USSR. Probably the only significant attempt at old-style armed guerrilla revolution was the 'Shining Path', brainchild of a fringe Maoist lecturer at the University of Ayachucho, who had not yet taken to arms when I visited that city in the late 1970s. It demonstrated what the Cuban dreamers of the 1960s had spectacularly failed to show, namely that serious armed politics were possible in the Peruvian countryside, but also – at least to some of us – that this was a cause that ought not to succeed. In fact, it was suppressed by the army in the usual brutal fashion, with the help of those parts of the peasantry whom the *Senderistas* had antagonized.

However, the most formidable and indestructible of the rural guerrillas, the Colombian FARC, flourished and grew, though in that blood-soaked country it had to deal not only with the official forces of the state but with the well-armed gunmen of the drugs industry and the landlords' savage 'paramilitaries'. President

Belisario Betancur (1982–6), a socially minded and civilized Conservative intellectual not in the pockets of the USA – at least in conversation he gave me that impression – initiated the policy of negotiating peace with the guerrillas, which has continued at intervals ever since. His intentions were good, and he succeeded in pacifying at least one of the guerrilla movements, the so-called M-19, favourite of the intellectuals. [...] Indeed, the FARC itself was prepared to play the constitutional game by creating a 'Patriotic Union' intended to function as that electoral party of the left which had never quite managed to emerge in the space between the Liberals and the Conservatives. It had little success in the big cities, and after about 2500 of its local mayors, councillors and activists, having laid aside their arms, had been murdered in the countryside, the FARC developed an understandable reluctance to exchange the gun for the ballot-box. [...]

What has happened to Latin America in the forty or so years since I landed on its airfields? The expected and in so many countries necessary revolution has not happened, strangled by the indigenous military and the USA, but not least by domestic weakness, division and incapacity. It will not happen now. None of the political experiments I have watched from near or far since the Cuban Revolution has made much lasting difference.

Only two have looked as though they might, but both are too recent for judgement. The first, which must warm the cockles of all old red hearts, is the national rise, since its foundation in 1980, of the Workers' Party (Partido dos Trabalhadores or PT) in Brazil, whose leader and presidential candidate 'Lula' (Luis Inácio da Silva) is probably the only industrial worker at the head of any Labour Party anywhere. It is a late example of a classic mass socialist Labour Party and movement, such as emerged in Europe before 1914. I carry its plaque on my key-ring to remind me of ancient and contemporary sympathies, and memories of my times with the PT and with 'Lula' (Luiz Inácio da Silva). [...] The other, more dramatic, landmark was the end in 2000 of Mexico's seventy years of unshakeable one-party rule by the PRI (the Institutional Revolutionary Party). Alas, one doubts whether this will produce a better political alternative.

So the politics of Latin America remain recognizably what they have long been, as does its cultural life (except for the vast global explosion in higher education in which its republics have shared). On the world economic scene, even when not shaken by the great crises of the past twenty years, Latin America plays only a bit part. Politically, it has remained as far from God and as near to the USA as ever. [...] For half a century journalists and academics have read secular transformations into tempo-rary political trends, but the region remains what it has been for most of a century, full of constitutions and jurists but unstable in its political practice. Historically its national governments have found it hard to control what happens on their territory, and still do. Its rulers have tried to avoid the logic of electoral democracy among populations which cannot be guaranteed to vote the way their betters would want them to, by a variety of methods ranging from control by local grandees, patronage, general corruption and occasional demagogic 'fathers of the people' to military rule. All of these still remain available.

And yet, during these past forty years I have observed a society being utterly transformed. The population of Latin America has just about tripled, an essentially agrarian and still largely empty continent has lost most of its peasants, who have moved into giant cities and from Central America to the USA, on a scale comparable only with the Irish and Scandi-navian migrations in the nineteenth century, or even, like the Ecuadoreans working on the Andalusian harvests, across the ocean. Emigrant remittances have replaced the great hopes of modernization. Cheap air travel and phone communica-tion have abolished localization. Life-patterns I observed in the 1990s were unimagined in 1960: the New York taxi-driver from Guyaquil who lived half in the USA and half in Ecuador, where his wife ran a local print-shop; the loaded pick-up trucks of immigrant Mexicans (legal or clandestine) returning from California or Texas for the holiday to Jalisco or Oaxaca; Los Angeles turning into a town of Central American immigrant *politicos* and union leaders. True, most Latin Americans remain poor. In fact, in 2001 they were almost certainly relatively poorer than in the early 1960s, even if we set aside the ravages of the economic crises of the past twenty years, for not only has inequality within these countries soared, but the continent itself has lost ground internationally. Brazil may be the eighth economy of the world by the size of its GDP, Mexico the sixteenth, but *per capita* they rank respectively fifty-second and sixtieth. In the world's league table of social injustice Brazil remains at the top. And yet, if one were to ask the Latin American poor to compare their life at the start of the new millennium with their parents', let alone their grandparents', outside a few black spots most would probably say: it is better. But in most countries they might also say: it is more unpredictable and more dangerous.

It is not for me to agree or disagree with them. After all they are the Latin America that I went to look for, and discovered, forty years ago [...].

2002

Notes

1   See chapter 14 'A Peasant Movement in Peru', above.
2   See chapter 29 'Murderous Colombia', above.
3   See chapters 6 'The Revolutionary Situation in Colombia' and 7 'The Anatomy of Violence in Colombia', above.
4   See 'Guerrillas in Latin America' (1970) and 'Latin American Guerrillas: a Survey' (1973), above.
5   See chapters 24 'Generals as Revolutionaries', 25 'What's New in Peru' and 26 'Peru: The Peculiar "Revolution"', above.
6   See Chapter 27 'Chile: Year One', above.

Dates and Sources of Original Publication

1 Cuban Prospects
   New Statesman, 22 October 1960.

2 South American Journey
   Extracts from an article published in *Labour Monthly*, July 1963.

3 Bossa Nova
   New Statesman, 21 December 1962.

4 Latin America: The Most Critical Area in the World
   The Listener, 2 May 1963. Based on the first of two talks for the
   Third Programme of the BBC.

5 Social Developments in Latin America
   The Listener, 9 May 1963. Based on the second of two talks for the
   Third Programme of the BBC.

6 The Revolutionary Situation in Colombia
   The World Today, June 1963. Based on a paper given to the Latin
   American seminar at the Royal Institute of International Affairs
   (Chatham House).

7 The Anatomy of Violence in Colombia
   New Society, 11 April 1963. Reprinted as 'La anatomía de la

violencia: La Violencia en Colombia' in *Rebeldes Primitivos. Estudio sobre las formas arcaicas de los movimientos sociales en los siglos XIX y XX* (Barcelona: Ediciones Ariel, 1968; Crítica, 2001), the Spanish edition of Eric's first book *Primitive Rebels* (1959).

8   Feudal Elements in the Development of Latin America
    Paper delivered at a meeting in Poland in homage to Witold Kula. Published in Witold Kula (ed.), *Miedzy Feudalizmem a Kapitalizmem. Studia z dziejów, gospodarczych i spoùecznych* (Wroçlaw: Zazùad Narodowy Imienia Ossolínskich – Wydawnictwo, 1976), pp. 57–74.

9   A Case of Neo-Feudalism: La Convención, Peru
    Journal of Latin American Studies, I (1) (May 1969), pp. 31–50. Based on a paper given at a conference in Rome in April 1968.

10 Peasants as Social Bandits
    Extracts from *Bandits* ([1969] 4th revised edition, London: Weidenfeld & Nicolson, 2000), pp. 20–33, 64–9, 116–19, 162–5.

11 Peasant Insurrection
    Extracts from an unpublished paper 'The Motives of Peasant Insurrection'.

12 Ideology and Peasant Movements
    Extracts from an essay 'Ideology and Social Change in Colombia' published in June Nash, Juan Corradi and Hobart Spalding Jr (eds), *Ideology and Social Change in Latin America* (New York: Gordon & Breach, 1977), pp. 185–99.

13 Peasant Land Occupations: The Case of Peru
    Extracts from an article published in *Past & Present*, 62/1 (February 1974). Reprinted in *Uncommon People* (London: Weidenfeld & Nicolson, 1998), chapter 12, pp. 223–55.

14 A Peasant Movement in Peru
    Essay based on a paper presented at an international conference held in Paris in October 1965. Published as 'Problèmes agraires à la Convención' in *Les Problèmes agraires des Amériques Latines* (Paris: Editions du Centre National de la Recherche Scientifique, CNRS, 1967), pp. 385–93. Reprinted as 'Un movimiento

campesino en el Perú' in *Rebeldes Primitivos* (Barcelona: Crítica, 2001), pp. 241–61.

15 Peasant Movements in Colombia
Essay written in 1969. Published in Commission Internationale d'Histoire des Mouvements Sociaux et des Structures Sociales, *Les Mouvements Paysans dans le Monde Contemporain*, 3 vols (Geneva: Librairie Droz, 1976), vol. III, pp. 166–86.

16 Peasants and Politics
Extracts from an article published in *Journal of Peasant Studies*, I (1) (1973). Reprinted in *Uncommon People* (London: Weidenfeld & Nicolson, 1998), Chapter 11, pp. 205–15.

17 Peasants and Rural Migrants in Politics
Extracts from an essay published in Claudio Veliz (ed.), *The Politics of Conformity in Latin America* (London: Oxford University Press for the Royal Institute of International Affairs, 1967), pp. 43–65.

18 The Mexican Revolution
Extract from Chapter 12, 'Towards Revolution', in *The Age of Empire 1875–1914* (London: Weidenfeld & Nicolson, 1987), pp. 286–92.

19 The Cuban Revolution and Its Aftermath
Extract from Chapter 15, 'Third World and Revolution', in *The Age of Extremes: The Short Twentieth Century, 1914–1991* (London: Michael Joseph, 1994), pp. 437–41.

20 A Hard Man: Che Guevara
New Society, 4 April 1968. Review of Che Guevara, *Reminiscences of the Cuban Revolutionary War.*

21 Guerrillas in Latin America
Article published in Ralph Miliband and John Saville (eds), *The Socialist Register 1970* (London: The Merlin Press, 1970), pp. 51–63.

22 Latin American Guerrillas: A Survey
Review article published in Colin Harding and Christopher Roper (eds), *Latin American Review of Books*, 1 (1973), pp. 79–88.

Index

Acción Democrática, Venezuela, 8, 45, 249n, 424
Acción Popular, Peru, 246
agrarian movements: Chile, 381, 383; Colombia, 67, 68, 164, 168, 198, 206, 210, 212, 215–21, 223, 239, 439; Latin America, 182, 241–2; Mexico, 256; Peru, 117, 120, 121, 165n, 194, 224, 229, 429
agrarian reform: Bolivia, 44, 167, 238, 441; Chile, 373, 374, 381–2; Colombia, 68–9, 73, 220, 235; Cuba, 29, 30, 31; Latin America, 317; Mexico, 142, 429; need for, 56; Peru, 179, 187, 189, 225, 318, 321, 327, 330, 332, 337–8, 340–1, 344, 349, 352; Venezuela, 171
Alape, Arturo, 402
Alessandri, Jorge, 392n, 423
allegados, Peru, 119, 182, 183, 241
Allende, Salvador: chances of success, 391; coup against, 12, 22, 393–7; EH's meeting, 15; election (1970), 12, 307, 384, 392n, 444; government, 305, 367–9, 371, 394–7; government achievements, 376, 378–9; land reform, 381–2; limits to

powers, 379–80, 387; Message to Congress, 367, 382; political skills, 371–2; political style, 389; presidency, 365, 389; support for, 374, 389
Alliance for Progress, 296, 298, 299, 300, 301
Almond, G. A., 429
Anderson, Benedict, 417, 418
Andrade, Raul, 158
anti-imperialism: Cuba, 30–1; Latin America, 48, 261–2, 310, 312, 331, 425, 426; Mexico, 301; Peru, 327, 331, 344–5, 347, 350
APRA (Alianza Popular Revolucionaria Americana), Peru: army relations, 329, 331, 335, 342; breakaway movement, 187; leaders, 184; Lima position, 246; military government view of, 342, 346–7; opposition to Belaúnde, 190, 320; political stance, 22; populist movement, 8, 45, 248, 328, 424–5; response to military government, 335, 347; role, 175; support for 1945 government, 229; supporters, 178, 184, 236n, 238–9, 320,

revolution (1952), 2, 43–4, 57,
238, 241, 249n, 276; separatist
movement, 431; unions, 238,
441; US relations, 299, 313, 415
Bourricaud, François, 339n, 340
Bravo, Douglas, 274, 280, 281
Brazil: bandit tradition 142, 143–5;
bossa nova, 40–2; *bourgeoisie*,
36–7; capital, 433; coffee, 90;
colonization, 323; *colonos*, 91;
Communist Party (PCB), 7,
36, 433; EH's visit, 436; GDP,
447; guerrilla warfare, 272;
guerrillas, 292–3; industry,
36, 57; labour tenancies, 106;
military coup (1964), 7, 274,
329, 383, 396, 397, 442; national
ideology, 155, 422; oligarchy,
57; peasant insurrection, 197;
peasant leagues, 35; populist
movement, 45; poverty, 34,
150; São Paulo, 35–7; separatist
movement, 431; slums, 57;
unions, 7, 243–4; urban
guerrillas, 282; US relations,
304; voting qualification, 236;
wages, 36; Workers' Party (PT),
445
Buarque de Holanda, Sérgio, 424
Buenos Aires, 52–3, 243, 244, 248,
423

Caceres, Andrés Avelino, 179
Caldas, Colombia, 78
Cândido, Antônio, 421
Cárdenas, Lázaro, 146n, 246, 258n,
301
Cardoso, Fernando Henrique, 15, 17
Carioca, Joe, 41
Carpio, Leónidas, 185
cash-crop economy, 101, 154, 221,
235, 241
Castro, Fidel: achievements,

32; agrarian policy, 31, 317;
background, 260; expropriation,
55–6; guerrilla movement,
272–3; guerrilla tactics,
259–61; inspiration, 9, 13, 259,
262–3, 298, 322, 443; national
movement, 49; political stance,
35, 44, 55–6, 311; political
style, 389, 431; slogans, 169;
US relations, 1, 299; victory,
1, 2, 260–1; view of Peruvian
Revolution, 342
Catholic Church: Colombia, 62n,
64, 65, 66, 70, 81–2, 403; Cuba,
31; dissidents, 283–4; Latin
America, 430, 442; Liberation
Theology, 438; Mexico, 429;
Peruvian Catholicism, 311,
344; progressive priests, 7;
revolutionary developments, 311
cattle: Brazil, 137; Colombia, 64, 76,
79, 97, 199, 201, 207–8, 210–12,
219–20; Mexico, 98; Peru, 39,
112, 135, 185, 338–9
Cayaltí, Peru 318–21
censuses: Colombian agricultural
(1960), 207, 209, 219; La
Convención, Peru,110–11,
111–12; Peru, 176
Chávez, Hugo, 19
Chevalier, F., 101
Chiclayo, Peru, 318–21
Chile: agrarian movements, 381,
383; agrarian reform, 373,
374, 381–2; Allende election,
365, 370, 371, 385, 391, 444;
Allende government objectives,
378–84; Allende's presidency,
365, 368, 379–80, 389, 395,
397; armed forces, 376–7,
383–4; changes of regime,
249n; 'Chilean Way', 367–8,
390–1; Christian Democrats

for, 235; expulsion, 186–7, 192; government support for, 107; land usurped by, 185–6, 210; Mexican, 95–6, 141, 256–7; Peruvian, 120–2, 125; relationship with *arrendires*, 182, 183, 241; relationship with *colonos*, 217; relationship with peasants, 98–9, 125, 191–2, 197–8; status, 96–7

hacienda system, 94–107, 167–8, 178–9; cash-crop economy, 235, 242; changing economic functions and structure, 242; collapse, 8, 11, 179; Columbian expropriation, 220, 438; Colombian Indian struggles, 216; Colombian sale of land, 215, 218; Colombian system, 200–1, 207–8, 210–12, 235, 242; expropriation of land, 100, 189–90, 220, 241, 257–8, 318, 438; Guatemala, 90–1; labour force, 100–6, 110, 115–18, 153, 183; management, 320, 338, 348; Mexico, 95, 98–9, 100, 226, 233, 257–8; nationalization of land, 443; occupations, 187, 189–90, 192; ownership, 94, 167–8, 185, 207, 215, 218, 332; Peruvian collapse, 8, 11, 179; Peruvian expropriation, 318–21, 327, 332, 338; Peruvian Indian invasions, 37–8, 39; Peruvian Indian labour force, 115–18, 122, 153; Peruvian La Convención area, 110, 113–15, 121–8, 181–7; Peruvian labour force, 153, 154; Peruvian land occupations, 186–90, 192; Peruvian land use, 98, 154, 164; Peruvian management, 338, 348; Peruvian nationalization,

443; Peruvian profits, 120–1; post-colonial history, 178–9; Spanish colonization, 200; uncultivated estates, 164

Handelman, Howard, 428

Haya de la Torre, Víctor Raúl, 8, 305, 328, 330, 335, 424

Hernández, José, 423

Hirschman, Albert O., 218, 221

Honduras, 98, 205, 427, 428, 430

Huamán Huamantica, Guillermo, 38

Huaranca Puclla, Clara, 38

Huasicancha community, 172–3, 228, 230, 428–9

Hugo, Victor, 438

Illich, Ivan, 436

imperialism: foreign, 344, 422; global, 254, 342; neo-imperialism, 343; Peruvian policies, 350, 351; US, 36, 255, 296, 304, 308, 377n; world economy, 106, 255; *see also* anti-imperialism

Incas: highland cultivation, 355; idealized, 340, 359; labour services, 89, 90n; millennialism, 177, 421; relics, 37, 111

independence: Brazil, 36–7, 143–4, 418; Latin America, 21, 45–7, 49, 199, 232, 417–21; Mexico, 21, 143, 254, 255, 256; Peru, 112

Indians: Andean, 193–4, 279; Arauco, 161; Bolivia, 15, 44, 238; Chibcha, 200; Chile, 382–3; *cholos*, 328, 339–40, 356, 441, 444; clothing, 37, 182, 441; Colombian areas, 199–201, 203, 204, 206; Colombian communism, 9, 159, 161–2; Colombian guerrillas, 75; Colombian outside ideological

Revolutionary Liberals, Colombia, 65, 67, 439

Revolutionary Socialist Party, Colombia, 205, 215

Ricardo Franco group, Colombia, 411

Rio de Janeiro, 17, 52, 434, 436

Rodríguez, Carlos Rafael, 2

Rodríguez, Leonidas, 341

Rojas, José, 238

Rojas, Teófilo, 81

Rojas Pinilla, Gustavo, 63–4, 70, 71, 357, 404, 406–7, 427

Romainville family, 114, 185, 187, 190

Roosevelt, Franklin D., 61, 298, 299, 301–3, 389

Rosas, Juan Manuel de, 421

Rosell, D. D. Enrique, 119

SAIS (Sociedad Agricola de Interes Social), Peru, 339

Salvador, 430

Sánchez, Gonzalo, 402, 404

Sánchez Cerro, Luis Miguel, 424

Sandino, César Augusto, 22

Santanon (Santana Rodriguez Palafox), 143

Santo Domingo, 249, 274, 282

São Paulo: description, 35–7; EH's visits, 17, 434; immigrants, 243, 434–5, 441; population, 52, 243; settlement, 91; shanty towns, 434; unions, 243–4

Sarmiento, Domingo Faustino, 421–2, 424

serfs: conditions of serfdom, 53–4, 96–7, 99, 101; Indians, 37, 47; La Convención area, 110, 115–16, 122, 125; labour costs, 101; peasant revolt, 118, 177; Peruvian highlands, 184, 325; rural society, 53–4

Sernaqué, R., 184

shanty towns: Brazil, 52, 57, 434–5; Chile, 374–5; Colombia, 411; community organizations, 342; migrants from countryside, 52–3, 328, 434–5; Peru, 37, 52, 174n, 353, 355, 435; political movements, 246; support for guerrillas, 411

sharecropping: advantages, 101; Brazil, 106; Colombia, 214, 219, 235, 242; La Convención, 115–16; land seizures, 68

Shining Path (Sendero Luminoso), Peru, 263, 444

Sieyes, Abbé, 418

Silvino, Antônio, 136, 138, 144

slave plantations, 93, 95, 105

slave-societies, 127–8

slavery, 92–3, 103, 107

slaves and ex-slaves, 35, 47, 97

Smith, Adam, 414

Smith, Gavin, 428

socialism, 30–1, 44, 47–8

squatters: Colombia, 199, 209–10, 211, 214, 223: individual, 122, 272; isolated families, 150; La Convención, 119, 122; organized land occupations, 165, 320; rights, 405; role, 153–4; types, 209–10; uncultivated areas of estates, 121; United Fruit lands, 211; urban, 337, 434; virgin land, 54

Stalin, Joseph, 335

Standard Oil, 255–6, 305

strikes: *arrendires*, 182n, 186, 188; banana-growers (1928), 153, 198, 206; Chile, 381, 395–6; Colombia (1928), 205–6; Costa Rica and Panama, 205; Peru, 190, 319, 348–9; students, 69; tenants, 215